WITTGENSTEIN: A LIFE

WITTGENSTEIN
A LIFE

YOUNG LUDWIG 1889–1921

Brian McGuinness

Duckworth

First published in 1988 by
Gerald Duckworth & Co. Ltd.
The Old Piano Factory
43 Gloucester Crescent, London NW1

ISBN 0 7156 0959 9

British Library Cataloguing in Publication Data
McGuinness, Brian
   Wittgenstein: a life.
   Young Ludwig, 1889–1921
   1. Wittgenstein, Ludiwg   2. Philosophers
   —Austria   —Biography
   I. Title
   192   B3376.W56.Z7
   ISBN 0–7156–0959–9

Typeset on a Lasercomp at
Oxford University Computing Service
and printed by
Redwood Burn Limited, Trowbridge

Contents

Illustrations

(between pages 180 and 181)

Preface

LONG a student of Wittgenstein's *Tractatus* and, with Mr David Pears (now Professor), a translator of it, I came to an interest in Wittgenstein's life through the discovery of various papers that called out for publication. First there were the literary remains of Friedrich Waismann, to which Dr James Griffin and Professor Robert Stoothoff drew my attention. From these it was possible to recover Wittgenstein's conversations with members of the Vienna Circle. This led also to contact with Professor Hans Motz and Mr J.Hevesi, the latter of whom told me of the writings of Paul Engelmann of Tel Aviv, then still alive, and of a typescript of the *Tractatus* in his possession. Here too, through correspondence only (for Engelmann was too courteous to allow me to undertake an arduous journey in order to see him), I was able to arrange a publication of letters and a memoir and to obtain the gift of the typescript for the Bodleian Library.

These publications required a certain knowledge of the biographical background (which, so far as I acquired it, appears in a preface and an appendix respectively). Already at this stage, some twenty years ago, I was aided by members of Wittgenstein's family, Thomas Stonborough, Arvid Sjögren, Clara Sjögren, Felix Salzer, Major John Stonborough, and Mrs John Stonborough, who took me into the houses that Wittgenstein had known (or even built) and who opened to me the treasures of the family, albums, letters, libraries, and possessions of every kind. Above all they spoke openly with me, showing every degree of trust, about all the circumstances of that fascinating world. It is a sorrow to me that the translation of my efforts into print has been so slow that the first four mentioned are not alive to read it, with whatever feelings of approval or disagreement it might occasion. In the case of Arvid and Clara Sjögren I should particularly mention the generosity that made their houses in Vienna and on the Hochreith (the Wittgenstein family country estate, as readers will learn) two bases for me as I worked in Austria. Here in England I have had constant contact with, and have been allowed to pester with questions Major John Stonborough, a faithful and vigorous correspondent: he and Mrs John Stonborough have shown me the Villa Toscana in Gmunden, where Margaret Stonborough, Wittgenstein's sister once lived in archducal splendour. In Oxford itself a distant niece, Mrs Heinrich Kuhn, has kept me in touch with the family. She and Dr Heinrich Kuhn welcomed me at

Thumersbach, and introduced me to further cousins and to the whole atmosphere of that family colony.

But by this time I was well under way on my voyage as a biographer. The launching, as so much else, I owe to Professor Georg Henrik von Wright. He had already smoothed my way to the Wittgenstein family and it was with him that I discussed the need to put such material as I had collected for other purposes into the hands of some one person who would eventually write a life. He felt that this should be someone who had not known Wittgenstein personally, and he encouraged me to undertake the task myself. Thereafter he furnished me constantly with materials, he made it possible for me to visit Helsinki and see his own collection of Wittgensteiniana, and he has read what I have produced with sympathy but also with a preparedness to demur. I hope I have learnt much from him.

The other two heirs to Wittgenstein's literary copyrights, Professor Elizabeth Anscombe and Mr Rush Rhees, have likewise shown me great generosity as well as giving their blessing to my project at its inception. Professor Anscombe, who was also an heir general, gave me sight of many mementoes, photographs, and diaries: she also gave me valuable indications in conversation (as indeed did her husband Professor Peter Geach). Mr Rhees made me free of Wittgenstein's small but interesting library and answered every query in careful and full letters, which must have taken him away from work more valuable to him personally.

To these three principally I particularly owe the inestimable advantage of having full access to the bulk of Wittgenstein's manuscripts, typescripts, diaries, letters, and documents of every kind. (Some I saw in the houses of the family in Austria, or in that of Professor Hermann Hänsel, the son of Wittgenstein's old friend, who has endured many visits and applications from me with great courtesy.)

Among the friends and family of Wittgenstein who have helped me a special place is occupied by Professor Friedrich von Hayek. He, a cousin, was the first, to my knowledge, to start collecting material for a biography. He corresponded with Wittgenstein's then surviving sisters and brother (who were, however, not disposed to further the project) and with many other valuable witnesses (as, for example, Ludwig Hänsel, just mentioned). Professor Hayek not only gave me the benefit of his recollections in person, but also made available to me the sketch (as he terms it) that he had written and also, here with extraordinary generosity, the correspondence on which it was largely based. Professor George Pitcher also very kindly made over to me material he had collected for himself.

The present volume covers only the first half (almost exactly) of Wittgenstein's life. I must, with some reluctance, leave thanking, or acknowledging my debt to, others to the preface of a second volume and confine myself here to those who helped me with the earlier period. The earliest, perhaps, was the late William Eccles, whom I met during his retirement in Ireland. Engelmann's friends, the members of the Olmütz Circle, naturally occupy an early place also: the late Heinrich Groag, with whom I had many fascinating discussions, and Dr Max Zweig, whom I last heard of alive at a great age in Jerusalem. Soon after comes Direktor Fritz Parak, who was a fellow-prisoner at the end of the First War. For the period immediately after that I owe an enormous amount of knowledge, freely imparted, to the late Rudolf Koder.

In the case of none of these heirs or family members or friends who survive can I be sure of complete agreement with my view of Wittgenstein—for a view it is that is here presented: a mixture, as Goethe said of his account of his own life, of fiction, that is to say of imagination, and truth. I do not here pretend to publish a reference book containing all that is known (and nothing but what *is* known) of Wittgenstein. Rather I attempt to present his life (part of it, at first) as an intelligible whole, as something capable of being seen as a unity, as the development of just such a *Daimon* as Goethe describes in a favourite poem of Wittgenstein's: I have made it the epigraph of this volume (and am very grateful to Anvil Press Poetry Ltd for permission to use Michael Hamburger's translation). I believe that Wittgenstein wanted to see his own life in such a way: what I have to describe is as much the character he tried to create as the character he was (if the two are really distinct). I also believe that he meant his life to be written: the sort of records of his state of mind that he kept reveal this. Later he even leaves instructions (to a literary executor, as it were) written in his private code. So I do not feel constrained by the feeling of Wittgenstein's brother (expressed to Professor Hayek) that biography simply means indiscretion. Of course, it is another question (and not for me to answer) whether I am, objectively, the right person to write that life. I should say perhaps that the apparent intrusions of my own opinions, of my judgements or comments on Wittgenstein or his family or other matters, are a literary device, copied to some extent from the chorus in Greek tragedy. The conventional views given serve to throw into relief the individuality of the protagonist and even of his family.

Subjectively I cannot regret the long years spent on the task. A variety of men and cities known can never merely bore, but I believe I have been exceptionally fortunate in both. For this first volume I seemed transported into an earlier age: at Trinity and in Central Europe I was able to relive in some way the experiences of the generation of my parents. And for good measure, there was also the interest of a particular refinement of German culture to be assimilated. In so far as that proved possible for me, I owe it to many Austrian friends. Some already mentioned became such friends: others I knew already—Emmy Wellesz, recently dead at a great age, introduced me to Stifter, to Grillparzer, to Keller, and to much else. Magda Minio-Paluello (also recently dead) and Dr Leo Ungar, her brother, gave me some understanding of the Vienna of Karl Kraus and Adolf Loos.

If a measure of the stimulus it has afforded me comes through also to the reader, I shall have achieved some success and he will be in a better position to make up his own mind about Ludwig Wittgenstein.

For information about and involving Bertrand Russell I am indebted to the late Dora Russell, to Lady Katharine Tait, to Professor Conrad Russell, and to the Bertrand Russell Archive at McMaster University, particularly to the late William Ready and to Mr Kenneth Blackwell. Letters from Russell to Lady Ottoline Morrell are quoted by kind permission of the Library of the University of Texas at Austin. At Trinity College, Cambridge, I am indebted for information about the period before the First World War to Dr Philip Gaskell (former Librarian), and among survivors of the period (no longer such, alas) to the first Lord Adrian, Sir J.R.M. Butler, Professor H. Hollond, and Professor J.E. Littlewood. The late Hester Adrian and her daughter Lady (Richard) Keynes helped with information about David Pinsent (extracts from whose diary were also made available to me in Trinity College Library). The late Dorothy Moore and Dr Paul Levy told me much about G.E. Moore and Dr Levy about the Bloomsbury circle generally. King's College Library (Dr Penelope Bulloch was there then) made Keynes's correspondence available to me, and I also received information from the late Sir Geoffrey Keynes: King's and Lord Kahn kindly gave me permission to publish. Dr Joachim Schulte generously read a draft and the final version with an especial eye for points of German idiom and literature. For constant advice on literary, publishing, and library matters I am happy to thank an old friend, Mr John Commander. At Duckworth's Mr Colin Haycraft, also an old friend, has shown himself capable of combining encouragement with infinite patience.

The Ministry of Defence Library in London, the Kriegsarchiv and the Innenministerium in Vienna, the Wittgenstein Museum at Kirchberg am Wechsel in Lower Austria, and their staffs have constantly assisted me. Without Bodley and Blackwell and his own college an Oxford man would be lost: I believe my college has provided particularly good facilities—leave, a good library, computing facilities, and excellent secretaries, Miss Patricia Lloyd (who typed most of this) and Mrs Fleur Walsh and Miss Jane Fewings who made it ready for the computer and helped in many other ways. The actual work of Mr Stephen Cope and Mrs Alison Cope in preparing the material for Lasercomp leaves me awestruck. I began with Dr Griffin and am happy to end thanking Mrs James Griffin for her advice on that system.

B.F.McG.   Queen's College, Oxford, July 1987

ΔΑΙΜΩΝ

Wie an dem Tag, der dich der Welt verliehen,
Die Sonne stand zum Gruße der Planeten,
Bist alsobald und fort und fort gediehen
Nach dem Gesetz, wonach du angetreten.
So mußt du sein, dir kannst du nicht entfliehen,
So sagten schon Sibyllen, so Propheten;
Und keine Zeit und keine Macht zerstückelt
Geprägte Form, die lebend sich entwickelt.

GOETHE, in *Urworte. Orphisch*

DAEMON

As on the day that gave you to this world
The sun stood in relation to the planets,
So from that moment forth and forth you throve
According to the law that ruled your birth.
So you must be, from selfhood there's no fleeing,
So Sibyls, prophets long ago declared;
And neither time nor any power can break it,
The living pattern latent in all growth.

Translation by Michael Hamburger

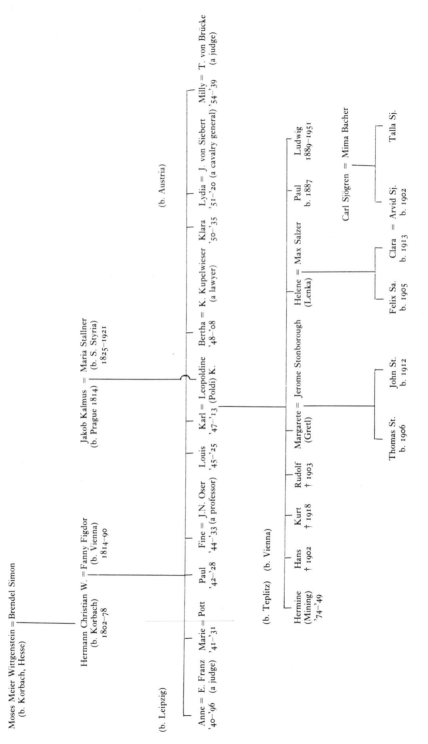

Family tree of Ludwig Wittgenstein

1 Family Resemblances

THE house of Wittgenstein with which we are concerned took its rise at the end of the eighteenth century in the village of Laasphe in the county of Wittgenstein not far from the castle of the princely family of that name. In some year unknown, or perhaps in no definite year, Moses Meier, the son of Meyer Moses of Laasphe and the prince's factor, adopted the name of the county as his surname. The love of legend, the need to fit every event into a familiar category, and later, perhaps, the desire not so much for a princely ancestor as for one who was not a Jew have surrounded the assumption of this name with incident and motive. The prince is said to have thrashed his presumptuous factor; the factor is said to have been expressing (surely in an improbable manner) his indignation at the fact that the son born to him in 1802 was in reality a princely bastard; the edict of Jerome Bonaparte that every Jew must take a family name has seemed to place the event in 1808. Perhaps this is the most probable explanation: the alternation Meier Moses, Moses Meier belongs to the old style of naming among Jews and Jerome's legislation explicitly forbade them to take a town name such as Laasphe. For this reason, no doubt, a number of families in or from the district took the name Wittgenstein, so for example one in Berleburg and another in Höxter. There is no reason to suppose them to be related to our Wittgensteins. If the name was adopted in 1808 Moses Meier had already moved to Korbach in the principality of Waldeck, where the son mentioned was born in 1802 and where his father died in 1805.

The portraits of Moses Meier Wittgenstein and his wife Brendel Simon, stiff and patriarchal and remote, still hang in the Viennese villa of their great-great-great-granddaughter but little is recalled about their originals. It is (surely) Moses' father that lives on in the less reverent side of family tradition as 'old Meyer Laasphe, who sold fish in the market-place at Korbach'. Here probably there is too acute a sense of the contrast between the cultivation and riches achieved in Vienna and the humble origins of the family, for the Wittgensteins had one of the largest businesses in Korbach and charitable foundations were instituted by the old man as well as by his son and by one of his grandsons.

But Jewish the family certainly was: '*pur sang*', as Moses Meier's grandson Louis said to his sister Milly, with something of the irony that we have just observed—they were proud, not of being, but of having been Jewish. And in the next generation when the suggestion of

Hermann Christian's illegitimacy was set afloat or revived,[1] Margaret Stonborough scornfully rejected this way out for her sisters: they preferred to base their claim to special treatment on the nineteenth-century achievements of their family and especially on the character of their grandfather about whose ways and life there was nothing specifically Jewish. This ambivalence to their Jewish origin was a feature determined by time and place. Jews of the assimilation, particularly in what became the German Empire, not only took pains to lose all traces of the old culture themselves but viewed its manifestations in others and even viewed the race itself as a sort of taint from which only good fortune and self-mastery had managed to free them, in so far as they were free. Thus when Hermann Christian's son Karl is reported as saying 'In matters of honour one does not consult a Jew'—and he was certainly capable of such directness of language—and when his son Ludwig (the particular subject of our study) speculated whether a Jewish thinker (such as himself) could ever be more than reproductive, they were only examples of a common phenomenon of their times, the Jew who understands antisemitism. Today, after Hitler, most families with Jewish blood, among them some of the descendants of Hermann Christian, have, with whatever justification, a different attitude towards their origin and see it as the source of their energy and intelligence, but Ludwig belonged to an earlier way of thinking, with something of the Jewish self-hatred of Karl Kraus and Otto Weininger.

In 1938 when the Nazi authorities investigated the ancestry of Ludwig's sisters they could not find any record of Hermann Christian's birth in the Jewish archives of his region of birth, even though Mrs Stonborough made them look twice. The name Christian of course could not have occurred in such archives and even Hermann is an unlikely name for a Jew and may have been taken at baptism. The date of baptism is uncertain: his granddaughter Hermine thought it was just before his marriage in 1839: other family accounts place it during childhood in 1811 (aet. 8) or 1815 (aet. 12) agreeing only that he was 'baptized standing'. We know that his future wife was indeed baptized just before marriage and it seems more likely that she was conforming with him than that both became Christians in order to be married. If he had for some time been a Christian it might help to account for a certain estrangement from his family implied by the words of his will, where, after thanking God for the fact that he need not feel unable to provide a modest existence for his wife and children, he proceeds:

---

1. The ruling suggestion then was that he was a bastard of the house of Pyrmont-Waldeck, in whose principality Korbach, his birthplace, lay. Some likeness to the Wittgenstein family has been seen or fancied among the ancestral portraits of the Pyrmont-Waldecks, but there is no record of contact with their family, as there is with the Sayn-Wittgensteins.

I began my career in other and troublesome circumstances. Thrown back upon my own powers I was never despondent, never solicited or received any man's favour, and, endeavouring to emulate my betters, I never became an object of their contempt.

Steif und würdevoll—stiff and dignified—the words used by his granddaughter Hermine to describe his manner are surely borne out by this brief testament of his life. He shows in it also a religious earnestness, a sense of life as a task, which was to reappear in many of his descendants. No less typical of him is the impression he gives that this task resides principally in the decent and orderly conduct of business in such a way as to win a solid position in the world. The means to this end were provided by the other commercial virtues of energy and persistence.

Photographs show him as an elderly man, ruddy, determined, and not a little irascible. He was probably just as formidable at 35 or 36 when he met Fanny Figdor, who was to marry him and who has left us the first personal impression of him. Her brother Gustav had met him in Pesth—he was active in the wool-trade and visited his sources of supply in Hungary and Poland as often as his customers in Holland and England. Some time in 1838 he was in Vienna for eight days with a Dutch business associate. Gustav brought both to his father's house and it fell out that Wittgenstein was assigned to Fanny as a table companion. His stern, cold, and forbidding expression and the seriousness of his conversation were· a striking contrast to the charming superficiality that even then characterized a Viennese dinner-table. Two further meetings produced some thaw: to her he now seemed, if no better-looking, at any rate more appealing, whereas on his side he had seen enough to apply for her hand. For the first time (she was already 24 and must have had many offers) she felt no positive aversion,[2] but papa had to go to Baden, Wittgenstein (after prolonging his stay so that he had known his prospective bride for nearly three weeks) could no longer put off his business in Frankfurt, Madame Obermeier in Augsburg had to be consulted about his character and financial standing, and so on. As was likely with two principals of decided views, all went well and in the course of 1839 the Biedermeier furniture was bought, the siver and the linen (much still in use today) was prepared, the dowry was paid over in 20-florin pieces, and Fanny went to Dresden first for baptism, and then for marriage, in the Lutheran church.[3]

Hermann Christian had evidently already settled on Leipzig as a centre. Trade in Korbach had declined by this time and he seems in any case to have become independent of his family's firm. After 1838 or 1839 (as later in Vienna) he was in partnership with his wife's family. The

2. So she had told a friend, forgetting perhaps, or silently suppressing, a Hungarian count that Papa had turned down.

3. The marriage seems also to have been registered in the Jewish records in Vienna.

newly married couple settled in Gohlis, then on the outskirts, now towards the centre of Leipzig. Here they rose to a solid prosperity, here most of their eleven children were born, and here their family life received its decisive stamp. It was the house and the life of a German merchant, living at the centre of the trade in books and wool alike, in the birthplace of Richard Wagner, and in the town where Gustav Freytag wrote his *Soll und Haben*,[4] a book possibly read for longer in the family than elsewhere. It does indeed need an historical eye to read it. The commercial values of the middle class: the order, the quiet, the austerity in the midst of plenty in the house of T.O. Schröder are too crudely contrasted with the idleness and luxury of the aristocracy, the envy and greed of the Jews (except for the favourite son Bernhard who becomes a scholar and dies young), and the disorderly circumstances (true *polnische Wirtschaften*) and aimless insurrection of the neighbouring Poles. Not that the later Wittgensteins identified themselves wholeheartedly with figures in this social novel, in which, if truth be told, there is a certain insensitivity: the author cannot quite convey the flavour or the content of a friendship or a personal problem and seems to describe them from a little way outside. In such matters the Wittgensteins judged by the highest standards and they saw the German period of their family through other glasses—that for example of Kügelgen's *In Bygone Days*,[5] which describes the revival of the German spirit through the first decades of the century but in the framework of a close family life with a mother's calm and unquestioning because unreasoned insistence on the highest standards of honesty and dutifulness and a father's quiet confidence in his work and his own worth: uncles, tutors, family friends all conspired to show the boys that the truest affection could and should be combined with justice. Only later is there added to this scrupulous bourgeois morality a religious element with the realization that one is, despite it all, still worthless. The book became for later generations of the Wittgenstein family a kind of mirror of right feeling—their *Sachsenspiegel*, so to speak. Another book with the help of which they looked back to that time was Fritz Reuter's *An Old Story of my Farming Days:*[6] here, as in life, some of the landowners are feckless, some of the Jews are grasping, and some of the peasants are curmudgeonly, but the main lesson is the way in which a man's honesty and diligence and the strength in him of simple and natural human feelings, though in one way they magnify misfortune when it arises, yet they also make it possible for him to support it, secure in his own conscience and in the confidence of a few who know him well and can judge him fairly.

4. 1855: translated into English with the title *Debit and Credit*.
5. *Jugenderinnerungen eines alten Mannes* (1870).
6. *Ut min stromtid* (1864). Ludwig's friends and his young relations had to struggle to get their thoroughly Austrian tongues round its Low German text. His sister Hermine's name in the form 'Mining' was taken from the book.

It was a world of deep feelings as well as of hard work but for all that a little austere and Fanny Figdor, who brought into it a breath of the more urbane world of Vienna, is said to have cried when she first saw the scoured and sandstrewn floors of her new Leipzig home. The story probably is her own: at any rate no one would have invented it to fit the future mother and grandmother who saw, indeed, everything that was amiss but was quicker to censure than to repine. It is consonant with the story, however, that the Wittgensteins moved after ten years to Austria, a move naturally but probably truly ascribed to Fanny's influence.

Anna, Marie, Paul, Fine, Louis, Karl, Bertha, Clara, Lydia, Milly, and finally Clothilde (who spent a long life in tutelage) were none the less brought up by this energetic and sharp-tongued lady in a strict household and more frugally than the family fortunes demanded. The girls wore clothes passed down from their sisters. Transgressions were punished by locking in a room or cellar and even as they grew up the daughters were, less literally, locked away from unsuitable admirers. In the family their very number protected the children to a certain extent and the others were able to mitigate the severity that occasionally fell to the lot of one of them. In some cases they inherited, in others they learned to live with, their mother's impatience and quickness of decision. (A favourite story was that of her taking a boat to Egypt as part of an Italian holiday.) Something of this rapidity of judgement, which goes with a brisk general intelligence, can be seen in later generations, only modified by an imbued politeness.

One quality very characteristic of the Wittgensteins Fanny did not possess or not in the same measure as her husband: it is a very general quality and hard to define but is immediately recognizable when one has to rely on another person—it is the ability to get a thing done, *etwas durchzusetzen*. This showed itself in an exaggerated form in the obstinacy with which Hermann Christian persevered with even a bad investment —an estate bought in ignorance of local conditions which he was determined to make pay. Another aspect of it was his complete confidence in his own authority in the family. When Fanny could not impose her authority on her younger cousin Joseph Joachim he advised her, sensibly enough, to find the boy a room in another house and concluded his advice by saying:

> I am so fully persuaded of the truth of what I write that I await your consent with confidence and turn to another subject.

It rankled with him that his son Karl always went his own way even though he recognized that it had led to success. Yet Karl, as will be seen, had been following in his father's footsteps and carrying out his precepts. Like Hermann Christian he had allowed himself to be cast back on his own resources and, as Hermann Christian had intended in the case of Joachim, he had learnt that a human being could be thrown from the arms of a comfortable life on to the hard paving-stones of privation with nothing to protect him except the induced toughness of a Stoic.[7] In this he was alone in the family, for though the mother's briskness conspired with the father's principles in teaching the children to be indifferent to comfort, none of the others was ever in real need. Karl was also alone, it seems, in going his own way. Some signs of it are visible in his sister, Fine, who jumped from a window when locked up as a child and retained some irreverence and originality throughout her 89 years. She was a favourite aunt of Ludwig's but the favourite of them all was the professional aunt, Clara, who remained unmarried and was taken as a model for her courtesy, her considerateness, her concern. for the moral and physical improvement of others, and also for the dignity and presence that made it only half a joke to call her the Empress of Laxenburg.

Paul and Louis, the two other brothers, fell in more readily with their father's wishes. One gave up his legal studies to help his father, the other did likewise so as not to vie with his brother. Cultivated and sensible men they trod the path prepared for them but it is hard to resist the impression that the education they had all been given suited the sisters best, and (apart from her father) it was to them that Ludwig's sister Hermine looked back when she wrote about the family at the end of the Second World War.

It was naturally part of Hermine's aim to make younger generations aware of the former distinction of the family at a time when its name had been obscured—and in some cases literally deleted from monuments—by Nazi rule, but the atmosphere and the reverence she sought to evoke was also that in which Ludwig had grown up. The brighter pages of the family history were always before his eyes and the number and variety of his relations and their various dependants and companions provided in itself a social world. What did their distinction and eminence consist in, as seen now with more dispassionate eyes and if Karl is treated as a special case? To see this it is first necessary to look at the social position of the family. Hermann Christian came to Vienna in the late 50's as one of a number of settlers from Germany proper who were to transform, perhaps too late, the Dual Monarchy. Typically he was at first an agent for the house of Esterhazy and he also managed or bought, and restored to rentability, properties with which their noble owners could do nothing. True, his wife came from an Austrian Jewish family, art-collectors, and friends of Grillparzer, but his own and his family's more notable associates in Vienna—Hebbel, Bonitz, Brücke, even Brahms—though famous names in Austrian history, also came from Germany

---

7. Phrases drawn from another letter of Hermann Christian's to Fanny about Joachim.

proper. Like many Americans living in England the Wittgensteins combined strong affection for the country with considerable impatience at its ways. They resented those ways rather as a husband is often irritated by the very qualities he married his wife for. It is entirely characteristic that admiration for Bismarck ran strong in them and no surprise that they favoured the German-speaking elements in the Monarchy and (in some cases) even union with Germany after the First War. Their Protestantism too (though in time diluted by marriage) put them into a slightly suspect class, and, more than the scholars and writers, they represented the new class of *entrepreneurs*, intruders on the ancient home of the Hapsburg empire.

The distinction that the family claimed for itself did not reside solely in its effectivness—in its wealth, its cohesion, and its outward success— but much more in the style of life that they combined with this— comfort, correctness, and taste without ostentation; private and public patronage for music and hospitals and churches and research institutes. They were connected by marriage with most departments of Austrian life—a brother and a sister married into the Franz family, leaders of the Protestant community, who were later ennobled and were represented in Ludwig's day by an army officer of some distinction and by an ambassador. The Franz's were connected with the Salzers (again Protestants) two of whom were adopted, and two of whom married into the Wittgenstein family, bringing into it surgeons and civil servants. Another sister married Karl Kupelwieser, son of the painter and friend of Schubert: the connexion was to bring Karl Wittgenstein into the steel industry. There remained marriages with a professor of forestry, a high-ranking officer (though this was possible only after Hermann Christian's death), and a judge, Theodor von Brücke (a son of the physiologist). Only Karl married a wife who was partly Jewish. On the whole the effect of these marriages was to produce a dynasty not of businessmen but of professional men with inherited property. It was as if they all aspired to something other than their origin and, while Karl resisted this tendency in his children, it must be taken into acount in assessing what sometimes seems to be the rise and fall of the house of Wittgenstein. The boldness and energy that characterized them during the *Gründerzeit* did not simply, though it did in part, vanish: it had all along been accompanied by ideals which eventually forced it into other channels.

From an external point of view this extended family provided for most of the contingencies of life—a cousin who could obtain a visa, an uncle who could procure an introduction to a general, a nephew who could direct a projected research institute, a brother who was competent to give advice on or actually assist with the children's education. As for the quality of the life thus led, it was partly conditioned by this very interdependence which led to a close involvement of the members of the family in one another's lives and only in rare cases (perhaps Ludwig and his brother were the most notable) provoked a measure of withdrawal and secrecy. It was also a life on a high cultural level. Hermann Christian who wrote out his own anthology of German poems and took his wife's cousin, the young Joachim, to be taught by Mendelssohn in Leipzig, also had his daughters taught by Clara Schumann and gave his children every opportunity to develop their musical and artistic abilities. These, though not startling, were not inconsiderable: one of the *Geschwister* Wittgenstein, Paul, painted portraits of the rest, another also painted, a third modelled busts, several themselves made music as well as supporting and encouraging it in their large houses and in the concert-room. They belonged to a spacious world with time as well as energy enough, and above all to a culture not yet fragmented and specialized, so that the music they made, or the pictures they painted, at home differed in degree perhaps but not in kind from the highest achievements of their age. In some ways this was a survival of older attitudes. The world of Biedermeier, of the Prince Consort, of Mendelssohn was already past but they still retained its attitudes, its perhaps illusory sense of the unity of culture, and its equation of civilized values with those that were *bürgerlich*. In this respect Ludwig was reflecting a family attitude, though with more self-consciousness, when he reflected that European culture had really come to an end in the 1840s. But it is not at all clear how far even he saw that the decline of this culture was connected precisely with the achievements of the *Gründerzeit*, which he also mentioned in a special tone of voice—for the faculty of reverence was as strongly developed in him, though as selective in its objects, as in any of the Wittgensteins.

'The Wittgensteins'—*Die Geschwister Wittgenstein*—how far were their descendants and friends right to see them as more than a large and variously successful family? Were there traits of character running through them? Were there elements in all or many of them that could truly be referred to (in a word often reverentially used) as *wittgenstein-isch*? The generation we are speaking of were taught under the frosty Leipzig starlight that Cassiopeia stood for 'Wittgenstein': a century later, in the Cambridge water-meadows, Ludwig would not hear the suggestion that it stood for 'Malcolm'. Perhaps the most general characteristic associated with the family was one ascribed to Hermann Christian, the determination to do a thing properly. Not the competitiveness that goes with a feeling of inferiority and is often ascribed to families of Jewish origin but a much more aristocratic attitude, a consciousness of their capacities and a strong feeling of a duty to realize them. It was not a matter of ambition: Ludwig's Uncle Louis was not of a type to vie consciously with other landowners yet he brought it about that his land near Puchberg was recognizable by the excellence of its crops alone. Nor a desire for recognition: they were too sure of their worth to behave like *nouveaux riches*; press attacks were a matter for disdain; and when the offer of ennoblement came (as to Karl and to Bertha's husband Karl Kupelwieser) reasons were found to decline it. Another quality that was in many cases a modality both of their intelligence and of their characters generally was the quickness and the nervous energy observed principally in Fanny. Their speed of thought appeared often in speed of decision, sometimes in impatience, occasionally in too hasty a judgement that a friend or an agent was to be trusted. They had exceptional loyalty to chosen friends but also a nervousness and a degree of sensibility which interacted with this and made many of them difficult to live with save for a companion endowed with an unusual placidity of temperament. Such a one was Karl Kupelwieser who answered his wife's excited account of the alterations her brother Karl Wittgenstein had planned in their house with a calm *Nix geschieht, nix geschieht, nix geschieht* ('Nothing is going to be done...') on a descending note. Another was Nepomuk Oser who was content to let his new wife travel on their wedding journey in a non-smoking compartment provided he could travel in a smoking one. These robust Austrians brought a very necessary element into the family, but nephews and nieces had no such resources against an uncle like Paul who could not be reconciled to Ludwig once he had presumed to give up philosophy for architecture or to Ludwig's brother and sisters once they had accepted (or rather failed to prevent) his distribution of his inheritance. It was hard for the *Geschwister* Wittgenstein to keep or restore a friendship when it fell away from complete intimacy, hard to overcome the series of offences too small for comment and too large not to be felt that in time diminish most human relationships. Thus Clara had to suffer the pain of seeing close friends turn to her less demanding sister-in-law Poldy. Her nature was of a refinement to be scarred by the loss without resenting the replacement.

Clara has been mentioned already as the paragon of the *Geschwister* Wittgenstein and one trait that ran strong in them she particularly exemplified: the need to improve and educate others. This need, with its demand for time and intimacy, partly conditioned the style of life of many of them. Companions, nieces, protégés, servants provided sufficient company when so much attention was given to each. The story of Clara's three successive identical lunches, the first made by the cook with the niece watching, the second by the cook with the niece helping, and the third by the niece alone can be taken as typical of the forethought involved.

Most of the eleven lived to a great age. In so large a family illness and sudden death was bound to take its toll of their children and, as luck would have it, its tendency was to increase the preponderance of women.

A darker side—then accepted largely as inexplicable—appeared in the severe nervous disorder of the youngest aunt and the suicide of one of Ludwig's male cousins and three of his brothers. In their own behaviour the aunts and uncles did all that their times required: that is to say, the aunts were beyond reproach and if one uncle lost a house at cards and another preferred to live with his sister-in-law rather than his wife, such failings were within the limits of toleration. These secure and self-sufficient figures form the background, itself remarkable enough, from which the lives of Karl and his children stand out.

Karl's ability was not from the first so evident as his originality and waywardness. His were the jokes and the imitations that were most in demand and it was he that christened the meal solemnly eaten with their father *das Hochamt* (high mass). He remained impatient throughout life, apt to cut off a serious conversation with a joke, fond too of practical jokes, quick to detect or suspect humbug. His escapades as a child were often enterprises—the castle clock mended that then struck all night, the violin pawned to pay for experiments in glass-cutting. These and others showed ingenuity and a practical bent. A larger undertaking was his running away from school (and home) at eleven. The family had by then moved from the castle at Vösendorf to Vienna and Karl got as far as Klosterneuburg where he failed to pass himself off as an orphan from Leipzig. (The children could still manage but regarded as faintly amusing the accent that had piqued Goethe.) Karl was much attached to his violin-playing but the schoolwork irked him. In a number of cases the Wittgensteins seemed to be late developers and some childish incapacities did remain with Karl for longer than usual, as for example an uncertainty of spelling and punctuation that appears also in Ludwig's letters and manuscripts. A truer account of the matter may lie in the *Gründlichheit* already mentioned: he needed to learn things for himself and reacted with perversity to the instruction in the Gymnasium. His elder brothers and sisters were much more content with the tutor they had at home—Herr Wessel, a learned man and a friend of the great Theodor Gomperz. Karl's dissatisfaction at school seemed to his father (about whose own formal education we know nothing) to be unwillingness to work, so that it is unlikely that he was doing particularly well even in Latin and Mathematics, the subjects he favoured for his own children. He was later much opposed to subjects such as history and geography, and here not only his impatience but his intolerance of received ideas played a role. It was an early instance of this, an essay denying the immortality of the soul, which was the proximate cause of his being given the *consilium abeundi* from his Gymnasium in 1864.

Karl was in his last year of school at this time and his father resolved that he must continue to study privately and sit his *Matura* the following Easter. 'He must be brought to see that a goal can be reached only by work and that it can actually be reached by that means. . . .' But in the event Karl disappeared from the house in January 1865 and was not heard from for a good part of a year.

At the end of his life Karl dictated some chastely factual autobiographical notes to his daughter Hermine, fuller for this period than for his business career. He left home with 200 florins of his sisters' and a violin. After two months in hiding—in the centre of Vienna—he bought the passport of a needy student and used it to reach New York, quite without money, in April. There he worked as a waiter, then as a violinist in saloons until Lincoln's assassination put a halt to public amusements. He was then a hand on a barge going to Washington, where he became a bar-tender and earned his first reasonable wages because, unlike the owner, he was able to distinguish one black face from another. In November he went back, with new clothes, to New York, sent word home for the first time, and supported himself for another year teaching the violin, the horn, mathematics, Latin, .Greek, mathematical drawing, and (as he says in a letter) everything possible in various parts of New York state. He records that he returned home at the beginning of 1867 with money and new clothes but, as his sister Fine recalled it, his clothes and person alike attested to the trials he had undergone and he seemed to be in the dispirited state of one not recovered from shock.

Such an adventure was bound to stamp Karl for a while as 'the son who turned out badly' (*der missratene Sohn*) and he himself felt that he had deeply offended his parents, from whom he needed forgiveness, and his brothers and sisters, whose continued affection surprised him. These feelings probably were what kept him in America so long, for his brothers and sisters sent him money (which he did not always immediately touch) and would no doubt have helped him to return earlier. His letters show that he wanted to be sure of a reconciliation with his father: his actions that he also wanted not to return in the style of a prodigal son. There is little evidence of what was thought at the time about the causes of it all, if indeed much thought was given to them. His daughter, reflecting on it much later, thought that while it seemed as if a deep rift had appeared in a fair young life it was really a matter of a bitter but necessary phase of transition.[8] A personality so out of the ordinary required, she thought, a development out of the ordinary. It was a healthy nineteenth-century instinct to see in the accidents of youth only aspects of the developing personality and those that appeared in Karl's case were indeed aspects of a strong personality. He turned his back on his family. He did not try to find the best solution or some compromise inside the framework presented for him. He broke with everything and above all he did it at one blow, without a long period of visible tension. One day he was as amusing as ever, the next he was gone.

8. Hermine Wittgenstein: *Familienerinnerungen.*

It is evident that his love of the bold and unconventional set him at odds with his father's formality and there was never (certainly not after America) a warm and open relation between them as there was between Hermann Christian and his son Paul. Yet the son exhibited in America precisely those qualities that the father prized—the ability to turn his hand to things, the willingness to support privation, the determination to carry through to the end something once undertaken. The difference between them was in part one of temperament. Hermann Christian was a father ill-suited to a son more remarkable for liveliness than for duty, but the two men also shared qualities which made either end of the relationship between father and son difficult for them. Both combined sturdy independence with decided views about what was good for others. Each therefore became in a measure a self-made man and each had difficulties with at least one son.

The influence of these *Wanderjahre* remained with Karl. He acquired confidence in his own powers. He was confirmed in the view that a variety of experience was preferable to a formal education. In America he came to know a capitalist system untrammelled by tradition. Many of the articles he wrote from 1888 on sing its praise. 'It is impossible to think of an apter school for the education of a human being than that which every immigrant passes through in his first years. He is placed under a dread necessity to strain his powers to the uttermost in order simply to survive.'[9]

As regarded independence from his father, Karl had carried his point. His further formation was in a pattern chosen by himself. In America he had thought his father would expect him to practise estate management, like his brothers, but in fact it was his mother's suggestion of a technical education that was followed. After a brief respite on a rented estate, he studied engineering for a year at the Technical High School in Vienna, working for the State Railway in the afternoons. His further training consisted in a succession of posts as draughtsman or engineer in railways, ship-building, and the construction of turbines. Often, as in the last case, he had to deal with matters he at first knew nothing about. But everywhere, in Budapest as in Trieste, his energy and determination and adaptability made him seem anything but the son who had gone to the bad.

His career proper can be seen to have begun in 1872 when he went to Ternitz in Lower Austria to work as a draughtsman under Paul Kupelwieser, the brother of his brother-in-law and a director of the Teplitz Rolling Mill, for which he was to draw plans. In the autumn of 1873 he moved to Teplitz itself in the Sudetenland as an engineer concerned with the construction of the Bessemer furnace there. At about

9. Article in the *Neue Freie Presse* of 15 August 1888 (reprinted in Karl Wittgenstein: *Politico-Economic Writings*, Amsterdam/Philadelphia, 1984).

the same time he records his engagement to Leopoldine Kalmus—the sister-in-law of an officer quartered since 1872 in the small castle at Laxenburg that was the Wittgenstein family home. Fräulein Poldy was well known to his sisters Clara and Fine and to his mother and he himself had come to know her principally through making music with her. Mother and sisters had long looked forward to the match.

> Karl has a good heart [wrote Fanny to her newly promised daughter-in-law] and a clear head but—he left his parents' home too young.
> The completion of his education, regular and orderly life, and self-discipline: these are things I hope he will obtain through your loving companionship.[10]

It is striking that Hermann Christian had not met Poldy and Karl was in some embarrassment when he had to tell his father of his intention to marry 'an angel'. 'That's what they all are, until they slough off their skins' (*Das sind sie alle. Aber später häuten sie sich.*) was the reply. It will be seen that the mother was more right in her expectations than the father.

In his autobiographical notes Karl records only his salary (1200 florins a year) at the time of the engagement. Before the first child was born he had given up his position out of a characteristically uncompromising loyalty to Paul Kupelwieser in a boardroom dispute. In the event Kupelwieser's opponent resigned within two years and Karl became a director, working from Vienna, but he cannot have calculated on this at the time. A year later, in 1877, he succeeded Kupelwieser as managing director though he continued to live in Vienna.

This was the time, fortunate for those who knew how to take advantage of it, at which the Austrian economy began to recover from the stagnation that followed the Stock Exchange crash of 1873. Wittgenstein's career was henceforth that of a manager and an industrialist and though a considerable technical knowledge was essential to his success the main reasons for it were his rapidity of decision, his daring, and his gift for the unexpected, which enabled him to think of a solution or a project which his customers or his rivals had not expected. Thus, in competition with Krupp and others, he secured a contract to supply the Russians with rails for their Turkish war of 1878 by suggesting to the minister that lighter rails would serve and by working out on the spot the saving in puds and versts. It was not even certain that the rails he promised would be released by a previous customer. Again, in 1880 he bought rights to the Bessemer process (permitting the use of the phosphoric Bohemian ore) not only for the Teplitz works but for all of Bohemia except Kladno.

10. Letter quoted in Hermine Wittgenstein: *Familienerinnerungen*.

It was important to cut out the Bohemian Mining Company which owned large deposits of phosphoric ore and could thus exploit the process more effectively than himself. Their representative, Duschanek, had not supposed it possible that so small a firm as Wittgenstein's could be seriously interested. Also he felt he must wait for Prince Fürstenberg's consent and turned up with it the morning after his option expired, only to find that Wittgenstein had dined with Massanetz (who held the patent) and had concluded the bargain at midnight. The natural reaction of the B.M.C., now largely under the control of Bontoux, was to attempt to take over the Teplitz Mill. Wittgenstein reacted with great daring and undertook himself to buy out the Gutmanns, who were chief shareholders in it. Friends and family money (including his wife's) assisted him but the success (as it proved) of the gamble really depended on his management of the Teplitz works in the next years and on the setting-up of the Austrian Rail Cartel and later the Tyre Cartel largely by his efforts and those of Paul Kupelwieser, now managing director of the Rothschild works at Witkowitz.

The Bohemian Mining Company was in any case a defeated competitor but the failure of Bontoux's Union Générale in France in 1882 enabled the Wittgenstein Group (Karl Kupelwieser, Weinberger, Wessely, Wolfmann, and Wittgenstein himself) to take it over on favourable terms. The organization of the Bohemian iron industry was completed in 1885 when the Prague Iron Industry Co. nominally took over the group's holdings, Wittgenstein managing the whole complex and placing trustworthy men at the head of the various enterprises. At Kladno he commemorated his wife by building a new works, the Poldihütte, still notorious as the Poldinka in Czech novels of social revolt. The remaining large ironworks in Bohemia was that of Witkowitz, and Wittgenstein had no difficulty in arranging with Paul Kupelwieser that they should have a joint sales office in Vienna. He also organized the Austrian Iron Cartel (now covering all products) in 1886.

> An industrialist must take risks [wrote Wittgenstein himself in 1898]: when the moment demands it, he must be prepared to place everything on a single card even at the danger of failing to reap the fruits that he hoped for, losing his initial stake, and having to start again from the beginning.[11]

The words were inspired by a tour of America, and indeed Wittgenstein himself seemed to those he supplanted, to Duschanek with his feudal loyalties for example, to be an aggressive businessman of the American style. His rise was part of another phenomenon of the time—the growth of Jewish and Protestant capital in the Monarchy. Bontoux's adventures there and in France were a forlorn attempt to counter this in the interests

11. 'Die Ursachen der Entwicklung der Industrie in Amerika', *Politico-Economic Writings*, pp. 22ff.

of Catholicism and the aristocracy. Prejudice and conservatism might have sufficed to create a climate of opposition in official circles to Wittgenstein and his associates but this opposition was at the same time a reflection of political realities. The tax and tariff policy of the government, the protection of the farmers, and above all the special position of Hungary were scornfully attacked by Wittgenstein in newspaper articles. He took it for granted that industrialization and the increase of productivity were the only sensible aims for a government. Failings in the national character and the stupidity of ministers had led to the Monarchy's falling behind Western countries. Many of its best workers emigrated

> because for decades not one of our many governments has had a single man whose capacity, experience, and influence might have entitled him to undertake the work required in the economic sphere.[12]

Thus Wittgenstein from his tent in the Alleegasse. But if Austria needed a Bismarck or even a Karl Wittgenstein, the Monarchy could not well support them. In some measure the struggle of its nationalities was indeed, as Wittgenstein said, a struggle for bread, but the growth of industry accentuated the contrast between the races and the more successful he was in expanding his enterprises and in employing Czechs for wages that Germans would not accept, the more he contributed (as Karl Kraus pointed out)[13] to Slavicizing the industrial regions of the Czech lands and to sharpening the racial conflict. For many reasons the future of the countries of the Dual Monarchy was not to be determined by capitalists and liberals of his stamp.

Wittgenstein himself gave something like this as his reason for his dramatic resignation from the boards of all steel companies at the beginning of 1898. The hostility of the government towards himself was, he announced, harming the works he directed. The *Berliner Bursen-Kurier* for 10 January gives as the immediate occasion of this some discussions between the Minister for Trade, Baron Di Pauli, and Wittgenstein's colleague Kestranek, in which the government put pressure on the steel cartel to reduce prices by threatening to increase taxes. This does not seem to have been the only point of difference, however. Wittgenstein was at the height of his career and might now have stepped into a really commanding position in the Austrian economy. Over thirteen years his group had purchased mines and factories in Bohemia and Styria to supply and be supplied by their steelworks. Finally, in 1897, their Prague company, having previously relied on a Prague bank, exchanged directors with the great Credit-Anstalt and transferred their business to

12. 'Neujahrsbetrachtungen' [1905], *Politico-Economic Writings*, pp. 167ff.
13. *Die Fackel* 31 (February 1900), p. 3.

it. Both bank and company now purchased considerable holdings in the Alpine Steel Company which no longer drew any advantage from its supplies of non-phosphoric ore and was not well-managed. Mauthner of the Credit-Anstalt denied that they had any intention of influencing the management but this was clearly the aim of the Wittgenstein group. They put in their own man, von Hall, who introduced new systems of accounting and revived the company. A full merger with the Prague Iron Co. was prevented, however, by the tax authorities who used their discretion in a way unfavourable to the Wittgenstein group.

Wittgenstein detached himself from his industrial affairs only gradually and not without controversy. Towards the end of 1898 his colleagues attempted to distribute some of the reserves of the Prague company which, in part, had been only recently accumulated. This seemed to be a transparent stock exchange manoeuvre and was severely criticized in the official newspaper. It is even said that the heir apparent, the Archduke Franz Ferdinand intervened. In the event the distribution was delayed for a year and the Credit-Anstalt directors left the Prague company's board while Wittgenstein himself left that of the Credit-Anstalt. It can hardly have been an accident that the value of the shares (which had fallen by 27 fl on the day Wittgenstein left the steel board) was driven up in this manner just when he was divesting himself of his interests: a year later Karl Kraus was able to point out[14] that on the one hand the dividend had in fact fallen from 60 to 50 florins and the shares by 100 fl and on the other Wittgenstein had declared that he had nothing more to do with the company. Another consequential change was the merger of two banks to provide the Prague company with an alternative to the Credit-Anstalt. The modalities of this too were criticized but Wittgenstein was able to claim that his meetings with Feilchenfeld, Kestranek, and Weinberger were of a purely friendly character.

So, at 52, Wittgenstein retired into private life. Not indeed completely: he wrote a few articles and he was in his office each morning, available, he said, if the Minister for Commerce wished to call. But he accepted no director's fees, and transferred his monies into property and foreign equities, thus securing his family's future, not out of pique or by a fortunate stroke but by the capacity—necessary for an industrialist—'to take into account not only all obvious factors but also those uncertain ones that the future holds.'[15]

14. *Die Fackel* 56 (October 1900), p. 7.
15. 'Die Ursachen der Entwicklung Industrie in Amerika' [1898], *Politico-Economic Writings*, pp. 22ff.

This capacity, and also the courage necessary for its exercise are not innate, like musical talent for example, but must be inculcated, must be earned by diligence and practice.[16]

Karl Wittgenstein was quite certain that he had deserved well of his country. He was always sure that he was right in employing all the devices of the market and while he referred to money as the by-product of sweat he clearly thought of it as the evidence of merit. He was a paternalistic capitalist who paid his workers what he and the market thought was due to them and used the profits that remained partly for the style of life that he thought due to himself and partly to assist his servants, his employees, or the community in the ways that he thought most fitting. Hence the hospitals built at his works, the specialist who had treated Bismarck brought from Berlin for an employee, the cigars handed out to railway-drivers, the double-eagles casually thrown onto the table at Monte Carlo on the way from the restaurant, the financing of the *Sezession* building with the extra gratification of a slight provocation to official art: all the arbitrary trappings of self-confidence and wealth. When the leading German economist Adolf Wagner defended in Vienna the thesis (which now seems, at least in theory, a modest one) that a city should take the largest part of the unearned increment in property values since this was produced by the economic activity of the whole community, Wittgenstein laughed him to scorn. *Every* economic activity owed its success to society as a whole. Wagner would be saying next that society should profit from all of them and give part of what it gets to its professors.[17]

Much of the criticism and envy that Wittgenstein incurred sprang from his doing more successfully and with more style what many others were doing. There was a touch of distinction too in the less controversial side of his life. His daughter thought he had acquired a taste for spacious surroundings from a childhood spent in the castles of rented estates but it was also a taste for the life of a *grand seigneur* which he shared with many a successful businessman. It was entirely characteristic of his class that he should buy a grandiose and frowning house in the Alleegasse which had been built by a Count Nako earlier in the century and should fill it with the best, though not always the lightest, of furniture and tapestry and bronzes. This became, though the family of course never called it so, the Palais Wittgenstein, the centre of their lives, with its *Dienstmann* sitting on his stool outside, the business-rooms on the ground floor, the card-tray where the children were careful to put the tame Princess's card on top, the imposing staircase, the large music room, and the numerous protégés and tutors and servants. But in it, as well as the equestrian portrait of

16. ibid.
17. Cf. *Die Fackel* 71 (March 1901), pp. 10ff.

himself by Krämer and later the fashionable portrait by Laszlo, which any successful businessman might have, he assembled a collection of pictures painted between 1870 and 1910 of much more modern inspiration—Segantini, Rudolf von Alt, and Klimt among them. These were set off by sculptures by Rodin and Mestrovic, and a famous one of Beethoven by Max Klinger. His eldest child and perhaps closest companion, Hermine, helped him to assemble the collection, though his taste, she said, was decisive. It was to form a unity: a Goya was rejected because it would have jarred with the others. It seemed to her that all the pictures, curiously enough, were characterized by a certain serious-ness and calm in their composition, a stressing of the verticals and horizontals that she wanted to call 'ethical'. 'Curiously enough'[18] because, no doubt, calm was the last quality she associated with her father. Yet there was something very *wittgensteinisch* in the idea of an intense and even febrile nervous energy channelled and contained in an apparent spontaneity. It appears again and again in Ludwig Wittgen-stein's life and in his work, in the exhortations to his sister and his friend's daughter Mareile Hänsel to draw honestly and decently, in his admiration for the sunniest and least forced works of Schubert written in the most miserable circumstances, in the obsessive rephrasing and rearrangement of his philosophical remarks in order to find the most natural and least professorial expression and sequence of thought. We find it too in the manner and subject of his sister's portrait by Klimt. Klimt had no good reputation for his attitude towards his models and there were those who smiled at Karl Wittgenstein's entrusting the young Margaret Stonborough to him. But the result justifies the father and shows all the energy and passionate intellectual intensity of the daughter somehow held in a repose emphasized by the rich but judicious ornament of the background. There is none of the brooding sexuality of many of Klimt's portraits of fashionable women. The father and the daughters at least remained untouched by this malaise at the end of the century.

Karl's taste, however, was uneven. His love of the unexpected led him to some strokes of originality—as for example the rich Sezession style interior by Josef Hoffmann for his *Blockhaus*, not even the main house of his country retreat, an extravagantly urban setting yet intended only for his wife and himself. In this vein were his paying for Klimt's fresco of *Philosophy* when it and the three that were to follow were rejected by an outraged professorate at Vienna University; and also his burying a statue by the proletarian artist Kundmann in his garden at Neuwaldegg. But he could also conform to the usual tastes or tastelessness of his class, as, perhaps, in the choice of the Alleegasse house and, surely, in the building of a pompous stone mansion near the *Blockhaus* already mentioned, a

18. Hermine Wittgenstein: *Familienerinnerungen*, p. 77.

surprise for his wife and daughter less welcome than he expected, or than they affected, to find it.

More perhaps than a house of pictures and statues, more than one of servants and wealth, the Alleegasse (as the family called it) was a house of music. F.R. Leavis remembers that Ludwig Wittgenstein told him there were seven grand pianos in his childhood home:[19] the emphasis placed on this fact is interesting, though it is hard to establish that there were more than three or four, unless one counts those in Karl's other houses at Neuwaldegg or on the Hochreith. Bruno Walter saw little of Viennese society: but the Wittgensteins' real feeling for music drew him to the Alleegasse.[20] Hermine Wittgenstein felt they had contact with the later classical composers, not merely with the romantics. The Joachim quartet played in the house and Joachim, who had sat under Mendelssohn, had heard musicians who knew Beethoven. Karl's sisters as we have seen had been taught by Clara Schumann and Brahms knew the family well. The high point of the Alleegasse was perhaps the evening in 1892 when Karl Wittgenstein arranged for a private performance, which he had been told Brahms wished to hear, of the clarinet quintet, already performed but only in public. Brahms came often enough after that and Hermine and her mother visited him in his last illness. A visit from him was a scene to remember—the daughters meeting him at the door, walking hand in hand with him up the stairs, the champagne brought up when he said one of them needed to put it on her hair, the old man left to sit alone on the landing so he could hear the music in peace—Uncle Paul the painter made a drawing of him there. He fitted into the house very well. He disliked being lionized, to be sure, but he found no party spirit in the Alleegasse, where the chidren indeed learned the *Meistersinger* by heart, and he could not object to the Wittgensteins' faculty of reverence when it so clearly took its origin, in his case, from their deep musicality. They divided the human race into great men (Karl himself was one such in his daughters' eyes) and ordinary mortals, and they did not allow (as will be seen in other cases) for development or for contradictions in a personality. Every trait in a great man was an aspect of his greatness. Not least, perhaps, Brahms's prickliness, of which he was himself rather proud and which had much in common with Karl's dislike of humbug. 'That's what the waste-paper-basket is for!' they would quote—Brahms's comment to the composer of a score submitted to him. But the greatness itself corresponded to their particular historical situation. Brahms was the last representative of the age, from Haydn on, which essentially constituted music for them. His was a structured music, not relying for its effect on orchestral colour, but accessible in chamber works and arrangements for four hands, which they could hear or play in the house.

19. In Rush Rhees (ed.): *Recollections of Wittgenstein* (Oxford, 1984), p.54.
20. Bruno Walter: *Theme and Variations* (London, 1967), p. 168.

Further, as well as his sunny side—*Brahms von der Sonnenseite*—there was his sense of the devils that might break out: Ludwig heard it, for example, in one of his quartets and it was to Brahms's music with these two aspects that he insisted on listening during his leaves from the Front in the First World War. Brahms was, like the older Wittgensteins, a German who found in Vienna an environment that complemented the too earnest or melancholy elements in his nature. His need for this appears in his admiration for Hungarian music and the waltzes of Strauss. Above all, however, Brahms represented no rebellion against inherited forms but an attempt to work out within them, though in a down to earth manner, as Ludwig said, and certainly in one more suited to his age, the very problems that had confronted Beethoven. The Wittgensteins had an executant's sense of the significance of every passage in a musical work and Brahms is remarkable for 'the appropriateness of each theme to the exact emotional state to be expressed'.[21]

The Alleegasse was a musical house. There were visits by Brahms, performances by the young Casals, by the Rosé quartet or by Josef Labor. There was the privileged position in the household of Brahms's favourite violinist Marie Soldat-Roeger and of the pianist Marie Baumayer (both women companions and practically protégées of Clare Wittgenstein). But above all the organ and grand pianos were for the family itself. Karl took his violin everywhere with him and played sonatas when on holiday with his wife and unaccompanied suites on his business trips. It was in his style to make a joke of the tears that certain passages brought to his eyes. But music was a need for him during his last illness. When he had to face a serious operation he spent the evening before it making music with his wife.

For Leopoldine Wittgenstein music was perhaps the mainspring of her life. Music was her chief means of real contact with her husband and children—music and perhaps the stories that she told to children so beautifully. Slight and transparent, with hands that could scarcely span an octave, and feet that could scarcely reach the pedals, she surmounted at the piano or the organ every physical disadvantage, every failure of co-ordination that age brought with it. Intellectual limitations, too, or what seemed to be such, vanished when it came to music, so that she who, by her daughter's account, was slow to follow a complicated sentence could play from sight the most elaborate pieces of music. A pupil of Goldmark's, a fit partner in four-handed playing for Bruno Walter, able to sight-read, to transpose, or to improvise charmingly, she was yet no professional or virtuoso. She could not play from an orchestral score—her music was the house music of the nineteenth century. All the emphasis was on the expression of the musical idea and it was this that was discussed with a minimum of technical terms and in the vocabulary of cultivated and perceptive participants in the long Alleegasse analyses that followed each Vienna Philharmonic Concert. It was at the piano that Poldy best performed her role of wife and mother, her part holding together the father and sons when they played chamber works, her accompaniment guiding a song. Few now remember her playing: those that do thought it superior to that of the son who became a concert pianist and it was said to be superior to that of the musical prodigy who was not allowed to. It was characterized above all by an avoidance of exaggeration, of any striving for effect, of any distortion of the logic of the music. In other spheres she was sure, indeed, of what she herself ought to do but perhaps too slow to detect or correct the failings of others. Here she had absolute confidence: How could she play with such a musical idiot? Did the piano have to be *belaboured*? The first was said to her grandson, the second (not in his hearing) of her son.

Poldy and her relations figured much less than the Wittgensteins in the picture that Ludwig and his brother and sisters had of themselves and their family. Partly this was due to the patrilineal emphasis common at the time, partly the Wittgensteins expressed themselves more vividly and really were more remarkable. Thus the younger generation spoke of the Kalmuses and Stallners less even than of the Figdors, the maternal line of the preceding generation. There they had the connexion with Joachim and with the art-collector Willi Figdor not only to pride themselves on but to enjoy. These Figdors belonged to their world and, in token of it, both Willi Figdor and Uncle Paul were married to Hochstetters, and so related to the eminent Protestant geologist. The Kalmuses had lived more simply. Jakob Kalmus, who died in 1870, was the mild and uxorious husband of Marie Stallner, a pretty girl from Lichtenwald, then in Styria now in Yugoslavia, who was Ludwig Wittgenstein's only attested non-Jewish grandparent, the daughter of a provincial merchant who had become a landowner.[22] A widower, he required from her little more than good manners and an elegant appearance: she was to owe her moral education to her mother-in-law. Jakob Kalmus, himself a reasonably successful merchant, had been born in Prague where Ernst Wehli, one of his maternal grandfathers, had been President of the Jewish community. But Sophie Kalmus, the daughter of this Wehli and the moral tutor of Marie, had accepted baptism late in life and was a devout Catholic. There were already converts on her husband's side for a cousin, Pater Kalmus, was well-known as a chaplain first in the army and then in a fashionable Ursuline convent, affecting, like all priests, to find the former much less trouble than the latter. It is

22. Professor F.A. von Hayek, the first to collect biographical material on Ludwig Wittgenstein, is descended from this family.

perhaps possible that some ancestral traces remained—dim memories of the frugal dignity of the Prague ghetto: but for Poldy's children the Kalmuses represented rather what was Austrian in their background— the slower and deeper, Catholic stream of German culture to which even Goethe looked with envy.

Poldy's mother lived in long widowhood until 1911, some early difficulties with Karl forgotten, cherishing the daughter who had been devoted to her. The two elder sisters, less agreeable in character, were not redeemed in the Wittgenstein eyes by any special distinction. Elsa von Bruckner (later Elsa Stradal), the daughter of one, was always welcome for her fine voice and a more distant cousin, Dora Hauser, for her painting and her independence of spirit. She continued to live in Cilli near the Stallner home until her house was burnt down (despite her vigorous defence of it) by the partisans in the Second World War. But these closer contacts were few and despite friendly relations with other cousins—the Gräzers in Zurich, for example, who provided a valuable neutral postbox in the First World War—Poldy Wittgenstein's relations did not form an important part of the framework of her children's lives. She and they were absorbed into the Wittgenstein connexion. Poldy herself, however, brought two elements of extreme importance into their lives: first music—her single talent well employed—and second a moral earnestness and a selflessness which it is proper to call extreme. Her son Ludwig was later to say that for all that he had written he had left half his life—the music in it—unexpressed. As for the moral life, Poldy's mother-in-law soon saw that it was after all not best to be 'an angel': 'Dear Poldy, there is such a word as "too": it is possible to be *too* good, *too* unselfish.'[23] The unselfishness which had made her the favourite daughter made her perhaps less than the perfect wife. It would have been difficult for a woman of the most decided opinions to provide a counterweight to the confidence and energy of Karl Wittgenstein. For Poldy whose main fear was to have incommoded someone else or to have failed in her duty, it was impossible: the more so as it was duty to her husband that filled her horizon. It was not only that she sacrificed herself completely to him in his last illness. Then indeed she may have been right to lie in pain rather than to disturb him, to bloody her nose rather than let him think the doctor's news had caused her tears. But by treating him so all her life she had (even his daughter thought) spoiled him and above all she had been unable to offer any rational opposition to his less well-judged plans or prejudices. In his marriage, as well as in his business enterprises, he had for better and for worse sleeping partners.

Of all the children of the *Geschwister* Wittgenstein a special place was occupied by the *Karl-Kinder*: there were scientists, managers, surgeons among their cousins, who indeed, on average, achieved at least as much

23. Fanny Figdor quoted in Hermine Wittgenstein: *Familienerinnerungen*, p.93.

worldly success as they, with less of the counterpoint of tragedy. But for promise, for intensity, for distinction, for the quality, in fact, of being *wittgensteinisch* these children stood out. Karl, the rebel, had alone married into a family with some Jewish blood and while, from one point of view his was the marriage of understanding with feeling, of aggressive practical ability with almost marked self-distrust, from another he had by marriage not offset but reinforced tendencies present in his own heritage—the moral earnestness, the scrupulosity and melancholy of Hermann Christian and the quick nervous artistic temperament of Fanny Figdor. Rather as (so it is thought) intermarriage has tended to produce among Jews a higher incidence of scientific and musical gifts and of the manic-depressive psychosis, so in this one instance what Karl and Poldy had inherited and transmitted, genetically and by the moral atmosphere they lived in and recreated, all of this conspired to form a generation of human beings remarkable much more for the exceptional gifts distributed among it than for its capacity to achieve harmony and happiness.

2   Childhood and Schooldays

LUDWIG Wittgenstein was born in the Alleegasse house at 8.30 p.m. on 26 April 1889, the last child and the eighth to live to maturity of Karl and Poldy Wittgenstein. It was one of a number of foibles he had in later life to insist that nice people must be born in April, which was in fact the month of his father's birth and also that in which he himself was to die. Photographs show him first as a fair and curly-haired baby with large blue eyes, later on as a small boy in a sailor-suit looking out from innumerable family groups, walking with a governess on the terraces, lawns, or meadows of one of his father's country-houses, endearing, a little earnest but by no means troubled—the typical Benjamin of a wealthy industrialist's family of that time and place. Typical too (at any rate for the first ten or twelve years of life) was his education and that of his brothers and sisters. They did not go to school but received formal instruction from a number of tutors and governesses. They were taught French and English from their earliest years by the well-brought-up native-speaking governesses or tutors available at that period. 'My French is poor but English I *know*,' Ludwig told an Austrian friend in the First War: but all his family, not just those who spent years in England or America, could write it all their lives and speak it with that out-of-date purity and refinement of accent and vocabulary that is now heard only from survivors of their generation or middle-aged members of foreign royal families. Their German, too, was of a beauty and elegance not often heard now—the German of culture and the stage in the Austria of that time, recognizably different from the German of the empire but in no sense a dialect. Indeed they had little contact with the people except as servants and dependants. Their contacts at children's parties or dancing schools were with the upper classes. Their outlook and all their habits were those of Austrians, indeed, but Austrians of those classes. Education in the home accentuated this remoteness: the normal way of life of most Austrians—not just of *das Volk* but of those that became writers and scientists—was alien to them. Ludwig, for example, always wrote in a bold Latin hand: when he became a schoolmaster he had to struggle to teach himself the customary *Kurrent*. Their education, then, was typical enough, but typical of a particular class at a particular time.

It was quite usual too that they should be in awe of their father, that they should see little of their mother, that they should be expected not to speak much in the presence of their aunts and uncles. They were impressed above all with the importance of honesty, of strict performance of duty, and of fulfilment of obligations towards servants and dependants. Formal religion, in comparison, played little part in their lives. Moral and cultural and material superiority to those that surrounded them (or the consciousness of each of the three) were inextricably interwoven and formed the atmosphere in which they lived.

Their household had, of course, its special atmosphere. The eldest daughter, Hermine (Mining, as she was called after the Fritz Reuter character), said that all the children felt it to be one of constant excitement, an unrelaxed tension that came in the first place from their father. His vigour and decisiveness would have put his stamp on any family—a father at the height of his business success, disposing instantly of problems that puzzled his subordinates, but with time and energy free to fence and to ride as well as any cavalryman, he could not but be overpowering. His intellectual powers were formidable—there are many stories of his rapid mental calculations and the most considerable of his posthumously published papers (an analysis of the industrial achievement of America) was a lecture delivered—tables, statistics and all— without notes.[1] A moral or human problem he would dispose of with the same rapidity: he did not like discussion and would cut it short with a pointed joke. Such a character is far from being without charm—indeed the very strength of the personality is an added charm when it is all bent to pleasing or gratifying or making comfortable. Good-looking, vigorous, confident, right (so far as they could tell) in his judgements, witty, adroit, a man who absorbed a wide general culture by casual reading, and in whom his business rivals recognized the power to charm a bird from a tree, Karl Wittgenstein was for his children the dispenser of all good things, the creator of the world of large houses, parks and estates which they took as a natural environment. Small wonder if his daughters especially, to whom he paid court, worshipped him. He remained their standard of manly excellence and long after his death if something was neglected by a servant, it was always 'If Papa were alive to see this!' and each spot on their walks was associated with some small incident involving him—say a treat given to a grandchild or the like.

Ludwig, too, and Paul, the second youngest brother, retained or allowed themselves to retain only good memories of their father. For both of them the idea of authority had great attractiveness: they were prepared to accept a world of moral absolutes which could be perceived immediately, not assented to on balance, and from which any deviation was complete failure. They were like Karl too in their dislike of humbug and their quickness to detect it. Until (for complicated reasons) the Second World War brought contact between them to an end, Paul's communications with Ludwig were for the most part 'nonsense'—

1. 'Die Ursachen der Entwicklung der Industrie in Amerika' [1898] in *Politico-Economic Writings*, pp. 22ff.

cuttings of self-evident absurdity from some newspaper, which Ludwig carefully kept in the collection of such things especially mentioned in his will.

Even these two youngest sons, however, though conscious of no resentment against their father, were clearly hampered in many ways by the upbringing he chose for them, though in their time he somewhat mitigated his régime. For his vigour and self-confidence were purchased, naturally enough, at the price of a certain insensitivity and even at times brutality. A man of great largesse he could also refuse a request most harshly if he thought it somehow foolishly or maladroitly presented. His dislike of humbug passed over into practical jokes at the expense of those who would feel themselves socially insecure—an entire house-party secretly changing for dinner to embarrass a newly-arrived guest (whom the servants reported to have arrived without evening clothes), the hoax of a specially engraved honorific invitation to a circus performance, and the like. Sure of himself and of his values, he imposed them on his sons with not much attention to their gifts and none to their inclinations. They were to learn mathematics and Latin and in later life they were destined—by him—to combine engineering and business as he had done. Other subjects they would pick up for themselves. As for music, if one of them had a native gift for it, that was a bonus, but not something that should be allowed to affect the pattern of his life. This attitude bore hardest on the second child and eldest son, Hans, who was undoubtedly a musical prodigy—a genius, said Professor Epstein—playing the violin in St. Peter's church at the age of 9, playing also the organ and piano, and exhibiting a variety of musical feats. It was not so much that he lacked the intellectual abilities demanded by his father's plan—his sister Hermine describes childhood fancies and games involving elaborate measurements and calculations that recall exactly his father's facility at mental arithmetic. Much rather he had no interest in the career chosen for him and he had not learnt such habits of regular even if distasteful application as a normal schooling might have given him. Thus when he was sent, without a proper tutorial training, to pick up the necessary knowledge in various enterprises in Bohemia, Germany, and England, he had no idea what was expected of him and concerned himself much more with organizing string-quartets. The atmosphere between him and his father when he was on leave was an uncomfortable one. He vanished from a boat in Chesapeake Bay at the age of 26 in circumstances suggesting suicide: as such, certainly, from whatever indications, his death was always regarded in the family.

The Wittgenstein family history (true to its time) contains many anecdotes that might have figured in the appendices to a treatise on psycho-analysis. Thus we are told that the first word Hans learnt was the name 'Oedipus'. There are obviously grounds for saying that he identified with his mother and rejected his father. The reasons for this lie much deeper in the dynamics of the family than in the ill-chosen system of education. But his mother's attitude to that too was typical. The father had no time to supervise the education he had prescribed and the mother had in the first place little time except for the father. Moreover, distrustful as she was of herself, she was reluctant to correct or control those who worked for her. The children were brought up in their first years by a curmudgeonly nursemaid who paid little attention to their activities, their behaviour, or even their corporal well-being. Poldi's mother and others saw this clearly and protested to her but she was evidently afraid to commit herself to a programme of improvement and intervention, so that Fräulein Elise stayed on for twenty-one years, until, in fact, Ludwig was six. It was the same when some of the tutors were useless. Above all, she said nothing to her husband about his harshness towards Hans (as she herself regretted in the retrospection of widowhood). It is impossible now to trace the conflicts between feeling and a strong sense of duty that led to her unquietness. Her children sensed them—certainly her daughter did from whose family memoir most of this account is drawn—and saw that in her devotion to her mother and her husband she had exhausted her abilities to remain calm. When it came to the children's problems she seemed to lack the necessary sense of their individual characters and, above all, she was too anxious to believe that all was well lest she should be drawn into struggles beyond her powers.

Her gentleness and courtesy and unselfishness were a constant model for her children. They saw too, and many of them inherited, her anxious concern not to have failed in any duty, but they suffered by reason of her inability to see clearly where her duty lay and to contrive and follow through the best policy available. For inner reasons and because of her marriage she was like a person holding her own in a storm and so far from giving strength to them she was someone whom they had to support and spare. This was more marked during her widowhood and the end of her life no doubt coloured their recollections of her. But the pattern of her widowhood itself illustrates that she needed someone to hold her up, and it seems that her sons especially required more devotion and insight and individual care than she was capable of giving them.

With regard to Hans, his elder sister doubted whether he would have been happy even if left free to live a life of music. There was a violence and nervousness in his playing that seemed to correspond to something in his whole nature. She thought that in all her brothers there was in youth a lack of the will to live—of *Lebenskraft*, *Lebenswille*, or *jugendliches Lebensgefühl*, as she variously called it.

The third son, Rudi, certainly committed suicide—he poisoned himself in Berlin. When he was seven, on the occasion of a test of

elementary education that he had to undergo, he seemed so frightened
and miserable that the examiner warned his mother that he was a
nervous child, who ought to be watched. This was always quoted by the
mother as a great joke. Rudi was remembered as the brother with the
most feeling for literature, perhaps not creative but with the gifts of a
critic. His suicide is usually attributed to his being or thinking he was a
homosexual—though one second-hand account mentions the difficulty of
making his own way in Berlin after the comfort of his father's house and
also suggests that he had a venereal disease. Both his suicide and Hans's
occurred in the early years of the century.

A third brother, Kurt, second in order of age, also killed himself, but
much later. He was to all appearances the least troubled of the sons
(though this may be partly the Wittgenstein way of saying that he was
not obviously gifted), remembered chiefly for the charming musicality
with which he would sit at the piano to play what he had heard at the
opera. His father had him appointed a director of a company. He
disliked the work but supported it with apparent cheerfulness. Two
attempts to marry failed and he seemed to be a rich and cultivated
bachelor with no especially serious obligations. A photograph of 1918
shows him sitting on the terrace at the Hochreith with the rest of the
family, the confident cavalry officer in dress, bearing, and expression. A
few months afterwards, at the end of the War, on the retreat from the
Italians he left the bivouac saying he must stretch himself, after which a
shot was heard. A number of reasons have been suggested—shame at
defeat, or at his soldiers' refusal to fight, a horror of being taken prisoner.
But (as in Rudi's case) the precise precipitant cause seems unimportant
compared with the the implications of the fact that there were three
suicides in the one family and that the two remaining brothers (so their
sister says) were also at times so near to it that it seemed the merest
chance that either of them survived to live a full life. She thought it was
perhaps a lack of *das harte Muss*, the stern sense of obligation, that the
father so much wanted to give them. But a variant of this explanation
seems more plausible—from both father and mother they had acquired
too strong a sense of duty: from their father they learnt that their role in
life was to act—to change the world in some way. Karl believed or at
any rate he put the whole force of his personality into the belief that
technical advances would solve every problem: he was the embodiment
of the idea of progress that later haunted and repelled Ludwig who
thought it the essential characteristic of the society of his time and the
reason why he himself was alien to it. But the temperament that the sons
inherited from their mother was one quite unsuited to these beliefs and
this role—it was a passive and sensitive and self-distrustful temperament.
It is not surprising if in the three elder sons this temperament lacked the
strength to assert itself and to enable them to find a way of life tolerable

for them. The father's own sudden changes of direction will be remembered. He too could not tolerate any degree of failure: but these sons perhaps lacked his almost manic belief that everything was possible. For their more depressive personalities any failure seemed absolute, whether in their careers, or in their moral life, or in the fortunes of their country.

All in all the three daughters adapted best to what was expected of them, no doubt because less was expected of them. Hermine, or Mining, the eldest of the family, became her father's real companion. It was with her that he collected his pictures, to her that he dictated his autobiography, and for her essentially that he bought and developed his country estate the Hochreith. She took something of her mother's place too in relation to the younger children. Later in life she became in effect the head of the family, sitting in the main houses—in the Alleegasse or on the Hochreith—*das gnädige Fräulein* as she was known in their circle, the repository of family tradition and the eventual author of its history. It was a harmonious life, something like that of the older Wittgensteins. She painted and drew—mostly family interiors and scenes on the Hochreith —with taste. She played the piano and arranged or permitted the arrangement of musical evenings. She entertained the numerous protégés of the family and sent presents with exquisite taste. Until the first war she devoted herself entirely to family duties but during it she worked in a hospital and after it she ran a day-home for children—naturally with many and, fortunately, well-chosen helpers; for she had inherited much of her mother's unpracticality though not the anxiety that went with it. Her life seemed to her nephews and nieces a rounded one—they could not imagine her married, for example. There were, of course, sometimes tempestuous scenes with her brothers and sisters, most of whom had clear ideas about how the others ought to behave, but for the most part she was respected without needing, as her mother needed, to be spared.

Harmonious too was the life of the second sister, Helene or Lenka. As happened from time to time in the family, the strength of her personality was not apparent in youth, when (by strict standards) she was judged rather frivolous. She was to marry a stable and humorous civil servant, Max Salzer, from a firmly Protestant family already connected with the Wittgensteins, who became an adviser of the family in all practical matters. She was one of the most musical of the family and organised a small choral group between the wars. The suspicion of frivolity vanished but she retained a lively form of the Wittgenstein strain of humour (the sort of thing that appears in her father's letters to his sisters) and she would talk nonsense by the hour with her brother Ludwig, who shared that strain. It was chiefly in this, in harmless jokes—a firework for her birthday present and the like, and in making music or talking about it that these two kept in contact. Lacking the maternal privileges of Mining and the unremitting zeal for human improvement of the remaining sister, she left him to manage his own life.

Margaret or Gretl—the nearest sister to Ludwig in age, in ability and in temperament—had a much greater influence on his development. She was all through her life an imposing personality. It was only in comparison with her and in their relations with her that the other two sisters sometimes seemed less than strong characters. For nephews and nieces and to the outside world *das gnädige Fräulein* and *die Frau Sektionschef* were powerful ladies with whom liberties would not be taken. Only Gretl (as she wrote to Ludwig) feared they might not be morally strong enough (she chiefly meant clear-sighted enough) in an emergency; only she sought to guide them; and only she could have taken over the responsibility for infusing a soul into one of Lenka's children.

She was also always more advanced than they were. True, she contrived like them to live, until the middle of the twentieth century, something like the life of the old Wittgensteins, a little snobbish perhaps, a little narrow-minded (in this respect Gretl was a friend of Freud's in vain), but essentially well-intentioned and happy, if moderate self-satisfaction be happiness. But in her impatience with mere tradition, her passion for new ideas—for psycho-analysis, say, or for socialism—her determination to understand, to analyse, to improve, even in the scale of her enterprises, she, perhaps most nearly of all his children, recalled the versatility and energy of her father. If this was applied now to human problems rather than technical ones, this was not just because she was a woman but because that was the spirit of the generation of Wittgensteins to which she belonged.

Paul and Ludwig were the two remaining sons, respectively five and seven years younger than Gretl, so that for the normal course of life they were thrown very much together. Paul's was a quite different nature from Ludwig's. He paid much less heed to the opinion of others. He wanted all his life to carry everything with a high hand. It was more important to be respected or even feared than to be liked. He certainly had the power and the determination necessary to secure this reaction. A pupil of Leschetitzky and destined for a career as a pianist (an evident sign of the mitigation of his father's regime), he made his concert debut in 1913. But in the early months of the war he lost his right arm on the Eastern Front. Returned by the Russians in an exchange of prisoners, he contrived both to be sent back to serve as an aide-de-camp and to teach himself to play with the left hand only (there was the precedent of Count Zichy for whom Liszt wrote pieces). He commissioned and performed pieces by Richard Strauss, Ravel, and others and continued his career as a concert pianist and a teacher with great success. It will already be apparent that the family provided its own severest critics and Paul's style of playing was not always to the taste of his brother and sisters, let alone of his mother. There was a violence about it which was only in part explained by the exigencies of execution with the left hand. They, who had heard Joachim and turned up their noses at Sarasate, were suspicious of any effect not strictly demanded by the music. (Ravel was to share these doubts.) On recordings and to a modern ear he sounds like a virtuoso indeed but an Austrian virtuoso and of the past, richer and less brilliant than a modern performer. The recordings, of course, are thicker than those of today and the unnaturalness of his mode of execution, which the Wittgensteins felt sharply, is not there to be seen.

He seemed in many respects to force nature and his own powers. It was scarcely necessary to learn to box—he, a pianist—with his remaining arm, even as part of his constant exercise to keep himself as upright and straight as a two-armed man. The incredibly long walks he took served that purpose too and were of a piece with his father's preferred way of spending a holiday, except that the father always wanted his wife, no vigorous walker, and his eldest daughter with him, while Paul went alone. He had, or came to have as a result of adversities and the strain of overcoming them, a harsh and secretive strain in his personality. Thus he lived with his family until the Second War but only some accident revealed to them anything of his private life. He left them then—in circumstances probably deeply misunderstood on both sides, in the lurch it seemed to them; for obvious reasons it seemed to him—and an unrevealed wife as suddenly appeared. The *Anschluss* proved even harder to overcome than the hardships of the First War and the humiliations of defeat. *Paul ist ein armer Kerl*—'Poor Paul!', Ludwig said for the first time; something symbolized by his relations with his family was finally broken by it.

Able, quick, well-read, with the manners of a grand seigneur, he seemed to carry with him as a professor in New York all the atmosphere of a vanished age. His time spent with the Starhembergs and with the officers of his old regiment (the 6th Dragoons) remained with him, for all that it was precisely the Germans that had excluded him. So did his wide culture and his interest in nature, again the qualities of an aristocrat. When he went on his long walks in Austria he would carry a Livy in one pocket and a botanical specimen in the other. Very characteristic of him at all times was a mocking sense of humour like his father's which deflated pretentiousness and cut discussions short. It is in this aspect that he first appears in his sister's reminiscences, a small boy torturing the now aging nursemaid with his flow of nonsense and only barely held in check by his grandmother's housekeeper, as tough a piece of timber as himself.

To all of these brothers and sisters whose attitude we know of, Luki or der Lukerl seemed at first someone that needed to be protected—and not only because of his age relative to them, for no one took this attitude

towards Paul. Luki was delicate and sensitive in temperament, and
almost certainly in health also. By the age of 14 it is known that he had
to be excused gymnastics at school and his history even before the
hardships of the First World War is one of minor operations and surgical
appliances (he had apparently a double rupture). At this time of his life
he both needed and invited affection.

Ludwig's later remarks about his childhood have to be treated with
great reserve, except of course as evidence of his later state of mind.
There is no absolute contradiction in them: it is possible to have the best
of fathers, the best of sisters, and the best of environments and still to be
unhappy, provided that the possibility of attributing the unhappiness to
a defect in one's own character is not excluded. And Ludwig, far from
excluding this possibility, embraced it. He looked back on his childhood
with an eye like that of St. Augustine, searching for sins and faults in all
the accidents and velleities of childhood. Often indeed it was precisely in
the context of a general confession that he spoke or wrote of those years.
At the same time he was proud of the sort of abilities that he developed
and of the sort of intellectual and moral culture that surrounded him.
This pride was a sort of affirmation of identity like that of the French
politician whom he quoted as saying that French was the only language
in which the words came in the order which one thought them.

A good intellectual nursery-training—*eine gute geistige Kinderstube*—so
he used to describe his earlier years, a remark covering, though not
restricted to, the fourteen years he spent at home. This was not, for the
most part, the merit of his tutors and governesses. They varied in their
competence and, above all, they themselves were not supervised, and it
would be an honest man indeed who would reveal to his employers that
he was unable to overcome their children's laziness or disinclination.
Even the piano Ludwig was taught by an unsuitable method and lessons
were discontinued. The incident is a little strange, because Paul, who
tells the story[2] and who stresses Ludwig's exceptional musicality, himself
managed to learn to play. It seems that Ludwig preferred subjects that
he could teach himself, as he later taught himself the clarinet: perhaps
also, where music was concerned, he preferred the role of critic or
director of others to that of executant. At any rate, for music he was
thrown back on the musical life of the household—the frequent concerts
visited or given in the house and the frequent performance by the family
of Mendelssohn's choral songs and duets, of Schumann's vocal trios, and
of chamber works and sonatas in which his mother and father and
brothers would play. He learnt to whistle with great accuracy and
expression and he found the technicalities of music easy to master. It
came as easily to him as if he had picked up a second language in the house.

2. In a letter to Professor F.A. von Hayek.

The nursery training however was principally the reading and discussion that went on in the house. Particular passages were dwelt on and learnt by heart. Works that seemed appropriate for an individual were put out for him. It was a constant discussion of life by means of literature and the emphasis was on the chaste and unrhetorical language in which it was expressed. Ludwig once said to a friend, 'It would not matter what you had done, you might even have killed somebody: what would matter would be how you talked about it, or whether you talked about it at all.' This is what he looked for in a literary work too—we find him recommending Tolstoy's *Hadji Murat* to Russell and Kleist's *Michael Kohlhaas* to one of his sisters: works in which the chief character shows not a stoical indifference to misfortune but, like an Aristotelian man, a readiness to do and suffer terrible things because, as matters had turned out, they too are part of the good or noble life that he has chosen. His life is ruined, ὅμως δὲ καὶ ἐν τούτοις διαλάμπει τὸ καλόν—but still the nobility shines through the misfortunes: it is true of the style as well as of the events related. In fact it is only from the style that one can see how these men accept their lot: in Wittgenstein's own phrase, that can only be shown, not said.

Of these particular works we know only that Ludwig read them before the First War. Of what works and writers he came to know actually in childhood we have only strong indications. The great writers—Goethe, Schiller, Moerike, Lessing—he turned to all his life. They were like suns he said, meaning that they were central to a culture and defined it. Goethe especially dealt with problems of Western culture, not as much to be sure as Beethoven did, but still with problems that no philosopher had touched: or perhaps Nietzsche had just touched them, but then Nietzsche (as he also said—and without a trace of deprecation) was more of a poet than a philosopher. These last remarks date from the thirties and their awareness that Western culture was simply one phase in the history of mankind is of a piece with his respect for the ideas of Spengler. Ludwig was not obsessed with the thought that the culture he himself represented was a thing of the past. He accepted it more simply—as the medium in which to form (and eventually to express) his understanding of the meaning of life. Music provides a good illustration of this: for him and his family music meant the music of Vienna, from Haydn to Brahms. He saw no need for a change: Berg's work, for example, seemed to him a scandal. The classical repertory contained more than enough to think about all one's life. His relation to music, so understood, was like his relation to his native language: he had no need to look outside it for means of expression. Towards music this remained his attitude throughout life; and such too was his relation in youth to a certain brand of (essentially) German culture, until maturity and the War added new dimensions to his sensibility. When he went to England as a student he took with him large numbers of the elegant but not luxurious editions then available of the works of these central writers. The books were sold after the First War and later in England he assembled a collection of cheaper second-hand editions—no doubt, in a favourite phrase of his, both inner and outer reasons played a part here.

He read intensively, rather than read widely: he would return again and again to a passage or a poem that 'said something to him' rather as he would when listening to music on the gramophone put the needle back repeatedly to some musical transition from which he wanted to extract everything. This was his attitude towards literature, also towards philosophy, well-reflected by his friend Engelmann's comments.[3] His reaction was not to say, 'Well, we understand that, what is the next step', but to stay with any profound utterance and attempt to deepen his understanding of it. Naturally enough, therefore, his notebooks abound in quotations from Goethe and Schiller.

Other writers and particular works became important later: those we are here concerned with formed part of the permanent furniture of his mind—of what he called, in fact, his *Kinderstube*. Lessing illustrates the inseparability in his eyes of ethics and aesthetics. The world changed in this respect and Ludwig came to think that culture had lost the integrity necessary if the best and strongest characters of an age were to turn to the arts, but he was himself a survivor of an earlier way of thinking. He often said that he belonged to a world that had vanished with the death of Schumann. In his admiration for Schiller too there was something out of date. The idealism, and the passion for freedom which attracted him took forms appropriate to the age before the Napoleonic wars. Moerike's merit was the simplicity and naturalness of his language: not exactly restraint but the exact fit of the emotion and hence of course the language to the situation. It is this quality that Ludwig found also in Gottfried Keller, whose works (as we happen to know) were among those he took to England with him and whom, Engelmann reports,[4] he passionately revered. The tone never a fraction too loud for the depth of the feeling—this is apparent in the Zurich stories that he liked to recommend to his friends—*Der Landvogt von Griefensee* and *Kleider machen Leute*, a typical case of his love for the apparently simple parable; but the figure of Heinrich Lee in *Der grüne Heinrich* is also very reminiscent of Ludwig and his judgements of himself, both in his shame over the betrayals of youth and in his sense (justified in Heinrich's case) that he had constantly refused and withdrawn when an opportunity was given him.

To say what Ludwig admired in Goethe would almost be to say what he found remarkable or worthwhile in life, so many are the themes and

---

3. P. Engelmann: *Letters from Ludwig Wittgenstein with a Memoir*, p. 132.
4. id. ibid., p. 86.

attitudes from Goethe that recur in his thought. The contempt for academic learning; the fertility and originality of a mind looking for fresh bases of comparison and not content even with the authority of a Newton; more generally, the completeness and harmony of a character that gave a distinctive stamp to every sentence that he wrote, so that for 'voilà un homme' one might substitute 'voilà un style'. No sensualist himself, Ludwig did not neglect—probably on account of their sense of liberation—the *Roman Elegies*. Above all Goethe was the man of the Enlightenment who had resolved for himself the conflicts of a life and an age of confusion and vicissitude.

Yet perhaps Ludwig had a deeper affinity with some Austrian writers. He said of Grillparzer: 'We do not know how beautiful he is.' That Grillparzer's classicism would appeal to him we can see from his selection of Goethe's *Iphigenie* for Russell to read and the theme of *Ein treuer Diener seines Herrn* (one play that we know to have been a particular favourite of his)[5]—the theme of the loyal servant who willingly puts up with every slight, judging that the worst affliction would be to commit a wrong himself, chimes exactly with Ludwig's own attitude towards lawful authority. But all of Grillparzer's plays were well-known in the Alleegasse, including those that suggest a noble and far from servile acceptance of the house of Hapsburg and a sense of the special moral role of Austria, not so much as a ruler of peoples but as contributing a true and perceptive and unexaggerated morality to German culture: in a related context Engelmann speaks of reason *with* emotion, head *and* heart—Grillparzer himself speaks of Austria as the young man placed between the childhood of Italy and the maturity of Germany

> Inmitten
> Dem Kind Italien und dem Manne Deutschland
> Liegst du, der wangenrote Jüngling, da.[6]

On the Rhine or in Saxony, he says, there may well be those who have read more in books but the Austrian strides far ahead when it comes to the heart of the matter: he has what most pleases God—a clear eye and a true and candid heart. He gives each matter what thought is due and lets others talk.

The epigrams and notebooks are yet more critical of the German national spirit, partly because many of them come from after the triumph of barbarism (as Grillparzer regarded it) in 1848. In politics, in literature, and in thought, Germany was characterized by conceit, abstraction, and bombast. For much of this Hegel was to blame and many of Grillparzer's epigrams are aimed, sometimes sourly, sometimes

5. id. ibid., p. 88.
6. *König Ottokars Glück und Ende*, Act III.

effectively, at him—'I'd rather believe [in] ten miracles than in one
Hegel,' he said about David Fredrich Strauss: 'The one merit of Hegel's
system is that it is as incomprehensible as the world itself,' and so on.[7]
Austrian literature on the other hand was characterized by modesty,
common sense, and genuine feeling. Grillparzer takes the comic poet
Raimund as an example to show the Germans that the task of art is not
ideas but giving life to an idea. In much of this opposition to nationalism,
radicalism, progress, and so on, Grillparzer was, no doubt, reflecting an
Austrian fear of forces that would divide the Hapsburg empire, but he
was at the same time representing himself as one of the true heirs of
Weimar classicism, now neglected in its own land. It is in a similar spirit
that he appeals to Kant. Such a feeling was not peculiarly Austrian: it
was shared by Schopenhauer and Nietzsche. Their names, with those of
Raimund and Nestroy and Grillparzer himself (all authors Ludwig
admired), serve to indicate a current—not the mainstream—in German
culture which he felt he belonged to and which accords with his nostalgia
for the period before 1848. The other typical representative of the
survival of classicism in Austria—Stifter—was not a particular favourite
of his, perhaps because too much of his simplicity seems contrived; he is
guilty of what Engelmann[8] calls 'artificial banality', or *Schlichtheit* in a
bad sense. Another Austrian writer who did impress Ludwig represented
a different strain—Lenau's Faust seemed to him a Catholic Faust
standing to Goethe's as Bruckner's Ninth Symphony did to Beethoven's.
In both cases he admired more the men of the Enlightenment but felt
sympathy with the Catholics. Lenau's Faust showed what despair was
like and showed the powerlessness of man: Ludwig likened himself and
his feeling of loneliness to that of *this* Faust.

Ludwig's familiarity with these authors requires no special explanation. They were part of his cultural heritage, their works surrounded
him in the libraries of his father's houses. His especial tastes seem to have
been formed under the influence of his sister Gretl. With Rudi, the
brother immediately older than himself, and his two friends the
Zitkovsky brothers, enthusiastic actors, she provided the cultural ferment
of the Wittgenstein household. The house performances of classical
drama were of course no offence to the aunts and uncles and there
Ludwig first got to know his Molière, always a moral teacher for him,
and Shakespeare, a unique figure in Western culture, he thought, like
nature or a landscape, a creator rather than a poet perhaps because he
was not a moral teacher. There naturally he heard Grillparzer again and
again: Gretl's performance as the unwittingly incestuous Berta in *Die
Ahnfrau* was particularly remembered. But as well as these respected
authors the young people affected modern writers and modern thinkers;

7. Cf. David Heald's 'Grillparzer and the Germans' in *Oxford German Studies* 6 (1971–2).
8. *Letters from Ludwig Wittgenstein with a Memoir*, p. 113.

Gretl's by no means muted championship of them though accepted sensibly and rationally by her Aunt Clara struck some other older members of the family as aggressive (a common reaction to directness in service of a cause not quite to our liking). Ludwig gave little sign at any period of interest in contemporary literature. Hofmannsthal was a distant family connexion and his idea of a return to the Baroque as a refuge from the decline of culture in his own day had some attraction. At any rate Ludwig liked to quote his saying

One has to behave decently
Some day, somehow, somewhere, it will pay off

But on the whole he was a stranger to Young Vienna and he hardly knew the names of the writers Ficker selected for his benefaction in 1914: Musil with whom he has often been compared he probably never read: there could have been no question of that before 1906 in any case. The chief exception to this disregard for contemporary literature—an exception proving the rule—was his respect for Karl Kraus, one of the chief influences on his thought, he said in the 1930s, listing those influences in the order Boltzmann, Hertz, Russell, Kraus, Loos, Weininger, Spengler, and Sraffa. Presumably this is a chronological order of their influence, but it also seems likely that he knew Kraus from adolescence on. The little brochures (*Die demolierte Literatur, Sittlichkeit und Kriminalität*, and so on) are to be found in their original editions on the shelves of family libraries and his sister Gretl (perhaps other family members too) had a complete set of *Die Fackel*, despite its fierce attacks on her father. It is obvious enough what he liked about Kraus—again, the style *and* the man. The satire, the exposure of shabby moral attitudes, the scorn were conveyed by a use and criticism of language which was more ethical than literary. Ludwig all his life had Kraus's habit of taking his opponent at his word and reading from a single ill-judged sentence a whole moral character. Further, the writers whom Kraus did respect and to whom he tried to lead his readers back were just those who belonged to that tendency in German literature that has been mentioned. The feuilletonist Kürnberger, from whom the motto of the *Tractatus* is taken, is one example: probably an example of coincidence of taste rather than of influence, for *Literarische Herzenssachen*, from which that motto is taken, was also on the library shelves. Another is Lichtenberg: the early nineteenth-century edition of the *Vermischte Schriften* was at hand, for the Wittgensteins tended to have early and fine rather than scholarly editions. Ludwig told von Wright that Lichtenberg was 'terrific',[9] and

9. Von Wright had already noticed parallels between Wittgenstein and Lichtenberg—see 'G.C.L. als Philosoph', *Theoria* 1942. Parallels between Lichtenberg and Wittgenstein's later work are noted and discussed in J.P. Stern's *Lichtenberg* (London, 1963), esp. pp. 158ff.

much earlier, before the First War, he had found a second-hand edition
for Russell. The theme of the errors and faults that arise from or are
reflected in the misuse or misunderstanding of language is prominent
here too; as is the aphoristic method of composition, which later became
Ludwig's own. It was the natural method for one who distrusted systems
and who believed in the inspiration of the moment—*der plötzliche
Einfall*—as if problems arose from an unhappy use of language and could
be solved by finding exactly the right turn of phrase. Thus we find him
longing for *das erlösende Wort*—the keyword, the solution, but also the word
of power that would release him; and in his letters to Engelmann he wrote:

> I know that brilliance—the riches of the spirit—is not the ultimate good,
> and yet I wish now I could die in a moment of brilliance.[10]

The ideas of Lichtenberg were certainly important to him and must be
discussed, but those of Kraus exercised a more indirect influence, for he
hardly recognized their existence, saying that, while raisins might be the
best part of a cake a bag of raisins isn't better than a cake: 'I'm thinking
of Kraus and his aphorisms, but also about myself and my philosophical
remarks.'[11] For his own part he was to spend a great deal of time
arranging and rearranging his remarks, but, true to this reflection late in
life, he always read Kraus for the raisins, laughing heartily at the rather
cruel jokes. 'He was a man of iron and steel,' ran one panegyric: surely
the wrong tense, said Kraus, he was a man of iron, and stole.[12]

As for modern thinkers, Rudi was studying science when he
committed suicide and Gretl also pursued studies in chemistry and
mathematics before turning to psychology. Besides it was then part of
general culture to read philosophy and much that passed for philosophy.
Rudi's copy of Emil du Bois Reymond's *Die Welträtsel* remained on
Gretl's shelves but it seems unlikely that Ludwig ever adopted anything
other than a negative attitude to this attempt to solve the problems of
metaphysics, or to see them as solved, by the methods of science: 'The
riddle does not exist,' he was to say in the *Tractatus*. Science did not
contain the explanation, it did not even touch our problems; and in the
rejection of its role as an explanatory agent he came nearer to Mach, a
cult figure of the time of his youth and undoubtedly known to him. But
much lies behind his remark to Russell that Mach's style made him sick,
for here again the style reflects the thought and shares its weaknesses.

10. Engelmann: *Letters from Ludwig Wittgenstein with a Memoir*, p. 55. Originally Wittgenstein wrote 'in a brilliant conversation' ('Gespräch'). Much more could be said, he thought, than written—the theme comes again and again in his letters. The letter is from August 1925; the cry for the word of power comes in *Notebooks 1914–16* in the entry for 20 January 1915.

11. L. Wittgenstein: *Culture and Value*, p. 66.

12. Actually Kraus made only typographical alterations: 'Er war ein Mann von Eisen und Stahl'—'Er war ein Man von Eisen, und stahl'.

The cumulation of instances, the lack of a central theme and of organization in Mach's writings correspond to the idea that all phenomena are equal, that science is an economical form of thinking forced on us in an evolutionary manner by the sheer repetitiveness of phenomena, that the self even is merely one prominent conjugation of impressions. Mach wrote without distinction, without epigrams and without striking images, because he did not think he was a philosopher: all unconscious of his own role he was embalming the science of his own day—an impressive achievement and justly influential but not always the best guide to its past history or the best help to an original thinker. Ludwig learnt much more from Hertz and Boltzmann: here he found the idea that science was a picture or model created by the mind, often with the utmost daring and freedom. He was to use Boltzmann's idea that different fundamental hypotheses—Ludwig called them networks— might equally fit the world, and he was to use the ideas of both scientists in developing his more general account of language as well as of science. 'The whole task of philosophy', he was fond of quoting from Hertz, 'is to give such a form to our expression that certain disquietudes (or problems) vanish.'[13] Boltzmann he certainly knew before leaving school, for there was talk (probably rather inaccurate) of an intention to study under him, frustrated only by Boltzmann's suicide in 1906. Boltzmann's *Populäre Schriften* were published in 1905 (many of course were available earlier separately) and the collection was dedicated to the shade of Schiller: it was he, closely followed by Beethoven, who had formed the man that Boltzmann supposed himself to be. The fusion of music, literature, and philosophy corresponds exactly to Ludwig's own habits of thought. That he came to know Hertz before undergraduate days is a conjecture based on his mentioning Hertz first among those that influenced him and also on the fact that Hertz and Maxwell were the sort of authors read in the Alleegasse.

These scientists apart, his earliest philosophical reading seems to have been in Schopenhauer: von Wright reports him as saying that his first philosophy was an epistemological idealism, in Schopenhauer's manner, until he was converted by the works of Frege. Certainly he later knew *Die Welt als Wille und Vorstellung* and was fond of quoting from the *Aphorismen zur Lebensweisheit*, indeed it was from there that he used to quote the epigram by Goethe which forms the motto of this book. Miss Anscombe has even suggested that he read and drew on *Die vierfache Wurzel*. Ludwig was far from possessing the scholar's virtue, or defect, of wanting to read everything in the obscurer and more original form, but he might have gone to this work if it had contained something of its own and if he had been particularly impressed by the work of Schopenhauer, but neither condition seems to have been fulfilled. As to the first, the

13. Quoted in *Philosophical Grammar* §89 p. 421.

reader who has a taste for German polemic must judge for himself: for the second, Ludwig later usually expressed reservations about Schopenhauer—'Schopenhauer is so clear you can see to the bottom,' he told his friend Drury, 'but Berkeley is really deep' (the contrast-figure chosen is surprising but characteristic): and in a similar vein he wrote, 'Where real depth begins, his comes to an end.'[14] The precise turn he gave to Schopenhauerian ways of thinking in his own writing must be traced later, but the attractions of Schopenhauer for any adolescent and particularly for Ludwig are clear. Elegantly written, for all its occasional shrillness, sprinkled with the quotations he was fond of, full of contempt for the professorial philosophy of philosophy professors, from which it differed so widely, original and personal in every line, it was the powerful expression of a proud and lonely spirit, fascinated on the one side by the clarity of its vision of the world, the plasticity of the world as an object of its knowledge, but horrified on the other side by the dark and mindless forces operative in that world and in itself. This loneliness, this fascination, and these obsessions were Ludwig's too; speaking often in correspondence of his evil spirits or *böse Geister*, he also thought with Schopenhauer that art, and particularly music, could incorporate these forces in such a way as to give him better understanding of them; and that, for the rest of life, some form of renunciation or denial of the will was the only way he could obtain release from them.

A similar set of problems, a similar agreement in attitude, attracted him to Weininger, whose *Geschlecht und Charakter* (*Sex and Character*) first appeared in 1903. It is tempting to look for parallels in the more restrained *Über die letzten Dinge* published posthumously in 1906 where Weininger says, for example, 'Every true and perennial problem is equally a true and perennial guilt; every answer is an atonement, every piece of knowledge won a conversion.' But the first and chief impact on Ludwig, and what he discussed with his friends later, was the popular book and the attitude it expressed. Here, as in the case of Schopenhauer, there are details to be discussed in a scholarly context—the theory of elements borrowed by Weininger from Mach and Avenarius and echoed by Ludwig in the *Tractatus*, the placing of logic and ethics on the same level; but the personal aspect was the important one. Weininger's thought about character, superficial and half-baked at times, came from a deep concern with ethical problems of his own life. This explains why Ludwig later said that his was an important book because of the questions it raised—you could even put the word 'not' before all his answers, the book was still worth thinking about. Weininger saw two ethical poles in human character—the one positive and creative and concerned with reality and truth; the other negative and amoral and concerned not with objective truth or goodness but with impulse and

---

14. *Culture and Value*, p. 36.

above all with sexuality. It is unimportant, though of course it is the most striking feature of his book, that Weininger identifies the one type or pole as the man and the other as the woman; that he conceives every human being as a mixture of man and woman, as it might be MMMW or MWWW; that he supposes the ground of this mixture to lie in the cellular constitution; and even that he anticipates, or as it was alleged plagiarizes, Freud in his reduction of the affective life to sexuality. These wild assertions, and the accompanying absurdities, are not the chief message of the book. Its merit is to have identified and expressed a moral ideal embracing truth, beauty, and goodness and all that is admirable and to have seen at the same time that there were principles in human nature, often residing precisely in what we value, that directly opposed this ideal. In his later aphorisms Weininger expressed his ideal thus:

> The highest expression of all morality is, Be!
> Let a man so act that his *whole* individuality resides in every moment

The paradox was that there were elements in a man that opposed this very expression. True, they were elements which, on Weininger's view, also opposed the formation of a soul, they did not belong to an ego, so that ideas like those of original sin or of the devil suggested themselves as a way of describing them. None the less those elements were there, and Weininger's second merit was to express, more from an ethical than from a scientific point of view, the virtual impossibility of overcoming them, indeed the actual impossibility for man in time of overcoming them except perhaps in an heroic act by what Weininger calls a genius. Finally the significance of Weininger for Ludwig resided in his attitude towards suicide—it was the decent man's way out when he felt he was finally becoming evil: so Weininger said, and his practice differed from it only a little, since he committed suicide shortly after his book appeared because with his inheritance (as he thought) he could not meet the moral demands he made of himself.

Weininger is sometimes defended on the grounds that, while his psychological theories are absurd, he presents very vividly the problems of his own life. The praise is feeble: Weininger is not just a text-book case; like every imaginative writer in so far as he suceeds he does so by expressing a

> . . . sorrow
> not mine but man's

All the same it is true that many upright people do not feel, and even reprobate, this sense of guilt and powerlessness, whether because they have not reached religion or because they have come to it by another way. In some cases, perhaps in Weininger's, its effects seem to be almost wholly bad; in others, perhaps in Ludwig's, friends and relations cudgel their brains to know why a man living an apparently decent life tortures himself with scruples and they are even exasperated that he concentrates on failings of his own instead of engaging immediately in some good work. Their nature is not therefore less divine—it is possible for the simple to see and act directly, appropriately to the nature of the case and to the best of their ability; within the human limits that apply to the others too they can attain a true moral insight and not necessarily a purely conventional or a utilitarian one without being afflicted with feelings of worthlessness and failure. But the way of a thinker—here meaning not an intellectual or scientist necessarily, but one who thinks about human life and his own life and feels the need to make sense of it—is bound to be other. It is not in itself a better way and is far from being a happier one, but it belongs to the economy of human life because it shows something also about the forces at work in the life of the simple.[15] It is for this that comfortable people read Augustine and Tolstoy, who followed this way, which was the way also of Weininger and of Ludwig.

Born in humble circumstances to an admiring father, physically rather unattractive, evidently near to madness, Weininger had yet two important features in common with the young Ludwig. First he was Jewish. He suffered from the consciousness of that fact. He identified the Jewish with all that was (on his theory) feminine and negative. It was a shame which nothing could wipe out and, together with the sexuality he detested in himself, it made up that radical inadequacy of character which he died to escape. The theme of the stamp put on a man's life and thought by his Jewishness often recurs in Ludwig's later notes, though, to be sure, he saw it more as an intellectual than as a moral limitation. Already in childhood he was preoccupied on a more practical level with dissociating himself for social and even moral reasons from all the different strata of Judaism in Austria. We shall see what remorse that cost him and can measure in that way how compelling the need for dissociation was. More basic even than this obsession with Jewishness, and in Ludwig's case, much more important, is the importance both he and Weininger attached to a man's character as something he could not escape from—$\mathring{\eta}\theta o\varsigma$ $\mathring{\alpha}\nu\theta\rho\acute{\omega}\pi\omega$ $\delta\alpha\acute{\iota}\mu\omega\nu$—so they, and Goethe, interpreted Heraclitus' dictum. This is connected with the second feature of Weininger important for an understanding of his attraction for Ludwig. Weininger too had a lonely youth, no doubt more for internal than for external reasons, and he became not so much introspective as (in an intellectual sense) self-centred or even solipsistic: that is to say, he was inclined to see the whole

---

15. I paraphrase here a letter of Wittgenstein's to his friend Arvid Sjögren, which itself draws heavily on the work of Kügelgen already mentioned.

world as related to his point of view. He was a microcosm of it and (perhaps the most important consequence) he felt whatever was evil in the world as his own guilt.

As for the especial guilt Weininger felt over his own sexuality, the more marked (on some accounts) because his homosexuality, like his Jewishness, marked him out as one of the most feminine of men, there is little sign that Ludwig shared it. Some concern with sexuality is inseparable from adolescence; and from slightly later in his life—the time of the First War—we have diaries in which he notes recurrences of 'sensuality' without evident guilt, simply as facts of life, distractions it is no use resenting. It seems that for him the dangers of an erotic relationship did not lie in its mere existence but as for most human beings in the risk that it might be conducted without straightforwardness or courage or with meanness and jealousy towards the other or towards some third person.

In discussing the literature and thought with which Ludwig was familiar in his first eighteen years we have been led to use religious terms. It is clear that in some sense the problems these authors dealt with were religious ones and we shall have continually throughout this book to try to define that sense. We know that Ludwig received formal religious instruction—a priest later to be a bishop and so presumably fairly highly regarded in Viennese society was brought in to give it. But (as he told his friend Arvid Sjögren) he lost his childish faith after conversations with his sister Gretl. She was at that time rather an enfant terrible in intellectual matters and her especial tendency was to reject tradition and externals and whatever smacked of humbug. Much later, demurring at von Wright's remark that Ludwig certainly did not have a Christian faith,[16] she mentioned the influence of the 'strong, severe, partly ascetic Christianity of my grandfather and his many children' and she said of Ludwig, 'He *was* a Christian in my reckoning.' Late in life, under the influence of a powerful spiritual director, she and her sisters came much closer to their church; but there was little church-going from the Alleegasse and (as she implies) the strongest religious influence was that of their grandfather and uncles and aunts, who were not, even formally, Catholics. Ludwig held aloof from formal religion all his life—it was difficult, he said, for him to bend the knee. That he prayed during the First War and that his reading then was intensely Christian, we shall in due course see, but this was noted as a striking change by Russell, who had the impression before the war that Ludwig was hostile to religion. Russell was surely right in detecting a change, but as far back as we have indications of Ludwig's inner life, his thoughts ran on sin and guilt and good and evil spirits: much of the machinery of religion and eschatology seemed to be for him the natural expression of moral realities.

16. In Norman Malcolm: *Ludwig Wittgenstein*, p. 20.

Such, then, so far as we know, was the intellectual nursery training that Ludwig received, the music, the books, and the thinkers that he came to know and respect and that, in most cases, continued to support him throughout life. Even in this part of his childhood and youth—though it was the part about which he expressed himself most positively—we have been forced to observe a sombre colouring. He himself said little about the formal instruction that he received. His sister tells of the grumpy and incompetent nursemaid; and his brother Paul follows this up by an account of the willing but not always competent tutors and governesses who had great difficulty in persuading the high-spirited boys (here Paul was clearly speaking chiefly of his own case) to apply themselves. At last one more honest than the rest frankly told the father that the boys were learning nothing. Appalled at so natural a consequence of a lack of parental supervision, Karl now intervened not without heat, first testing the boys and confirming their ignorance, and then altering his plan for their education and sending them to normal schools. As for the change of plan, it is to be remembered that Karl was now considerably older than when he had last had a son to educate (these were the youngest boys and separated by some years from any older brother). Moreover, at just this time—it was 1903—the news of Hans's suicide had come (that of Rudi was to follow later), bringing home the defects of the former system of education.

That the boys had learnt nothing was no doubt an exaggeration on Paul's part but Ludwig in fact did not show any particular ability in school subjects until later in life. We have already noted the phenomenon of late development in his family. The particular form it took in his case—as in his father's—was that he proved able to learn very rapidly what he required for some immediate purpose in any subject. Examples are how quickly he mastered the problems (then a great novelty) of the foundations of mathematics, and, on a humbler plane, the ease with which he could read Latin when the Vulgate and St. Augustine's *Confessions* became important for his spiritual life. He was never one for learning a multiplicity of things because it was expected of him or in order to vie with his contemporaries or out of a general and undiscriminating appetite for knowledge or information. It may be that he came to formal schooling, which favours such motives, too late; but it seems more likely that he was one child at any rate to whom his father's methods were intellectually suited. There was something very practical about his habits of mind. He did not, like many academics, lay in large stores of miscellaneous information which might some day turn out useful. His mind was not a compost heap in which disregarded scraps, lovingly preserved, eventually became a principle of fertility. Nor was it even a particularly efficient machine for collecting, sorting, storing, and retrieving whatever information it received. Obviously he did possess all necessary abilities of this kind, and he did become a man of wide general culture; but the peculiar excellence of his mind was his capacity for concentration. Once involved with a problem or question he could very rapidly master all necessary techniques. On the other hand he needed involvement with a problem if he was to make any progress. It was, agreeably with his father's wishes, an engineer's habit of mind, fitted to the analysis of a problem in fundamental and concrete terms and the envisaging and exploration of every possible combination that might solve it. It was a paradox, but perhaps the source of his fruitfulness, that with this disposition he became involved with problems generally considered, as he himself said, the most abstract that there are.

He had also in a more literal sense the abilities of future engineer and his sister Hermine noticed the contrast with his brother Paul's interest in nature—in flowers, animals, and landscape. At the age of ten his technical interests were so far advanced that he made a model with wood and wire of the house sewing-machine, a model that actually sewed a few stitches. He retained throughout life an interest in the logic of machines and in his last years used to go to the Science Museum in South Kensington to look at the steam engines. He liked to think with the machine—to understand every detail of its functioning—and this accounts both for his interest in the older and more perspicuous types of mechanism (motor cars never fascinated him) and for his success in repairing mechanisms that had gone wrong. Always it was achieved by the most careful observation of the machine from every side and deep and concentrated reflection until he had internalized the principle of the machine. It was thus that he had observed the distrustful sempstress in the Alleegasse and it was thus that he would examine the searchlight or boiler or whatever it was, sometimes rather to the irritation of onlookers, only intervening (like a well-trained doctor examining a patient) when the course to be followed was absolutely clear to him. His notebooks and the scraps of paper that he left often contain schematic drawings of machines. One, that comes in his philosophical writings, is particularly interesting because it recalls his youth: it is a sketch of an apparently especially efficient machine whose principle occurred to his father but which will in fact not move at all.[17] It is an early example of a favourite theme for Ludwig: the mind's liability to be misled by a superficial resemblance between the picture that it draws of a situation and other pictures it is familiar with. The essential thing is to have and to understand aright a picture that corresponds to all the real complexity of the situation. Ludwig seems to have been alone in the family in sharing such interests with his father.

Such, then, was the cultural and intellectual atmosphere in which Ludwig lived until the age of 14, such the education he received, and

17. The example is used in *PhGr* 194.

such the interests he displayed. It was, as our whole account of the house of Wittgenstein will have shown, very much a life inside an extended family. Visits to aunts and uncles apart, the year would be spent chiefly in the frowning Palais on the Alleegasse, with stays of a month or so in spring and autumn in Neuwaldegg, where Karl owned a couple of houses with large gardens stretching up into the hills behind them and forming a private Wienerwald. In the summer, the family would go to the Hochreith—Karl bought the estate when Ludwig was five and throughout Ludwig's childhood was busy rounding off his purchase, constructing a road and houses and arranging for planting and clearing. It was a place where no one save the family and its intimates could penetrate. Even the small town of St. Aegyd nearby was part of the Wittgenstein world—Karl had owned the factory there and there he also built, like a confident landowner, a church of his own confession and in the now rather pompous-looking Sezession style that he preferred. A rich and varied, but none the less an enclosed, environment, it reinforced in more than one way Ludwig's feelings of isolation. First it confined him to a small circle in which, as we have seen, the parents for all their good will could not, by reason of character and preoccupations, supply a vital sustaining warmth. There was affection from the brothers and sisters, to be sure; a slightly off-hand masculine kind from Paul, an enthusiastic and demonstrative kind from the sisters for their dear, their good Luki. It was clear that they wished him everything good, even, as Gretl once said, the good things he could not wish for himself, but they were sisters, with the normal tensions of a family relationship heightened by the open concern evident in that family for each other's spiritual as well as physical well-being; they were, moreover, (by the standards of childhood and youth) much older sisters. Ludwig needed, and always felt the need of, a friend. Here another influence from his home environment came into play—the moral, cultural, and even social fastidiousness which made most human relationships irksome for him, the more so, no doubt, because he was not at first exposed to a great variety of them. During the First War he was fond of quoting Schopenhauer's parable of the porcupines who crowded together for warmth on a winter's day and then drew apart to avoid one another's spines and so moved to and fro until they found a moderate distance that they could support. So it is with men too:

> The middling distance that they eventually find, which makes life together possible, is politeness and good manners.

True it gives an incomplete satisfaction to the need for mutual warmth, but to make up for that no one gets pricked by the spines. But a man who has a great deal of inner warmth (a man of great qualities) will prefer neither to cause nor to receive annoyance and will avoid the society of others:[18] if such men there be, Ludwig was certainly not one of them. He possessed in a high degree—too high for what most people would count as happiness—both the need for affection and for warmth and a sensitivity to the frictions and differences inseparable from any relationship. It is not necessary to think of these qualities—or these degrees of these qualities—as morbid. No doctrine of the mean can be applied to them simply. Both seem to belong to human good, even though a high degree of both makes many things difficult in life. Together with the intensity and concentration that he brought to any task, they made it certain that he would always be regarded as a *Sonderling*, an eccentric, someone out of the normal run.

In later life Ludwig rarely recurred voluntarily to his childhood. He used to say that it was an unhappy time and that he was lonely, but there was no element of blame for others in what he said, least of all for his parents. Just as he was proud, we have seen, of his intellectual nursery training, so he was glad to have been brought up to have 'standards'— standards which applied to intellectual work, to publication, to all cultural and moral matters from the greatest to the smallest. He accepted and affirmed just the things (it might be thought) which made his a difficult life.

We have mentioned that he looked back on his past with the eye of an Augustine, detecting faults and motives he may hardly have been conscious of at the time and subjecting them to as ruthless an analysis as he would (occasionally) apply to analyse the gestures or the turns of phrase of a friend. One such survey is preserved for us schematically in notes that he left among his papers. It is not clear whether he was preparing a confession for his family and friends or an account of his life for a psychiatrist (for he once had to be examined). In either case his purpose would have been the same:

> I do not want to be satirical at my own expense (he writes), rather I am trying to be just.

The draft begins with continuous passages and then turns to notes. The few at the end that deal with his time in Linz will be given later.

> As far back as my memory goes I was an affectionate child but at the same time of weak character.
>
> Very early in life I recognized the greater strength of character of my brother Paul. When he had been slightly sick and was recovering and was asked whether he would like to get up now or would prefer to stay longer in bed, he would calmly say that he would rather stay lying down;

18. *Parerga und Paralipomena* vol. 6 (Frauenstädt), p. 690 (cf. vol. 5, p. 452).

whereas I in the same circumstances said what was untrue (that I wanted to get up) because I was afraid of the bad opinion of those around me.

When I was about 8 or 9 I had an experience which if not decisive for my future way of life was at any rate characteristic of my nature at that time. How it happened, I do not know: I only see myself standing in a doorway in our house and thinking 'Why should one tell the truth if it's to one's advantage to tell a lie?' I could see nothing against it.

It is not as if I then set to work with the wickedness of a devil, unless one calls lies in themselves something devilish. I was not wicked and my lies had the aim of making me appear agreeable in the eyes of others. They were simply lies out of cowardice.

I do not want to be satirical at my own expense, rather I am trying to be just.

From my 10th or 11th year I remember the following incident:

box on the ear

looking for a gymnasium   Aryan origin

Gymnasium   love for Erich

fight

relation to Paul

to Gretl

to Rudi good memories

Wolfrum   I attempt to win him over and to entice him away from my brother

being in love   Paul a mischief-maker

innocent expression

lewdness

Latin exercises for Papa   thoughts of suicide[19]

It was entirely characteristic of Wittgenstein, at any rate when these notes were made in the twenties or thirties, to be fiercely concerned about any departure from the truth even for the sake of giving pleasure to others. It was the sort of problem that exercised his sister Gretl too. Brought up (it was perhaps more the style of the nineteenth century than of the present one) to consider always in a conversation what would gratify the other person and what way of saying it was most appropriate to him, they had to reconcile this aristocratic courtesy with a severer, perhaps a Protestant, tradition of saying the exact truth. She often spoke or wrote of how it might be done—a person, say a child, must never be rebuked unless he could be made to feel that you would far rather be praising him; a criticism should never be conveyed in a letter but only face to face, so that it could be adjusted to the reaction it provoked and the good will underlying it could be allowed to appear. Ludwig did not always follow these precepts and his rebukes in later life often seemed too fierce. All the more striking that he saw himself in childhood as having

19. The paper (in the possession of Wittgenstein's literary heirs) is fairly heavily corrected, like many of Wittgenstein's drafts, despite the absence of punctuation and some small slips.

the opposite fault of wanting too much to please. The need he later (and not long later) felt to tell the unpleasant truth was a conscious reaction against an earlier tendency to complaisance. Probably he was right both in suspecting this tendency in himself and in supposing (as he hints in these notes) that most aspects of it had been left behind after his childhood. He did give in first youth the impression of a sensitive person, anxious to please: the real force of his character (which came as a surprise to many) only appeared—perhaps it only developed—later. He managed in some way and at great cost to himself to put his life in order, and the effort this cost him bore heavily also on those that became at all intimate with him.

The general picture these notes give of a discontent with his attempts to conceal his failure to do all that he realized was expected of him, discontent with the innocent face that covered unconfessed weakness, cannot now be filled out with much detail. The episode of the search for a gymnasium is one he related to his friend Arvid Sjögren: then, as later, such clubs were extremely nationalistic and Aryan origin was usually required. It was so at any rate with the one Paul and Ludwig would have liked to join. Ludwig thought they could simply pretend to it: Paul, older and more realistic, saw that they would never get away with it. They found another. Wolfrum was the name of one of his father's close colleagues. The Latin exercises evidently date from the end of his period of private education and fit in with Paul's account of their father's discovery of the inadequacy of it. Ludwig remained unusually sensitive to duties of this kind: he reproached himself bitterly in the war, using his usual phrase *Ich bin ein Schweinehund*, when he had neglected to learn the organization of a K.u.k. infantry division or some similar piece of military pedantry.

Most of the incidents referred to are, we can guess, of a type fairly usual in adolescence, especially when allowance is made for the greater sexual segregation of those days. Even thoughts of suicide were common enough at 14 in 1903—the year of Otto Weininger's suicide. It is customary to draw attention to the prevalence of suicide among prominent Austrians at this time and to relate it to the loss of identity of their society, the wide divergence between the forms by which it lived and the real forces at work in it.[20] It is obvious that Ludwig and his brothers were affected by belonging to a society which recognized suicide as an acceptable way out, but beyond that their suicides or thoughts of suicide seem to have been only rather obliquely the expression of the moral constitution of their society. We have seen that their family formed a sort of enclave, fortified against the corruption and inadequacy that surrounded it by severe and private moral standards, which, it seemed, some of them had not the temperament to match or meet. Ludwig's case,

20. So for example Janik and Toulmin: *Wittgenstein's Vienna* (London, 1973), pp. 64–5.

about which we know most, if still little, seems to have been that of a phenomenally strong assent and attachment to these standards, often at war not only with the normal human failings that became glaring in their light, but also with a particularly soft and affectionate nature. Even if the thoughts of suicide are juxtaposed with exercises done (evidently inadequately) for his father, Ludwig was not one to see his problem as that of being unable to do what his father required. It was a struggle inside himself which led him constantly, for years after 1903, to doubt whether he could ever do anything worth while, and hence to the thought sometimes of suicide, sometimes of impending (because wished-for) death. In 1912 he told David Pinsent—

> that for nine years, till last Christmas, he suffered from terrific loneliness (mental—not physical): that he continually thought of suicide then, and felt ashamed of never daring to kill himself: he put it that he had had 'a hint that he was de trop in this world', but that he had meanly disregarded it...[21]

These thoughts recurred even after 1912 and we shall see that he was at least once on the point of suicide (though there was much that held him back, and not fear only).

In 1903, then, it was decided to send Paul and Ludwig to state schools. Paul went to a gymnasium in Wiener Neustadt, Ludwig to a *Realschule* in Linz. This is perhaps a sign that he seemed more fitted than Paul for the scientific or technical education that such a school would prepare him for. Also he was thought to be below the severer standards of a Gymnasium, which gave a classical education. The choice of Linz too was partly dictated by the thought that he would more easily pass the entrance examination to the appropriate form in that town than in Vienna. But it must also have been thought desirable both to separate the boys and to take them out of the atmosphere of the family home in which they had not achieved either much learning or much happiness. Ludwig welcomed the change in prospect at first: he later told Arvid Sjögren that he had wanted to go to Linz: it was as far west from Vienna as he had any prospect of getting.

It was a school for dayboys and he lived with one of the masters at the local Gymnasium, a Dr Strigl. It is typical of the style of generosity of his family that the Strigl family thereby became protégés, receiving tactful presents and help on important occasions, as when the daughter studied in Vienna and needed to have a couple of operations. Luki (as he was known to them too) was fortunate in this choice of lodgings, where he was held in great affection. Diffidence and the desire to please were in him allied to an originality which made them long remember his

---

21. Extracts from Pinsent's diary that deal with Wittgenstein have been copied and deposited in Trinity College Library. This one is dated 1 June 1912.

opinions and sayings. Even his formality had its charm. With the son of the family, Pepi—*Herr Pepi* as Ludwig at first called him—he had a particularly close though characteristically stormy relationship.

The *K.u.k. Realschule* in Linz has its small place in history, since Adolf Hitler attended it from 1900 to 1904. Hitler was a few days older than Ludwig, but during the year in which they overlapped he was in the IIIrd class while Ludwig was in the Vth. It seems that he was a year behind and Ludwig a year ahead of the average. The school counted as a stronghold of German nationalism and Hitler in *Mein Kampf* mentions one history master who traced all that was glorious back to the Teutonic tribes. There were a handful of Jews, rather isolated, but, by the rough standards of schoolboys, not persecuted. One former pupil explained that if a Jew were called *Saujud!* in a quarrel, this would only be in the formulaic manner in which a Bavarian would refer to a *Saupreuss*. Hitler's contempt for his contemporaries was more general. 'All future civil servants,' he is reported as saying, 'and with this lot I had to sit in the same class.' There is a slight inaccuracy here, for they would most be destined for technical or commercial occupations, but the inaccuracy may be Hitler's. Hitler, who was rather lazy in his schoolwork, and even in art relied on his facility, got little from his time in Linz, except for some contact with the musical life of the town, which was of rather a high level—though to be sure this would be so in comparison with Passau, not with Vienna.

Ludwig's first reaction to the boys in his class was more violent than Hitler's: *Mist!* (perhaps: 'What a shower!') he thought. One of his contemporaries later told his sister that he seemed to come from quite another world. His way of life was entirely different, he addressed them as *Sie* (surely a deliberate distancing of himself from them) and all his reading and interests were quite different from theirs. It was painful for him (then as later in life) to sit in a class, and, in the event, though he completed his three years successfully, his performance in school subjects was far from distinguished. Paul thought that his main interest was in physics and that this was the only subject in which he obtained *Vorzüglich*—the highest mark. This may correspond to his interests, but in fact on the five-point scale then used,[22] he obtained in his *Matura* certificate a 1 only for Religious Knowledge; a 2 for Conduct and English; a 3 for French, for Geography and History, for Mathematics, for Natural History, and for Physics, and a 4 for German, Chemistry, Descriptive Geometry, and Free-hand Drawing. Religious Knowledge, taught and examined by priests rather than professional teachers, was often rather generously marked: Ludwig later in life often speculated about the meaning of, as it were the moral truth behind, this or that element of

---

22. Vorzüglich, lobenswert, befriedigend, genügend, nicht-genügend. Say: excellent, good, fair, satisfactory, unsatisfactory.

traditional Christianity; perhaps he did so all the more effectively for a lack of that automatic consciousness of qualifications and definitions which is the chief by-product of a thorough training in Christian doctrine by the methods that have usually prevailed. The other marks on his *Matura* certificate, mediocre in themselves, are ludicrous in comparison with his later knowledge in these various fields. A lack of early training in scientific subjects is not a sufficient explanation for a result obtained after three years at school. It was more that his background and his temperament alike made the cumulative methods of a school distasteful to him. Depth, and not mere rapidity, was what he instinctively sought. However strong these temperamental reasons may have been, he himself saw them as failings; and in 1931 he remarked:

> My bad spelling in youth, up to the age of about 18 or 19, is connected with the whole of the rest of my character (my weakness in study).

This special difficulty with spelling presumably explains why, in German, he was actually given the failing mark of *nicht-genügend* in the written examination, redeeming himself only by obtaining *lobenswert* in the *viva voce*. It always cost him some effort to spell correctly and there are a fair number of mis-spellings, sometimes quite expressive ones, in his rougher drafts. His written English naturally varied with the length of time he had been in or away from England; but at all times the spelling was shakier than the idiom. This shadow of a defect, possibly hereditary, can be associated with the slight stammer that Engelmann observed. The stammer had disappeared by the twenties, when he spoke with the clear high voice not uncommon among those who have overcome an impediment.

Ludwig's remaining notes on his inner life, fragmentary as they are, show a concentration of his affection on one friend and the first attempts to make a general confession.

> *Realschule* class first impression. 'A shower.' Relation to the Jews. Relation to Pepi. Love and pride. Knocking hat off. Break with P.
>   Suffering in class.
> Halfway reconciliation and further break with P. Seeming innocence I learn the facts of life. Religiosity, G's influence on me, talk about confession with my colleagues. Reconciliations with P. and tenderness
>   Inventions
> Halfway confessions to Mining but ones in which I manage to appear to be an excellent human being.
>   Berlin.

Ludwig was of course registered at the school as a Roman Catholic; his origins will have been little known in Linz. It is probable that he felt he had denied or minimized his Jewish blood—for this was a common theme of his confessions. We shall see that at the time of the First War and in the years just after it he felt himself to be thoroughly Austrian and indeed in the cultural sense German.

Pepi was the forerunner of a series of attempts to find a friend: David Pinsent, Arvid Sjögren, and Francis Skinner are the best-known examples. Sometimes the friend was the same age, sometimes a little, sometimes a lot, younger. Sometimes there was a great intensity or erotic charge on Ludwig's side (often unperceived and usually not shared by the other). At least once the other was a girl. But in all there tended to be angry outbursts arising from Ludwig's pride and from his too accurate perception of the other's occasional failure to place the highest value on his friendship or to give first consideration to what his feelings might be. These difficulties were additional to the concern for the other's well-being and decent behaviour which made even his less emotional friendships an exacting privilege. Whether they led to breaks depended on the calm, as well as the depth of affection, of the other. Ludwig needed, and sometimes found, a friend more simple-hearted than himself. We shall probably never know how it went with Pepi, who fell in August 1914. Ludwig himself counted Pinsent as his first friend.

The influence of Gretl and the abandonment of childish faith, we have already seen. From these notes alone it is clear that a darker religion took its place: a consciousness of sin without a ground for hope of redemption. It became an important aim to set his own house in order (*mit mir selbst ins reine kommen*), to recognize in the first place, in order to detest, the weaknesses and dark places of his own nature. This was one purpose of his confessions: he said something of the kind later about a nephew's psycho-analysis—that the good it would do him would be the disgust with himself that he would feel when he had to tell all those things to the analyst. Another purpose was to get rid of one bad element at any rate, namely the pretence that the others were not there. Here, however, there were various temptations, among them that of making the fault appear something to be proud of—a *vitium splendidum*. To this temptation he felt he had yielded in his early confessions to his sister Mining. It was in this spiritual condition, carrying the seeds of much future distress, that he left Austria for Berlin.

3 Engineering Studies

LUDWIG left school in the summer of 1906: the years from then until the end or towards the end of 1912 were, he told von Wright, ones of constant unhappiness. The unhappiness appeared in, and probably it was largely caused by, the difficulty he had in choosing an occupation. He was unusually free in this respect, because his father's wealth made it possible for him at any time to change his place or subject of study. He told von Wright also that it was his original wish to study under Boltzmann in Vienna, but that Boltzmann committed suicide precisely in the year he left school. Some details in this story are not quite clear: Boltzmann taught at the university and Ludwig's *Matura* certificate from the *Realschule* sufficed only to obtain him admission to a *Technische Hochschule*. In order to enter the university, he would have had to spend a further year at some other school. Probably he had at most a vague wish to study under Boltzmann, but arrangements had already been made for engineering training before Boltzmann's suicide.

The wish to study under Boltzmann is interesting as being the first signs of his divided vocation, for it must have been the philosophy of science in Boltzmann that attracted him: he had not yet the necessary knowledge to appreciate the mathematical elegance of Boltzmann's strictly physical work.

Ludwig was, however, to study mechancial engineering; and that being settled the choice of the *Technische Hochschule* at Charlottenburg is easily explained. It was the most renowned and the best of German engineering schools and Ludwig long retained a belief in the superiority of Germany in engineering matters—a year or two later he told his friend Eccles in Manchester that an engineering training demanded a stay in Germany: England's days as a leader were long over. Besides this there may well have been a desire (as we have seen about the school at Linz) to move away from Vienna. At every point in his life he was apt to see very clearly the deficiencies of the place where he happened then to be living. True, in 1914 and even, fleetingly, in 1938 he felt that he belonged to Vienna and must share its fate but before the First War he was quite clear that everything technical was better in Germany and everything to do with human relations better in England.

To Berlin, then, he came, *der kleine Wittgenstein*, seventeen and a half years old, and about five foot six in height, still with the winning ways of his childhood but now especially formally dressed and serious-looking. Naturally contacts had been found for him there: there were the

Rieders—relations of the Sjögrens—to be called on, and a Professor Jolles in whose house he could stay.

He was registered at the THS on 23 October 1906 as a student of mechanical engineering (*Maschinen-Ingenieurwesen*) and was to stay for three semesters—a year and a half in the German system. He was given his leaving certificate—*Abgangszeugnis*—on 5 May 1908. No records of his course of study appear to remain. His sister Mining thought that from the start he was concerned with aeronautics and he certainly came to Manchester in 1908 already full of projects connected with it. She says that at some point unknown to her he was gripped almost against his will by philosophy. Again, we do not know in what form. It is only certain that there seemed at that time to be many possibilities for his future—Mrs. Jolles said as much when she learnt in 1930 that he had become famous as a philosopher. At the THS he would have access not only to many specialized departments of engineering but to theoretical study of mathematics and physics at a university standard. There was however no institute of philosophy and it is unlikely that he made his way across the Tiergarten to the University proper to hear Stumpf or Dilthey.

Wittgenstein, as he was now known—for in their brusque Berlin way even ladies would call him that—was given to a form of innocent boasting about any feature of his former life that seemed larger than lifesize: the remark about the nine grand pianos, already noted, was perhaps one instance of it. To this habit we owe our first detail of the Berlin period. He used to say that while there he had heard *Die Meistersinger* thirty times. The number *must* be an exaggeration, but the concentration on one great work is characteristic and reminds us again of the constant putting back of the gramophone needle to a crucial passage. Wittgenstein's reaction was not: '*Die Meistersinger* is a great work, I must hear more of Wagner' (or 'I must study his development', as a scholar might say) but '*Die Meistersinger* is a great work, I must hear more of it.' As a matter of fact he would later sometimes avoid a concert or a part of a concert in which passages from *Tristan* or *Parsifal* were played. It is possible to guess why just this work said so much to him, partly because we know the qualities that made it a favourite of his family. It was a treatment of problems of music and life at the same time—and its solution lay in the need for rules that can be discovered even within spontaneity but only when a note of reverence has been introduced. The opera contrives to show this and to lead to the happy ending necessary for so positive a message without overlooking the resignation and, from a human point of view, the loss involved in every achievement. It was entirely suitable to the tastes and preoccupations of these Wittgensteins that this general theme should be developed in connexion with music, for them not just a reflection but a part of life, and within a civic rather than mythological setting. The deep merit of the work resides in the extent to which these themes, sometimes banal, are grasped and felt and worked into a unity: it is one opera which seems for its five or six hours to present a world. Other works may be more completely Wagnerian but, by common consent, this is the most fully realized of Wagner's creations. It is perhaps a little too conscious; sententiousness is what makes the text so quotable. Forty years later Wittgenstein made a number of entries in his notebooks whose general effect was to give Wagner a high but a second rank—he was an imitator of Beethoven and in him Beethoven's terrible or cosmic irony had become earthly or bourgeois; his motifs were a sort of musical prose and did not amount to a melody and similarly his drama was not inspired by a succession of events. On the prelude to *Die Meistersinger* in particular he commented:

> Where genius wears thin, skill may show through.[1]

Too much contrivance, a theme not fully, perhaps not capable of being, mastered: the criticism is not unusual and perhaps not unfair, but in those Berlin years the work seemed to represent as well as to preach all that was *deutsch und echt*, all that was genuine in the culture he belonged to.

During these years Wittgenstein took up a practice which he followed at many periods of writing down thoughts about his own life.

> Strange [he wrote in 1929 or 30] that for so many years now I have scarcely ever felt the least need to make notebook entries. In the very first time in Berlin when I began to write down thoughts about myself on slips of paper, it was a need. It was an important step for me. Later it came partly from the impulse to imitate (I had read Keller's diaries) and partly from the need to preserve something of myself. So it was in large part vanity. But it was also a substitute for a person in whom I could confide. Later I added in an imitation of Pepys's diary. Of course, it is hard to be fair here, as always, because natural motives and vanity were thoroughly intermixed in what I was trying to do.[2]

The idea of laying by something of himself, not only on days of dispiritedness for which he had nothing else to show, but also on happy and successful days, was in fact one of Keller's chief aims. By Wittgenstein's own account this motive came to *him* only later and his original aim was to talk about himself as if to a friend in whom he could confide. It was his method later to write down his thoughts as they occurred to him on slips of paper and to enter them later in a large notebook. The question of the vanity involved in making and copying

1. *Culture and Value*, p.43.
2. Code diary.

such entries often exercised him, but clearly writing was a necessity for him—as he told a friend during the First War, 'If I had no paper I would write on sand'—and its fundamental purpose, as far as he could see it, was to reach a true understanding of, to come to terms with, his life as it actually was: to settle accounts with himself.

> If my notebook is to be in order, I must, as it were, step straight out of doors from it—into life—and not have either to climb up into the light as if from a cellar or to jump down onto the earth again from a higher level.

No diaries or notes of this kind from before the First War have been preserved as far as is known.

His family and friends did not know, or at any rate left no record, of what led Wittgenstein to leave Berlin. Perhaps he simply wanted to pursue his aeronautical experiments and investigations in England. But his brother Paul had the impression that it was occasioned by some disappointment.[3] In fact we know indirectly that there was some painful episode between him and the family with whom he stayed though its date is uncertain. At this distance of time it may be not unfair to reproduce an exchange of letters in 1930 between him and the wife of the professor with whom he stayed—an emotional lady, evidently, and enamoured of intellectual life—*schöngeistig* is the German expression—but these were qualities for which he had in earlier years more use than later. The first is dated from Berlin-Halensee, Kurfürstendamm 120, 20 September 1930:

> Dear Mr. Wittgenstein,
>   How long—how very long—it is since I wrote to you. Probably the last time was after my great misfortune. —And I know—you will not be at all delighted at the sight of my letter. I can just see your embarrassed face in Vienna. 'What on earth am I to do about these strangers?'—these 'extras' perhaps—'how can I get out of it?' For some weeks now I have been struggling against an overpowering desire to write to you. How can I bring myself to someone's attention when he has unambiguously and finally dropped us old friends? It's very perverse of me, of course, to do it all the same. But, good God, you have your own ways—and that's your affair. Why should I behave in your way and not in my own, even if it means that I have to poke my head for a moment out of the trapdoor so kindly allotted me by your 'Enough of that!', even if my pride has to take another beating. How much longer before there will be a definitive 'Enough of that' and it will be too late for writing or not writing and pride will be food for worms.—That's enough of an introduction. So. We went again, for the first time in very many years, to a scientific congress, in

---

3. Letter PW–F. v Hayek.

Königsberg,[4] and there I met a number of Viennese from the learned fraternity and found out in this way that our former friend—'our ex-friend' would be a ruder but more accurate expression—'little Wittgenstein' had after all turned into something more than a village schoolmaster and was very highly thought of there. Now, whether or not this is a matter of indifference to you or even unwelcome, I *have to* tell you how exceptionally, really exceptionally, pleased I was. After all, I believed in you when your prospects were—how shall I put it?—very chequered and it wasn't at all so clear where your 'ladders' would take you. I could easily offer you a regular correspondence in which you would write to me once a year and tell me how things were with you despite, or because of, the circumstances ('Enough of that!') which I have already mentioned and which you insist on. But, I shan't do it. I allowed myself, long ago to burn your letters and scatter the ashes to the winds. So be it. To my husband, who was attached to you like a father, as you know, you were a bitter disappointment, to him but not to me. Indeed, you will always belong to the few bright and dear memories that I have; that's to say you won't, but that 'little Wittgenstein' and dear person will, whom you scarcely wish to know about any longer. I don't know the Wittgenstein of today. Loyalty may well be a lack of mobility, a clinging to what's dead and gone, stagnation, a hindrance to progress and growth. I understand all that perfectly, but it is a disease I suffer from. And as a matter of fact I haven't made progress but have remained stuck in the rearguard. —Well, that is all over and not to be changed.

In the next room my cousin Margareta J., a well-known pianist who lives with us, is playing Brahms's B minor concerto. Oh, God, how times have changed since then. —(Do you remember how we played it three-handed?) Life is hard...[5]

Wittgenstein kept among his papers a pencil draft for a reply to this:

Dear Madam,

I received your letter today. It was indeed of course a surprise for me, though not of the unpleasant kind you supposed. On the contrary I feel it to be a piece of good fortune that fate has given me this opportunity to get in touch with you again. But now that I set about writing to you, I am faced with the choice of writing something not quite natural for me just in order to answer you, in order, as it were, to give you some sort of answer or else of writing what I think but what will possibly be quite unintelligible to you. I think it is better that I should write in the way that is natural to me and so make understanding *possible* for you, even if

4. 'Königsberg'. At the second Conference on the Epistemology of the Exact Sciences at Königsberg in September 1930 Wittgenstein's ideas on mathematics were presented by Friedrich Waismann and discussed at length. This marked Wittgenstein's return to philosophy after the twenties, as far as the continent was concerned. See *WWK*, pp. 19 and 102. 'Great misfortune': evidently a reference to the death of a daughter of the Jolleses after an accident in the home.

5. Letter in the possession of Wittgenstein's literary heirs.

difficult, rather than writing something that sounds halfway plausible but that can in no circumstances be understood, because it is not true.

First of all, you are quite right: it is indifferent to me whether people in Königsberg think highly of me or not. With all the good will in the world I can't think much of myself and the good opinion of professors of philosophy and mathematics (with some exceptions) does more to confirm me in my unfavourable judgement than to give me encouragement. (To be sure, the good opinion of the few exceptions won't mislead me either—or so I hope—in my judgement about myself and my work, but I accept it gratefully as a piece of personal friendliness.) Well, when I read that you had attended a scientific (???) congress, I was overcome by the violent repugnance and disgust that I always feel at the fact that the wives of the professors participate in congresses and have discussions with 'members of the fraternity'. The only reason, though, that I write this to you, is that it is *one* symptom of all *those characteristics/things* that have become so alien to me. When I was in Berlin and even later I did not feel this repugnance. Later it grew very strong in me and made mutual understanding or indeed contact with you impossible for me. Indeed when I received your last letter but one, the letter in which you told me of your great misfortune, your unnatural and—forgive me the word—journalistic ways of expressing yourself caused me such repugnance and the feeling of such a difference between us that I put aside as absurd any idea of achieving an understanding with you.

But I now see (and I saw even then, though less clearly) that it was wrong of me to allow myself to be ruled by such feelings when feelings of gratitude and loyalty should have come first. For that reason your reproach of disloyalty is unfortunately not quite unjustified even though the case is not quite what you, naturally enough, suppose it to be. I knew and regretted that I had to disappoint your husband but *that* was not where my fault lay, because I had to disappoint a number of people precisely by doing the right thing. What I want to say is that my fault did not consist in regarding the achievement of understanding as out of the question, because it was—and *perhaps* still is—out of the question: no, my fault consisted in treating gratitude and loyalty as less important than mutual understanding, whereas in comparison with them it is of no account whatever. So I did after all not behave decently and I beg you and your husband to forgive me for that, if you can do so whole-heartedly. I will further say that three passages in your letter affected me in a good sense: that in which you write that I had my ways and that was my affair, but you must behave in your own way. That is true and I often think the same thing. Then the passage where you express your pleasure at my success in Königsberg and this passage pleased me although it rests on a false assessment of the judgement of 'men of the learned fraternity'. And finally the words 'Life is hard'. That was a tone that I understand...[6]

6. Draft in the possession of Wittgenstein's literary heirs.

Wittgenstein also kept Frau Jolles's rather calmer reply thanking him for
his candour and a letter of 1939 with the project (unrealized) of a
meeting during his visit then to Berlin. There were some family
keepsakes that she wanted to go to him rather than to anyone else.
Written in widowhood, old age, and the shadow of impending war, it too
is emotional but with the emotions of resignation and final leave-taking:

> I send you my kindest thoughts and wish you many good and nice things
> and when I am dead remember me with friendship and don't call me too
> many names.
>   What from time to time put you off was perhaps involuntary
> affectation. Or was it voluntary?[7]

We are given only an impression of the friendship, but it contains
much that was typical of Wittgenstein—the music played together,
Wittgenstein contributing only one line but no doubt most of the musical
direction; the intensity and affection of Frau Jolles first invited and
welcomed, then rather harshly rejected, ostensibly, and up to a point
really, because of some theatricality and artificiality in her (as if that
were not part of what brought them together), but more deeply because
she threatened his privacy; then, as a further stage, his recognition that
he had failed in affection and loyalty, a recognition expressed in a letter
carefully and of course painfully explaining what he had been right to
resent. Even the element of confession in his letter is in a way
self-defeating, because what was required was not to admit to coldness
but to show warmth. This was a feature that made some of his relations
critical of Wittgenstein's confessions which seemed to them to be aimed
at recording his faults rather than at putting them right. Still in the case
of Frau Jolles the open explanation did have its success and there
supervened a fourth and calmer stage, not full friendship but the
memory of it. Wittgenstein (who wrote a number of letters rather like
this) may have been right in thinking that only by way of such openness
was a friendship *with him* possible and sometimes (as perhaps in the
present case) he managed to judge rightly what his correspondent could
take. Generally, however, as he himself saw in theory, such adjustments
in a friendship require meetings and not letters, and even then belong to
the realm of what can be shown rather than said. The letters, carefully
retained, with what mixed feelings we can only guess, are themselves one
token of a contradiction in Wittgenstein's attitudes: another is given by
their whole subject-matter, which suggests not only a demand for
affection greater than his capacity to receive it but a full awareness of this
tension.

---

7. Letter in the possession of Wittgenstein's literary heirs.

This is an impression obtained chiefly from the later remarks and reactions of Wittgenstein, and, as he himself indicates—he was often to comment on it—there had been a change in him. Partly the change was simply a matter of growing older and becoming surer of his own powers and clearer about his own needs. In his first years as a student he clearly accepted the companionship and concern of Frau Jolles and the affection and ambitions for him of her husband. Later he found he had to pursue his own path and the professor saw a promising pupil shake off his guidance and immerse himself in a succession of disparate inquiries and experiments, each of which generated new questions before any result was reached. The process culminated, after a development accelerated if not distorted by the war, in Wittgenstein's becoming a schoolmaster. To one who did not know the success or the value or perhaps even the existence of the *Tractatus*, it would seem like a waste. Yet in fact one central idea of that work—the idea of the proposition as a picture—owes much to reflection on Professor Jolles's subjects, which were Descriptive Geometry (his study of methods of representing solids and other figures in three dimensions by drawings in one plane) and Graphical Statics (a method of reducing a system of forces graphically and showing the resultant force, couple or equilibrium). As for Frau Jolles, it is only a guess, though a probable one, that his move away from Berlin was a move away from the oppressiveness of her affection. He was still glad enough of it during the war, when a warm letter from her was a relief after a businesslike and impersonal note from Keynes in England.[8] But after the war (it seems) he made a decisive break with her as with so many of his past attachments, fiercely trying to work out his own life.

The move to England, then, seems to have been an early stage in his development into an independent scientific workerwho consulted the professors and discussed things with them rather than followed a regular syllabus leading to a general examination. In this respect, Manchester was an excellent choice for a place to study. There were few research students, no definite plan of work for them, and ready access to the professors: Horace Lamb,[9] the Professor of Mathematics, instituted a seminar so that they could bring their problems to him. The professors and junior instructors were in many cases men who had achieved or were destined for great distinction. Lamb himself is best known as the author of a still classic work on hydrodynamics. This specialism led to his being one of the leading advisers on the construction of aeroplanes during the First War. He had been a pupil of Clerk Maxwell whose views he developed in general lectures on Statics and Dynamics. He argued vigorously for the theoretical development of statics on the basis of Newton's laws: there was no need for further experimental data to be

8. Code diary 5 and 28.10.14.
9. See *Obituary Notices of Fellows of the Royal Society* (*ONFRS*) 4 (1935).

brought in. A summary of theoretical statics by him can be read in the eleventh edition of the *Encyclopaedia Britannica*.

J.E. Littlewood, whom Wittgenstein was to know again in Cambridge as a Fellow of Trinity and later as Professor of Mathematics there, was lecturing under Lamb from 1908 to 1910 and Wittgenstein attended at least some of his lectures, well-known for their elegance of presentation, on the Theory of Mathematical Analysis. (Over the years Wittgenstein acquired something like a second-year undergraduate's knowledge of Pure Mathematics. He used to examine later the proofs in Hardy's *Pure Mathematics*, but his interest was, in early years, in the foundations or lack of foundations of the proofs, and later in their significance.)

Littlewood[10] in the late 1960s thought that Wittgenstein came to Manchester to learn what was behind engineering and that for this purpose he intended to sit at the feet of Rutherford. The general motive is probably correctly ascribed, and it was indeed the case that a year before Rutherford had arrived at Manchester. Curiously enough in the very year that Wittgenstein came to Manchester there was a large loan of radium made to the University from the Austrian Academy of the Sciences to enable Rutherford to carry further his work on radioactivity. There may well have been some direct or indirect link—his father's patronage, perhaps—between this loan and Wittgenstein's coming, but we know nothing of any contact between him and Rutherford or of any interest of his in Rutherford's work. (It was in these years that Rutherford established the structure of the atom.) Naturally we may assume that the atmosphere of 'getting on with the job' that Rutherford always created round him contributed to Wittgenstein's ideas about how serious work on science was done, but the affinities of his own thinking and his search for the foundations (if the term may here be used) of engineering were much more with the work of Lamb already mentioned. To some extent Wittgenstein when he arrived was under the protection of Rutherford's predecessor, Arthur Schuster,[11] who had retired in order to devote himself to the organization of science but was still an honorary professor in the University. Schuster, a younger son of a rich family of converted Jews (still flourishing), had discovered in fairly early life that he had more devotion to science than to the family business. So far from being opposed in this, he brought a good deal of his family money with him to finance scientific projects and posts in the university, including meteorological work on the upper atmosphere at the Howard Estate Observatory, where Wittgenstein first went.

Schuster, a pioneer in the development of meteorology as a university subject, had arranged for kites or balloons (according to the weather conditions) to be sent up with recording instruments, essentially in order

10. Personal communication.
11. See *ONFRS* 4 (1935).

to measure the temperature at various heights and to relate these measurements to other conditions in the upper air. These measurements would then be compared with results at other stations, and were in fact published daily in the *Daily Telegraph* and in midland newspapers. The lecturer in meteorology from 1908 (and thus the person in charge of the experimental station) was a distingushed physicist, J.E. Petavel.[12] Among his other gifts he was particularly ingenious at designing and adapting machinery for experiments and it was for this reason that he was called in to improve the winch used for the instrument-carrying kites and hence became interested in the whole project.

Petavel, already a Fellow of the Royal Society and later Director of the National Physical Laboratory, could have served as the prototype of many British scientists in war fiction. He was in fact the son of a Swiss divine and educated partly in Switzerland and Germany. From his English mother he inherited a respectable fortune. He was chiefly distinguished by a remarkable versatility: he had done important work on explosions, devising the Petavel gauge, long used for ordnance purposes; he had worked on low-temperature phenomena, the expansion of gases, gas engines, reactions at high pressures. Now, after a visit to the kite and balloon station at Glossop, he made a free balloon ascent and became interested in aeronautics. He was appointed to the original Advisory Committee set up by the government in 1909 and was soon a leading authority on all aspects of the subject. He first learnt to fly himself and put in what was then the average number of hours in a flier's life. The last flight of this programme resulted in a severe accident, but the sequel to it was not only that he escaped from hospital while still crippled but that when the war came he was once again up with de Haviland testing the stability of a new plane. The indifference to danger was characteristic of him and appeared at Glossop too when he calmly went on using the winching gear of a kite during a thunderstorm and stopped only thirty seconds before it was destroyed by lightning. He had other traditional eccentricities and, as Professor of Engineering, would provide considerable amusement by driving round Manchester in a one-cylinder motor which was liable to stop every hundred yards.

Yet he was, of course, not a figure of fiction but a figure of his times, when a scientist could and must turn his hand to every aspect of a problem that concerned him, when he expected to design and make his own equipment and would often be involved (as Petavel was) both in devising new instruments and in theoretical work, and when many branches of science now specialisms with their own accumulation of data and techniques were in their infancy and could be advanced by a resourceful use of general principles. It was a natural consequence of this atmosphere—though perhaps it was particularly marked at Manchester

12. See *ONFRS* 5 (1936).

—that the division into departments did not dictate the studies or limit the collaboration of the scientists working there. Schuster had been Professor of Physics and Applied Mathematics; he handed over the latter subject to Lamb when he arrived: Petavel was Lecturer first in Physics, then in Meteorology, until he became Professor of Engineering. The seminars or laboratories or workshops of one department would be made available to researchers from another and members of Rutherford's team would—as a holiday or a hobby—go out to Glossop and try some meteorological experiment with the kites. The especial degree of freedom and mobility at Manchester was owed partly to the small size of the departments and indeed of the university, partly to the marked scientific ability of those working there. The sheer size and competence and method of Charlottenburg might be missing, but Manchester had its own tradition of self-taught and independent scientific genius—to this day a visitor can expect to be reminded of Dalton and Joule. These men of 1908 were also—here too in contrast perhaps with Charlottenburg, certainly with our own age—easily accessible, ideal teachers or helpers for the young Wittgenstein with his succession of interests and problems. He was to have similar good fortune in Cambridge. Even his perfect manners (when not in the heat of argument) would not have won him so ready or so informal a hearing in Germany.

Wittgenstein came to the Research Station at Glossop in the summer of 1908 apparently shortly after leaving Charlottenburg. For obvious reasons the station was more fully manned during the summer months and much more frequent ascents were made. The arrangement seems to have been that he could use the machinery for tests with his own kite, and, in partial return for this, he would assist with constructing, sending up and recovering the instrument-bearing kites, which were in practic- ally continuous operation during the summer. The station was three miles from Glossop, near a then isolated inn, The Grouse Inn, situated among moors chiefly used for game, over which the scientists were allowed to stumble to recover their kites and wire. Roads were few and rarely used. The observers, as they were called, would stay at the inn and shared a sitting room. In a letter to his sister Hermine dated 29 May 1908[13] (perhaps the earliest of his letters preserved) he tells how he and the meteorological observer, Mr Rimmer, are living there alone with the landlord and his wife. The food and the lavatory arrangements are rather rustic (*ländlich*) and this is hard to get used to (this complaint, as a whole, at any rate as regards the food, is very unlike the later Wittgenstein). His own job is to provide the kites, which were previously ordered from outside. So far he has only observed but now he is capable of making a kite. He needs a friend and is looking for one among the students who visit the station on Sunday. He is sleeping well and (a

13. Seen when in the possession of Dr Thomas Stonborough.

characteristic ending) if only his own self didn't rankle with him all the time, he ought to feel really well there for the time being (*und wenn nicht mein eigenes Ich immer an mir nagte, so müsste ich mich vorläufig hier wirklich wohl fühlen*). The friend seems to have arrived when William Eccles came to do a spell as observer[14] and, finding Wittgenstein's books and papers littering the table, tidied them up and placed the books in neat piles. Something about the simplicity of this action attracted Wittgenstein as well as amused him and the two men became friends even beyond the needs of living together in the small inn for some weeks.

Eccles was a qualified engineer, four years older than Wittgenstein, ostensibly doing research, assisting indeed with the meteorological programme, but principally waiting for a suitable post. One turned up in August of 1909 with Westinghouse, and he spent the rest of his working life with that firm, the first few years in Manchester. Wittgenstein told Eccles that they got on so well together because Eccles had a soothing effect on him. J. Bamber (then of the Engineering Department) confirms this, in so far as he says that Eccles and Bradley, the other friend that Wittgenstein made on the moors, were the exact opposite of Wittgenstein in temperament.[15] Eccles had certainly an exceptionally open and cheerful and friendly disposition. Far from stupid he was yet simple, in the sense that he did not complicate his life by allowing the thought of how others would view his actions to enter into his motivation. And he took things as they were, not as they might be represented to be: for him Wittgenstein was not a comic foreigner, he did not strain to hear the foreign accent;[16] and if Wittgenstein was given to being lost in thought and would dislike being interrupted, that was a fact about him to which one could easily enough adjust. They talked a lot about technical problems, though more those of the work they were jointly engaged on than any arising out of Wittgenstein's work: Eccles did not think that Wittgenstein knew any subject thoroughly—it would have been surprising at nineteen if he had—but he admired Wittgenstein's ingenuity: he used to quote the example of a door that had to be difficult for strangers to open, though not locked—Wittgenstein hit on the idea of a handle that had to be lifted instead of depressed. In this respect Eccles thought he himself appealed to Wittgenstein and in a measure resembled him

14. Eccles gave an account of his friendship with Wittgenstein to Dr W. Mays of Manchester for an article in *Mind* (reprinted in K. Fann: *Ludwig Wittgenstein: The Man and his Philosophy*, 1967, pp. 79–88). Wittgenstein's letters to Eccles, with a few notes by the latter, were published in *Hermathema* XCVII (1963); see also L.W.: *Briefe*, 1980. Subsequently Eccles gave a number of interviews, including one to the present writer.

15. Letter to the author.

16. Witnesses differ about exactly how good Wittgenstein's spoken English was. No doubt it varied with date and circumstances. Occasionally, it is clear, a German idiom would betray him, but the accent is generally agreed to have been good. Those with whom he was most relaxed tend to say he had no foreign accent whatsoever.

because of his desire to get to the bottom of things, by his ability to analyse and find out what the problem really was.

Wittgenstein told Eccles that he was the only friend he had—it was the sort of avowal he used to make; and in fact both men were rather lonely at the time. How deep the friendship was it is hard to judge but it does illustrate a feature of himself that Wittgenstein explained to his friend Postl (who became a family servant)—'I am a collector of good human beings,' he said (*Ich bin ein Sammler von guten Menschen*). He liked especially the naturalness and directness which, for himself, was a quality to be striven for. They talked, of course, of personal things. Wittgenstein told Eccles of his mother and his sister Hermine (an important figure in his life at that time), of a brother who had committed suicide because he was so brilliant he could do anything (presumably Hans): but on the whole, and especially when it concerned the future or plans, they spoke of Eccles's life—where he should go to work, how he should furnish his house, are the topics of the two pre-war letters that Eccles printed. The younger man was taking the leading role—but, it is important to note, without giving offence: the relationship suited both of them.

Eccles's accounts also illustrate another feature which recurs in Wittgenstein's friendships: they depended on or originated in long periods spent together. The work at the station was arduous and continuous. Sometimes there would be eight or ten ascents a day until as late as nine or ten at night. The kites would be sent up as high as 5,000 feet—naturally this demanded a train of kites. Sometimes the kites would escape or come down and then a correspondingly long distance would have to be traversed on foot to recover them. There were the dangers, too, of storms, which Eccles and Wittgenstein were exposed to as well as Petavel.

So passed the first period of their friendship in the summer of 1908. It was continued, however, during the succeeding year when both men were in Manchester. Wittgenstein would go often with Eccles to the house of his aunt Mrs Moore, the wife of a doctor in the poor district of Manchester, still remembered in the television series *Coronation Street*. The comparatively humble, simple and useful life of these people appealed to Wittgenstein. He liked innocent friendships and minor attentions. Small but carefully chosen presents were characteristic of him, and Eccles retained all his life a particular rather attractive biscuit-box, the remains of a present that had been given by Wittgenstein to Mrs Moore. They would go for little expeditions together (not walking, for that was too much part of their job on the moors). One incident often related is that of the proposed visit to Blackpool, when Wittgenstein, in default of regular trains, wanted to hire a special. Eccles dissuaded him and they went to Merseyside and indulged in the alternative luxury (in those days

it must have cost a penny) of a trip on the ferry. Further afield they
visited Eccles's family home in the north of Ireland.

Some things they did not share. Eccles had the impression, surely false
and partly contradicted by his own story of the inn, that Wittgenstein
was not much of a reader. Eccles had not much of an ear for music,
though he went occasionally to the Hallé concerts with Wittgenstein and
heard him whistle through what he took to be whole symphonies. Like
all observers he was impressed by the intensity and concentration with
which Wittgenstein listened to music. Their relationship was probably
all the less stormy because of the differences in their character and and
outlook: it did not occur to either of them to expect the other to have the
same tastes and reactions as himself. In one respect they perhaps shared
more than Eccles was aware of. He thought of himself as having no taste
for art at all as opposed to Wittgenstein, the connoisseur. Yet the two
discussed the furnishing of Eccles's new house and were at one
(Wittgenstein as usual was the critic and the guide) in excluding
ornament. Thus he wrote to Eccles in July 1914:

> I can't see any drawing of a bed, or do you wish to take the one which the
> furniture manufacturers submitted? If so *do* insist that they cut off all those
> measly fancy ends. And why should the bed stand on rollers? You're not
> going to travel about with it in your house!? By all means have the other
> things made after *your* design.

At the same time he approved the absolutely straightforward and
unadorned drawings that Eccles made for a wardrobe and medicine
chest and so on. He only wanted (it was more unconventional then) to
have the horizontal crosspiece on the doors in the middle, so that the top
and bottom panels should be of the same height. As for the decoration of
the room later—at least it was Eccles's recollection that this belonged to
a later period—Wittgenstein prevailed upon the Eccleses to plan a room
with a self-coloured royal blue carpet, black woodwork, and yellow
walls. Echoes of the Wiener Werkstätte.

Wittgenstein admired Eccles's form of intelligence as well as his
character: indeed the two were part of the same phenomenon—an open,
inquiring turn of mind. He said that Eccles was a man who could make
use of any amount of experience, because his experience was alive in him.
Straightforwardness, no nonsense, balance, the capacity for happiness
and for an essentially masculine comradeship—these were qualities that
belonged to one sort of friend that Wittgenstein made—Raymond
Priestley is a later example. Eccles had something in his nature that
would preserve him through vicissitude and make him always valuable
to those capable of appreciating him: this seems certainly to have been
the case and also to have been the sense of Wittgenstein's inscription on a

photograph of himself given to Eccles—words whose precise meaning Eccles never troubled himself about:

> Much are we given by time, much also robbed of, but may you,
> Winning the best as your friends, ever rejoice in their love.[17]

Wittgenstein *knew* his friend: it is striking that he knew at once (although a hundred accidents might have accounted for it) that Eccles's failure to reply to a rather too hearty wartime letter was in fact caused by scruples at corresponding with an enemy—the sort of consideration that would not weigh for a moment with Wittgenstein and his sophisticated Cambridge friends.

It was on the moors in the summer of 1908 that Eccles and Wittgenstein met: in the following academic year Wittgenstein was registered as a research student working five days a week in the Engineering Department. Eccles and Mays explain this as follows:

> His experimental work with kites did not last long as he soon realized that until some form of engine was available it was not much use developing an aeroplane. By a stroke of good fortune the plans still exist of his experimental engine. It is not known how he arrived at the idea of having a reaction jet at the tip of each blade of a propeller, but he soon realized that the discharge nozzle was all-important and accordingly transferred his interests from the moors at Glossop to the laboratory of the Engineering Department where he had a variable volume combustion chamber constructed by Messrs. Cook nearby and had it arranged for a variety of fuel spray and gas discharge nozzles.
>
> The whole assembly was workmanlike and practical for its purpose and the jet of hot gas from the discharge nozzle on top was arranged to impinge on a deflector plate where its reaction could be measured. This apparatus was operated successfully, but before much experimental work was done with it, Wittgenstein got interested in the design of the propeller and as this lent itself to a complete mathematical treatment his interests in mathematics developed and eventually in turn the propeller got forgotten.
>
> It is interesting to note that Wittgenstein's idea of a combustion chamber together with a tangential reaction nozzle at the tip of a propeller blade was brought into practical use for the rotor blade of a

---

17.　　　　Vieles giebt uns die Zeit, und sie nimmt's auch, aber der Besseren
　　　　　　　　frohe Neigung sei auch Dir froher Besitz.

A slight misquotation, from memory, obviously, of a distich (that actually translated) which Goethe addressed to his son:

　　　　　　　　Vieles gibt uns die Zeit und nimmt's auch; aber der Bessern
　　　　　　　　Holde Neigung, sie sei ewig Dir froher Genuss.

Wittgenstein's version speaks of joyful friendships joyfully possessed.

helicopter by the Austrian designer Doblhoff during the second world war
and is now adopted by Fairey's for their Jet Gyrodyne as well as by others.

The account is rather schematic and it must be remembered that Eccles
did not know everything that Wittgenstein was doing. He seems to have
kept up *some* interest in the kites even after starting to work in the
laboratory, for he is listed as the 'Voluntary Observer' at the station in
the university prospectus of 1909–10; and we know, as will be seen
shortly, that he was thinking about the foundations of mathematics
before April 1909. Probably his progress was not so linear as Eccles
supposed. After all it must be supposed that he knew before going to
Manchester that a flying-machine would need an engine, and at the end
of his Manchester time, when he went to Cambridge, he still represented
himself as a would-be aeronaut or aviator. As long as he worked in
aeronautics at all his aim seems to have been to design, build and fly a
machine himself. The ambition itself was intelligible at the time. When
Wittgenstein started on the project, the Wright brothers had not yet
made the powered flights, hundreds of times longer than any previous
ones, to which they owe their fame. But it had long been clear—
Boltzmann represents the view in a lecture of 1894—that theoretically
the most promising line of development in aeronautics was not the
dirigible airship but the aeroplane propelled by airscrews. Boltzmann
spoke when Maxim had already flown such a machine, but there were
then found to be enormous difficulties in the steering. To overcome these,
to discover a method, was, so Boltzmann thought, a task for a genius who
should at the same time be a hero. In 1908 nearly every aspect of
powered flight was still in the stage of trial and error. Eccles observed
this with dismay about the experiments on the moors, but it was entirely
characteristic of the aeronautics of the time. Every form of wing was
tried out—often with fatal results: it was only in succeeding years tht
wind-tunnels were used and a conventional wing-shape and design of
machine was evolved. The engine too was a crucial factor: it must not be
forgotten that until the time that Wittgenstein was actually working on
the question, no flying machine had yet been fitted with a sufficiently
light but powerful engine to permit sustained flight. True the petrol
engine had been developed and nothing as big as Maxim's steam-engine
was necessary. The Wrights fitted a modified motor engine. The French
developed the rotary aero-engine in the immediately succeeding years.
Wittgenstein's project may have been over-sophisticated: it would have
been rather foolhardy to fit a flying machine with so experimental an
engine, since even with conventional petrol engines one of the main
problems for aviation was that of reliability; but for all that it was an
attempt to deal with a pressing problem of the time, no more
fanciful—though one might say more imaginative—than many that were

then put forward. Some engines were tested on an unused railway line in the Manchester area,[18] which suggests a fair degree of development. We do not know, however, that Wittgenstein himself actually flew: he certainly meant to, and Russell, when he came to know him, occasionally referred to him as an aviator or aeronaut. It is entirely possible that he did: we should not necessarily have heard of it, for he was very selective in what he told his friends—he did not set out to give an account of his life, but would tell an anecdote à propos of something from time to time. And, naturally, not all even of these have been recorded.

These various projects in Manchester were work not for weeks but for years, and he did in fact spend three years there and planned to spend at least a fourth. He seemed an odd fish, Littlewood says. Bamber and Mason, then of the Engineering Department, both describe him as charming but as of nervous or excitable temperament. This indeed was his oddity to an English eye—the extreme formality and charming manners in everyday matters coupled with an intensity, a concentration, and an extreme dislike of being interrupted or thwarted in things that mattered to him. 'He was doing work' (Bamber says) 'on the combustion of gases and his nervous temperament made him the last person to tackle such research, for when things went wrong, which often occurred, he would throw his arms about, stamp around and swear volubly in German.' He used to ignore the midday break and carry on till evening. In the autumn of 1909 Mason helped him to install some heavy apparatus which he had removed from the Physics Department to the new research laboratory in the Engineering Department. It was a matter of a heavy-duty compressor used in research into high-pressure gases. 'A charming, enthusiastic man, not then very well accustomed to the handling and assembling of engineering machinery,' says Mason. The qualification is important: Wittgenstein was a learner; by the time of the First War he made an excellent director of work in an artillery workshop.

Wittgenstein himself took his 'nervous temperament' more seriously, it was an aspect of the self that rankled with him, and in another letter to his sister Hermine (dated from Glossop, 20 October 1908) he speaks first of his work—how Lamb, the professor, 'doesn't know whether his equations are soluble by present methods'—and then goes on to the sort of personal problem typical of him. 'My evil spirits induce in me the most tiresome moods you can imagine.' After talking to Lamb he went into the drawing room and saw the assistant, 'a very dangerous person' for him, and began to scold him about the way the drawing had been done. He got more and more excited—he was upset that the assistant was so

18. L. Goodstein's account of Ludwig Wittgenstein's reminiscences in A. Ambrose and M. Lazerowitz's *The Philosophy of Wittgenstein*.

indifferent—when fortunately the assistant was called away and Wittgenstein came to himself. It was a common pattern before the First War and later in his time as a teacher: some people were a danger to him because he was hypersensitive to them, he would react too violently and betray himself. He wanted to be natural and spontaneous and yet in these cases his automatic reaction was a disproportionate one which he could only dislike but could not correct. It added to the unpleasantness that he disliked the violence of his own reaction without condoning the real fault—the laziness, the *Schlamperei*, or the meanness that had evoked it.

Manchester University records show that Wittgenstein's registration as a research student in the Engineering Laboratory was renewed for 1909–1910, when, as we have seen, he was also the Voluntary Observer for the Kite Station. In 1910 and again in 1911 he was elected to a research studentship by the Senate. The second year of this studentship he did not take up. It was a small honour and an indication that he was then at any rate accepted as a serious student. Financially it meant little to him. He seems to have financed his own experiments with kites and combustion chambers, and to have had a shed built on the moor; and in general he lived not ostentatiously but the life of a rich man. Eccles estimated that he had an income of £5,000 a year, an enormous sum for those days. The episode of the proposed special train naturally stuck in Eccles's mind. Bamber mentions lodgings at Fallowfield, where Wittgenstein's only pastime was to relax in a bath of very hot water (there was more of his innocent boasting—this time about how hot the water was). His address in 1911 is known to have been 104 Palatine Rd (now 154); Palatine Rd was on the borders of Withington and West Didsbury—Fallowfield adjoins and is perhaps a venial error of Bamber's. It is of some interest that the district was one of comfortable large houses, with a fair sprinkling of successful Jews and Armenians. 104 in particular was not a house that usually took in lodgers and there is an impression in Vienna that a friend of the family was found for him to stay with. At all events it was a comfortable life and Wittgenstein showed perhaps a severe taste but no austerity in his ways, apart from supporting the comparative rigours of the moor as well as the next man. He dressed carefully and apparently expensively. He took full advantage of the lively musical life of Manchester and every informant mentions visits to the Hallé concerts for more serious composers—Wagner, Beethoven, Brahms—and the concentration with which he would listen and the enthusiasm with which he would then talk about music.

Three years in Manchester: it was to be twenty years before Wittgenstein again spent so long in a single place. It is to be supposed that there—or between there and Charlottenburg—he learnt a lot; but these were not years in which he imposed himself or in which his powers broke through. Charming, erratic in temper, able, eccentric—he might have been no more than that. He had yet to break out of the chrysalis. Partly he lacked there the sort of stimulus that Russell was to give him. Partly (a connected point) he was still casting about for a vocation. None of the projects he was involved in were carried more than half-way: some of them were doomed to failure because they were too ambitious. It seems that he was carrying out his father's wish that one of his sons at any rate should turn into something useful and that his heart was not in it, with the the result that, while he was enthusiastic enough about individual projects, he had no determination to carry the whole thing through to a finish.

4 Cambridge 1911–12

IN THE autumn of 1911 Wittgenstein took a step which was to prove decisive. Instead of returning to Manchester according to plan, he went to Cambridge to attend Russell's lectures. No previous arrangements had been made with Russell, nor with the university or any college, and Wittgenstein was not in fact matriculated until February 1912. His coming there had all the marks of an impulsive decision and of an experiment. Various accounts have been given of the events that led up to it. Von Wright, repeating what he was told by Wittgenstein, says that an interest in the construction of flying machines led to one in engine construction, then to one in the design of a propeller, and hence to a preoccupation with the mathematical treatment of this problem and finally to a concern with the foundations of mathematics. Eccles's account, we have seen, supports this; so does Russell's in his *Autobiography*[1] and in various memoirs which appeared after Wittgenstein's death:

> Wittgenstein had intended to become an engineer, and for that purpose had gone to Manchester. Through reading mathematics he became interested in the principles of mathematics, and asked at Manchester who there was who worked at this subject. Somebody mentioned my name, and he took up his residence at Trinity.

Russell could, of course, easily have been mentioned by someone at Manchester—by Littlewood, for example, though Littlewood himself does not recollect such a conversation. But Wittgenstein's own account of the matter, given to von Wright,[2] was that, resolved to study the philosophy of mathematics, he went first to Jena to discuss his plans with Frege and that it was Frege who advised him to go to Cambridge to study with Russell.

Wittgenstein must have said this to von Wright in the 1940s: at about the same time his sister was writing her account of him in Austria. Speaking of the Charlottenburg period she says:

> At this period or a little later he was suddenly gripped by philosophy—that is to say by reflection on philosophical problems—so violently and so

1. Volume 2, pp.98ff. This part of the autobiography was published in 1968 but evidently substantially written in 1933.

2. Biographical Sketch, p. 5, in *Ludwig Wittgenstein: A Memoir* by Norman Malcolm. As will appear, there are grounds for thinking that Wittgenstein, when he went to Jena and to Cambridge, had already decided to give up his studies in engineering, as von Wright states.

much against his will that he suffered severely from the twofold and conflicting inner vocation and seemed to himself to be torn in two. One of the many transformations which he was to go through in his life had come over him and shook him to the depths of his being. He was engaged in writing a philosophical work and finally made up his mind to show the plan of this work to a Professor Frege in Jena, who had discussed similar questions. Ludwig in these days was constantly in a state of indescribable, almost pathological excitement, and I was very much afraid that Frege—whom I knew to be an old man—would not be able to muster the patience and understanding needed to go into the matter in a way commensurate to its seriousness. Consequently I was very worried and anxious during Ludwig's journey to Frege. It went off however much better than I had expected. Frege encouraged Ludwig in his philosophical quest and advised him to go to Cambridge as a pupil of Professor Russell's, which Ludwig indeed did.

This is the account of one who was a party to Wittgenstein's deliberations at the time and is thus independent of his own later account. It would seem probable that the visit to Jena was made from Vienna and in the summer of 1911, though presumably the philosophical writing had begun some time earlier. Both this account and Wittgenstein's own conflict with Russell's impression (recorded in 1951) that Wittgenstein 'at this time'—i.e., presumably, when he came to Cambridge —did not know Frege personally.

Such contemporary records as exist—it is the common experience of biographers—do not agree completely with any of these recollections: they are perhaps different fragments of the mosaic. When Wittgenstein first called on Russell in October 1911, he told him—and Russell recorded it in a letter to Lady Ottoline Morrell on the same day, 18 October 1911—that he 'had learnt engineering at Charlottenburg, but during his course had acquired, by himself, a passion for the philosophy of mathematics, and has now come to Cambridge on purpose to hear me'. A fairly early date for the interest in the philosophy of mathematics is also implied by another shred of evidence: P.E.B. Jourdain kept a correspondence book[3] in which he recorded a conversation that he had with Russell on 20 April 1909:

> Russell said that the views I gave in a reply to Wittgenstein (who had 'solved' Russell's contradiction) agree with his own.

These views (which revolve round abstaining from assuming that there are any such things as classes at all) do not fall for examination here, but it is clear that already in his first year in Manchester Wittgenstein had

---

3. Now in the Institut Mittag-Leffler, Djursholm, Sweden. I am very grateful to the Institute for providing me with a copy of the entry and to Dr I. Grattan-Guinness for telling me of its existence.

read enough to propose a contribution of his own, and it is probable that he had read some Russell before he met Frege. His later enthusiasm for both books leads one to suppose that he had read both Frege's *Grundgesetze der Arithmetik* and Russell's *Principles of Mathematics*. The latter and the second volume of the former were both published in 1903, and each author has an appendix mentioning the other.

There is a certain tradition among Wittgenstein's pupils that he was in fact led to Frege by the appendix in Russell's book, but one pupil's account of Wittgenstein's memories suggests a source from which he might have learnt of Frege independently. The professor of philosophy in Manchester—it was thought surprising there should be any students of it in that businesslike town—was Samuel Alexander, an eccentric character held in much affection. After combining Darwin and Hegel in a book on ethics he had lapsed into a long silence and seemed spent as a writer. But in the years from 1908 to 1912 he poured forth a stream of articles which were thought, so his obituarist says, to reveal a 'surrender to Moore'.[4] He was, in those years, a propagandist against idealism and for the view that the object we perceive or image or ideate is entirely distinct from us and that consciousness is only another thing along with it. He certainly knew the work of Frege and Russell and their definition of number. It is entirely plausible that it should have been he (as R.L. Goodstein relates) that told the young Wittgenstein of Frege, though we have no other evidence than Goodstein's of Wittgenstein's story that Alexander called Frege 'the greatest living philosopher'.[5] This advice of Alexander's may have occurred at any point between Wittgenstein's arrival in Manchester and his visit to Frege—though it presumably left time for him to become familiar with and formulate some views of his own on Frege's work (see p. 83 below). Of Wittgenstein's attitude to Alexander we know little. Drury[6] recollects Wittgenstein's admiration for the title of Alexander's main work *Space, Time and Deity* (1929)—'That is where the great problems of philosophy lie'—but it is unlikely that its content, with its assimilation of philosophy to natural science, pleased him, if he knew it at all. Some of Alexander's interests in experimental psychology are echoed, perhaps by chance, in Wittgenstein's own avocations.

Wittgenstein's correspondence with Frege no longer exists, and the notes made by Scholz (before this part of Frege's papers was destroyed in the war)[7] begin with a request for a meeting in October 1913, which was

4. J. Laird in *Proceedings of the British Academy* 24 (1938) 386.

5. Goodstein's account is given in Ambrose and Lazerowitz: *Ludwig Wittgenstein, Philosophy and Language* (1972), pp. 271–2. One or two points in the story as Goodstein heard it are hard to reconcile with the remainder of the evidence but, fallible though memory is and colourful though anecdotes tend to be, it can hardly be doubted that there was some consultation with Alexander.

6. Personal communication.

7. See G. Frege: *Briefwechsel* (1976), pp.264–8.

quite certainly not their first meeting, since Wittgenstein writes to Russell about a visit in the winter of 1912. Besides which we have Hermine Wittgenstein's circumstantial account, which is quite incompatible with a first visit to Frege later than the summer of 1912: whatever else she may have misremembered, she could not have been so anxious about Wittgenstein's visit to Frege after hearing Russell say (as she did in that summer), 'We expect the next big step in philosophy to be taken by your brother.'

The rough pattern, then, is a growing interest in the philosophy of mathematics, caused by coming across Russell's or Frege's book in Charlottenburg (1906–8), encouragement from Alexander in Manchester (1908–11), an attempt to solve the main problem then outstanding, leading to a correspondence in 1909 with Jourdain—perhaps occasioned by Jourdain's own articles on this subject in the *Philosophical Magazine* for 1905,[8] followed by a period during which, as an avocation, he planned a philosophical work: finally the visit to Frege, the advice to study under Russell—very reasonable, since Frege himself, though confident that a solution could be found, did not himself work on one or even mention in his lectures what the possibilities were.[9]

'He acquired, by himself, a passion for the philosophy of mathematics' —this remark, if true, and it is a report of Wittgenstein's own account of the matter, seems to defy expansion. We can assume that he had no mentor—and it is indeed difficult to trace a probable one at Charlottenburg or Manchester. We can point to the books he knew well and the passages he later quoted. But what it was that first caught his eye seems to be a matter of fruitless conjecture. Yet there is a certain puzzle to be resolved—and one that ran through Wittgenstein's philosophical life, namely the puzzle of the connexion between his passion for the philosophy of mathematics and his other interests, or indeed passions. He was never a mathematician. For him as an engineer, mathematics was a tool. His mathematical education and sophistication barely qualified him to discuss the foundations of mathematics in the way he did. So it was not by difficulties or obscurities in his everyday work that he was led to these problems. Yet perhaps half of all that he wrote was concerned with mathematics. And on two occasions, this one of his coming to Cambridge, and the later one of his resuming passionate philosophical discussion after long silence in 1928, it was a problem in the foundations of mathematics that excited him (here Frege and Russell's difficulties with the paradoxes, there Brouwer's exposition of intuitionism). These problems were not only unconnected with his technical concerns as an

8. Vol. 6, pp. 42ff and 61ff. If it is necessary to explain how Wittgenstein came across this, Dame M.L. Cartwright has pointed out to me an article in the same number by Horace Lamb, one of Wittgenstein's professors, that he might well have consulted.

9. Not as far as R. Carnap, who heard his lectures at this time, could remember. See *The Philosophy of Rudolf Carnap* (ed. Schilpp), pp. 4–5.

engineer; at first sight they also seem to be quite different from his other preoccupations. He was a musician. He read passionately works of literature that 'said something to him'—something, that is, about human life. He brooded over his own defects and difficulties. He was a fierce critic of failings, especially those of honesty, in others. He came to write a book whose main point (he said himself) was an ethical one. What had the foundations of mathematics in common with propensities like these?

The question is the expression of a confused feeling that not quite everything fits. An answer can be attempted on various levels. The first is this: why should Wittgenstein be an engineer rather than a philosopher of mathematics? We may of course try to say *what* particularly interested him about it, but there will come a point at which no explanation can be given of why he was interested in this or that. He himself did not try to justify his own interest. Russell wrote to Lady Ottoline in March 1912:

> What he disliked about my last chapter [of *Problems of Philosophy*] was saying philosophy has *value*; he says people who like philosophy will pursue it, and others won't, and there is an end of it. *His* strongest impulse is philosophy.

On another level, Wittgenstein seems to have thought that what was wrong was *saying* that philosophy had value. It was a craft, a discipline—he said in his notebooks for 9 November 1914 that he had a strong scholastic feeling about it—and its value consisted in its being well done. So one should do it well and not preach about it: in his slightly later terminology, showing not saying was important. Like all crafts, its exercise at its highest produces beauty, a beauty which it requires an intellectual effort to grasp:

> He is the ideal pupil [said Russell in the same letter]—he gives passionate admiration with vehement and intelligent dissent. He spoke with intense feeling about the *beauty* of the big book [probably *Principles of Mathematics* rather than *Principia Mathematica*], saying he found it like music. That is how I feel about it, but few others seem to.

It is true that Wittgenstein came to think, at the time of completing the *Tractatus*, that as well as possessing intrinsic beauty his logic could throw light on the possibility of metaphysics, the nature of ethics, and, in however oblique a manner, the meaning of life; but it is not clear that these implications were obvious to him from the start. For various reasons, to be discussed later, Russell was shocked to find Wittgenstein a mystic after the war; but one reason appears in the letter already quoted twice. Wittgenstein had been horrified to learn that a man he liked was a monk.

He abominates ethics and morals generally; he is deliberately a creature of impulse and thinks one should be.

(There follows the passage first quoted, with its reference to Wittgenstein's strongest impulse.)

'I wouldn't answer for his technical morals,' Russell concludes. However *this* form of abominating ethics is perhaps not so far from the *Tractatus*: it is a dislike of preaching, and hence of preachers. More significant of a change of mind is Wittgenstein's own remark in his notebooks (2 August 1916):

Yes, my work has broadened out from the foundations of logic to the nature of the world.

The notebook in which this is written is the first (of those that have survived) to show a clear realization that the logical inquiries he had been engaged in have implications for all the areas I have just mentioned.

All the same, it seems that there was from the start a connexion between the interest he acquired in the philosophy of mathematics and the first gropings of his thought about the philosophy of life. Von Wright recalls Wittgenstein's saying that it was Frege's conceptual realism which made him abandon his earlier idealistic views derived from his reading of Schopenhauer.[10] The theme is a complicated one, because Wittgenstein not only began with a sympathy for idealism and indeed solipsism, but retained that sympathy throughout the period of writing the *Tractatus* and (it can be argued)[11] well beyond it: we shall see that the insights which that sympathy gave him were incorporated in the *Tractatus*. In his notebook for 15 October 1916, among many passages deeply influenced by Schopenhauer, he described his own development thus:

The way I have travelled is this: idealism singles men out from the world as unique, solipsism singles me alone out, and finally I see that I too belong to the rest of the world; so that on the one side *nothing* is left over, and on the other side, as something unique, *the world*. In this way idealism, strictly thought out, leads to realism.

(The passage is echoed in *Tractatus* 5.64.) Our concern here is with the starting-point of this progress: Wittgenstein gave Schopenhauer's idealism a solipsistic twist which its author (feebly enough, as Hacker argues) always disclaimed:

10. Biographical Sketch, p. 5, in *Wittgenstein: A Memoir* by Norman Malcolm.
11. This point is elaborated by P.M.S. Hacker in *Insight and Illusion*.

The whole of nature outside the knowing subject, and so all remaining individuals, exist only in his representation. He is conscious of them always only as his representation, and so merely indirectly, and as something dependent on his own inner being and existence.[12]

It was not in fact against so radical an idealism (let alone against solipsism if that is implicit in it) that Frege was arguing. He was attacking it, in the first place, because of its inadequacy to account for the truths of mathematics, the common picture of the world as consisting on the one side of physical objects and on the other of our ideas. There was also a third realm which housed concepts, propositions (thoughts, as Frege called them), numbers, and countless other categories of object. These were not the products but the objects of our thinking and what he hoped to do was to recognize the eternal relations subsisting between them. One example of his way of looking at them is given in a famous passage in that introduction to the *Grundgesetze der Arithmetik* that Wittgenstein knew nearly by heart:

The point can be put yet more generally: I recognize a realm of what is objective though not actual, whereas the psychological logicians immediately assume that anything not actual is subjective. Yet it is by no means apparent why something that has existence independent of the judging subject must be actual, which, after all, presumably means that it must be capable of directly or indirectly affecting the senses. No such conceptual connexion can be detected. Indeed examples can be produced that show the contrary. Thus the number one will scarcely be thought to be actual, save by followers of J.S. Mill, and on the other hand we cannot attribute a private one to each individual, since then there would have to be a preliminary investigation of how far these ones agreed in their properties and, if someone said, 'Once one is one', and someone else, 'Once one is two', we should be reduced to registering the difference and saying, 'Your one has the former property, mine the latter.'[13]

The recognition of objects from this third realm was essential, according to Frege, for a correct view of many philosophical problems; thus it was essential if we were to be able to say, as common sense would demand, that a thought (in the sense of what can be judged, thought, or entertained not in that of the judging, thinking or entertaining of it), if true, is so quite independently of whether anyone ever judges it to be true. But the recognition of those objects was especially necessary if we were to understand the nature of the universality and validity of the so-called laws of thought—the laws of logic or of truth itself:

12. Quoted by Hacker: op.cit., p. 71 from *Die Welt als Wille und Vorstellung*.
13. *Grundgesetze der Arithmetik* vol. I (1893), p. xviii.

By logical laws I do not mean psychological laws of taking something to be true but laws of truth itself. If it is true that I am writing this in my study on 13 July 1893, while the wind howls outside, then it is true even should all men later hold it to be false. And if being true is in this way independent of being recognized to be true, then too the laws of truth are not psychological laws but boundary stones set in an eternal soil: our thinking can indeed submerge, but it cannot displace them.[14]

What was true of logic was true also, in Frege's view, of arithmetic, and, in Russell's, of all of pure mathematics: they gave an account of eternal relations holding between objects which did not affect the senses. The existence of these objects and the holding of these relations could not be thought of as depending on the representations of the knowing subject. Not, of course, that Schopenhauer, or Kant before him, had thought of exactly this dependence. They had held that logic was *a priori* inasmuch as it contained the form of thought and its laws were to be discovered simply by reflection on the exercise of the understanding. It was not at all apparent to sceptical critics why these laws of thought were valid or what force they had as laws. Boltzmann, in a scornful attack on Schopenhauer, urges changes in the laws of thought whenever (as he thought to be the case with the infinite divisibility of matter) they lead to absurd consequences:

These laws of thought can be called a priori because many thousands of years of experience by the species have made them innate in the individual. But it seems to be nothing but a logical howler of Kant's when he proceeds to infer that they are infallible in all cases.[15]

Against such views Frege and Russell seemed to oppose a picture of a world—a crystalline world, Wittgenstein was later to say[16]—of eternal objects eternally possessing those properties and relations that the truths of logic and mathematics ascribed to them. It was not the form of thought that was embodied in them but the form of reality itself. It was the discovery amid the uncertainties and the relative character of human thinking of something whose existence and nature was absolute, and it seemed to Wittgenstein, though we do not know precisely how early, to have implications going beyond logic and mathematics and extending to the problems of ethics and of the meaning of the world.

His first concern then, true to what had attracted him to these authors, was with the fundamental logical concepts—the logical cons-

14. ibid., p. xvi.

15. *Theoretical Physics and Philosophical Problems*, p.195 (from an attack on Schopenhauer given as an address to the Philosophical Society of Vienna in 1905).

16. e.g. *Philosophical Investigations* I §97.

tants, which Russell at this time thought of as eternal objects like Frege's numbers:

> The discussion of indefinables—which forms the chief part of philosophical logic—is the endeavour to see clearly, and to make others see clearly, the entities concerned, in order that the mind may have that kind of acquaintance with them which it has with redness or the taste of a pineapple. Where, as in the present case, the indefinables are obtained primarily as the necessary residue in a process of analysis, it is often easier to know that there must be such entities than actually to perceive them; there is a process analogous to that which resulted in the discovery of Neptune, with the difference that the final stage—the search with a mental telescope for the entity which has been inferred—is often the most difficult part of the undertaking. In the case of classes, I must confess, I have failed to perceive any concept fulfilling the conditions requisite for the notion of *class*. And the contradiction discussed in Chapter X. proves that something is amiss, but what this is I have hitherto failed to discover.[17]

It is probable that already in 1909, when he proposed a solution of Russell's paradox, Wittgenstein too faced the question whether the notion of class was one of the logical constants; it is certain that he very soon began to question not only which logical constants had to be retained but also what ontological status should be assigned to them. The first written philosophical remark of his that has been preserved is in a letter to Russell of 22 June 1912:

> Logic is still in the melting pot, but one thing gets more and more obvious to me: The propositions of logic contain only apparent variables and whatever may turn out to be the proper explanation of apparent variables, its consequence must be that there are no logical constants.
>
> Logic must turn out to be a totally different kind than any other science.

This was vehement dissent indeed—and from the very features of the doctrines of Russell and Frege that had first, so it seems, attracted him. But it was entirely in their spirit—or at any rate in Frege's—to see logic as totally different from all other sciences. The general path that Wittgenstein followed in his use of logic to reveal, or to point to, the transcendental features of the world, while denying it the status of a substantive science of one category of objects, will be traced in another chapter. Not only does it not lend itself to an exact chronological account interspersed with other biographical matters, but we lack the continuous documentation necessary to show the precise order in which various ideas occurred to him.

---

17. From the Preface to the first edition (1902) of *Principles of Mathematics*, pp. xv–xvi of the second edition.

Of the three logicians with whom Wittgenstein first came into contact, Frege was the one for whom he exercised that organ of reverence which was so strongly developed in him, though it found so few objects. This can be seen in the references in his *Tractatus*—the acknowledgement of the stimulation that he owed to 'Frege's great works and to the writings of my friend, Mr. Bertrand Russell', the note of incredulity in some of the criticisms: 'It is remarkable that a thinker as rigorous as Frege appealed to the degree of self-evidence as the criterion of a logical proposition.' Russell is mentioned rather oftener (29 times against 18) but with less ceremony. Respect for him is implicit—I think that Wittgenstein nowhere discusses an author he does not respect—but Frege was a special case.

It was by a rare and fortunate perspicacity that Wittgenstein saw in Frege a figure to be mentioned in the same tone of voice as he would mention Kant. A neglected and passed-over professor—an Ordinarius but only an honorary one—at Jena, he had reached the age of 63 without either the recognition he deserved or the success in his logical enterprise that he had hoped for. Small, shy and extremely introverted, he regarded most acknowledged authorities on the foundations of mathematics with the contempt but not the tolerance that they would have felt for the superstitions of a charcoal-burner. For perhaps twelve years he had known that a school of logicians, led by Peano, had adopted ideas akin to his own (which were earlier), but even here he seems to have been more aware of their errors than of their support. In Jena itself a handful of students attended his lectures out of curiosity: Carnap records that in the summer semester of 1913 he and a friend and a retired major pursuing a hobby formed the entire audience.[18] To have inspired both Carnap and Wittgenstein is already some measure of Frege's genius, but he counts for more. First, he was the founder of modern logic, chiefly because of his account of the logic of statements involving multiple generality, an account and an insight summed up in the device of quantification. Before this discovery the logical analysis of many parts of human language remained in the stage of scattered insights without system, rather like the tips given in Aristotle's *Topics*, some acute and some misconceived, as compared with the palmary treatment of the syllogism in the *Prior Analytics*.[19] Naturally not all parts of human language were covered or even touched by Frege's work, but even the discussion of tenses and modalities, to take examples from areas he on the whole ignored, follows a pattern set by him. Second, he was able, partly because of his newly-won knowledge of the potentialities of logic, to open

18. *The Philosophy of Rudolf Carnap* (ed. Schilpp), p. 5.
19. This account of Frege's importance follows that of Michael Dummett: *Frege: Philosophy of Language*, pp. xiiff.

up new fields also for philosophical logic, to such an extent that discussions in this subject are still carried on in his terms.

Dummett points out that since the time of Descartes epistemology had been the basic part of philosophy:

> The whole subject had to start from the question, 'What do we know and how?, ... Descartes's perspective continued to be that which dominated philosophy until this century, when it was overthrown by Wittgenstein, who in the *Tractatus* reinstated philosophical logic as the foundation of philosophy, and relegated epistemology to a peripheral position.[20]

It is clear that this change in philosophy is confined to the 'analytical', Anglo-American tradition; and even there it is by no means universally recognized. Russell, who came to philosophy before the change signalized by Dummett, perhaps never realized that it had taken place. Despite all his own discoveries in logic and philosophical logic, he tended to think that the Cartesian question was the one with which philosophy began, and the large number of his admirers, together with their conviction that today the main questions in philosophy are somehow not being answered, is an indication that this attitude (on which it is not our immediate purpose to pass judgement) is still alive.

There is no doubt that, while Frege made no profession of the greater importance for philosophy of philosophical logic over epistemology, the example that he gave by avoiding any epistemological prolegomena in his own philosophical discussion of logic and language had a very great effect on Wittgenstein.

Wittgenstein's own account of his visits to Frege is given by Peter Geach:[21]

> I wrote to Frege putting forward some objections to his theories, and waited anxiously for a reply. To my great pleasure, Frege wrote and asked me to come and see him.
>
> When I arrived I saw a row of boys' school caps and heard a noise of boys playing in the garden. Frege, I learned later, had had a sad married life—his children had died young, and then his wife; he had an adopted son, to whom I believe he was a kind and good father.
>
> I was shown into Frege's study. Frege was a small neat man with a pointed beard, who bounced around the room as he talked. He absolutely wiped the floor with me, and I felt very depressed; but at the end he said 'You must come again', so I cheered up.

20. op.cit., p. xv (2nd edn., p. xxxiii).

21. In *Three Philosophers* by G.E.M. Anscombe and P.T. Geach. The account given to R.L. Goodstein echoed the phrase about Frege's wiping the floor with Wittgenstein but mentioned only the discouragement, not the cheering effect of the invitation to come again. See above. Hermine Wittgenstein's account and the objective effect of the visit agree better with the account given to Geach as a whole than with that given to Goodstein.

I had several discussions with him after that. Frege would never talk about anything but logic and mathematics; if I started on some other subject, he would say something polite and then plunge back into logic and mathematics. He once showed me an obituary of a colleague, who, it was said, never used a word without knowing what it meant; he expressed astonishment that a man should be *praised* for this!

The last time I saw Frege, as we were waiting at the station for my train, I said to him 'Don't you ever find *any* difficulty in your theory that numbers are objects?' He replied 'Sometimes I *seem* to see a difficulty—but then again I *don't* see it.'

So far as these things can already be judged, Frege was a deeper though a narrower philosopher than Russell and has accordingly had a greater effect on philosophy: but it was Russell who had the greater immediate impact on Wittgenstein. This is at least consistent with the list Wittgenstein gave in 1931 of the influences on his work (each representing a step onward):

There is truth in my idea that really in my thinking I am only reproductive. I believe that I have never invented a new line of thought: that has always been given me by someone else. I have only seized on it immediately with a passionate urge for the work of clarification. That is how Boltzmann, Hertz, Schopenhauer, Frege, Russell, Kraus, Loos, Weininger, Spengler, and Sraffa influenced me.[22]

The passage comes from a section where he is thinking of the Jewish elements in his own nature—he says on the same page:

It is typical of the Jewish mind to understand the work of another better than the other himself understands it.

Jewishness apart, this was the impression Russell himself soon had of the disciple who combined passionate admiration with vehement dissent, and he began to feel he could leave his own work to Wittgenstein, in whose early writings the voice is perhaps the voice of Frege but the problems are the problems of Russell. Hertz and Boltzmann gave him the idea of a mental picture or correlate of reality in which all that was esssential was the logical structure of (in their case) the scientific theory involved. Russell, however, provided the tools for the extension of such analysis to the whole of our language. With the help of these tools Wittgenstein thought we could see what had to exist or be the case and what might (and might as well) be one way or the other. No matter that his conception of logic and language finally differed from Russell's: it arose from Russell's question what logic could show us about the nature

22. *Culture and Value*, p.19 (my own translation).

of language and it was the Archimedean point in his book, the logical insight that solved the problems of philosophy. The attitude to the world that resulted, the conception of the tasks that might still be performed, was perhaps the contribution of Kraus.

In October 1911 Russell was beginning his second year as a lecturer at Trinity. The appointment had been a considerable honour. It met no obvious college or university need and did not fit into the then normal pattern of elections. Like his election to the Royal Society two years earlier, it was owed principally to his work on the foundations of mathematics and to his association with Whitehead. It came at an opportune time. The stipend was certainly useful—in those days £200 per annum was not a small sum; but more important than that was the circumstance that the concentrated and private work—Russell himself called it the mechanical work—of writing out the three volumes of *Principia Mathematica* had just been completed. 'My intellect never quite recovered from the strain,' Russell said.[23] 'I have been ever since definitely less capable of dealing with difficult abstractions than I was before.' The transition to less abstract forms of philosophy was made in these years at Cambridge and was influenced by his contacts there, not least that with Wittgenstein. Some relaxation from the severe and limited task of *Principia* had already begun before Wittgenstein came: Russell during 1911 composed what he called his 'shilling shocker', *The Problems of Philosophy*, a book still widely read as an introduction to the subject: the proofs were arriving during Wittgenstein's first term in Cambridge and the book came out in January 1912. It is written with great elegance and betrays in many passages the possession of a logical apparatus much greater than that common in philosophical works of that or any time. Its approach, however, is exclusively epistemological, for it conceives philosophy as the criticism of knowledge. Within this sphere it fails to deal with the complete sceptic:

> Against this absolute scepticism, no *logical* argument can be advanced. But it is not difficult to see that scepticism of this kind is unreasonable.[24]

Thus philosophy cannot succeed in doubting the indubitable—the existence of sense-data, for example—but may lead us to reject some beliefs at first sight obvious—such as that physical objects exactly resemble our sense-data. Its aim in short is to diminish the risk of human error and in some instances it does indeed render the risk so small as to be practically negligible. The answer is a little feeble, since from a practical point of view, no one would do philosophy at all. On the other hand, all attempts to provide knowledge concerning the universe as a

23. *Autobiography*, vol. I, p. 153.
24. *The Problems of Philosophy* (OPUS), p. 87.

whole, to prove that in virtue of the laws of logic such and such things must exist and such and such others cannot, are rejected. The chief tool used for this purpose is the distinction between knowledge of things and knowledge of truths. It cannot be claimed as the Hegelians (and Russell himself in youth) believed, that the nature of each thing involved all of its relations with other things, and hence that the universe formed a single harmonious system. For a thing may be known (and hence, in normal parlance, its nature may be known) even when very few propositions (theoretically even when none) are known about it. 'Theoretically'—the word suggests some uneasiness. What would such knowledge by bare acquaintance amount to? It seems to be not so much a phenomenon everyone is familiar with as a consequence deduced from an antecedent picture of the world, seen as consisting of independent objects which may stand or fail to stand in any one of a number of independent relations with one another. And is not such a picture itself (useful though it is if the logic of relations is to be applicable to the world) a piece of knowledge about the universe as a whole? Russell could hardly answer such questions in a shilling shocker, and in fact he had, or developed, answers to them as satisfactory as those of most eminent philosophers. But there was an air of something not completely worked out about *The Problems of Philosophy* and it was to a completer and rounder view of epistemology that Russell next devoted his thoughts.

Russell's private life, at the time of which we speak, underwent a change and a diffusion somewhat similar to those in his thinking: the parallelism is hinted at but hardly stressed in his *Autobiography*. The years from 1902 to 1910 had, intellectually, been ones of painful work, first searching for a solution to the paradox that had seemed to frustrate the purpose of *Principles of Mathematics* to show that all mathematical statements were deducible from a small number of fundamental logical principles; then working out the consequences of his own insights and Whitehead's. Which was harder—to stare at a blank sheet all day, or to work on comparative minutiae for ten or twelve hours a day—Russell does not say. But these were also the years between his discovery that he no longer loved his first wife (Alys) and his breaking with her. The break actually came at Easter 1911 and was precipitated by his relationship with Lady Ottoline Morrell, whose lover he had just become.

We were both earnest and unconventional, (Russell wrote), both aristocratic by tradition but deliberately not so in our present environment,
both hating the cruelty, the caste insolence, and the narrow-mindedness of
aristocrats and yet both a little alien in the world in which we chose to
live, which regarded us with suspicion and lack of understanding because
we were alien. All the complicated feelings resulting from this situation we
shared. There was a deep sympathy between us which never ceased as

long as she lived. Although we ceased to be lovers in 1916, we remained
always close friends.

Ottoline had a great influence on me, which was almost wholly
beneficial. She laughed at me when I behaved like a don or a prig, and
when I was dictatorial in conversation. She gradually cured me of the
belief that I was seething with appalling wickedness, which could only be
kept under by an iron self-control. She made me less self-centred, and less
self-righteous. Her sense of humour was very great, and I became aware of
the danger of rousing it unintentionally. She made me much less of a
Puritan, and much less censorious than I had been. And of course the
mere fact of happy love after the empty years made everything easier.
Many men are afraid of being influenced by women, but as far as my
experience goes, this is a foolish fear.[25]

Always amative, Russell had in fact keenly enjoyed friendships with
women before this—notably with Lucy Martin Donnelly, with whom he
kept up a lively correspondence, but Lady Ottoline was the first, apart
from Alys, with whom he had (in his own phrase) full relations. The new
freedom did not confine him to Lady Ottoline and in the years that
followed he was to have casual relations with a number of ladies, the
occasion being some internal or external difficulty in his relations with
Lady Ottoline, some frustration in his philosophical work, sometimes
perhaps just the impulse of the moment. The change was not total:
Russell had before been deliberately provocative, unconventional, and
involved in public work. But it was essentially in these years that he
became the Russell of legend, serious and censorious about public issues,
but with less of a need than before for profundity, more of a tendency
towards superficiality and easy victories both in his personal and in his
intellectual life, became in fact the Mr. Apollinax who visited the United
States.[26] Russell himself compared the change between 1910 and 1914
with the life of Faust before and after he met Mephistopheles, a change
produced in his case by Lady Ottoline and the war. There is no evidence
that Wittgenstein felt objections directly to Russell's 'technical morality',
and the cleverness and quickness attracted him enormously—'Russell

25. *Autobiography* vol. 1, p. 205.
26.   When Mr. Apollinax visited the United States
                His laughter tinkled among the teacups.
                I thought of Fragilion, that shy figure among the birch trees,
                And of Priapus in the shrubbery
                Gaping at the lady in the swing.
                . . .
                I heard the beat of centaur's hoofs over the hard turf
                As his dry and passionate talk devoured the afternoon
                'He is a charming man'—'But after all what did he mean?'—
                'His pointed ears. . . He must be unbalanced,'—
                . . .

T.S. Eliot was a pupil of Russell's during the latter's visit to Harvard in 1914, though his later
association with him is better known.

was terribly bright then', he used to say. But he detected very early that
Russell was past the age of his best discoveries. More serious for their
relations was Wittgenstein's awareness of the new complex of attitudes in
Russell. They led perhaps to a way of life that suited Russell, but they
were to prove the exact converse of his own, for his tendency was to look
for the difficult thing to do in private life and in intellectual work, while,
where public affairs were concerned, he became fiercely convinced that
there was nothing worthwhile to be done beyond the most obvious duties
of a citizen.

Russell's circumstances in autumn 1911, then, were these: he had left
his wife and he lived in rooms in Nevile's Court of Trinity. Alys would
not divorce him; Lady Ottoline did not wish for a divorce for herself.
There was no question of living with her, or even of spending a night
with her. He kept a flat in London and would go down to see her,
returning to give his lectures and spend the evenings in Cambridge. In
his College rooms he was an easy mark for callers; that apart, he often
held 'squashes' or 'evenings'—the few survivors remember them as a
place first of all to hear Russell talk and then to meet the interesting
newcomers or visitors to Cambridge. As well as this, Russell made time
to write each day to Lady Ottoline, going over the events of the day,
naturally with a desire to be amusing and no attempt not to be
outrageous, but still giving us, as it gave her, his immediate reactions.[27]

Busier in more varied ways than before and also happier, Russell was
open to influences: a change was preparing in him when Wittgenstein,
who was in part to provoke the change, first called on him, shy but
unannounced:

> this raised a lot of complicated problems, which we were in the middle of
> when an unknown German appeared, speaking very little English but
> refusing to speak German. [There follows the passage about becoming
> interested in the philosophy of mathematics at Charlottenburg.][28]

He came back the next day, after Russell's lecture, and argued till dinner
time:

> obstinate and perverse, but I think not stupid.

It was to be the common pattern: Wittgenstein would call on Russell at 4 or
5 and stay until Hall, talking even while Russell dressed. As time went on,

27. I owe my knowledge of the correspondence (like much else) to Mr Kenneth Blackwell. The
Russell side of it is held in the Library of the University of Texas in Austin, Lady Ottoline's side in
McMaster University Library as part of the Russell Archive.

28. Letter 225 to Lady Ottoline Morrell (18 October 1911). Subsequent letters are identified by
date in the text. The shyness (typical of Wittgenstein on first acquaintance) is here inferred from the
untypical imperfection of his English. Wittgenstein was always slow to accept that his English friends
could understand German, no doubt rightly.

it became his custom to go away during dinner and come back for more talk afterwards, staying in the room while callers came and went. Naturally Russell's judgement and his patience fluctuated:

> My German friend threatens to be an infliction. (19 October)
>
> My German, who seems to be rather good, was very argumentative. (25 October)
>
> My German was very argumentative and tiresome. He wouldn't admit that it was certain that there was not a rhinoceros in the room. [This apparently during a lecture, because afterwards he 'came back and argued all the time I was dressing'.] (1 November)
>
> My German engineer, I think, is a fool. He thinks nothing empirical is knowable—I asked him to admit that there was not a rhinoceros in the room, but he wouldn't. (2 November)

This is the incident, surely, of which Russell made an anecdote:

> Quite at first I was in doubt as to whether he was a man of genius or a crank, but I very soon decided in favour of the former alternative. Some of his early views made the decision difficult. He maintained, for example, at one time that all existential propositions are meaningless. This was in a lecture room, and I invited him to consider the propositon: 'There is no hippopotamus in this room at present.' When he refused to believe this, I looked under all the desks without finding one; but he remained unconvinced.[29]

The dispute seems to be connected with a thesis held by Wittgenstein at the time, and mentioned in the next two letters (7 and 13 November), namely that there is nothing in the world except asserted propositions. The exact point at issue can hardly be recovered, but it is clear that Wittgenstein was harking back to earlier views of Russell's and G.E. Moore's. The sense of assertion involved is not the social or psychological sense in which true and false propositions alike can be affirmed or credited, but that described in *The Principles of Mathematics* (p. 49), where being asserted is said to be the extra quality that true propositions possess to differentiate them from false propositions. A proposition also is nothing psychological, but is a complex of concepts in the sense described by Moore in his article 'The Nature of Judgment' (*Mind* 1899). Concepts on this view are the objects of thought (not modes of it) and, as such, are the only things that exist. The truth of a proposition (its being asserted in the above sense) will consist not in a correspondence or other relation between a complex of concepts and something else, but in a certain property of the complex itself.

29. From *Mind* 60 (no. 239) 1951.

The view described will best be understood if it is seen as a reaction (rather in the spirit of Frege) against any confusion between what is judged and the judging of it. If we call what is judged a proposition, and if there is nothing mental about it, then the proposition cannot stop short of actual things involved in the judgement, and, if it is a true proposition, it will be identical with a fact.[30] Thus (Moore thought) contemporary accounts of truth as consisting in correspondence between a proposition and a fact arose from a failure to distinguish between a mental act and its objects.

To say that asserted propositions exist will, therefore, be to say that facts exist, though the reasons for saying it in this way are of considerable philosophic interest. Some further reason is needed for saying that only asserted propositions exist. A man would have such a reason if he held the second of two views described by Russell in an early discussion of Meinong:

> Among objects ['objects' here are the same as what Moore called 'concepts'] there are two kinds, the simple and the complex. The latter are characterized by a certain kind of unity, apparently not capable of definition, and not a constituent of the complexes in which it occurs. On one view, a complex is the same thing as a proposition, and is always either true or false, but has being equally in either case; on the other view, the only complexes are true propositions, and falsehood is a property of such judgements as have no Objectives.[31]

Russell himself held the former view; that was what led him to make the remark criticized in the *Tractatus* (6.111) that some propositions are true and some false, just as some roses are red and some white.

> What is truth, and what falsehood, we must merely apprehend, for both seem incapable of analysis.[32]

On the other view (taken, so it seems, by Wittgenstein) a general difficulty about negative propositions, mentioned but dismissed by Russell, becomes apparently more acute:

---

30. For present purposes logical truths will be disregarded.

31. 'Meinong's Theory of Complexes and Assumptions', *Mind* 1904, reprinted in B. Russell: *Essays in Analysis*, this passage p. 62. 'Objective' is Meinong's term and here means, essentially, what Russell and Moore meant by 'proposition'. Readers will notice in this passage more pre-echoes of Wittgenstein's early writings than it is necessary to go into at this point.

32. *Essays in Analysis*, p. 76: similarly Moore says (*Mind* 1899, p. 180).

> What kind of relation [between its constituent concepts] makes a proposition true, what false, cannot be further defined, but must be immediately recognized.

It is hard to regard A's non-existence, when true, as a fact in quite the same sense in which A's existence would be a fact if it were true.[33]

It must be remembered that in the present discussion a fact is a true or asserted proposition, that is to say a complex concept, which on the first view possesses a certain property and on the second view (that ascribed to Wittgenstein) simply exists. Now: what complex can reasonably be supposed to exist in virtue of there not being a rhinoceros in the room?

There are two levels of difficulty here. First, there is the question whether there exist any complexes having 'not' or negation as a constituent—this shortly became the question whether there are negative facts. Second, there is the question whether there exist any complexes having existence as a constituent—whether there are existential facts. Both difficulties were felt about this time: in his *Notes on Logic* (autumn 1913) Wittgenstein said that there were both positive and negative facts; in a letter to Russell (apparently from November 1913) he feared that '($\exists$ x). x = L.W.' would turn out to be meaningless.[34] It is, of course, paradoxical to say that only facts (or asserted propositions) exist and also that there are no existential facts among them. What is meant is that we can speak of existence only when we are referring to the truth of some proposition not itself existential.

Waiving the special point about existential propositions, the claim that only asserted propositions exist is clearly intended as a correction of Moore's position in his 1899 article according to which (p. 182) the world is formed of concepts. On Moore's view the furniture of the world could consist of all objects of thought and thus would include all constituents of propositions and all complexes of such constituents (and thus all propositions whether false or true). Wittgenstein's correction consisted in denying existence in this sense to everything except asserted propositions or facts. Thus he had already reached the position expressed in the first propositions of the *Tractatus* that the world consists of facts. 'The world is the totality of facts, not of things' (*TLP* 1.1.) i.e. things, objects, or what Moore called simple concepts do not go to make up the world; nor obviously do states of affairs (combinations of objects) that do not exist (these are what Moore called propositions or complexes of concepts possessing the property of falsity). Much later Wittgenstein was to tell Drury, 'My fundamental ideas came to me very early.' Again and again (as will appear) we have the impression that he was comparatively

33. id.ibid.

34. *Notebooks 1914–16*, p. 94, and *Letters to Russell, Keynes, and Moore*, p. 34. The position of the *Tractatus* on both issues is rather complicated: certainly negative and existential propositions can be used to give true partial descriptions of the world, but they owe their truth to the states of affairs or atomic facts that exist and to those being all the atomic facts. The 'existence' of an atomic fact is affirmed by an elementary proposition, which is not general, contains no quantifiers, and is thus not an existential proposition in the sense here in question.

little affected by new discoveries or advances made by others; and that, important though discussion and reflection were to him, their function was to enable him to articulate and clarify some initial insight, some inspiration or *Einfall* that had come to him in his earliest reading on a subject—in the present case in the reading of works that Russell and Moore thought they had left behind.

Exactly what conclusions about our knowledge Wittgenstein drew from the earlier form of his view about the contents of the world admits of conjecture too wide to be profitable. It may have seemed to him that we could know the truth of a proposition only by being acquainted with the asserted proposition, that is with the actual connexion of concepts or constituents; and that this was possible only when the connexion between them was necessary. But it is hard to state such a view without falling into a confusion with different and more usual assumptions about the nature of propositions. Moore, to be sure, thought that all combinations of concepts into judgements were necessary, but for very different reasons. And the difficulty in the *Tractatus* of supposing that there is any knowledge of empirical propositions arises chiefly from its adherence to the correspondence theory of truth (here implicitly rejected) and the obscurity of how a comparison with reality could be instituted by any mind.

Intimations, then, of later views which, even if false, many were to find compelling had already appeared in Wittgenstein's first month of work with Russell. They were no doubt obscurely formulated and not recommended by arguments that Russell could recognize—'My German ... is armour-plated against all assaults of reasoning—it is really rather a waste of time talking with him,' he once exclaimed. On 27 November, Wittgenstein made (apparently) his first personal appeal to Russell:

> My German is hesitating between philosophy and aviation; he asked me today whether I thought he was utterly hopeless at philosophy, I told him I didn't know but I thought not. I asked him to bring me something written to help me judge. He has money, and is quite passionately interested in philosophy, but feels he ought not to give his life to it unless he is some good. I feel the responsibility rather, as I really don't know what to think of his ability.[35]

Meanwhile the two got better acquainted: Wittgenstein got tickets for Lady Ottoline, Russell called on Wittgenstein, discovered that he was

35. Russell told this story several times (e.g. *Autobiography*, vol. 2, p. 99; *Portraits from Memory*, p. 23) usually in a livelier form: 'Will you please tell me whether I am a complete idiot or not?'—'My dear fellow, I don't know. Why are you asking me?'—'Because, if I am a complete idiot, I shall become an aeronaut; but, if not, I shall become a philosopher.' The written work was to be done (and indeed was done) in the vacation.

really an Austrian, that he was literary, unusually pleasant-mannered, and (he began to think) really intelligent.

Thus ended Wittgenstein's first and unofficial and altogether provisional term in Cambridge. He was not yet intimate with Russell, he had ideas but had written nothing or nothing presentable, he had not yet got the measure of Cambridge society: indeed he seems to have met no one but Russell and to have been altogether preoccupied by philosophy and the question whether he should devote his life to it. What personal complications surrounded this uncertainty, we do not exactly know. His father was now in his last illness. He had still two years to live but the vigour and the sarcastic newspaper articles had stopped since about the time Ludwig left Austria and Karl now lived for his family. To be sure he did not insist upon Ludwig's becoming an engineer, but Ludwig well knew (and told Russell before March 1912) that Karl had been disappointed in all his other sons and was very anxious this one should do something respectable like engineering and not waste his time over such nonsense as philosophy. Karl's condition could only make this problem more severe. Also, for this and other reasons, Ludwig was still plagued by evil spirits and his own nature still rankled with him. It was apparently about this time, perhaps even in Vienna and over the Christmas vacation that now followed, that he found some solution for these problems. The next June he talked about it with his new friend, David Pinsent:

> He was very communicative and told me lots about himself: that for nine years, till last Xmas, he suffered from terrific loneliness (mental—not physical): that he continually thought of suicide then, and felt ashamed of never daring to kill himself: he put it that he had had a 'hint that he was *de trop* in this world', but that he had meanly disregarded it. He had been brought up to engineering, for which he had neither taste nor talent. And only recently he had tried philosophy and come up here to study under Russell. Which had proved his salvation: for Russell had given him encouragement.[36]

Certainly it was after this vacation that he began to be effective, that his powers—in work and over people—began to appear. Probably the change was more gradual than the account he gave to Pinsent suggests, and even after that vacation it was interrupted by periods of self-doubt. Still, some change of heart over Christmas seems to have occurred. One possibility is that he found it possible to write, always for him the first index of spiritual well-being. It is tempting to place at this period also an incident related to Malcolm in connexion with religion:

36. From Pinsent's diary for 1.6.12.

He told me that in his youth he had been contemptuous of it, but that at about the age of twenty-one something had caused a change in him. In Vienna he saw a play that was mediocre drama, but in it one of the characters expressed the thought that no matter what happened in the world, nothing bad could happen to *him*—he was independent of fate and circumstance. Wittgenstein was struck by this stoic thought; for the first time he saw the possibility of religion.[37]

The play was Ludwig Anzengruber's *Die Kreuzelschreiber*.[38] Undoubtedly Wittgenstein's religious awakening will have been associated with the scene in which one character describes the 'special revelation' or '*afflatus*' (*extraige Offenbarung, Eingebung*) that he has had: previously his life had been one of unalleviated misery but one day when he had thrown himself, at the point of death as he thought, into the long grass in the sunshine, he came to himself again in the evening to find that his pain had gone, to be visited with unreasoning happiness as if the earlier sunshine had entered into his body, and to feel as if he were being spoken to: 'Nothing can happen to you! The worst sufferings count for nothing once they're over. Whether you're six feet under the grass or know that you've got to face it all thousands of times more—nothing can happen to you!—you're part of everything, and everything's part of you.[39] Nothing can happen to you!' *Es kann dir nix g'schehn*! the phrase was almost proverbial in Vienna,[40] and Wittgenstein was to return to it again.[41]

Wittgenstein went back to Cambridge in January, 'very vigorous', it seemed to Russell, bringing 'some MS he had written in the Vacation, very good, much better than my English pupils do. I shall certainly encourage him. Perhaps he will do great things. On the other hand I think it very likely he will get tired of philosophy.' (This from a letter of 23 January.) A week later he brought more manuscript, and clearly it had been decided that it was worth while his going on with philosophy, for on 1 February he was admitted a member of Trinity College, with Dr J.W.L. Glaisher as his tutor.[42]

37. In *Ludwig Wittgenstein: A Memoir*, p. 70. Marcus Aurelius (*ad se ipsum* 10.6) has a striking parallel to the passage referred to, but the thought is too general in its occurrence to be called Stoic.

38. See Erich Heller: 'Ludwig Wittgenstein, Unphilosophical Notes', *Encounter* 72 (1959), 423. The passage in the play that I refer to occurs in Act III, Scene I: Professor P. von Morstein long ago helped me to locate it.

39. '*Du g'horst zu dem all'n und dös all g'hort zu dir*'—a typical expression of the nature mysticism that I have sought to identify in the *Tractatus* (*Philosophical Review* 1966, pp. 305–28).

40. Cf. S. Zweig: *Die Welt von Gestern* (1955), p.366.

41. 'Lecture on Ethics', *Philosophical Review* (1965), pp. 6ff. *Wittgenstein and the Vienna Circle* (1979), p. 68.

42. Information from Trinity College records, kindly communicated to me by Professor von Wright. J.W.L. Glaisher was a distinguished mathematician. No record of communications between him and Wittgenstein survives. By the summer Wittgenstein had W.M. Fletcher as his tutor. A tutor at Trinity was and is responsible for the administrative relations between a student and the college and not directly for teaching or research.

The Cambridge and the Trinity that Wittgenstein joined—that is to say the circles in which he moved—were tiny institutions by modern standards. Three or four undergraduates a year would sit the Moral Sciences Tripos (this covered philosophy and experimental psychology, but no longer economics). There were two professors, Sorley and Ward, with whom Wittgenstein had no contact that we know of. W.E. Johnson, the philosophical logician, was a lecturer, so was G.E. Moore. Wittgenstein became friends with both, though he scouted Johnson as a philosopher. Russell and McTaggart and Keynes also sat on the Moral Sciences Board. So did C.S. Myers, the experimental psychologist, whom Wittgenstein was to work with. There were eighteen undergraduate members (apart from six women) of the Moral Sciences Club in 1911–12 and thirty-four (apart from nine women) in 1912–13. They included Whitehead's son North; future philosophers such as A.D. Ritchie and A.J. Dorward; psychologists such as B. Muscio (with whom Wittgenstein worked), C.A. Mace, and F.C. Bartlett; and the future translator and editor C.K. Ogden. I.A. Richards, who was to write *The Meaning of Meaning* with Ogden, was not yet a member of the club, but was one of the ten or so who attended Moore's lectures along with Wittgenstein. Dorward and Muscio were friends: we have no record of contacts with the others. It was to be the same at Trinity. We find no record of his meeting Whitehead until 1913, by which time Whitehead was teaching in London. Littlewood was already known to him from Manchester and Littlewood's close colleague G.H. Hardy was also a Fellow: both of these were friends, as was the classicist Donald Robertson, and H.A. Hollond got to know Wittgenstein at one of Russell's 'squashes' but it seems doubtful whether Wittgenstein knew well any other Fellows apart from necessary contact with his two Tutors. G.H.S. Pinsent, J.R.M. Butler, E.D. Adrian, J. Burnaby, and K.W.M. Pickthorn were among the Senior Scholars, of an age and status similar to his own. He was later to know them (though in varying degrees) fairly well and to think highly of them: before the First War they made no impression. David Pinsent (a cousin of G.H.S. Pinsent) alone became a friend: again following on a meeting in Russell's rooms. Slightly later Wittgenstein got to know Keynes, and, as we shall see, the small and select group that formed the Cambridge Conversazione Society, secret but known from numerous memoirs and biographies as the Society or the Apostles. Like them, his whole circle was small but of high distinction and not unconscious of the fact. Keynes has told us how *Principia Ethica* and *Principia Mathematica* were regarded as fundamental works, ushering in a new era in their respective subjects. Keynes, not yet of course a world authority, had made his name in Whitehall by his work on the Indian Currency Commission, was an influential lecturer for the infant Economics Tripos, as well as the chief source of informal instruction by means of his Political

Economy Club. At the same time he was completing the first draft of his *Treatise on Probability*, written under the influence of the two *Principias* already mentioned; it appeared after the war, in 1921, not, like some of his works, a book to amaze the world but probably till today (as Harrod forecast in 1951)[43] unmatched in scope and erudition. Hardy and Littlewood had already begun the collaboration that made them (as Hardy—modestly enough—says of himself) for a while among the five or six best analysts in the world.

Through these contacts Wittgenstein found himself at Trinity, more even than in Manchester, at the centre of the most fundamental scientific work then in progress in England. Gowland Hopkins, one of the junior fellows, was doing the work that entitled him to be called one of the discoverers of vitamins; they would hear at high table that J.J. Thompson (the discoverer of the electron) had found a new element of atomic weight 3;[44] or Hardy and Littlewood would tell them of some remarkable result they had received from a self-taught Indian (this was Ramanujan). Russell's philosophical work on the foundations of mathematics and his attempts during these years to introduce scientific method into philosophy[45] were regarded as integral parts of science; and, by the autumn of 1913, they would at that same table discuss Wittgenstein's theories of logic, evidently with equal respect.[46] Russell, Moore, Keynes, Hardy, Littlewood, perhaps Whitehead—this gives us some impression of the group of whom Russell said to Hermine Wittgenstein, 'We expect the next big step in philosophy to be taken by your brother.'

Towards this circle and this eminence among them he made a first step by enrolling himself at Trinity. No room in College was found for him at first, nor would it have been usual in a by-term. He lived a couple of hundred yards from its great gate at No. 4 in Rose Crescent, a curved passage running from Trinity St. to the Market Place, full then of lodging houses, tobacconists, and tailors, now of health food stores, coffee houses and steak bars, though Calverley might still find his cigars in Bacon's corner shop.

Formally speaking Wittgenstein became an Advanced Student (in 1913 these were renamed Research Students) under the Moral Sciences Board. He would have a supervisor, and after two years' residence and on submission of a dissertation embodying the results of his research

43. See R.F. Harrod: *A Life of J.M. Keynes*, pp. 150–1.

44. It turned out to be a form of hydrogen. Reports of High Table Conversation at Trinity are taken from G.E. Moore's manuscript diary (now in Cambridge University Library).

45. The slogan of *Our Knowledge of the External World* and *Scientific Method in Philosophy* (Herbert Spencer Lecture), both published in 1914, but the aim is apparent also in 'On the Notion of Cause' (*Mysticism and Logic* (1918), chapter 8), which had been the presidential address to the Aristotelian Society in November 1912.

46. 'Hall opposite Russell and Hardy, hear them talking about Wittgenstein's logical theories, but have to attend to Glaisher.' (From Moore's diary, 18 October 1913: there are other similar entries not all involving Russell.)

would be given a B.A. degree. An M.A. would follow after the usual lapse of time and on payment of the appropriate dues. (The degree of Ph.D. was not introduced at Cambridge until after the war.) Wittgenstein took this seriously and wished to obtain the degree. His motive was not, or not at first, that the degree might enable him to obtain an academic position. He had no clear aims of that sort; Russell understood that he would at some time 'finish his work in engineering' (that is to say, presumably, obtain some engineering qualification as well) but meanwhile do some philosophy.

Wittgenstein's academic status was not formalized until June, and at that time Russell was appointed his supervisor, but originally Russell advised Wittgenstein to 'coach with' Johnson. Johnson was then 53, a widower, rather withdrawn from the public life of college and University, oppressed by poor health and a small income—for in those days the combined stipend of a University Lecturer and a Fellow of King's was small enough, and he was in constant danger of not being renewed in the latter post because of his failure to publish.[47] Yet he was, apart from Russell, the only considerable logician (today he would count as a philosophical logician) then working in Cambridge. He had contributed suggestions when Keynes's father was writing his *Formal Logic*, still one of the best and most technical expositions of syllogistic logic; he had written on 'The Logical Calculus' in *Mind* in 1892, and had sent a paper to the International Congress of 1900 where Peano's contribution to the discussion opened Russell's eyes to the importance of new logical methods (essentially those of Frege) for the philosophy of mathematics. Now for some time Johnson had been working on a review of *Principles of Mathematics*, which, Broad says, would have filled several numbers of *Mind* if it had reached publication. His lectures, though idiosyncratic and divagatory, were highly valued. Much of their substance appeared after the war in an ordered form when, with the assistance of pupils, he brought out the three volumes of his *Logic*. This was the work in which an Oxford critic claimed to distinguish twenty different senses of the term 'proposition'; but Broad's defence of the richness and depth of the thought of the book is confirmed by the long survival of distinctions and terminology drawn from it. Johnson suffered the common fate of those who do their thinking away from the philosophical market-place and who crystallize it in later life. Individual insights may impose themselves (in Johnson's case they certainly did) but the system as a whole is too remote and eccentric to win admirers among those who, while the writer lingered, have moved on to new pastures. It is not given to every solitary thinker to be, like Frege, ahead of his time.

---

47. On Johnson see the Obituary Notice by C.D. Broad in the *Proceedings of the British Academy* XVII (1931). Harrod (*The Life of J.M. Keynes* (1959), p. 162) records that in 1912 the dividend for a Fellow of King's was £120 a year.

The arrangements for coaching or supervision proved a failure, as Russell told Lady Ottoline on 2 March:

> While I was preparing my speech Wittgenstein appeared in a great state of mind because Johnson (with whom I advised him to coach) wrote and said he wouldn't take him any more, practically saying he argued too much instead of learning his lesson like a good boy. He came to me to know what truth there was in Johnson's feeling. Now he is terribly persistent, hardly lets one get a word in, and is generally considered a bore. As I really like him very much, I was able to hint these things to him without offending him... Wittgenstein says Johnson's own ideas seem to him muddled, but his comments on W's ideas seemed excellent; evidently however J. resented W. not taking his word as law... It was a delicate matter talking to Wittgenstein.

Moore's recollections[48] were to much the same effect—it was Johnson, not Wittgenstein, who put an end to the arrangement. Probably there was not much to choose between the two as partners in a discussion, for Johnson, to judge by Broad's account of his lecturing and examining, was apt on any one occasion to neglect what was essential in order to get absolutely right some particular point that attracted his attention. Wittgenstein, for his part, was hardly more flexible: then as always some fundamental intellectual sympathy was needed before he could be stimulated even to disagreement—Russell, Schlick, and Moore (in his views on belief and certainty) are instances.

No less typical of Johnson and Wittgenstein is the fact that this failure did not affect their good relations. One important bond was music: Johnson's house was by family legend supposed to have been built round his grand piano, and at the tea-parties that were his main form of social life, serious conversation was followed by his playing himself or getting his guests to play. They made music—the phrase is almost affected in English, but for Wittgenstein *das Musizieren*, especially in a patriarchal atmosphere, was as natural as the air he breathed. Much later, on his return to Cambridge, in the short interval before Johnson's final illness, he was to revisit Ramsey House on at least one such occasion and to have a brief clash with F.R. Leavis that led to an uneasy friendship.[49]

Wittgenstein retained a great fondness for Johnson, as he told von Wright,[50] which indeed appears in the messages in his letters to Keynes during and after the war. 'Please give my love to Johnson whom I appreciate more and more the longer I haven't seen him' (4 January

48. Given to Hayek in a letter.
49. F.R. Leavis in *Recollections of Wittgenstein* (ed. R. Rhees), 1984, pp.51ff.
50. *Letters to Russell, Keynes and Moore*, ed. Von Wright, editor's note on K.14. Von Wright adds: 'Johnson seems patiently to have endured the demolishing attacks on his logic which Wittgenstein launched in their conversations before the war', but as will be apparent this was not quite the impression of Russell and Moore.

1915) is a typical passage. Johnson's feelings appear in a note written to Keynes when there was a prospect of a visit from Wittgenstein (24 August 1925):

> Tell Wittgenstein that I shall be very pleased to see him once more; but I must bargain that we don't talk on the foundations of Logic, as I am no longer equal to having my roots dug up.

Keynes had since childhood known Johnson, and was besides a Fellow of King's. He was Wittgenstein's avenue to Johnson for another purpose too. In the first half of 1913 Wittgenstein mentioned to Keynes a wish to give some money to any research fund King's might have to assist Johnson in his work by freeing him from some of his financial difficulties. By June he had decided on the form of the gift—it was to be £200 a year. Whether and in what way an instalment was paid before the war, we do not know, but Keynes and Wittgenstein corresponded again about the matter in 1914–15—at least this is the obvious meaning of 'The money will be sent to the registry as soon as the war will be over', in the letter from Wittgenstein last quoted. No doubt the routing of the money was designed to conceal the donor's identity.

The proposed donation matches a number made in Austria at the beginning of the war, to be described later. It seemed entirely natural to Wittgenstein to give money for such a purpose, as later to accept it himself, whether from Trinity or from friends. Such gifts were in the tradition of his family and appropriate to his time, when it could by no means be expected that a serious thinker would support himself adequately by teaching and publication. Johnson's dependence on his academic earnings attracted comment because it was so common to have access to other sources of income: Petavel and Moore were more typical than, say, Whitehead, who had great difficulties in supporting family life on an academic income. This gives added significance to the decision made by Russell and, as we shall see, by Wittgenstein, to live on their earnings—it meant giving up the normal way in which an independent thinker lived.

Thus Wittgenstein continued to derive the main intellectual stimulus that he found in Cambridge from Russell. Russell gave a number of anecdotal accounts of their relationship. In these he inevitably tended to dwell on Wittgenstein's eccentricities, for which he had an aristocrat's fondness. He was not sparing, either, of tributes to the great influence the association had on him:

> Getting to know Wittgenstein [he said in an obituary notice] was one of the most exciting intellectual adventures of my life. In later years there

was a lack of intellectual sympathy between us, but in early years I was as willing to learn from him as he from me.[51]

He was perhaps [said Russell in his *Autobiography*, a passage probably writen in the early 30s] the most perfect example I have ever known of genius as traditionally conceived, passionate, profound, intense, and dominating. He had a kind of purity which I have never known equalled except by G.E. Moore.[52]

But what his later accounts do not always bring out is the strength of the intellectual attraction between the two men, which made Wittgenstein exclaim that the happiest hours of his life had been spent in Russell's room (a spontaneous outburst like that to Eccles already mentioned), and which made Russell in letters to Lady Ottoline refer to him as 'a dear man' and say 'Wittgenstein makes me feel it is worth while I should exist.'

I like Wittgenstein more and more. He has the theoretical passion *very* strongly—it is a rare passion and one is glad to find it. He doesn't want to prove this or that, but to find out how things really are. (BR to OM 8.3.12)

W. is very excitable: he has more passion about philosophy than I have; his avalanches make mine seem mere snowballs. He has the pure intellectual passion in the highest degree; it makes me love him. His disposition is that of an artist, intuitive and moody. He says every morning he begins his work with hope, and every evening he ends in despair—he has just the sort of rage when he can't understand things that I have. (id. eid. 16.3.12)

He even has the same similes as I have—a wall parting him from the truth, which he must pull down somehow. After our last discussion, he said 'Well, there's a bit of wall pulled down.' (id. eid. late March 1912.)

These were Russell's reactions to the frequent discussions when Wittgenstein brought him some written work, or continued a discussion begun at his lecture, or (as it soon became their practice) came before the lecture to read it in advance, or simply brought a 'suggestion' on a point of mathematical logic—Russell on one occasion mentions an account of logical form as opposed to logical matter, but usually he spared Lady Ottoline the technical details.

Through the next two terms they met more and more often. Wittgenstein was the most constant auditor at Russell's lectures—indeed the only auditor once they were overtaken by the Tripos examinations, the days on the river, and the balls that mark the deliquescence of a

51. *Mind* 60 (1951), reprinted in *Ludwig Wittgenstein: The Man and his Philosophy*, ed. K.T. Fann, p. 31.
52. *Autobiography*, vol. 2, pp. 98–99.

Cambridge year. He would also often come back after the lecture, sometimes with the rather Continental present of roses or lilies of the valley. He would have lunch with Russell and then a long walk. He himself loved the water meadows that surround Cambridge: no town could have been better situated from the point of view of one who much preferred the flat *Praterauen* to the hills of lower Austria. But Russell took him further afield: they lay in fields listening to larks and cuckoos and trespassed in the woods round Madingley:

> To my great surprise [said Russell] he climbed a tree. When he had got a long way up a gamekeeper with a gun turned up and protested about the trespass. I called up to Wittgenstein and said the man had promised not to shoot if Wittgenstein got down within a minute. He believed me and did so.[53]

Harmless eccentricities of behaviour and childlike jokes were always to remain Wittgenstein's form of relaxation and he shared with Russell an aristocratic attitude towards minor regulations. Twenty years later he proposed a similar trespass to Leavis and prompted a rebuke voicing a different and perhaps more centrally English tradition of property, and indeed propriety.[54] On other occasions Russell and Wittgenstein would meet for tea. The hours from 5 to 7 were usually devoted to work, though sometimes Wittgenstein would call on Russell before Hall (this seems to have been usually at 7.45). We do not hear of Wittgenstein's dining at High Table with Russell, or indeed with any other of his friends (perhaps it would have been unusual to invite a Research Student) but the two men might dine together at the Union Society or go to a private dinner party. After dinner there might be a meeting of some Society and a paper discussion heard, followed perhaps by private discussion in more caustic terms, and a parting late enough to ensure no early start for the next day; or else one of Russell's evenings with a like sequel; or a concert. He would go back to Russell's room from some meeting and talk until midnight—not yet every night[55] nor yet in despair.

This programme of a day—though it is not suggested that Russell and Wittgenstein ever or often completed the whole of it together—is perhaps of some interest as exhibiting a way of life that survived in the ancient universities down to the 1950s. It was no quirk of these two men: Wittgenstein saw other friends (when he began to make them) in the interstices of the same framework and differed from them only in

53. *Portraits from Memory*, pp. 18–19.
54. *Memories of Wittgenstein*, p. 57.
55. In *Autobiography*, vol. 2, p. 99 Russell says he came every evening at midnight. We shall see that something sufficient to make this a pardonable exaggeration began in October or November 1912.

requiring rather longer stretches of a friend's company. Like the Jew in the joke, he was just the same as other people, only more so.

From the frequency of meetings alone it will be clear that Russell had become fond of Wittgenstein and that the initial temptation to think of him simply as a bore had quite vanished. This first impression (Russell reports it as the general one, and occasional contemporary letters confirm this) had evidently two rather different sources. First, people were surprised by the contrast between Wittgenstein's exquisite manners, index of a higher degree of sensibility than was usual among the educated English, and the force and fire and persistence with which he talked when a subject gripped him.

> In argument he forgets about manners and simply says what he thinks. (BR to OM 8.3.12)

But there was another side—occasions when manners were not enough and inspiration and brilliance (*Einfall* and *Geistreichtum*, to use Wittgenstein's own terms) deserted him. Russell goes on to say:

> In spite of it all something about him makes him a bore. In his flat moments, he still talks, slowly, stammering, and saying dull things. But at his best he is splendid. (ibid.)

'At his best he is splendid'—Russell exulted not only in Wittgenstein's penetration but also in his complete candour:

> No one could be more sincere than Wittgenstein or more destitute of the false politeness that interferes with truth; but he lets his feelings and affections appear and it warms one's heart. (BR to OM 10.3.12)
>
> He is always absolutely frank. (id. eid. 16.3.12)
>
> He is not a flatterer but a man of transparent and absolute sincerity. (id. eid. 17.3.12)

During these months, as we shall see, Russell could accept the criticism and the intensity did not make Wittgenstein tiresome to him. The summer of that year probably saw the peak of their intimacy. Wittgenstein was 'a treasure':

> I think he is passionately devoted to me. Any difference of feeling causes him great pain. My feeling towards him is passionate, but of course my absorption in you makes it less important to me than his feeling is to him. (BR to OM 1.6.12)

The affectionate phrases in Wittgenstein's summer letters to Russell,[56] while not enough to prove a passionate attachment, are quite consistent with one. Russell is quite frank about his own feelings:

> I had a letter from Wittgenstein, a dear letter which I will show you. I love him as if he were my son. (BR to OM 22.8.12)

Later he (5 September) mentions his strong protective feeling. There is no doubt that Russell meant exactly what he said. He was now forty and passionately wanted children but saw no prospects of having any. While Lady Ottoline supplied the part of a wife, as Alys had for long failed to, Wittgenstein to some extent made up for the children he had missed. Thus these two relationships were for the time being the most intense that he had and he constantly compared them with one another.

Forty, and with an immense piece of technical work behind him in mathematics, precisely the area in which inventive power first develops and first decays, it is not surprising that Russell felt spent, so far as work of this kind was concerned. By the summer of 1912 others noticed this too and the Whiteheads advised him to let technical work be. During that summer he began to think of Wittgenstein as a successor as well as a son. He asked himself often whether his teaching a subject in which he could not make fresh discoveries was worthwhile. After a conversation with Wittgenstein in April he wrote:

> Yes, I think my daily round here *is* useful—Wittgenstein alone would have made it so. (BR to OM 23.4.12)

And when, at Whitsuntide, it became clear that Wittgenstein wished to do philosophy in the regular way and perhaps to teach, Russell could say:

> Oddly enough, he makes me less anxious to live, because I feel he will do the work I should do, and do it better. He starts fresh at a point which I only reached when my intellectual spring was nearly exhausted. (BR to OM 1.6.12)

It was, of course, a difficulty that Wittgenstein attached little importance to developing a systematic and reasoned presentation of his views and putting them in their right place in the philosophical controversies of the day. Partly this was a literary preference: Wittgenstein always looked for the striking, even the syncopated, expression of an insight—it should become dazzlingly obvious; and for refutation he relied on a rephrasing of views he disagreed with that made them seem absurd. But we shall see,

---

56. R.1–6 in *Letters to Russell, Keynes and Moore*: 'I need not say that I miss you awfully' and the like.

in connexion with the *Tractatus*, that the very novelty of Wittgenstein's standpoint demanded a different form of expression from conventional treatises. Russell was in two minds about this feature of Wittgenstein's philosophizing:

> I told him he ought not simply to *state* what he thinks true, but to give arguments for it, but he said arguments spoil its beauty, and that he would feel as if he was dirtying a flower with muddy hands. He does appeal to me—the artist in intellect is so very rare. I told him I hadn't the heart to say anything against that, and that he had better acquire a slave to state the arguments. I am seriously afraid that no one will see the point of anything he writes, because he won't recommend it by arguments addressed to a different point of view. (BR to OM 28.5.12)

But 'that must take its chance', Russell thought. So must the fact that Wittgenstein only knew 'a small proportion of what he ought to know'[57] as Russell had noticed earlier. At the end of May 1912 Pinsent notes that

> Wittgenstein has only just started systematic reading [in philosophy] and he expresses the most naive surprise that all the philosophers he once worshipped in ignorance are after all stupid and dishonest and make disgusting mistakes.

The main point was that Wittgenstein could detect and remedy defects and mistakes that Russell himself no longer felt equal to deal with. Russell thought therefore of giving up his teaching at the end of his five years (this would have been in 1915) by which time Wittgenstein would be able to take his place:

> He gives me such a delightful lazy feeling that I can leave a whole department of difficult thought to him, which used to depend on me alone. It makes it much easier for me to give up technical work. (BR to OM 4.9.12)

The technical work referred to does not seem to have been a continuation of *Principia*. The production of a fourth volume, on geometry,[58] was entirely in the hands of Whitehead. Russell seems to have felt that what was needed was another and more fundamental account of the fundamentals of *Principia* itself, an explanation of the nature of logical truth, and a justification of apparently accidental axioms like the Axiom of Reducibility. And this was—all Russell's references imply—precisely what Wittgenstein worked on. It was to be the autumn of 1913 before he produced for Russell his 'Notes on Logic',

57. BR to OM 15.3.12.
58. It never appeared, though Whitehead got rather further with it than Russell expected.

originally entitled 'Logic', but it seems likely that Wittgenstein was attempting to write just such an account of the nature of logic in the summer of 1912. Russell himself did not engage directly on such an enterprise until the autumn of 1912, with what success we shall see. The work was to be called 'What is Logic?' and this was after all the question left open by *Principia*.

Yet, as said, Russell himself was engaged in other directions. When Wittgenstein arrived in Cambridge the second and third volumes of *Principia* were in the course of production—they appeared in 1912 and 1913 respectively. There were proofs to be read but, for Russell, no original work to be done, though Whitehead had had to introduce extensive revisions into the second volume.[59] In April 1912 Russell wrote to Lady Ottoline:

> I have been thinking over the work I have done this last year—the shilling shocker, the article on religion, the Aristotelian paper, the paper on Bergson [the autobiography], and I shall have Matter done within the year.

The Aristotelian paper was 'On the relations of universals and particulars',[60] written and delivered before Wittgenstein became intimate with Russell. Its theme is the existence of an unanalysable relation of predication holding between a subject and a predicate and there is an echo of this in *Tractatus* 4.1274, where Wittgenstein says that the question 'Are there unanalysable subject-predicate propositions?' cannot be asked. In this paper Russell also argues for the existence of particulars which are not, like the traditional substances of philosophy, indestructible. Wittgenstein may well have this in mind when he insists in the *Tractatus* (2.02–2.2072) that the substance of the world must be unalterable. But we have no contemporary discussions on the paper, and it is notorious that the *Tractatus* gives no clear indication whether its 'objects' are universals or particulars—that whole way of thinking seems to be shunned.[61]

'Matter' was to occupy Russell for much longer than a year: this phase of his thought ended only with *The Analysis of Matter* in 1927. *The Problems of Philosophy* had treated the existence of matter as a reasonable but not an absolutely certain inference from our sense-data. Russell now began to question this inference, to doubt the force of the *a priori*

59. In particular the Prefatory Statement of Symbolic Conceptions, which ought properly to have come at the beginning of the whole work. This, and the knowledge of its authorship, is probably the source of Wittgenstein's reference to 'Whitehead's "Conventions"' in his notebook of 22.6.15 (*Notebooks*, p. 70). I owe my knowledge of this detail of the production of *Principia* to Dr. I. Grattan-Guinness.

60. *PAS* 12 (1911–12) 1–24, reprinted in *Logic and Knowledge*, 103–24.

61. It is arguable that the 1911 paper represents a temporary aberration in the development of Russell's thought. See R. Jager: *The Development of Bertrand Russell's Philosophy*, pp. 95–6.

principles invoked in it, and to incline with some changes of mind to the view that matter was instead a logical construction from sense-data. What must be assumed, if physical science has any validity, is that there are unsensed sense-data (Russell was later to call these 'sensibilia') very like the sense-data we actually experience, and that the things of physics are collections of such (perceived and unperceived) sense-data. Russell did not think that the demand of physics for such entities was enough to prove them to exist. The only metaphysical argument he could produce for that was our instinctive belief in the independent reality of the qualities that we perceive. His general aim at this time was to find, either in immediate experience or with the help of self-evident general principles, grounds for rejecting solipsism and accepting the truth of science.

Returning to Cambridge after Easter 1912, Wittgenstein was rather brisk and dismissive about this programme:

> I argued about Matter with him. He thinks it is a trivial problem. He admits that if there is no Matter then no one exists but himself, but he says that doesn't hurt, since physics and astronomy and all the other sciences could still be interpreted so as to be true. (BR to OM 23.4.12)

Wittgenstein had a temperamental and a philosophical hankering after solipsism: it was somehow to be accommodated, not quite dismissed, in the *Tractatus*; and bulks ever larger in the last of the wartime notebooks.[62] He also continued to think it obvious that the laws of physics employed all their logical apparatus in order to talk about the objects of the world, whatever these were (*TLP* 6.3431), so that no conclusions about what the world must be like could be drawn from them. In this latter point he was, perhaps, not so far from Russell as he supposed: for Russell was to devote a large part of his efforts to discovering the sort of interpretation of physics that would apply it to just those objects (the sense-data) that he thought we had good grounds for assuming.

Wittgenstein's attitude towards matter seems to have pleased Russell by its radicalism. It was of a piece with something he observed about Wittgenstein a day or two later on the occasion of Wittgenstein's meeting Lytton Strachey at tea:

> He is the only man I have ever met with a real bias for philosophical scepticism; he is glad when it is *proved* that something can't be known. (BR to OM 2.5.12)

---

62. *TLP* 5.6–5.641; *Notebooks*, pp. 73–89; there is a useful collection of passages in P.M.S. Hacker: *Insight and Illusion*, pp. 67–76.

This is not precisely a feature of Wittgenstein's that we can observe in his preserved writings: the nearest approach to it is in his scrupulous avoidance of questions of the theory of knowledge—if this is thought of as the attempt to find a number of things that we certainly know. He could give a mark of all logical truth: he did not attempt to give a mark of all known truths. However, if he was a sceptic at this time it is not at all surprising that the opening of Russell's paper on matter delighted him when he actually read it:

> In what follows, I shall endeavour to maintain three theses:
> (1) That all arguments hitherto alleged by philosophers against matter are fallacious;
> (2) That all arguments hitherto alleged in favour of matter are fallacious;
> (3) That, even if we had reason to suppose that there is matter, we could have no means of finding out anything whatever as to its intrinsic nature.[63]

The close, which Wittgenstein also liked, recommends the hypothesis of the existence of actual and possible sense-data as the hypothesis most consonant with our instinctive beliefs, though there may be conclusive arguments against it and can be none in its favour. As far as these parts went, Wittgenstein thought the paper on matter was the best thing Russell had done, but he disagreed with the central section, the chief function of which is to sketch the ways in which science might be interpreted to dispense with the hypothesis of matter. (This section was in fact extensively revised by Russell later in October.)

The shilling shocker, *The Problems of Philosophy*, we have already briefly described, and we have mentioned its reliance on the feature of self-evidence to account for the certainty of logic. This, which Russell himself felt to be inadequate, is the chief of the doctrines of the book to get reflected, in the form of criticism, in Wittgenstein's writings.[64] Of talk that the two men may have had about the book, Russell records only Wittgenstein's disgust with the last chapter, which is devoted to the Value of Philosophy. This was one of the conversations which led Russell to say that Wittgenstein was absolutely frank. He thought it wrong to argue that philosophy had an end outside itself or has value (we have quoted him on this point above). As a fact, Russell at this period was given to perorations and even complete papers in which he returned to the theme of 'A Free Man's Worship'—a paper first published in 1903:

---

63. Quoted from the as yet unpublished manuscript in the Russell Archive. The text is quoted as it was before correction, on the assumption that corrections to the April/May paper were inserted in October 1912. One feature of the corrections is that they make the paper less negative and provocative.

64. See for example *Tractatus* 5.1363 and 5.4731.

> To abandon the struggle for private happiness, to expel all eagerness of temporary desire, to burn with passion for eternal things—this is emancipation, and this is the free man's worship. And this liberation is effected by a contemplation of Fate; for Fate itself is subdued by the mind which leaves nothing to be purged by the purifying fire of time.[65]

But whereas then he had concentrated on the proud defiance of a weary but unyielding Atlas, solaced only by the consciousness that he was aware of the good denied him by a hostile and evil world, now he saw reason to suppose that the disinterested use of the intellect in philosophy would have desirable effects for practical life too:

> The mind which has become accustomed to the freedom and impartiality of philosophic contemplation will preserve something of the same freedom and impartiality in the world of action and emotion... Contemplation makes us citizens of the universe, not only of one walled city at war with the rest.[66]

Moreover contemplation itself had become, in Russell's eyes, a means no longer to condemn but to accept the universe. This was perhaps connected with that loss of faith in the objectivity of good and evil to which he drew attention in his comments of 1917 on 'A Free Man's Worship'.[67]

The 'article on religion' Russell referred to in his letter of April 1912 was evidently 'The Essence of Religion' published in the *Hibbert Journal* for October 1912. There he attempted to reject the dogmas of religion but to retain the good elements of worship, acquiescence and love. The animal part of man, he thought, finds it intolerable to suppose that the universe is unaware of the importance of its own desires but

> the divine part does not demand that the world shall conform to a pattern: it accepts the world, and finds in wisdom a union which demands nothing of the world... Every demand is a prison, and wisdom is only free when it asks nothing.

Wittgenstein did not see this article until it appeared and we shall see that his mood when he returned to Cambridge in October was often fiercer and more critical than that exhibited during the academic year at present under consideration. His reaction then led to a number of painful talks with Russell. He detested the paper.

---

65. *Mysticism and Logic and Other Essays* (1918), pp. 55–6.
66. *The Problems of Philosophy* (OPUS 1959, p. 93).
67. Preface of *Mysticism and Logic and Other Essays* (1918), p. v.

He felt I had been a traitor to the doctrine of exactness and wantonly used words vaguely; also [he felt] that such things are too intimate for print. I minded very much, because I half agree with him. (BR to OM 11.10.12)

Wittgenstein's criticisms disturbed me profoundly. He was so unhappy, so gentle, so wounded in his wish to think well of me. (id. eid. 13.10.12)

Wittgenstein was always distrustful of the attempt to convey any moral teaching in print. Even for the private discussion of problems of life he thought conversation a much preferable medium to a letter. The moral significance a man attached to an activity or an action, the meaning he saw in an utterance, these were things that could usually and then only with difficulty be conveyed face to face and to one who knew him well. The aesthetic objection to putting something personal into a treatise or sermon is not really distinct from the intellectual and moral objections to attempting to distil the moral content or principle out of an activity or a life and to present it on its own. Thus Wittgenstein, as we shall see, liked Moore very much and the quality of Moore's life attracted him, but Moore's attempt to express his ideals in *Principia Ethica* seemed to him to fail:

> I have just been reading a part of Moore's *Principia Ethica* [he wrote to Russell in June 1912] (now please don't be shocked) I do not like it at all. (Mind you quite apart from disagreeing with most of it.) I don't believe—or rather I am sure—that it cannot dream of comparing with Frege's or your own works (except perhaps some of the *Philosophical Essays.*) ... Unclear statements don't get a bit clearer by being repeated!!

What Moore had to say about ethics was bound to be unclear when he attempts to *describe* the nature of good itself and to say what things are good. In doing this he could be compared to Russell in 'A Free Man's Worship' singing the praises of a certain attitude towards the world.[68] The best that could be done in this direction was to involve the reader in some worthwhile activity without protesting too much that it was worthwhile. Thus Wittgenstein said he liked that sort of thing (a defence of the value of philosophy) when it had 'something solid at the back of it', as in the peroration to Russell's discussion of the philosophy of Bergson.[69] Here the praise of contemplation is an integral part of the argument against Bergson's preference of instinct to intellect:

---

68. *Philosophical Essays* (1910), the collection to which Wittgenstein referred, contained 'The Elements of Ethics' (1908), 'A Free Man's Worship' (1903), 'The Study of Mathematics' (1907) and four essays on pragmatism and truth.

69. Read to the Heretics in Cambridge in March 1912, published in *Monist* July 1912 and in a pamphlet in 1914.

Those to whom activity without purpose seems a sufficient good will find in Bergson's books a pleasing picture of the universe. But those to whom action, if it is to be of any value, must be inspired by some vision, by some imaginative foreshadowing of a world less painful, less unjust, less full of strife than the world of our everyday life, those, in a word, whose activity is built on contemplation, will find in this philosophy nothing of what they seek, and will not regret that there is no reason to think it true.

Because this passage occurs as a conclusion (or more strictly a corollary) of a philosophical argument of Russell's usual kind, its very style is also characteristic of Russell, pointed, humorous, simplified and yet cogent, preferable (for most tastes) to the rather laboured elevation of 'A Free Man's Worship' or 'The Essence of Religion'.

Print must be impersonal, Wittgenstein thought, it must not preach. A later anecdote records his condemnation of Tolstoy's *Resurrection* for this reason. Tolstoy is best, he said, when he 'turns his back on the reader', as, no doubt, in *Hadji Murad*, which Wittgenstein read with such enthusiasm in the summer of 1912. We look over the author's shoulder, he describes a life, and we see, rather than are told of, the values it exhibits. Paul Engelmann offers a similar analysis of the effect of Uhland's poem 'Graf Eberhard's Weissdorn' which he and Wittgenstein admired.[70]

The idea that higher things could only be indirectly communicated became a central one in Wittgenstein's *Tractatus*: in its words (6.522), they could be shown or they made themselves manifest. And of course the *Tractatus* was itself meant to show something, chiefly by what it did *not* say. It would communicate, Wittgenstein thought, only to one who thought through all its propositions and eventually recognized them as nonsensical (6.54). Now this at least means that communication regarding what is higher (which became the main point of the book in the author's eyes) is possible only for those who go through the thoughts of the book with the author and in the right spirit. That is the chief reason why in the preface Wittgenstein says that it will be understood, perhaps, only by one who has already had the thoughts expressed in it and that there may be only one such person.

It is worth mentioning these later developments, though we cannot yet see them in their philosophical context, because the attitude involved is already present in his reactions to Russell. It is not that we find all his opinions fully-formed whenever he first expresses himself on a subject, but rather that there is generally a pattern of them present in his thinking from the start. Thus in tracing the course of his thoughts we are

70. *Letters from Ludwig Wittgenstein with a Memoir*, pp. 82–5. For *Hadji Murad* see LW to BR [summer 1912], *Letters to Russell, Keynes and Moore*, Letter R.6. It is interesting that Wittgenstein himself turned his back on the audience when he read poems by Rabindranath Tagore to a handful of philosopher friends in 1927–8.

much more presented with a development or unfolding than with a convergence of influences. Parallels are perhaps easier to find. Janik and Toulmin[71] have drawn one with Hofmannsthal's distrust of language first expressed in the Chandos Letter of 1901. It is questionable what sort of an explanation of Wittgenstein's views such a parallel gives: elected silence in the face of phrases all sullied by misuse is not the same as the belief that anything worth saying is in principle incapable of being directly communicated, unless of course the latter is a mistaken and exaggerated acknowledgement of the need for the former. It may be that Janik and Toulmin want to ascribe this mistake to Wittgenstein, holding, as they seem to, that no man can express more than his own historical situation. But, quite apart from general objection to their methodology (as, for example, that it must itself be the expression of a particular time), it is clear that Wittgenstein's belief in the inexpressibility of value is compatible with the recognition that its indirect expression is much easier in periods when culture is not fragmented. This recognition did indeed come to Wittgenstein but apparently at a later period than that of which we now speak.

The criticism or the pain expressed by Wittgenstein when Russell wrote about matters too intimate for print itself illustrated that such matters were talked about by the two friends. Russell was not now as frequent or as simple-hearted a participant as G.E. Moore continued to be in discussions of the problems of life with clever young men, but in his relationship with Wittgenstein, he recaptured, for a while, the openness and flexibility of youth. This was another aspect of the reflowering we have already observed.

It took time, of course, before Russell saw, or Wittgenstein was able to communicate, his attitude towards these matters. At first Russell noticed the vehemence and the apparent hostility to religion and morality:

> He is far more terrible with Xtians than I am. He had liked F., the undergraduate monk, and was horrified to learn that he is a monk. F. came to tea with him and W. at once attacked him—as I imagine, with absolute fury. Yesterday he returned to the charge, not arguing but only preaching honesty. I wonder what will have come of it. He abominates ethics and morals generally; he is deliberately a creature of impulse, and thinks one should be. (BR to OM 17.3.12)

Six months later Wittgenstein was still exhorting F. 'to read some good book on some exact science, and see what honest thought is',[72] which F. seems to have taken in good part, assuming, no doubt, that his chief offence was to be a monk. Russell admired the intensity and the strong impulses:

71. A. Janik and S. Toulmin: *Wittgenstein's Vienna*.
72. Pinsent's diary for 9 November 1912.

He lives in the same kind of tense excitement as I do, hardly able to sit still or read a book. He was talking about Beethoven—how a friend described going to Beethoven's door and hearing him 'cursing and howling and singing' over his new fugue; after a whole hour Beethoven at last came to the door, looking as if he had been fighting the devil, and having eaten nothing for 36 hours because his cook and parlour-maid had been away from his rage. That's the sort of man to be. (BR to OM 23.4.12)

Sure enough, in the summer we find Russell reading the lives of Mozart and Beethoven, and Wittgenstein expressing his pleasure at this—'These are the actual sons of God'[73]—and sending him immediately five volumes of Beethoven's letters.

'That's the sort of man to be.' Wittgenstein was not merely overcome from time to time by a compulsive admiration for a life like Beethoven's but made the same absolute demands in his own and in Russell's, with none of the concessions to English life and practices that Russell allowed himself. Thus in November 1912 Russell wrote:

I had a passionate afternoon, provided by North and Wittgenstein. I had arranged to walk with Wittgenstein, and felt bound to see North's race, so I took Wittgenstein to the river. North was beaten, not by much; he was rather done afterwards. The excitement and conventional importance of it was painful. North minded being beaten horribly, though he didn't show much. Wittgenstein was disgusted—said we might as well have looked on at a bull fight (I had that feeling myself), that *all* was of the devil, and so on. I was cross North had been beaten, so I explained the necessity of competition with patient lucidity. At last we got on to other topics, and I thought it was all right, but he suddenly stood still and explained that the way we had spent the afternoon was so vile that we ought not to live, or at least he ought not, that nothing is tolerable except producing great works or enjoying those of others, that he has accomplished nothing and never will, etc.—all this with a force that nearly knocks one down.

He makes me feel like a bleating lambkin. I soothed him down at last, and came home and soothed down North. You would think that I had never felt the slightest excitement over anything, but was a mere bundle of common sense.[74] (BR to OM 9.11.12)

---

73. LW to BR 16.8.12. The reference is to *die echten Göttersöhne* in the Prologue in Heaven in Goethe's *Faust*:

> But ye, true sons of Heaven, it is your duty
> To take your joy in the living wealth of beauty.
> The changing Essence which ever works and lives
> Wall you around with love, serene, secure!
> And that which floats in flickering appearance
> Fix ye it firm in thoughts that must endure.

(trsln. by Louis Macneice and E.L. Stahl)

74. T.N. Whitehead was the elder of Whitehead's sons. On 9 November he was honourably defeated in the first heats of the Colquhoun Sculls by the President of the C.U.B.C., who went on to win the competition.

We shall see that at this time Wittgenstein was particularly severe in finding fault with his friends and himself and particularly energetic in trying to put things right.

Russell was both touched and amused (two elements in many of his friendships) to find his own ideals and intolerance present in Wittgenstein in a more uncompromising form. But, as regards Wittgenstein's hatred of parsons and monks and his abomination of ethics, Russell soon found that it was other than he had at first supposed and different also from his own attitudes.

Wittgenstein surprised me the other day; he suddenly said how he admired the text 'What shall it profit a man if he gain the whole world and lose his own soul' and then went on to say how few there are who don't lose their soul. I said it depended on having a large purpose that one is true to. He said he thought it depended more on suffering and the power to endure it. I was surprised—I hadn't expected that kind of thing from him. (BR to OM 30.5.12)

Wittgenstein was usually pessimistic, Russell often so (hence the rhetoric about fate in 'A Free Man's Worship'): but Russell inclined towards defiance and tended to see those who thought suffering itself valuable as subscribing to the religion of Moloch, the submission of slaves. Wittgenstein could see suffering as an integral part of a decent life.[75] On the next day:

Wittgenstein began on Dickens, saying David Copperfield ought not to have quarrelled with Steerforth for running away with Little Emily. I said I should have done so; he was much pained, and refused to believe it; thought one could and should always be loyal to friends and go on loving them. We got on to Julie Lespinasse, and I asked him how he would feel if he were married to a woman and she ran away with another man. He said (and I believe him) that he would feel no rage or hate, only utter misery. His nature is good through and through; that is why he doesn't see the need of morals. I was utterly wrong at first; he might do all kinds of things in passion, but he would not practise any cold-blooded immorality. His outlook is very free; principles and such things seem to him nonsense, because his impulses are strong and never shameful...

I told W. the story of Julie and then gave him one of her letters to read. He was much moved. I had represented Guibert as the cause of her misery. He said she was bound to be unhappy, since she could love like that. I had never talked with him before about things of that sort. (BR to OM 1.6.12)

75. A parallel with Aristotle in this respect has been drawn above (p. 33) and a further similarity now appears, in Wittgenstein's belief that all of a good man's impulses and feelings would be right.

The idea that suffering is preferable to ease if it flows from the whole-hearted following of those generous impulses that make up one's individuality, so that the attractiveness of avoiding or lessening it is really the temptation to lose one's soul, is of a piece with Wittgenstein's admiration for Weininger. It was natural for him (as we indicated when considering Weininger) to clothe his thoughts in religious terms, but formal religion seemed to him to involve dishonesty, since it was an attempt to reduce something essentially private and spontaneous to the status of an institution and consequently to investigate and propound moral truths in impersonal terms and by the methods appropriate to other intellectual activities. It therefore involved a cheapening both of the object sought (in the present context, saving one's soul) and the means used. Hence on the one hand the overtones of moral disapproval and on the other the injunction to see what honest thought about an exact science is. Certainly Wittgenstein did at this time allow for a religious experience and he told the Apostles,[76] when Moore read a paper on Conversion, that, as far as he knew, it consisted in getting rid of worry, having the courage that made one really not care what might happen. Here obviously he had in mind his 'experience' of utter safety induced by *Die Kreuzelschreiber*,[77] and, as he later pointed out, the expression of this did not literally make sense, did not pretend to belong to a science. This description of Wittgenstein's attitude towards religion is not meant to recommend it: much in it is banal and everything depends, obviously, on how it is applied. But it will be clear that he denied and altered much less in religion than Russell and that, while the two agreed on the importance of great works, Wittgenstein found the moral equivalent of religion more in personal life than in impersonal aims. Certainly later he was profoundly sceptical of political or social programmes or movements and particularly of Russell's involvement in them.[78] There is no accounting for a friendship. Russell's extraordinary quickness—his 'brightness' as Wittgenstein called it—was an important element. It was the first time Wittgenstein had prolonged an intimate contact with so powerful a mind. He never forgot it—just as he never forgot the contribution to his later thought of Ramsey and Sraffa, who were intellectually friends of the same sort. (Keynes probably cannot be

76. Russell recounted Wittgenstein's remarks to Lady Ottoline. We know independently that the date given (16 November 1912) was that of Wittgenstein's election as an Apostle; see below, p. 151.

77. See above, p. 94.

78. Two anecdotes will illustrate this. Paul Engelmann had a story about a League for Peace and Freedom projected or founded by Russell, the Women's League for Peace and Freedom, which Russell was on his way to address when he met Wittgenstein at Innsbruck in 1922. Russell told Wittgenstein, 'I suppose you would prefer a League for War and Slavery' ('für Krieg und Knechtschaft'). 'Better that! Better that!,' Wittgenstein replied with emphasis. ('Eher noch! Eher noch!') Wittgenstein told Drury that Russell's writings on logic and mathematics ought to be bound in blue, and everyone be made to read them, but his writings on ethics, marriage, and so on in red and no one be allowed to read them.

put in this category: there was never the same frequency of meetings in his case.) But there was more to the intellectual sympathy Russell spoke of than this: it is likely that the friendship would not have prospered but for those features of Russell's life at the time which not only made him such a valuable combination, from Wittgenstein's point of view, of maturity with openness to new ideas but also contributed to his being concerned (outside his philosophy) more with personal than with public matters.

The friendship thus favoured by time and chance was, particularly during this first year, a great source of happiness to both and gave a meaning to their lives. Their discussions of philosophy were their chief work: each was stimulated by the other and confirmed by the other's reaction in the feeling that some advance was being made. They shared too nearly everything else that they thought important. Russell began to go to many more concerts, first taken by Wittgenstein and then even when Wittgenstein was away. Anecdotes of the Alleegasse, talk about the greatness of Beethoven, the remark that hearing the Choral Symphony with Russell was one of the great moments of his life: small enough matters, but they led to Russell's hearing much of Beethoven and Brahms for the first time or with new ears. All the same, Russell felt that music alone did not do enough to civilize people:

> it is too apart, too passionate, and too remote from words. [Wittgenstein] has not a sufficiently wide curiosity or a sufficient wish for a broad survey of the world. It won't spoil his work on logic, but it will make him always a very narrow specialist, and rather too much the champion of a party—that is when judged by the highest standards. (BR to OM 6.3.13)

So at this time (admittedly when their differences were becoming more apparent to the two men) he told Wittgenstein that it would do him good to read French prose, because he was in danger of being narrow and uncivilized. We have commented above on the narrowness[79] that went with depth in Wittgenstein's reading. Paul Engelmann confirms that French literature was almost omitted. Partly perhaps it was accident, partly his not feeling at home in that language, though for him that is too temperamental a matter to be called an accident. Pascal impressed him—the *Pensées* at any rate, not the *Lettres Provinçiales*—it is hard to imagine him reading Rousseau. The French writer that he did turn to fairly often was Molière,[80] and it is possible to see why: Molière's

79. p. 34. All these judgements are relative. By modern standards Wittgenstein was very well-read. Russell too (it should be remembered in what follows) had learnt and read French and German from earliest childhood.

80. See above p. 136 and Engelmann: *Letters from Ludwig Wittgenstein with a Memoir*, pp. 4 and 68. *Les Femmes savantes* was the only French book among those he left at death. His favourite quotation from it was: 'Un sot savant est sot, plus qu'un sot ignorant.' Engelmann's remark about French literature comes from a personal communication.

epigrams emerge inevitably from the dramatic situation, in a favourite phrase of Wittgenstein's he 'has the right' to make them. If we had only the quotations or if they were supported by analysis or theory, they would lose all their fittingness. While Russell was urging French prose, Wittgenstein tried to interest Russell in German poetry, 'raving', as Russell put it, about Mörike and leaving a volume in Russell's rooms (quite in the tradition of the Alleegasse). Russell eventually took to Mörike when he heard some pieces read by Franziska von Hügel, and Wittgenstein (a little surprised) then urged him to move on to Goethe, naturally not new to Russell but previously not appreciated by him. With more hope Wittgenstein found a copy of Lichtenberg's aphorisms (still in Russell's library) for his friend. It is hard for an English (and I suspect for a French) reader to understand the enthusiasm inspired by Lichtenberg. As with much German literature of the eighteenth century, the thought is sinewy enough but the starting-point is a little naive for one steeped, as Lord John Russell's grandson was, in literatures that became urbane rather earlier. The author seems to find it too much of a novelty that men, and especially learned men, can be fools, and his language seems to lack some resources of pointedness and irony so that the epigrams—aphorisms is in fact the better word—do not quite come off.

With such exchanges of talismans, with the discussion of books, of men and women, of ideals and aspirations, each trying passionately to convince the other, Wittgenstein with more hope but less prospect, Russell with some parental tolerance, sitting back himself secure and enjoying the effect of Wittgenstein on his friends, they met each other's needs.

Only gradually did Wittgenstein come to know Russell's friends and to make some of his own. His first term (Michaelmas 1911) was devoted, we have seen, to Russell and the philosophy of mathematics. During the next—his first official—term, he took a wider interest in philosophy and, apart from his coaching with Johnson, went to Moore's lectures on psychology. Wittgenstein's public appearances did not at first impress the young men: perhaps he was too inclined to raise fundamental objections (to a learner this can often seem like mere obstruction) and to recommend them by assertion rather than argument. Moore could be very fierce in discussion with any view which he saw, or thought he saw, to be nonsense but his opponents rarely took this (on reflection) as a personal affront. No doubt they sensed what his friends knew and his letters and diaries show, that he was the most modest of men, diffident about his own powers and the correctness of views he had been led to. Certainly he showed this feature of his character with Wittgenstein. He told Russell that he thought enormously highly of Wittgenstein's brains ... —says he always feels W. *must* be right when they disagree. He says during his lectures W. always looks frightfully puzzled, but nobody else does. (BR to OM 5.3.12)

Not long afterwards Russell heard the other side:

Wittgenstein ... said how much he loves Moore, how he likes and dislikes people for the way they think—Moore has one of the most beautiful smiles I know, and it had struck him. (BR to OM 16.3.12)

Wittgenstein came often to Moore, usually after his lectures (which were on Mondays, Wednesdays and Fridays at 11), staying until '1¾' with a certain disregard for lunch. The lectures were discussed, Wittgenstein 'discoursed' after Russell's lecture and brought Frege for Moore to read but Moore records,[81] and his diaries of the time show, that their friendship became much closer in the next academic year, and it will be appropriate to give a fuller account of it under the events of that year. Some more or less external facts are however relevant here. At the beginning of 1912 Moore was 37, a year younger than Russell. After a classical education he turned to philosophy as an undergraduate at Trinity and stayed on as a Prize Fellow until 1904. These years saw his reaction against idealism, in which he influenced Russell and which we have described above principally in connexion with his article 'On Judgment' of 1899. They were also the years of the composition of *Principia Ethica* (Moore was probably alone in preferring *Ethics*, which appeared in 1912). For seven years after this Moore, who had independent means, lived as a private scholar; during the first half of this time he was occupied, he tells us, in trying to understand Russell's *Principles of Mathematics* and in writing one or two papers. During the second half (immediately before the period of which we speak) he wrote the book on ethics already mentioned and a set of lectures now published as *Some Main Problems of Philosophy*. In 1911 he returned to Cambridge as University Lecturer in Moral Science and was thus in his second term of office when Wittgenstein attended his lectures. As a Past Fellow he was allowed to occupy rooms, though not a Fellow's rooms, in Trinity and he dined regularly in Hall. (Moore married in 1916 and became Professor, and a Fellow of Trinity again, in 1925.)

Wittgenstein's letters to him suggest that he thought Moore in important ways more flexible and younger than Russell. Moore indeed always retained an unusual candour of speech and manner but in 1912 he was also young in appearance, stouter now, and rubicund, but still

---

81. In his 'Autobiography' in *The Philosophy of G.E. Moore* (ed. P. Schilpp) 1942, reprinted in K.T. Fann: *Ludwig Wittgenstein*, p. 39 and the Bibliography in the same volume.

recalling the undergraduate who for some years fulfilled Russell's ideal of genius:

> He was in those days beautiful and slim, with a look almost of inspiration, and with an intellect as deeply passionate as Spinoza's. He had a kind of exquisite purity.[82]

Moore's influence on the young men and on the occasional revenant from those who had recently gone down was if anything stronger than Russell's. It is fair to assume that Moore's was the most powerful recommendation that led to Lytton Strachey (up from London) seeking Wittgenstein's acquaintance: through Russell naturally, for they regarded him as Russell's protégé:

> Then Lytton came to tea to meet Wittgenstein, which he wished to do. Everybody has just begun to discover Wittgenstein; they all now realize that he has genius. He was very good at tea. (BR to OM 2.5.12)

This was the occasion when Wittgenstein's bias for philosophical scepticism struck Russell. Strachey's visit had a particular purpose:

> Somebody had been telling them [Lytton, Gerald Shove (later a well-known economist), and Sheppard (later Provost of King's)] about Wittgenstein and they wanted to hear what I thought of him. They were thinking of electing him to the Society. I told them I didn't think he would like the Society. I am quite sure he wouldn't really. It would seem to him stuffy, as indeed it has become, owing to their practice of being in love with each other, which didn't exist in my day—I think it is mainly due to Lytton. (BR to OM, further letter 2.5.12)

Russell too had been a member of the Society, an Apostle, like Moore (and indeed Whitehead and MacTaggart) but it seemed to him to have changed for the worse since his undergraduate days, and not only in the respect mentioned:

> We were still Victorian; they were Edwardian. We believed in ordered progress by means of politics and free discussion. The more self-confident among us may have hoped to be leaders of the multitude, but none of us wished to be divorced from it. The generation of Keynes and Lytton did not seek to preserve any kinship with the Philistine. They aimed rather at a life of retirement among fine shades and nice feelings, and conceived of the good as consisting in the passionate mutual admirations of a clique of

82. *Autobiography*, vol. 1, p. 64. It is interesting that it was Wittgenstein who replaced Moore as Russell's pattern of genius: 'He was perhaps the most perfect example I have ever known of genius as traditionally conceived, passionate, profound, intense, and dominating. He had a kind of purity which I have never known equalled except by G.E. Moore' (ibid. vol. 2, pp. 98–9).

the elite. This doctrine, quite unfairly, they fathered upon G.E. Moore, whose disciples they professed to be.[83]

Wittgenstein was to hear more of the Society later. For the moment he was being looked over and drawn out by a figure legendary at Cambridge and in London already at the centre of the literary and artistic circle known as Bloomsbury. It says much for Strachey's tact that Wittgenstein, who was not easily impressed, did take the trouble to shine at that first tea-party. Strachey's first two comments provide an example of that fluctuation in Wittgenstein between brilliance and apparent dullness which Russell had already observed:

> Herr Sinckel-Winckel lunches with me, quiet little man. (LS to JMK 5.5.12).

Keynes himself did not meet Wittgenstein until October. But another opportunity for philosophical conversation occurred on an evening in the rooms of Strachey's brother Oliver:

> Oliver and Herr Sinckel-Winckel hard at it on universals and particulars. The latter oh! so bright—but quelle souffrance! Oh God! God! 'If A loves B'—'There may be a common quality'—'Not analysable in that way at all, but the complexes have certain qualities.' How shall I manage to slink off to bed? (LS to JMK 17.5.12)[84]

The second passage refers perhaps to the same occasion, certainly to the same day as that on which Wittgenstein held the floor at one of Russell's 'evenings':

> Wittgenstein maintained the paradox that mathematics would improve people's taste because taste comes of thinking honestly—we were all against him. (BR to OM 17.5.12)

We shall see that Wittgenstein much preferred the older members of the Society (angels as they were called) to the unlicked undergraduates, and Strachey was certainly one of the most active of these older members, but he could not join in the general admiration of Strachey's work—witness his comment on *Landmarks in French Literature*

> [Wittgenstein] had been reading Lytton's little book, which he didn't like—he said it made an impression of effort, like the gasps of an asthmatic person. I got out the book, but couldn't see what he meant. (BR to OM 23.4.13)

83. *Autobiography*, vol. I, pp. 70–1.
84. Then an undergraduate.

Wittgenstein was to be drawn more into the circles of the Society and
Bloomsbury, but for the present he had made another friend from the
fringes of that circle. David Hume Pinsent, a collateral descendant of the
philosopher Hume, had been an embryo (a person considered for the
Society) in 1911, but had in the event not been elected. He at first read
mathematics but later studied law. He was the son of a musical and
cultivated family in Birmingham. His mother, later well-known in her
long widowhood as the social campaigner Dame Ellen Pinsent, was the
daughter of a clergyman and had written a number of improving novels
(one in fact is little more than a temperance tract), rather in the spirit of
Fritz Reuter. Pinsent himself was an unaffected and likeable young man
with what passed for a good education and rather more than the usual
taste for music. He had a wide circle of friends and made himself
welcome everywhere by a generous and lively enthusiasm for the
interests of others, usually having something amusing but unsatirical to
say. He kept an open and unself-conscious diary (to judge from the
extracts concerning his unusual friend); the personality suggested by it is
of a type familiar to all who have read letters and youthful productions
from that more than decimated generation of English public schoolboys
and undergraduates. We should perhaps read them with different eyes if
the young men had grown old. As things are, Pinsent seems to us (no
doubt he seemed to Wittgenstein, who had much wider experience and
much keener nerves than he) young, enthusiastic, not conventional but
still somehow proper, his aspirations and judgements unquestioned, and
none the less genuine for that; in short, very English, as Englishness was
then understood. This undoubtedly was part of what attracted Wittgenstein, at that time an admirer of much in English patterns of behaviour
and personal relations. It was only human nature that he occasionally
saw in his adopted country and in his friend defects associated with those
virtues, while it was his own individual almost morbid sensitivity that
made him feel and express this distaste so strongly. Naturally, also, he
was sometimes right and sometimes wrong in detecting traces of the
unfeelingness or hypocrisy of a certain stereotype in this particular
product of a cultivated and progressive upper-middle class family with
its Low Church roots, a family with something of the atmosphere of the
Schlegels of *Howard's End*. Three instances will perhaps illustrate the sort
of conversation this gave rise to:

> Wittgenstein and I had an animated discussion on public schools—
> eventually getting quite angry with each other until we found we had both
> misunderstood the other. He has an enormous horror of what he calls a
> 'Philistine' attitude towards cruelty and suffering—any callous attitude—
> and accuses Kipling of such: and he got the idea that I sympathized with
> it. (Diary 12.9.12)

Wittgenstein has been talking a lot, at different times, about 'Philistines' —a name he gives to all people he dislikes! I think some of the views I have expressed struck him as a bit philistine (views—that is—on practical things (not on philosophy)—for instance on the advantage of this age over past ages and so forth), and he is rather puzzled because he does not consider me really a Philistine—and I don't think he dislikes me! He satisfies himself by saying that I shall think differently as soon as I am a bit older! (Diary 19.9.12)

We talked about Woman's suffrage: he is very much against it—for no particular reason except that 'all the women he knows are such idiots'. He said that at Manchester University the girl students spend all their time flirting with the professors. Which disgusts him very much—as he dislikes half-measures of all sorts, and disapproves of anything not deadly in earnest. Yet in these days, when marriage is not possible till the age of about 30—no one is earning enough till then—and when illegitimate marriages are not approved of—what else is there to do but philander. (Diary 7.2.13)[85]

Pinsent's reaction to these occasional disagreements (which we can be sure were conducted with some vigour on Wittgenstein's side) gives a clue to his success in establishing a deep friendship with Wittgenstein. The quality that counted was not yieldingness and malleability (though it was important that Pinsent had an open mind and was prepared to learn about human beings and particularly about himself) but on the contrary the strength and the confidence that he showed inside the relationship. Much later Wittgenstein said in one of the code passages in his notebooks, 'In love, what counts for most is courage.' This is what Pinsent had, that enabled him to accept the intensity that Wittgenstein brought to their friendship, observing without resentment the cycles in the mood of his difficult friend, not managing him but reacting frankly, not necessarily calmly but without ill-will or jealousy, remembering the good qualities and agreeable aspects when they were least apparent.

We had a long discussion about plans for tomorrow: I wanted to go straight back to Reykjavik and he to stay a day here and go on Wednesday: at first I gave in to him and said we would stay here two nights: but he got very worried about my concession (eventually we hit upon the compromise we actually carried out: he is morbidly afraid of my giving in just 'to get a little peace' and so forth: of course that was not my motive: I did so as a favour to him and in order not to be selfish: I think I persuaded him so in the end. (Diary 23.9.12)

On the train we had to change our seats at the last moment because he insisted on being alone from other tourists. Then a very genial Englishman came along and talked to me and finally insisted on our coming into his

85. Passages from the diary are quoted by kind permission of the Master and Fellows of Trinity College, Cambridge.

carriage to smoke—as ours was a non-smoker. Witt. refused to move, and of course I had to go for a short time at least—it would have been violently rude to refuse. I came back as soon as I could and found him in an awful state. I made some remark about the Englishman being a weird person—whereat he turned and said 'I could travel the whole way with him if I pleased'. And then I had it all out with him and finally brought him round to a normal and genial frame of mind. I had been meaning to have it out all the morning—I can always reconcile things with him when I get a chance of being frank and open—but one trivial circumstance after another had made it impossible. When I did get the opportunity, we made it up in ten minutes. He is a chaotic person. (Diary 2.9.13)

These are examples of what Pinsent, with a rare discrimination, was able to treat as unimportant. Of course such scenes might derive from a feeling of Wittgenstein's that the friendship was more important to himself than to Pinsent—the latter of the two certainly originated in one of Wittgenstein's outbursts ('we had got on splendidly so far, hadn't we?') to which Pinsent, though he had been thinking exactly the same thing, was too shy to give more than a flippant answer. Behind the shyness were youth and Englishness, not any doubt about his true feelings, so that his explanations to Wittgenstein of what caused tension when they were together for long—his own occasional irritability or Wittgenstein's occasional fussiness—had a weight and sincerity and hence an effect that no conventional smoothing-over of difficulties could have had. Moreover he was sorry for his friend, not irritated with him, when some mood that Wittgenstein himself would regret took him out of what Pinsent recognized or regarded as his normal frame of mind. 'These sulky fits of his, I am afraid, distress him very much.' Naturally he found Wittgenstein different from his other friends ('he is if anything a little mad'), but this did not encroach on his awareness of the charm, the cleverness, the affection, the concern that Wittgenstein showed him.

It is worth dwelling on these difficulties of adjustment because they reappear in the majority of Wittgenstein's close friendships and figure perhaps excessively in the impression of his personality that has become general. Certainly he demanded much of a friendship. Everything must come from the heart, difficulties must not be swept under the carpet, differences of opinion and of taste must be explored—like nuances of conduct towards third persons they might reveal important divergences in value judgements. In any case they were the stuff of life, they were what a friendship would have to be about. The *ideal* is not uncommon. Everyone would want to agree with St. Augustine that 'a friend is one with whom one may dare to share the counsels of one's heart'.[86] But many things stand in the way of attempting to put it into practice—the desire for comfort, a disinclination to reveal parts of oneself that one is

86. Peter Brown, *Augustine*, p. 10: perhaps *de div. qq.* 83. 71. 6.

ashamed of, above all a lack of that courage we have spoken of. Wittgenstein himself faced not less of these difficulties than usual but more, being exceptionally sensitive to unworthy impulses in himself and others and at the same time persuaded that only a spontaneous life was worth living. There were bound to be outbursts on his side which required both robustness and understanding from his friends: Pinsent showed these qualities, Keynes too when Wittgenstein misinterpreted a slight tension betwen them.[87] Russell and Moore, we shall see, differed, Russell proving able to deal with the first outburst but later moving away from Wittgenstein, Moore being shattered by the first serious rift but later overcoming many differences.

High though the demands thus were, it is important to see that they were an essential part of what made friendship with him worthwhile. The sort of completely sincere discussion of one's own and others' life that seemed to open his friends' eyes to new aspects of life, or perhaps more accurately seemed to bring them back into touch with a reality they had almost forgotten, could not be lightly engaged in or lightly dropped. (Much later he was to say to Malcolm not only that trying to think honestly about your own and other people's lives was often both nasty and important but also that the attempt to do so in the frame of a friendship was likely to lead to clashes.)[88] It would be absurd to think of Wittgenstein as a saint (though his sister Mining did so for a while) but his friends could see that he had the idea of perfection in every area, in the serious matters of everyday life, in his work, or in the choice of a handkerchief for a present. Especially he wanted it in his friendships, and nearly all his friends reacted to this as to a kind of revelation, even if (perhaps for good reasons) they did not continue to live in this way and even if they had at times to suffer from his impatience at his own or their inability whether to be perfect or to have the right attitude (as he conceived it) towards one's own imperfection. Usually they felt as Pinsent did that their ideas on all sorts of subjects had been reconstructed.

The two first met at one of Russell's 'crushes'. They fell in with one another again at a concert 'including a very fine piano trio of Schubert's' on 4 May. Schubert was in fact the chief of their shared tastes. Pinsent would play arrangements on the piano—on one occasion an arrangement for four hands with his sister. The two friends would borrow music from the Musical Union and take it to Pinsent's rooms. Eventually they developed a method of performing Schubert songs, Pinsent playing and Wittgenstein whistling (the truth and expressiveness of his whistling were often commented on). In this way, on holiday, they learnt 40 or 50 songs.

---

87. See LW to JMK of May 1929 and Keynes's reply, JMK to LW 26.5.29, under K.21 in *Letters to Russell etc.*
88. *Ludwig Wittgenstein: A Memoir*, pp. 39–40.

Of all musical tastes that for Schubert requires least explanation. We have scattered comments of Wittgenstein: in one he draws attention (with his fondness for physiognomy) in accounts of music to the particular way in which Schubert was an Austrian:

> Bruckner's music has no trace of the long and narrow (nordic?) face of Nestroy, Grillparzer, Haydn etc but has quite simply a full, rounded (alpine?) face of a yet purer type than Schubert's.[89]

He spoke too of a feature that made Schubert particularly suitable for this sort of performance:

> One can say of Schubert's melodies that they are full of turns of thought, which one cannot say of Mozart's. Schubert is baroque. One can indicate certain places in a Schubert melody and say 'You see, that is the point of his melody, that is where the idea reaches its apex.'[90]

An example of one of these *pointes* or turns occurs in the last two bars of the theme of 'Death and the maiden':

> One is liable to think at first that this figure is conventional, commonplace —until one understands what it more profoundly expresses; i.e. until one understands that here the commonplace is filled with significance.[91]

The commonplace filled with significance—it might alone express Wittgenstein's ideal, but Schubert attracted him also for another reason, in which the ethical and the aesthetic were intertwined: the contrast of the misery of his life and the absence of all trace of it in his music, the absence of all bitterness.

Schubert was an old love of Pinsent's; and Beethoven, of course. Brahms—it seems strange today—was comparatively unknown to him: a concert the friends went to in London was the first time he had heard the First Symphony. Another time, in Birmingham with Pinsent's family, the two heard a festival concert conducted by Henry Wood—Brahms's *Requiem*. Wittgenstein had heard it often but never enjoyed it more. Then, after lunch:

> The second half of the concert began with two selections from Strauss's *Salome*: Wittgenstein refused to go in for them, and stayed outside till the Beethoven, which followed. He went out after that and went back to Lordswood by himself.

89. 1931, *Culture and Value*, p. 22 (my translation).
90. 10 August 1946, *Culture and Value*, p. 47 (my translation).
91. 24 September 1946, *Culture and Value*, p. 52 (my translation).

The *Salome* was rot, but very clever and amusing in consequence. (Diary 4.10.12)

Wittgenstein was, of course, the more fastidious of the two: hardly older, he already knew what he could tolerate. As for leaving early (before the Bach!), it was like him, who listened so intensely, to avoid too rich a musical feast.

In Cambridge the two went often together or separately (for both had other friends) to concerts of the Musical Club or Union, usually classical chamber music performed by semi-professionals. Through Pinsent Wittgenstein met 'musical undergraduates' who would defend 'modern music'—heaven knows what they meant, perhaps an amalgam of Richard Strauss and Mahler and Rutland Boughton, certainly not the atonal music already burgeoning in Vienna. At any rate Wittgenstein and Pinsent opposed it vigorously. The only modern music we hear of Wittgenstein favouring at this time was the chamber music, closely based on classical models, of Josef Labor, the blind organist, a protégé of his family. In Vienna they arranged a concert for the old man in the *Musikverein* and saw to it that seats were filled and applause swelled by friends and even gardeners. Now in Cambridge Wittgenstein tried to arrange for Labor's string quintet to be played. Numerous discussions were held and possible performers expressed some interest, but in the end the project ran into the sand. If Wittgenstein had stayed in Cambridge longer ... but perhaps it is better regarded as one of several plans taken up and abandoned by him during these years, which were, after all, those of his youth.

Another interest of Wittgenstein's that brought him and Pinsent together was his work at the time in psychology: Pinsent, perhaps because he was musical, was enlisted practically on first meeting as a subject for Wittgenstein's experiments. These were golden years for experimental psychology in Cambridge. F.C. Bartlett, Miss E. Smith (later Lady Bartlett), and C.A. Mace were among the young researchers. C.S. Myers had moved the department from cottage rooms to a building of its own, and now, in 1912, a new laboratory was being built. (It is typical of the social and economic conditions of the time that Myers could and did contribute as well as collect money for its building— perhaps also that Myers was Jewish.) Moreover, the researchers, and Myers in particular, were free, in the infancy of their subject and the ample atmosphere of those days, to pursue questions of theoretical or human interest with very little concern for practical applications or even for the likelihood of quick results. The war was to scatter them and to concern them with shell shock and industrial psychology and intelligence tests. But for the moment not Myers alone but Pear (in Manchester) and Valentine and Muscio devoted much time to the psychology of music, whether to the study of its development in what were then called primitive societies or to the analysis of musical appreciation among the inhabitants of Cambridge or Würzburg. The youthful *British Journal of Psychology* abounds with articles on the localization of sound, on the perception of tone differences, on synaesthesia, on individual differences in musical appreciation, and so on. Myers himself contributed studies of primitive music to the *Journal* and to a number of expedition reports and anthropological collections. Here two interests conspired: he had been intensely musical from early youth and after his training as a physiologist he had at first devoted himself to physical anthropology. His study of the special senses among primitive peoples revealed, after much care, little difference from what could be found in laboratories in Europe and America—though his successor and obituarist F.C. Bartlett believed that a subtler statistical analysis would have revealed interesting divergences.[92] Such differences in musical discrimination as he found seem to be fairly easily explicable: where differences in tone are the important element, absolute pitch seems to be much more widespread than in our society; where rhythm predominates, the primitives show a remarkable ability 'to regard many successively different intervals of time as a co-ordinated whole—as a phrase'. The change in direction of Myers's interests after the war prevented him from bringing this work to a conclusion, had it even been possible, but the general view of the development of music that emerged from his researches and perhaps in some measure from his preconceptions was the attractive one that none of the existing unitary explanations of its origin was exhaustive. There was a parallel with language, but probably it was better to think that both language and music developed out of a more primitive system of communication. Besides, in its rhythmical aspect, music was connected with bodily movements and activities, though this connexion too was inadequate to explain the whole of it. The same considerations applied to the sexual explanation of music. All this was before ethnomusicology and the heightened awareness of the different social role of music—and of different kinds of music—in different societies. The main application that Myers could make of the study of primitive music was the isolation of the various factors in music appreciation as we know it, chief among them the perception of pitch and pitch-difference, of rhythm, and of *Musikgestaltqualität*—the property of being musically meaningful, of constituting a phrase or tune. This last distinguishes music from mere noise and Myers describes interesting cases of loss of the sense for it—sometimes by highly musical people, who could still distinguish all the differences in what they heard but were unable to hear it as music.[93]

92. *ONFRS* 5 (1945–8) 772.
93. See, for example, Myers's 'The Beginnings of Music' in *Essays Presented to W.M. Ridgeway* (Cambridge, 1913) and the chapter on music in his *In the Realm of Mind* (Cambridge, 1937).

Wittgenstein's acquaintance with Myers and his interest in all this is easily explained. He would meet Myers in the musical world of Cambridge or in the Moral Sciences Club: perhaps he heard in early February the talk Myers gave on Primitive Music, in the course of which Myers sang some of the pieces he had brought back. And the subject was one that always exercised Wittgenstein, particularly the analogy to be found between music and language, or more exactly between a musical theme or idea (in German *Gedanke*, or thought) and a proposition or sentence:

> Musical themes are in a certain sense propositions. And so the recognition of the essence of logic will lead to the recognition of the essence of music. (*Notebooks* 7.2.15)
>
> A melody is a sort of tautology, it is self-contained, it satisfies itself. (*Notebooks* 4.3.15)

and in the *Tractatus*:

> A proposition is not a medley of words. —(Just as a theme in music is not a medley of notes.)
>   A proposition is articulated. (*TLP* 3.141)

The parallel with language, the appeal to logic or grammar, remained one (though only one) of his most constant ways of talking about music. It was a way of thinking particularly characteristic, for example, of Labor—Wittgenstein tells us that when Labor played, people used to say, 'He is speaking!' and that Labor himself would talk of musical thoughts as being crumpled and not fit for use any more. Wittgenstein came to think the analogy less important and applicable only to some music, not to all (he mentioned that it applied to Bach more than to Beethoven or Mozart), but at this time—perhaps because he was then, even more than later, dominated by the thought of the single musical tradition to which he belonged—it is the aspect of music most often referred to in his writings.

It is only a speculation, though a probable one, that the questions of aesthetics that lay behind his psychological experiments were connected with this. Muscio, who collaborated with him, died young, and Myers's detailed work on music, in the framework of which his experiments were conceived, never reached the point of publication. Those experiments were on rhythm and the sort of result achieved was a determination of conditions under which subjects heard or read into a sequence of beats a rhythm which was not in fact there. The phenomenon of subjective accentuation occurs very obviously when a regularly functioning metronome is heard as striking groups of beats. The conditions may be varied

by placing the metronome in a box, raising the lid unobserved by the
subject, and comparing the beats thus stressed with those heard as
stressed by the subject.[94] Pinsent records many hours of experiments and
mentions conversations too in which rhythm was discussed. The project
was a cement for their friendship. As for what it revealed about the
grammar or logic of music, it seems to have been, like Myers's own work,
suggestive and promising but not easily capable of a rigorous development. Perhaps that is what psychology ought to be like. At any rate it
ranked as professional work and, when the British Psychological Society
met at Cambridge in July 1912, Wittgenstein gave what he described to
Russell as 'a most absurd paper on rhythms'.[95] He also gave a
demonstration 'of an apparatus for psychological investigation of
rhythm' at the ceremonial opening of the new laboratory for experimental psychology in May 1913.[96] So he retained some interest in the
project in that academic year although Pinsent mentions no more
experiments. Pinsent, the keen photographer, thought it unwise of
Wittgenstein to have no hobbies, but in fact psychology was his hobby.
He did not think of it as having any connexion with his work, which he
called logic (at this time 'philosophical' was almost a word of abuse in his
mouth). He seems to have attempted to explain this point to Myers:

> I had a discussion with Myers about the relations between Logic and
> Psychology. I was very candid and I am sure he thinks that I am the most
> arrogant devil who ever lived. Poor Mrs. Myers who was also present
> got—I think—quite wild about me. However, I think he was a bit less
> confused after the discussion than before. (LW to BR 22.6.12)

Other hobbies—or other pastimes—were to come later. For the
moment (Easter term 1912) Pinsent and Wittgenstein met in the context
of the experiments, of concerts, of tea taken together, and the like.
Wittgenstein, with this friend, moved in the direction of a normal
undergraduate's life. He was prepared (a tribute to his friend) to go to
Chapel when Pinsent read the lesson, and we later hear of his attending
a Union Society Debate in his company.

Pinsent may have been wrong about Wittgenstein's lack of interests
outside his work but he was right about the loneliness which he supposed
to result from it. Wittgenstein still needed a friend, someone with whom
he could spend a long time together. Russell did not satisfy this need; his

94. This technique is described in C.S. Myers. Another method he described is that of tightening
the elastic with which hammers are held so as to produce *tones* louder. Wittgenstein was very
interested in the mechanics of experiments like these: one may instance his considerable ingenuity as
a laboratory technician in the Second World War.

95. LW to BR 1.7.12. The *British Journal of Psychology* records it as 'Experiment on Rhythm
(Demonstration), L. Wittgenstein and B. Muscio (Introduced by C.S. Myers)'.

96. BR to OM, 15.7.13. There is also a message to Muscio (presumably still in connexion with
the project) in a letter to Moore of 1914.

attention and affections were too divided, his character was perhaps too firmly set: for all his capacity for enthusiasm he was not, in the end, a person whose life and values Wittgenstein could take part in shaping. Pinsent was a quite different case and Wittgenstein recognized it immediately:

> He suddenly asked what I was doing during the vac: and proposed that I should come with him to Iceland. After my first surprise I asked what he estimated the cost would be: upon which he said—'Oh, that doesn't matter: I have no money and you have no money—at least, if you have, it doesn't matter. But my father has a lot'—upon which he proposed that his father should pay for us both! ... I have known Wittgenstein only for three weeks or so—but we seem to get on well together... (Pinsent's diary for 31 May 1912)

Pinsent's inclination was to go, and his parents sensibly supported it, so the trip was fixed for the coming September.

Wittgenstein stayed on in Cambridge, after term, until the middle of July. Russell was away from Cambridge for the month of June and we owe to this fact the first three of Wittgenstein's letters to him. Distracted though he was by his paper on rhythms, Wittgenstein was working on the foundations of logic. It is likely that the comparative isolation of these few weeks (for Pinsent too was away for most of June) made them particularly fruitful for Wittgenstein. What remains from them in writing is the pregnant discussion we have already quoted (p. 81 above) which leads to the remark that there are no logical constants—the fundamental idea of the *Tractatus*; and a suggestion that general propositions have meaning only in the context of inferences leading to propositions about individuals. In time he came to see or think that the problems of logic were not those of dealing with a special subject-matter, say connectives between propositions or the notions of generality, but were present already in the simplest proposition. But his thoughts, that June, were also on other matters:

> Whenever I have time I now read James's 'Varieties of religious experience'. This book does me a lot of good. I don't mean to say that I will be a saint soon, but I am not sure that it does not improve me a little in a way in which I would like to improve *very much*: namely I think that it helps me to get rid of the *Sorge* (in the sense in which Goethe used the word in the Second Part of *Faust*). (LW to BR 22.6.12)

Apart from the psychological meeting on the 13th of July there were two further external events that affected Wittgenstein before his departure. The first was a visit from his sister Hermine. 'Would you mind me introducing her to you?' he wrote to Russell. 'She ought to see everything worth seeing!' They came to lunch and stayed to tea.

> She is not at all fatal [Russell wrote—alluding no doubt to what he had anticipated]—older than he is, and very plain, pleasant but not exciting. It was rather uphill work at times—I think she was rather shy. At last he and I fell to arguing as if she were not there. She says he is quite different since he came to Cambridge—so much happier; she feels it is the right place for him. (BR to OM 10.7.12)

She was, in fact, deeply impressed: she had great loyalty and respect for those who had helped her brother and Russell always seemed to her one who had come along at the right time for Luki.

> Ludwig and I were invited to tea in Russell's beautiful College room. I can still see it in my mind's eye, with its huge bookcases covering all the walls and its tall, old-fashioned windows with their finely proportioned stone cross-work. Suddenly Russell said to me 'We expect the next big step in philosophy to be taken by your brother.' Hearing that was something so extraordinary and incredible for me, that for a moment I became literally dizzy. Ludwig was fifteen years younger than me and, despite his being twenty-three, I still thought of him as simply a young man, a learner. Small wonder that I never forgot that moment.[97]

It was from this time, it seems, that his family's belief in his distinction dates: his powers they knew already—how he could dissect and criticize unerringly. His earliest surviving letter (1908 or before, to judge from the hand) contained absolutely confident instructions to this very sister on how to draw. They knew too how quickly he could grasp the principles of some new subject-matter. What had been lacking was concentration, an interest that would absorb all his powers, and an indication that he would produce something of his own. They now had some asssurance of all of this, and it followed naturally that Ludwig was happier. In his diaries and letters it is usually by ability or inability to work that Wittgenstein measures happiness and unhappiness. In this he was very obviously his father's son, only for him (imaginatively if not theoretically) logical concepts and operations had the same reality as furnaces and girders and engines, and a day's work was done by reshaping or rearranging these in his mind or in his pocket-notebook. He was like his father too in finding his way through a number of occupations and interests, completing none in the regular way, but taking from each what he needed, and starting the career of his maturity at the age of 23. (Karl was in fact a year older when he went to Ternitz.)

97. *Familienerinnerungen*, p. 108. The phrase about the next step in philosophy also occurs in a wartime letter from Russell to Wittgenstein's mother.

Russell's tribute at such an age was perhaps even more surprising than Hermine Wittgenstein thought. To be accepted so young not as a promising young man but as a guide, to have written a major work before the age of 30, these have been the lot of few philosophers. Descartes's dream, to be sure, occurred when he was 24, but it was suppressed for at least nine years. Even the prodigies, Leibniz and Mill, produced their philosophical work mostly late in life. Of early beginners Hume and Schopenhauer, perhaps even Berkeley, received less recognition at first than Wittgenstein.

The second event of these weeks was Wittgenstein's choice of a room for the following year. He could now move into college and, for some reason now obscure, Moore wished to or was prepared to move from the rooms (not Fellow's rooms) given him on his return to Cambridge.[98] The transfer was arranged early in July. K.10 in Whewell's Court—they were situated at the top of a Victorian gothic tower at the furthest end from the main college of a complex of buildings (two narrow quadrangles, they seem, connected lengthwise) across Trinity Street from the main college. Here at the quiet limit of the college, in it but not completely of it, Wittgenstein could live privately and impersonally looking out away from the college over the streets of small shops and lodging houses towards the river landscape. Later, when he became a Fellow, still more when he returned as a Professor, he could have obtained rooms like those of Russell that impressed his sister, rooms where Newton may have lived, near the glory of the Wren Library, but each time he preferred to return to this less than prepossessing dark tower, to climb all the steps, and to live in these comparatively narrow rooms without the comforts—the bathroom, for example—that his age and health would have demanded. Some of this taste for the Spartan and uncomfortable was a later development, but the liking for small, narrow, and manageable quarters seems always to have been his and, as for life in a tower, we find him attempting to do the same thing at Olmütz in 1916, acting out, perhaps, his impulses towards withdrawal and isolation. At all events these Cambridge rooms were the nearest thing to a home that he had for many years. He left at his death a few mementoes, and of the very few relating not to his friends but to himself, one was a little snapshot of this tower.

The room arranged, he went out with Pinsent (now back in Cambridge) to view furniture at various shops. The expedition was amusing but not altogether fruitful, since Wittgenstein exclaimed 'No! Beastly!' at ninety percent of what the shopman showed them. It was the same when he resumed his shopping in London in September: the first day he bought nothing at all. He disliked all ornamentation that was not

98. Curiously enough Moore moved back into these same rooms when Wittgenstein vacated them a year later.

part of the construction and could find nothing simple enough. Eventually he had most of the furniture specially made for him—'rather quaint but not bad,' Pinsent thought. The best materials were used and numerous modifications were carried out—in March 1913 he was replacing the white marble top of a sideboard with one in black marble, specially cut and polished in London. Simplicity has in modern times become an expensive luxury. It does not seem that the subordination of design to function, in the sense of intended use, would be an accurate description of Wittgenstein's tastes. These were connected, very typically for him, with his views on the value of abstract education. He used to say that mathematics would promote good taste, 'since good taste is genuine taste and therefore is furthered by whatever makes people think truthfully'.[99] Speaking to Russell he emphasized construction as the decisive feature. A thing must be fully the thing it was: and life must go on around it in the way appropriate to that. Thus Eccles's bed, as we have already seen,[100] was not to have rollers—it was to be a thing around which people moved, and this would have to include whoever did the cleaning. Similar features appear later in his architectural work—for example the centrally or symmetrically placed light-bulbs giving an even illumination, impersonal, not carefully adapted to some special need or preference of the user.[101] For his Cambridge rooms, he chose porcelain beakers bought from a medical supplier or laboratory outfitter in London instead of cups, 'because they look so much nicer—but they are less convenient!' said Pinsent. His room had at least one *Prunkstück*, a large, almost square dining table, seating eight. It was made of peculiarly dark sombre mahogany with ornate carved Victorian legs. This later became Russell's possession, when he bought the books and furniture Wittgenstein had left in England. Conrad Russell recalls that it was used only on state occasions—so that his parents would discuss whether to dine on 'Wittgenstein'.[102]

Wittgenstein left for Vienna on 15 July. In April he had been to the Austrian Embassy in London to be examined for military service: a rupture had been discovered (he had had it before) and it was decided that an operation was necessary. He planned to have it now immediately on his arrival in Vienna, though the circumstances were far from favourable:

> He tells me his other sister (not the one I saw) [Gretl is the sister meant] has been very ill with a baby, his father has had cancer for 2 years and has

99. BR to OM, 17.5.12. 'A very fine theory,' Russell said, 'but facts don't bear it out.'
100. p. 67.
101. See Bernard Leitner: *The Architecture of Ludwig Wittgenstein*, pp. 99–101.
102. I am indebted to Mr Conrad Russell for this description of the table. Russell's letters mention that the table was so big that during a move it had to be brought in through the window. Lady Katharine Tait tells me that Wittgenstein's bed has turned up in the attic of her mother, Dora Russell's house.

been operated seven times and suffers intolerably; his mother, who feels everything very intensely, hardly knows where to be or what to do; she doesn't know he [Ludwig] is to be operated and he dreads the moment of her being told; he says she never thinks a moment about herself or has any pleasure except through others—except music, but she never goes to hear music. (BR to OM 15.7.12)

In the event, the case was even worse. Wittgenstein's father was just about to have another operation, and Ludwig felt he could not give his family the worry of an operation on him too. It would have been impossible to have the proper operation performed secretly, so instead he had a minor, temporary operation performed secretly.

Ludwig divided the summer between his father's estate, the Hochreith, and the house of his uncle Paul Wittgenstein at Hallein near Salzburg. It was, despite the circumstances, a happy time. He was quite well again, 'philosophizing for all he was worth,' he told Russell. The weather was excellent and he could do most of his thinking in the open air:

There is nothing more wonderful in the world than the true problems of Philosophy.[103]

He was often to find these familiar surroundings and the absence of strangers and acquaintances whose personalities might grate on him a help to work. It was also noticeable throughout his life that while discussion helped him and was indeed essential for him, its results really appeared and he made most progress when he had a prolonged period for solitary reflection. Such reflection might well take place out of doors, for his habit was to make notes, to formulate his ideas in epigrammatic sentences or questions in a pocket-notebook or on slips of paper and to transfer them later into a larger notebook. His work now concentrated on the logical constants, the fundamental concepts which form the subject-matter of logic. For the moment he was concerned with what he called apparent variables, that is to say with the notion of generality, and with propositional connectives such as 'v', '.' and '⊃' (roughly equivalent to 'or', 'and', and 'only if' in ordinary language). Together with negation and identity, these constitute the primitive ideas of Whitehead and Russell's logic and that logic may be regarded as the science that consists of all and only the propositions that are true in virtue of the character of these primitive ideas.[104] The question is, however, what is the 'logical' truth that these propositions possess? What

103. Letter 4 in *Briefe* (1980).
104. It is assumed here that the notion of existence (the fulfilment of a propositional function by *some* arguments) can be defined in terms of generality (fulfilment of a propositional function by *all* arguments) together with negation. If not all men are mortal, then a mortal man exists.

makes these primitive ideas a unified and not an arbitrary collection? What is their character, in virtue of which the propositions of logic are true? Wittgenstein was trying to find some theory of symbolism which would answer these questions. His letters to Russell mention one or two false starts (as they later proved), but his general conclusion was one that turned out to be extremely fruitful.

> I believe that our problems can be traced down to the *atomic* propositions. This you will see if you try to explain precisely in what way the Copula in such a proposition has meaning.
>   I cannot explain it and I think that as soon as an exact answer to this question is given the problems of 'v' and of the apparent variable will be brought *very* near their solution if not solved. I therefore now think about 'Socrates is human.' (Good old Socrates!)[105]

'Their problems' were those of discovering the nature of logical truth—or, as they would have put it at the time, of defining what sort of complexes corresponded to logical propositions. We have seen (pp. 81 and 129 above) that Wittgenstein felt that their peculiarity was not that they contained some special constituents, the logical constants, but something else. Various candidates presented themselves, and Russell and Wittgenstein spent much time discussing whether the notion of logical form would provide the necessary explanation. In these summer letters from Austria Wittgenstein first suggests that the answer may lie not in some special feature of the complexes corresponding to logical propositions but in the nature of any propositional complex. The tone of his letters is so positive and his pleasure in the progress of his work so evident that it seems necessary to read the postscript to that of 16 August, 'I feel like mad', as an expression of the feverish intensity of his intellectual work rather than as evincing any real distress. He seems to have been free for the time being from that feeling of the worthlessness of all his endeavours, the pointlessness of life, the *Sorge* he wrote about from Cambridge, and it was at this period that he reported to Russell the strong effect exercised upon him by *Hadji Murat*, which we have already commented on.[106]

The letter in which Wittgenstein did so was written from Hallein, where Wittgenstein was staying with his uncle Paul. Paul Wittgenstein was the eldest son of Hermann Christian. He had given up his legal studies to manage estates for his father and had in fact continued his father's career. This he did efficiently, but without enthusiasm. That he reserved for his own painting and for the works of the *Sezession*, of which he was a notable patron. Tasteful, well-dressed, and (in his youth)

105. LW to BR [summer 1912], letter 7 in *Briefe* (1980). (This letter is evidently the one received by Russell on 2 September.)
106. Letter 7 again. On *Hadji Murat* see p. 33 above.

handsome, he was a quick-tempered but warm-hearted man, much freer in his life and easier and more approachable in his manner than most of his brothers and sisters. He was a particular support to Karl's family in the distressing years of Karl's last illness and probably took steps to remove Ludwig for a while from the tense atmosphere, as it was then bound to be, of the Hochreith. There are other instances of his keeping a fatherly eye on his nephew and of his being alive to inner difficulties which had escaped the eyes of other members of the family, who accepted a quite high level of tension as normal. Besides, Ludwig's devotion to philosophy had caught his rather romantic fancy and he wished to encourage him in every way.

From Austria Wittgenstein returned to England for a few days in early September, to do further shopping for his Cambridge rooms before setting out on his holiday. He stayed in Russell's flat in Bury St., the first house-guest. Russell was impressed anew by Wittgenstein's powers:

> He is a great contrast to the Stephens and Stracheys and such would-be geniuses. We very soon plunged into logic and have had great arguments. He has a very great power of seeing what are really important problems. (BR to OM 4.9.12)

Russell urged him not to put off writing until he had solved *all* the problems, because that time would never come:

> This produced a wild outburst—he has the artist's feeling that he will produce the perfect thing or nothing—I explained how he wouldn't get a degree or be able to teach unless he learnt to write imperfect things—this all made him more and more furious—at last he solemnly begged me not to give him up even if he disappointed me. (BR to OM 5.9.12)

Only Wittgenstein's health seemed to Russell precarious: he gave one the feeling that his life was very insecure. And Russell thought (there was surely no physiological basis for this) that Wittgenstein was going deaf.

Iceland, though a strange choice, might at any rate be wholesome. And so indeed it proved: though Wittgenstein, who was a nervous traveller, nearly gave up the whole scheme on hearing from his brother that it was exceptionally cold there that year. Pinsent persuaded him out of this hesitation and they left in considerable style. Each was supplied with £145 in notes, theoretically by Wittgenstein's father, and Wittgenstein carried letters of credit for another £200. They travelled everywhere first class (it seems to have been Wittgenstein's practice at this time) and stayed at the best hotels. On the boat (Wittgenstein was disgusted it was so small) each would have a two-berth cabin. Wittgenstein brought three boxes and was shocked at Pinsent's having only one, persuading him indeed to buy various further items in Edinburgh. Their tips were lavish, their ponies in Iceland a cavalcade in the eyes of hardier travellers. A special occasion would be celebrated with whatever kind of champagne was available. In short none of those harmless luxuries were scanted with which the rich were then accustomed to infuse a measure of comfort into a holiday chosen for its simplicity.

The holiday itself (recounted in detail by Pinsent) was like every other such holiday: the deck-quoits and the simple card-games on the boat, the occasional piano and the chance to play Schubert, the talkative and sometimes obtrusive fellow-travellers, the well-informed guide, the sure-footed ponies, the strange and treeless landscape, the aurora borealis, the big geyser that would not erupt though they waited several days, the varying fare and the sometimes inadequate beds, the photographs developed at night. Both would get annoyed or nervous if things seemed to go wrong, both were very soon restored to good temper. Wittgenstein was not a very robust traveller: on the boat, if not actually sea-sick, he kept to his cabin rather a lot; his stomach would not always stand the unaccustomed food on land; rock-climbing made him extremely nervous and he would beg Pinsent not to risk his life. Wittgenstein in later life sometimes seemed to embrace hardship but it was certainly not his natural element.

The two friends managed their time carefully, allowing for occasions when each would go off without the other. None the less, there were endless talks—about people they knew, or met, about 'Philistinism', and so on.[107] Perhaps one sign of 'Philistinism' in Pinsent was his too easy tolerance. On one occasion when they had to share a table, Pinsent was amused by 'a very splendid bounder' with whom he talked. Wittgenstein however took a violent dislike to the man and the two had to give orders for their meals to be served separately from the table d'hôte.[108] 'A thing not so absurd as might be thought,' Pinsent goodnaturedly says, 'as table d'hôte hours are all ridiculously late': none the less it led to some awkwardness. Finally they talked about Wittgenstein's work. It is a striking fact that Wittgenstein was extremely good at exposition of those parts of a subject that are in their nature capable of being grasped thoroughly. There are instances later of his teaching elementary arithmetic to friends' children, and explaining to a complete amateur the difference between deduction and induction; and of course he later chose the vocation of a schoolmaster. Like many of his family he had a strong pedagogic drive. It was not, therefore, either incapacity or disinclination

107. Two such conversations are reported on pp. 120–1 above.

108. Russell tells a rather similar story about a walk he took with Moore: 'We fell in by accident with a husky fellow, who began talking about Petronius with intense relish for his indecencies. I rather encouraged the man, who amused me as a type. Moore remained completely silent until the man was gone, and then turned upon me, saying: "That man was horrible"' (*Autobiography* 1.64).

that made his own philosophical work, whether in lectures or in writing, much harder to follow or to see the point of. There he was always trying to convey new insights that usually went against the grain of his listeners' or readers', and indeed his own, prejudices; there he was not simplifying or training pupils in a technique. In Aristotelian terms, his method was bound to be dialectic rather than apodictic. But the apodictic method suited very well his explanation to Pinsent of the elements of Whitehead's and Russell's logic and their definition of number, as it did his account of how the engines of the ship functioned, and Pinsent found him an excellent teacher.

The two returned to England at the beginning of October, reaching Birmingham on the 4th. Wittgenstein stayed the night with Pinsent's family. They found a large party there and attended the last concert of the Musical Festival, already described. Wittgenstein, rather shy at first, was put at his ease and Pinsent enjoyed showing him off to his parents—he could explain logic to Father and discuss the education of young children with the future Dame Ellen.

Thus ends the most glorious holiday I have ever spent! The novelty of the country—of being free of all considerations about economizing—the excitement and everything—all combine to make it the most wonderful experience I have ever had. (Diary 5.10.12)

5   Cambridge 1912–13

WITTGENSTEIN took up residence in his new rooms on about 12 October 1912, Pinsent helping him to move in his furniture, and began his first complete year of residence in the Cambridge in which he was already a legend. Naomi Bentwich, a pupil of Johnson's, recalled[1] that he was generally supposed to live the life of a rich man, going up to London for all the good concerts and decorating his rooms in his own individual style (he was said to have painted the walls black). Some truth there was in this, we have seen already that he had his furniture specially made; and Pinsent's diary recounts one expedition to London on which he accompanied Wittgenstein to a concert conducted by Steinbach and stayed the night at the Grand Hotel.

Already well-known in psychological circles, and in musical ones (for he attended nearly every concert in Cambridge), Wittgenstein was sought out now by further members of that intellectual aristocracy that was centred in the Society.[2] Russell introduced him both to McTaggart, an elder statesman of the Society, and to Keynes, who (as in so many matters) was probably the most active and managing of the Angels:

> I had him to meet Keynes yesterday, but it was a failure. Wittgenstein was too ill to argue properly. It is funny how one person's presence will throw a new light on another person's; Keynes seemed to me soft and woolly, not nearly as able as I have always thought him. This was not from anything Wittgenstein said, for he hardly talked—it was the mere effect of his being there. Keynes, like most people, will accept a view without accepting its consequences, which is what makes me call him soft. —I also took Wittgenstein to see McTaggart, and that was more successful, though Wittgenstein found it hard to understand how McTaggart could believe such fantastic things. (BR to OM 31.10.12)

The meeting with McTaggart was a mere incident in Wittgenstein's life, but that with Keynes was much more important. It seems that both men were a little shy at that first meeting, or rather: Wittgenstein may have been shy, but it was in Keynes's style to be rather gentle and attentive, to mask his brilliance and quickness with a new acquaintance whom he wished to get to know properly. Russell, who was a little under Wittgenstein's spell at this time, probably misinterpreted the woolliness.

1. Personal communication.
2. See above, p. 118.

At any rate Wittgenstein and Keynes soon recognized one another. Keynes had at first given his friend Duncan Grant some less flattering account but shortly afterwards wrote:

> Wittgenstein is a most wonderful character—what I said about him when I saw you last is quite untrue—and extraordinarily nice, I like enormously to be with him. (JMK to Duncan Grant 12.11.12)

Satirical, brilliant, often malicious, Keynes could also be sympathetic and perceptive and open to new ideas and influences. Of all Wittgenstein's friends he had perhaps the widest palette. Philosopher, economist, writer and advocate of rare persuasiveness and elegance and economy of style, he was also an administrator and businessman of great energy and resource. In all the areas in which he interested himself he had an instinct for the best, the habit of a connoisseur—this appeared in his book-collecting, in his patronage (when he became rich and important) of music and art (in this area, to be sure, friends from Bloomsbury thought it was more intellectual conviction than heartfelt enthusiasm that inspired him). Nowhere more than in his choice of friends: if Wittgenstein was a 'collector of good human beings' Keynes had more of love for the unusual and the exciting. It was 'the student of character in all its forms',[3] his first biographer tells us, that was fascinated by the newly-met Wittgenstein. Friends, once made, were assisted and promoted by Keynes, both by his interest in their work and ideas and in practical ways—he would anticipate their needs or arrange what they wanted. So it was with Wittgenstein, when each had overcome some initial hesitation. They could have long talks about the ideals of that Cambridge which Keynes embodied and to which Wittgenstein only half belonged. The love of paradox, the outrageous exaggeration, the frequent irreverence, the impatience with the slow-witted, the prejudices, even, that sometimes alarmed Keynes's colleagues and impeded (though far from completely) his successes in the larger world outside the Society, will not have shocked Wittgenstein. The practical side was important too: to Wittgenstein Keynes soon came to represent official Cambridge, partly because his father was Registrary at that time, chiefly because he was fitted for the role. He was a kind of manager in Wittgenstein's life—he organized communication with him in the prison-camp, his hand was behind Ramsey's visits to the villages in the 1920s, he made possible a visit to England in 1925, he brought Wittgenstein back to Cambridge in 1929, he was an intermediary with the Russians in 1935, he advised on the question of Wittgenstein's nationality in 1938, and in 1939 he was the most active member of the electoral syndicate that made

3. R.F. Harrod: *Life of J.M. Keynes*, p. 161. For an admirable summary of Keynes's gifts see pp. 646–50 of that book.

Wittgenstein professor. By that time, indeed, the long discussions of ideas and ideals had ceased and Keynes's role was something like that of one of the family advisers in Vienna—the director, say, of the *Kanzlei Wittgenstein*, the family secretariat. Wittgenstein both liked and needed to involve friends in managing his affairs: we find him employing Pinsent ('often', we are told) to draft the right reply to a lost invitation or the like, and later he made Gilbert Patisson his accountant and almoner. A certain unpracticality and the habit of dependence lay behind this; also some shyness—he felt safer with an intermediary: A could explain his reasons or doubts to B better than he could himself, even when he knew B quite well; finally, it was part of friendship and an important part of life to work out decisions and procedure, important or trivial, with a companion. It is interesting that his role could continue even when there was, for whatever reason, some break in intimacy. Wittgenstein would never hesitate to help or to ask help from one who had once been a friend. He might indeed hesitate over whether the friendship was still a live one. In this connexion observe his letters to Keynes of June and July 1913. He asks for help with the benefaction for Johnson described above (p. 99). Keynes in reply evidently expressed some regret that they had not met often in the Easter Term; to which Wittgenstein replied:

> *My* reason for not seeing you oftener last term was, that I did not wish our intercourse to continue without any sign that *you* wished to continue it. (LW to JMK 16.7.13)

An echo, perhaps, of some misunderstanding over the Society.

The idea was current in 1912 among members of the Society, including the former members who came down from Bloomsbury, that Russell tried to make his friendship with Wittgenstein exclusive of the rest of Cambridge. Michael Holroyd reports this as the view of Moore and Desmond McCarthy (though it should be noted that the latter's acquaintance with Wittgenstein was slight).[4] According to them, it was only Keynes's intervention that brought Wittgenstein into contact with the Society. Lytton Strachey certainly held this view:

> [Russell] kept Wittgenstein to himself until Keynes insisted on meeting him and saw at once that he was a genius ... [Russell thought] the Society so degraded that Wittgenstein would certainly refuse to belong to it. (LS to Sydney Saxon-Turner 20.10.12)

All the same, the idea was fanciful: it is not surprising that Russell had no recollection of feeling mortified by the affair when Holroyd consulted him. Wittgenstein had all sorts of contacts in Cambridge and was in no

4. Michael Holroyd: *Lytton Strachey*, vol. 2, p. 71.

sense under Russell's control. What is true, and known to us independently of Russell's later recollections, is that Russell believed at the time
that it was a mistake to think of electing Wittgenstein—he would be
bored by the Society or refuse to have anything to do with it, and this
would lead to some undefined trouble. It will be seen shortly that in this
Russell was right up to a point. But of the jealousy that their too keen
eyes saw there is no trace in his letters to Lady Ottoline.

It is particularly surprising if Moore thought Russell possessive where
Wittgenstein was concerned, since just at this time his own association
with Wittgenstein became a much closer one. It began in a way that for
nearly any other pair would have been highly inauspicious. Wittgenstein
began to attend, as in the previous year, Moore's lectures on psychology,
but found in them faults similar to those that had disgusted him in
Principia Ethica in the summer.[5] Now he told Russell that Moore had not
only this trick of repeating himself *ad nauseam* but also an inclination to
spend his time on unimportant questions. 'He *loves* Moore,' Russell told
Lady Ottoline (15.10.12), 'but doesn't admire him as much as the others
do.' Wittgenstein did in fact go to Moore after his lecture on 18 October
in order to tell him to pull himself together—this from the comparative
beginner in philosophy to a man 15 years his senior. He was met with
great mildness: Moore promised to mend if possible and (so he told
Desmond McCarthy) still respected Wittgenstein enormously.[6]

> He came [Moore himself noted in a set of diary extracts about
> Wittgenstein] to one or two lectures but expostulated violently against my
> spending so much time in trying to find the meaning of and refute Ward's
> view that psychology differs from physics not in subject-matter but only in
> point of view. He said that what I ought to do was to give my own views
> not attack other people's. After that he ceased to attend my lectures but
> was quite friendly, coming to see me in my rooms and inviting me to his.

Moore's contemporary diaries bear this out:[7] the meetings become

5. See above p. 109.
6. Information derived from Russell's letter to Lady Ottoline of 24.10.12.

7. These, like the set of extracts mentioned above, were shown me by Mr Paul Levy with the
kind permission of Mrs Dorothy Moore. They cover these pre-war years. Moore seems to have
destroyed the later volumes of his diary covering his married life, but before doing so extracted all,
or presumably all, entries concerning Wittgenstein. The above remark is an introduction to these
extracts, and presumably incorporates his memories. The actual diary entry for 18 October 1912
reads:

> W comes up after lecture and tells me my lectures have become very bad. Then we get on to
> definition and he stays till 3.

The view of Ward's mentioned occurs in his article 'Psychology' in *Encyclopaedia Britannica*[11], vol.
22, p. 548. In his 'Autobiography' Moore mentions this as one of the texts on which he lectured. He
also says, in general, that the main stimulus to philosophizing in his case had been the things other
philosophers had said about the world or the sciences (*The Philosophy of G.E. Moore* [ed. Schilpp], pp.
13 and 29).

frequent—perhaps twice a week, by appointment (this was a rare feature for Moore in his meetings with friends). There were also undesigned meetings at a concert, in Russell's rooms, or at a dinner-party. Wittgenstein would come at tea-time or after dinner, and 'try to explain' about Russell's theory of classes, or what Russell and he now thought about the assertion-sign, or the sense and reference of propositional symbols, or his objection to Russell's theory of identity. But it was unusual for the whole time to be spent on philosophy:[8] by a sort of economy in their friendship they would begin by, or turn to, discussing music, or German lyric poetry, or Russell, Johnson, or some other friend. Music and poetry were two of the great loves of Moore's life. He was the brother of the poet Thomas Sturge Moore, and of his own two sons one became a poet and the other a musician. He tells in his autobiography of his enthusiasm for music at school and particularly for the songs of Schubert.[9] He had a pleasant tenor voice and would sing at length to Wittgenstein—'many songs' from the *Winterreise* on one occasion, Brahms's *Mein Mädel* and *Vier ernste Gesänge* on another. No mere interlude in either case. Or they would perform chamber-music together, Wittgenstein, as usual, whistling one part.

Moore was diffident: he was prepared to believe that Wittgenstein must be right even when he did not understand him—though it is impossible to imagine Moore writing down or agreeing with something unless he thought he understood it fully. He was diffident too, as his diaries show, in social relations: appreciative when people 'talked well', made uneasy by moments of silence and his own failure to draw out, say, a neighbour at High Table. It was in fact part of his charm: his insights and his perceptive reactions were all the more appreciated because he was in no sense, as Keynes and Russell surely were, a performer. And before the First War he was most of all diffident in his personal relations with Wittgenstein: 'Music Club, behind W.,' he would note in his diary; 'fancy he is disgusted at me' (24 May 1913): another passage throws some light too on the sort of social occasion Wittgenstein took part in:

Supper at Robertson's: go there with Hardy, W., and Miss T. Jones. Hardy opens about hypnotism, which I have just told him [about?] and W. talks well about that during dinner. Then Hill and Vivisection. After I sing and am afraid W. doesn't like it. Then we talk of morals and W. seems disturbed. I wait to [word indecipherable: meaning 'leave'?] till

---

8. Thus it is probably because it was an exception that Moore notes on 31.1.13: 'to tea with W by invitation $4\frac{1}{2}$–$7\frac{3}{4}$ he discusses probability all the time'. The length of this tea-time visit is not exceptional however.

9. *The Philosophy of G.E. Moore* (ed. Schilpp), pp. 6ff.

Hardy has finished talking, after 11. W. walks on ahead of us, which makes me afraid I am disapproved. (Diary for 21.5.13)[10]

Wittgenstein's criticisms of Moore's lectures by no means indicated loss of confidence in him. In fact at just this time, Wittgenstein set on foot a scheme by which Moore (as Moore put it on first hearing of it) should 'act as a kind of dictator at the Moral Sciences Club'. Wittgenstein always liked to attend this Club (though much later, when he was teaching in Cambridge, there were periods when it seemed better that he should absent himself). The comments of his from this period that have come down to us (mostly in Russell's letters) are naturally enough chiefly of a negative character. Wittgenstein was more likely to expostulate to Russell about his dislike of talking for effect, of subterfuges and refusal to face questions, and of preaching, than to enthuse about what he thought worthwhile in the meetings. His criticism of two or three members who happened to be clergymen was particularly severe, and Russell thought that he was there inclined to take confusion for dishonesty. Still, Wittgenstein believed that something could be made of the meetings, particularly if they were used primarily for the purpose of discussion and not for delivering and listening to a long paper.

His plan, then, was, and the Club adopted it on 15 November, that a Chairman should be elected to guide the discussion and that papers should be limited to seven minutes. It was also arranged that there should be supplementary meetings not open to those of M.A. standing. This provision was re-introduced from time to time in the Club's history, and of course later served to exclude Wittgenstein himself. It was no part of Wittgenstein's plan in 1912, and he vehemently opposed it, misled (Russell thought) by hatred of 'the parson' who had proposed it. Russell thought the parson's point—that the young did not dare to talk when Moore and Russell were present—was a good one, but Wittgenstein undoubtedly regarded the two senior men as a protection against precisely such people as the proposer. Moore was duly elected Chairman of the ordinary meetings.

A supplementary meeting at which W. Tye spoke was held on 22 November, but the first ordinary meeting under the new dispensation was held in Wittgenstein's rooms on 29 November, Moore being in the chair. The minutes, in the handwriting of Wittgenstein's friend Dorward, are of some interest:

Mr. Wittgenstein read a paper entitled 'What is Philosophy?' The paper lasted only about 4 minutes, thus cutting the previous record established

10. Robertson was Donald Robertson, later Professor of Greek, recently married, and a close friend of G.H. Hardy's. Miss Jones was the Principal of Girton, whose academic interest was in philosophy. On hypnotism see below.

by Mr. Tye by nearly two minutes. Philosophy was defined as all those primitive propositions which are assumed as true without proof by the various sciences. This definition was much discussed, but there was no general disposition to adopt it. The discussion kept very well to the point, and the Chairman did not find it necessary to intervene much.[11]

Perhaps the most significant thing here is the implicit identification of 'philosophy' with logic. Wittgenstein seems to have been drawing his first conclusions from the insight, already mentioned, that all the problems of logic could be traced back to the nature of the atomic proposition. Logic was thus not the science of any special set of objects—not a science that came into operation with the introduction of, say, generality or implication, but was the science of what was presupposed by saying anything whatsoever. As such it would be an equal part of every science.[12] The idea that the principles of logic are included in those of every science is quite a traditional one. Only the reasons for it and the view that nothing outside logic is assumed without proof in the sciences will be new (if indeed our account of Wittgenstein is correct in both these respects). But the idea is not one that in itself suggests any account of why the truths of logic are true. In his attempts to give such an account, Wittgenstein was soon to come to see that the propositions of logic differed from all others—'Philosophy gives no pictures of reality' is how he put it in the summer of 1913; and in the *Tractatus*, having said that the totality of those propositions that correctly represent the existence and non-existence of states of affairs constitutes natural science, he goes on to distinguish philosophy from science:

> Philosophy is not one of the natural sciences.
> (The word 'philosophy' must mean something whose place is above or below the natural sciences, not beside them.) (*TLP* 4.11)

Philosophy was not only not a special science but not a part or the common part of the other sciences.

Moore did not think well of Wittgenstein's performance and Russell (who had been prevented from coming at the beginning of the meeting) found Wittgenstein perhaps depressed by it:

> Then I went on to the tail end of the discussion on Wittgenstein's paper, and after the rest were gone I got into talking about his faults—he is worried by his unpopularity and asked me why it was. It was a long and difficult and passionate (on his side) conversation lasting till 1.30, so I am rather short of sleep. He is a great task but quite worth it. He is a little too

11. I am grateful to Prof. D.H. Mellor, when Librarian of the Faculty of Philosophy in Cambridge, for supplying me with information about and xeroxes from the minute books of the Moral Sciences Club.

12. The view reported is of course capable of other interpretations—philosophy might be supposed to consist of or to include the different principles assumed a priori by the several sciences. But this is the interpretation nearest to the other views of Wittgenstein's reported from about this time.

simple, yet I am afraid of spoiling some fine quality if I say too much to make him less so. (BR to OM 30.11.12)

There was indeed simplicity, even naiveté, in Wittgenstein's way of judging and treating people at this time, in the intolerance which led him to think that a clergyman who tried to wriggle out of questions was 'the most stupid, the most wicked, the most utterly worthless creature that ever lived' (so that Russell had the unaccustomed task of urging the importance of not misjudging those whose thoughts were vague); but still more in Wittgenstein's unawareness that only someone of Moore's childlike simplicity would be likely to profit from his radical criticism. Pinsent recorded the scene of Wittgenstein's trying to induce the undergraduate monk, F., to read some good book on some exact science:[13]

> Which would obviously be very good for F.—as indeed for anyone—: but Wittgenstein was very overbearing and let F. know exactly what he thought of him, and altogether talked as if he was his Director of Studies! F. took it very well—obviously convinced that Wittgenstein is a lunatic. (Diary November 1912)

Wittgenstein's criticisms of this same F. led to a quarrel (so Russell termed it) between Wittgenstein and North Whitehead. Naturally enough, therefore, Pinsent used more than finesse to shake off C, 'a mindless ass', whom he was sure Wittgenstein would not like. In this situation there was room for unpopularity. All the same, with many chance acquaintances Wittgenstein managed to have lively conversations, sometimes to Pinsent's surprise. When Wittgenstein returned to Cambridge at the age of 40, he learnt or resolved within a year or two to restrict his acquaintance to those with whom he was likely to get on well. This is how he became the withdrawn Wittgenstein of legend, a surprise, very often, to those whom he took the trouble to get to know. But before the First World War, when he had some of the optimism of youth—this was the simplicity Russell noticed—probable and improbable friends were alike exposed to his vigour in argument and his frankness. His eccentricity, his outspokenness, his wider experience, his apparent seriousness (we have seen that even with Pinsent, the simple sense of humour characteristic of his later friendships seems not to have appeared)—all these qualities marked him out from the run of clever undergraduates. Yet we have no evidence of real unpopularity: North Whitehead seems to have disliked him, and the elder Whiteheads had to be won over, but it seems that for the most part, as Pinsent implies, his oddities were taken as part of the madness easily ascribed to any

13. See above p. 111.

foreigner. At all events, he was clearly accepted as a lively guest and (at clubs and societies) as a manful contributor to discussions.

It was in this same month of November that Wittgenstein was elected to the Society. The project had occurred to Lytton Strachey and others in May,[14] but was now taken over and brought to a conclusion by Keynes. Technically the election was made by the 'active members', the undergraduates of the Society, but it is clear that the influence of the Angels or former members who still attended meetings was decisive. And so many of these were friends, even admirers, of Wittgenstein: Russell, Moore, Hardy, Keynes himself. Whitehead, McTaggart, Sheppard, Shove, and Lytton Strachey had all looked him over. Strachey was now inclined to think him 'a fearful bore': 'Poor Pozzo! will he never learn?' he exclaimed later when things went wrong about the election.[15] The view of the younger members can be judged perhaps from James Strachey's letter to his brother (3.11.12): Rupert [Brooke], Keynes, and Gerald [Shove] wanted him 'though they all thought he would be too awful for words'.[16] The Society was not looking for simple agreeable men: for distinction and independence it was worth tolerating a little grit. In a similar exaggerated vein Lytton Strachey wrote to Keynes after the election:

> The hopeful aspect of affairs for the future was particularly exhilarating. Our brothers B. and Wittgenstein are so nasty and our brother Békássy is so nice that the Society ought to rush forward now into the most progressive waters. I looked in on B. on Sunday night and he seemed quite as nasty as Rupert [Brooke] ever was. It was indeed cheering! (LS to JMK 20.11.12)

First, however, Wittgenstein himself had to be persuaded that the Society was worthwhile. Its nature and history were no doubt explained to him by Russell. It was a small society—one or two people from each year on the average.

> It has existed since 1820, and has had as members most of the people of any intellectual eminence who have been at Cambridge since then.[17]

They met every Saturday night, to hear a paper by one of their number, after which everyone present was expected to contribute to the discussion.

---

14. See above pp. 118f..

15. Letter to James Strachey, November 1912: I am indebted to Mr Paul Levy, who showed me these letters, as also those between Keynes and Duncan Grant, Keynes and Lytton Strachey, Moore and Lytton Strachey, and James Strachey and Rupert Brooke. 'Pozzo', after Pozzo di Borgo, was Lytton's nickname for Keynes.

16. Rupert Brooke had in fact not yet met Wittgenstein.

17. Russell, *Autobiography*, vol. 1, pp. 68–70.

It was a principle in discussion that there were to be no *taboos*, no
limitations, nothing considered shocking, no barriers to absolute freedom
of speculation. We discussed all manner of things, no doubt with a certain
immaturity, but with a detachment and interest scarcely possible in later
life. (id.ibid.)

Numerous accounts of the Society now exist: Harrod, in his *Life of Keynes*
gives one by Dean Merivale (a contemporary of Tennyson's), another by
Henry Sidgwick, and adds his own description as an outsider. Russell's
we have drawn on here. The account most bathed in golden light is that
of E.M. Forster in his memoir of Lowes Dickinson:

> Shortly before becoming a fellow he had been elected to one of those
> discussion societies which still flourish at Cambridge and play an
> appreciable part in its mental life. The characteristics of such societies vary
> but little. The members are drawn from the older undergraduates and the
> younger dons, they meet of an evening in one another's rooms, a paper is
> read, lots are drawn to determine the order of the speeches, the order is
> observed or ignored, there are developments and digressions, and finally
> the reader replies to his critics, handing round as he does so some such
> refreshment as anchovies on toast or walnut cake. Some of the discussions
> are logical in their tendency, others informative or whimsical, but in all
> cases formality is avoided, presidents and secretaries are reduced to their
> minimum, and there is no attempt to be forensic or even parliamentary.
> The young men seek truth rather than victory, they are willing to abjure
> an opinion when it is proved untenable, they do not try to score off one
> another, they do not feel diffidence too high a price to pay for integrity;
> and according to some observers that is why Cambridge has played,
> comparatively, so small a part in the control of world affairs. Certainly
> these societies represent the very antithesis of the rotarian spirit. No one
> who has once felt their power will ever be a good mixer or a yes-man.
> Their influence, when it goes wrong, leads to self-consciousness and
> superciliousness; when it goes right, the mind is sharpened, the judgement
> is strengthened, and the heart becomes less selfish. There is nothing
> specially academic about them, they exist in other places where intelligent
> youths are allowed to gather together unregimented, but in Cambridge
> they seem to generate a peculiar clean white light of their own which can
> remain serviceable right on into middle age.[18]

That was the ideal—a mite precious, perhaps, a little laboured in its
fantasies, its rituals, and its private language drawn impartially from
German metaphysics and half-remembered Christian heresies—embryos,

18. E.M. Forster: *Goldsworthy Lowes Dickinson* (1934), p. 65. He does not overestimate the effect of
the Society on his subject: see Lowes Dickinson's *Autobiography* (1973), p. 68: 'When young men are
growing in mind and soul, when speculation is a passion, when discussion is made profound by love,
there happens something incredible to any but those who breathe that magic air.'

birth-pangs, apostles exempt from time and space, who in due course take wings and become angels (for so they described the cessation of active membership). But still it was something to follow in the footsteps of Clerk-Maxwell and to draw lots to speak with the cleverest young men of the day. And, looking ahead, membership gave a man contact in each generation with the best and brightest of the young: its own reproduction is always one of the chief preoccupations of such a society. To belong to an elite would certainly not distress Wittgenstein, provided it really were an elite; and the unworldliness, the sense of intellectual and moral standards other than success though not incompatible with it, that pervaded the Society will even have attracted him. It had, of course, the airlessness of Cambridge, of which he later spoke, but that was preferable to the atmosphere at Oxford where the aims of Jowett's Balliol still prevailed and the best of the young men looked forward to ruling their own or some other country. Oxford always evoked an *horresco referens* in the letters of members of the Society: when Russell heard that journalism was taught at Harvard he commented, 'I thought that was only done at Oxford'. In many respects Wittgenstein always remained a Cambridge man.

We have seen why Russell thought that the Society had declined since his own day: Keynes, in his account,[19] confirms that in their ideals the members of the Soceity departed to some extent from those of Moore:

> We accepted Moore's religion, so to speak, and discarded his morals. Indeed, in our opinion, one of the greatest advantages of his religion was that it made morals unnecessary—meaning by 'religion' one's attitude towards oneself and the ultimate and by 'morals' one's attitude towards the outside world and the intermediate... Nothing mattered except states of mind, our own and other people's, of course, but chiefly our own. These states of mind were not associated with the action or achievement or with consequences. They consisted in timeless, passionate states of contemplation and communion, largely unattached to 'before' and 'after'... The appropriate subjects of passionate contemplation and communion were a beloved person, beauty and truth, and one's prime objects in life were love, the creation and enjoyment of aesthetic experience and the pursuit of knowledge.

They repudiated, Keynes says, not only Moore's view of the obligation to produce the most probable maximum of eventual good for the whole of the future, but also his account of the individual's duty to obey general rules. For our purposes it is of no account whether, as Harrod argues,[20] these are half-hearted and unconvincing parts of *Principia Ethica*, or

19. For Russell see above p. 118: for Keynes, 'My Early Beliefs' in *Collected Writings*, vol. 10, pp. 433ff.; also in *Two Memoirs* (1949).
20. *Life of Keynes*, p. 78.

whether, as Russell suggests, Moore's principle of organic unity (precisely one of the features they admired) would have entailed these consequences. Wittgenstein too was not far from rejecting both of these features of Moore's thought. Where he was not at one with the Society, as Keynes himself notes, was in the view of human nature on which their repudiation of these things was based:

> We repudiated all versions of the doctrine of original sin, of there being insane and irrational springs of wickedness in most men. We were not aware that civilization was a thin and precarious crust erected by the personality and the will of a very few, and only maintained by rules and conventions skilfully put across and guilefully preserved. We had no respect for traditional wisdom or the restraints of custom. We lacked reverence, as Lawrence observed and as Ludwig with justice also used to say—for everything and everyone.[21]

It will be seen that even in retrospect Keynes gives a grudging and external acknowledgement of the importance of reverence. It would be good if such and such beliefs, though groundless, where held.

A difference of attitude on these points was not enough to determine Wittgenstein to have nothing to do with the Society. He could, after all, talk by the hour with Russell, Moore, and Keynes, from all of whom he differed profoundly. He was prepared to shock the contentious dinner-parties of progressive Cambridge by actually opposing women's suffrage. He thought order could be introduced into the discussions of the Moral Sciences Club. Why not try to pull the Society itself together? This aim (Russell puts it in so many words) did in fact lead Wittgenstein, despite doubts, to accept election.

The doubts, his own and Russell's, arose from another source. Besides his own friends, were the young men, the active members, serious discussion-partners? Was the atmosphere of the Society the right one? Keynes confirms, up to a point, Russell's retrospective condemnation quoted earlier:

> As the years wore on towards 1914, the thinness and superficiality, as well as the falsity, of our view of man's heart became, as it now seems to me, more obvious; and there was, too, some falling away from the purity of the original doctrine. Concentration on moments of communion between a pair of lovers got thoroughly mixed up with the, once rejected, pleasure. The pattern of life would sometimes become no better than a succession of short sharp superficial 'intrigues', as we called them. Our comments on life

---

21. *Coll.Writ.* 10.447. This paper, written in 1938, was occasioned by some reminiscences voiced at the same club of D.H. Lawrence's reactions (in 1914 or 1915) to the circle that Wittgenstein knew so well. The Nietzschean in Wittgenstein often recalled Lawrence.

and affairs were bright and amusing but brittle ... because there was no solid diagnosis of human nature underlying them.[22]

Moore and Russell were essentially untouched by the personal complications to which this atmosphere gave rise; and though Keynes, with his zest for all forms of life, took an amused part in them, they were strictly a small compartment of his activities. But, for some of the younger men, they seemed for the time being to be all-important, and would Wittgenstein, with his hatred of superficiality and half-heartedness, be able to tolerate them or the discussions of them?

Some doubts of this kind Russell put to the meeting of the Society on 9 November. He left some members with the impression that he thought the Society too degraded for Wittgenstein. In any case his doubts were brushed aside, partly ascribed, as we have seen, to jealousy. Was not Wittgenstein one of them already? He came, indeed, to breakfast the next morning in Keynes's rooms with many of them and with the other embryo, B. Russell was overborne and undertook to persuade Wittgenstein to accept election.

> All the difficulties I anticipated have arisen with Wittgenstein. I persuaded him at last to come to the first meeting and see how he could stand it. Obviously from his point of view the Society is a mere waste of time. But perhaps from a philanthropic point of view he might be made to feel it worth going on with. (BR to JMK 11.11.12)[23]

From this letter Keynes emerges as the promoter of Wittgenstein, as indeed from his own to Lytton Strachey:

> Have you heard ... how our new brother's only objection to the Society is that it doesn't happen to be apostolic? and what an amazing character he is?
>
> I believe it might be a very good thing if you were to come to the Society this week, or if not, then the week after...
>
> Our new brother vastly prefers angels. He says to see active brothers is to see those who have not yet made their toilets. And the process though necessary is indecent. At any rate he couldn't say that you've not made your toilet, could he? (JMK to LS 13.11.12)

But Wittgenstein was already

22. *Coll.Writ.* 10.449. On the point of brittleness, Keynes includes Russell in this judgement. Russell's own remarks about the 'intrigues' are given above p. 118. The correspondence of various members of the circle, though clearly not free of wilful exaggeration, bears out Keynes's and even Russell's description. An important negative point is that these sharp tongues impute no intrigues to Wittgenstein. At most they dwell on the supposed jealousy of Russell (obviously not in this sense an intriguer) at Wittgenstein's election.

23. Letter among the Keynes Papers in King's College Library.

horribly bored by the Society, and wishing to get out of it. B. [the other embryo] is a great obstacle—he can't stand him. I told him there was nothing for him to get out of the Society but that in former days it had been good, and might become so again if he stuck to it. He promised to wait a week before deciding. The discussion was *very* difficult. (BR to OM 10.11.12)

Wittgenstein did indeed go to the Society the next Saturday, from which day his membership is dated. This was the meeting at which Moore read 'On Conversion' and Wittgenstein reported that for him this consisted in getting rid of worry.[24] But by the beginning of December 'The Witter-Gitter man,' James Strachey wrote to his brother, 'is trembling on the verge of resignation.' Resignation! It was hardly a concept for them. One man had resigned—or sent word he was too busy to come to meetings—far back in the nineteenth century, and his memory was—perhaps still is—held up to comic execration in their rites. Lytton put the word itself in inverted commas when he wrote in alarm to Moore and to Keynes and offered to come up and see what he could do. Keynes, Moore, Gerald Shove, all availed nothing. B. was intolerable, discussions with B. and with Békássy were not worth while. Békássy, an Hungarian grandee who lived in splendour near Budapest, had been educated at a progressive school in England. (He was killed in Bukovina in 1915 and Keynes saw to the posthumous publication of his poems.) Inherited prejudice may have stood between him and Wittgenstein but he was in any case much attached to B. He later told Hungarian friends that he had voted against, and even had excluded, Wittgenstein. So on 8 December Moore wrote to Strachey to say that Wittgenstein had resigned.[25]

This was not quite the end of the matter. Strachey came down and had an intercessorial tea with Wittgenstein. Moore's diaries are full of the repercussions:

9.12.12 Lytton comes in about 12¼ [midnight] and stays till 1¾ talking about W.

10.12.12 At Feast I talk to Lytton about his tea with W., what W. thought of me ... Talk to Norton about W.

2.1.13 Find it hard to talk to Desmond MacCarthy about W.

1.2.13 James [Strachey] comes 6¾–7¼ about W. To Society at 10¼, Norton, James, Keynes, Brooke, Shove, etc. about W., lasts till 1¾.[26]

24. See above p. 114.
25. So also Russell—'Wittgenstein has left the Society'—in a letter to Lady Ottoline of 6 or 13 December.
26. Russell was drawn in too: 'à propos of Wittgenstein, I shocked him [Sanger] by saying I thought the present Society a feeble lot' (BR to OM 2.2.13).

A compromise was reached: no resignation was recorded, Wittgenstein was not expected to attend meetings—he certainly never read them a paper—but he continued to take an interest in their affairs—discussing them with Moore (19.3.13) and asking in a letter from Norway whether a candidate of Hardy's had been elected.[27] As a final token of his continued membership, he underwent the formality of 'taking wings' when he returned to Cambridge in January 1929.

No one who has been a member of a small self-selected body, who has observed a College election or a candidacy for an Academy, will be altogether surprised by the triviality of the events we have described or by the importance attached to them. Yet there is something peculiar to Cambridge, to the circle and the atmosphere that Wittgenstein adopted as his own, in the fact that on this occasion all the effort was expended to retain association with a young man, of considerable charm, certainly, but obviously a *mauvais coucheur* from the Society's point of view. Keynes's circle had the merits as well as the limitations of an elite. Real excellence would be furthered in despite of rules and precedents. They wanted the best man, let him be as unclubbable as he might. It was the same with the benevolent oligarchy that ruled Wittgenstein's College, the high Trinity society described by C.P. Snow.[28] They, who found ways to support Ramanujan and Kapitsa, made a special case of Wittgenstein too, even though he was at times not on speaking terms with some of them. (Trinity's depriving Russell of his lectureship during the First World War was, and was soon felt to be, an aberration, due largely to absences at the Front.)

But what of Wittgenstein's side of this affair? Did he, was he ever prepared to, see himself as an apostle, especially tied to his brothers, older or younger, a little remote from the rest of the world, sharing, pursuing, and analysing an incommunicable ideal? We come here, in a minor example, both upon contradictions in his nature and upon development in his character. Wittgenstein, we are forced to suppose, wanted to belong to a society, a group, a profession, even; to have the tasks, the conventions, the status associated with it. Far from feeling any false modesty, he knew that any group he could properly belong to would be under some aspect the highest. His search for a calling was in part a search for a role. For the moment he had tried to be an aeronaut, even briefly a psychologist; now it seemed he was becoming a philosopher. He was to make two or three other attempts later. Each time he came without quite the usual formation, each time he looked for, often he found, a quite new way of approaching the task. He sometimes doubted whether he possessed true originality, but he never questioned that everything he did was marked with his own individuality. The style

27. Moore's diary of 19.3.13 and LW to GEM 18.2.14.
28. Foreword to G.H. Hardy: *A Mathematician's Apology*, pp. 25ff.

of his most casual letters is a clear instance of this. Though he often asked, in a material sense, very little, he demanded that this individuality should be recognized. Exception must be made for it, rules must be circumvented. The world must be remade to fit his gifts. It was the only way he could make use of them. The demand, we can now see, is triumphantly vindicated by his works. It was recommended to his friends when he was young by sincerity and force; when he was older, these took the form of authority.

But we are not speaking here of friendships as such. Difficulties arose there because of the intensity with which Wittgenstein pursued them and were the inevitable counterpart of the rewards that he and his friends drew. The difficulties that concern us here are those that he found in being a member of a group. Recognition and acceptance he required: but to tolerate a bore, to suppress disapproval, to conform his own actions to the practices of a small society, were all abhorrent to him. Useless to ask whether the habits of privilege or the consciousness of genius voiced these claims: both determined his attitude towards the world. Every word and action—Russell knew him best and saw this—had to be spontaneously his own; and if he himself was satisfied, if he lived up to his own upbringing, no hint from outside need be regarded. Neither socially nor intellectually was he prepared to receive one. In his moral as in his intellectual life, there was a drive towards solipsism. Two beings alone were luminous for Cardinal Newman— God and his own soul: Wittgenstein too saw principally his own nature and his own world, and these two had to be grasped and structured aright and put in the right relation if he was to realize the standards he so passionately affirmed.

And yet—he was young; he hankered after a wider companionship, a position not on the fringes of society. Later he generally found a different kind of group, more centred on himself, and perhaps for that reason more artificial and less satisfying. But in these early Cambridge years (of which the incident with the Society will serve as a type) he still thought it possible to belong. Russell was, being an observer, more clear-sighted and, by temperament, more consequential than Wittgenstein himself: he saw it would not do. Jealousy is not needed to explain this, but Lytton Strachey and the others perhaps better answered Wittgenstein's immediate needs when they found him a position of his own, of the Society but not in it, so to speak, and Michael Holroyd is to that extent right in saying that Strachey was instrumental in putting Wittgenstein in touch with 'the other Cambridge'.

Russell had more reason than the others knew to be apprehensive of any serious personal difficulties that might arise over the Society. Not only would his own loyalties be strained, but the effect on Wittgenstein might have been much worse. Throughout this Michaelmas Term, despite the activities we have described, Wittgenstein's health and spirits had preoccupied and even tortured both himself and Russell. His temperament was cyclical, and this was one of the longer depressed periods that we know of, alleviated by a couple of occasions when he felt he had made a significant advance in his work. At first he complained to Pinsent about rheumatism; later he told Russell that he had seen a doctor.

> Wittgenstein is on the verge of a nervous breakdown, not far removed from suicide, feeling himself a miserable creature, full of sin. Whatever he says he apologizes for having said. He has fits of dizziness and can't work—the Dr. says it is all nerves. He wanted to be treated morally, but I persisted in treating him physically—I told him to ride, to have biscuits by his bedside to eat when he lies awake, to have better meals and so on. I suppose genius always goes with excitable nerves—it is a very uncomfortable possession. He makes me terribly anxious, and I hate seeing his misery—it is so real, and I know it all so well. I can see it is almost beyond what any human being can be expected to bear. I don't know whether any outside misfortune has contributed to it or not. (BR to OM 31.10.12)

It is unlikely that the rupture and the minor operation for it had left Wittgenstein in real discomfort—we shall see that he was capable of a fairly active life—but the serious situation of his father must have affected him. Pinsent tells us how depressed Wittgenstein was in November by the news of yet another operation. Russell came to think that the real cause was the nature of Wittgenstein's work:

> he strains his mind to the utmost constantly, at things which are discouraging by their difficulty, and nervous fatigue tells on him sooner or later. (BR to OM 5.11.12)

Russell was remembering, no doubt, his own days spent sitting before a blank sheet of paper, the elusiveness of the subject-matter, the lack of a routine when no spark came, the new difficulties raised by each small step forward. Wittgenstein was determined to overcome all obstacles and prolonged concentration was his usual method. No wonder that he told Russell in a later phase of the same kind that logic was driving him into insanity. Both men agreed that 'Logic was hell!'[29] Physical remedies might alleviate Wittgenstein's condition, but no more. Lady Ottoline suggested cocoa, a remedy much valued by progressive thinkers of the period—and this, like riding, was urged upon the reluctant Wittgenstein.

---

29. BR to OM 2.5.13; Russell constantly used this phrase in their discussions, as Wittgenstein recalled on 29.9.37 (von Wright p.218); cf. also LW to BR November or December 1913, 'I often think that I am going mad'.

He accepted, though determined to think, as Russell puts it, that there was nothing the matter except 'premature decay of his intellect'.

So Wittgenstein went riding—with Littlewood, the most cheerful and companionable of Russell's friends, or else with Pinsent. They would hack out to nearby villages, Grantchester, Trumpington, Madingley, and back by another road, two or three hours in all. 'A tame ride,' Pinsent comments on one occasion, 'compared with the one I took with C—as there was no jumping etc.—but quite pleasant.'[30] Later in the academic year they played tennis together: Wittgenstein had to learn the game and was rather clumsy. Many family games at Neuwaldegg and on the Hochreith must have gone on without him, and his rupture hardly seems a sufficient explanation. Now, with Pinsent, though not especially adept at physical activities, he was enthusiastic. They even, more strenuously, went canoeing. In this, as in other ways, his friendship with Pinsent led him into a normal undergraduate life. Rather late, of course, but that was a common pattern in his life—his introduction to school, to philosophy, to military service, to training as a teacher, and subsequently to other occupations and positions, came later in life than that of most beginners—he approached them all as one who had his own habits already, not malleable, a critic, one who found it difficult to conform. Pinsent made this sort of thing much easier for him, and as for his health, the exercise was some antidote to the late night thoughts and monologues and the subsequent sleeplessness. Pinsent noticed that Wittgenstein customarily revived and was cheerful after lunch, Russell that he was in better spirits when he had something to do as well as philosophy.

Yet it was not of his father or of his health that he talked, but of his faults. This must have been the period of the agonizing night talks that Russell remembered so vividly.[31] Russell used to say it was wearing him out (and his letters show that he often really feared that Wittgenstein would commit suicide):

> I told Wittgenstein yesterday [he went on] that he thinks too much about himself, and if he begins again I shall refuse to listen unless I think he is quite desperate. He has talked it out now as much as is good for him. (BR to OM 12.11.12)

Thus we may date to this period one of Russell's most often repeated anecdotes:

---

30. Diary 8.11.12: C was the 'mindless ass'.
31. See above p. 101 and Russell *Autobiography*, vol. 2, p. 99. 'He used to come to see me every evening at midnight, and pace up and down my room like a wild beast in agitated silence.' Also in *Portraits from Memory*, p. 23.

> Once I said to him: 'Are you thinking about logic or about your sins?'
> 'Both', he replied, and continued his pacing. I did not like to suggest that
> it was time for bed, as it seemed probable both to him and me that on
> leaving me he would commit suicide.

Logic *and* his sins—Russell often recalled only the absurd aspect of things
that seemed menacing at the time. Wittgenstein evidently somehow saw
a connection between the difficulty of his philosophical problems—the
'decay of his intellect'—the objective grounds he had for depression and
his own shortcomings. Perhaps a clearer, a more concentrated view—it is
the final message of the *Tractatus* too—would enable him to see the
world aright. At any rate, if there was no real prospect of this: if he could
not reach this insight, and if he could not get rid of his troubles by
reconciling himself to the world, then his life was pointless. We have tried
to describe something of his attitude in reporting[32] his adolescent
thoughts of suicide and many of the themes there mentioned have
recurred in our account. His whole background led him to see life as a
task, to demand of himself some achievement. He was conscious of
exceptional abilities, yet discontented with the work he was producing.
On another side, he wanted to give and receive affection, which for him
meant to have some positive and productive relation with others, and yet
constantly found himself put off by them and constantly himself put
them off. Resolved to accept the circumstances of his life, he daily
rebelled against them. And so he felt that his life had no meaning, he was
afflicted with the sense of futility, the *Sorge*,[33] he mentioned to Russell in
the previous summer. He could recognize his own condition in William
James's chapter on 'The Sick Soul'.

Yet what we are describing here is no disease. As Tolstoy says:

> These questions are the simplest in the world. From the stupid child to the
> wisest old man, they are in the soul of every human being.[34]

Take a typical expression of Wittgenstein's discontent:

> I ought to have done something positive with my life, to have become a
> star in the sky. Instead of which I remained stuck on earth and now I am
> gradually fading out.[35]

Everyone has this feeling at some time: no psychiatrist would regard it as
a clinical indication of any importance. James suggests that those whom

32. p. 50.
33. p. 129.
34. 'A Confession', quoted by William James in *The Varieties of Religious Experience*, p. 155. (In the
World's Classics edition of Tolstoy the passage occurs on p. 24.)
35. LW to PE 2.1.21: later we shall consider his whole spiritual state at that time.

it oppresses to the degree that Tolstoy and Wittgenstein were oppressed have a lower 'misery-threshold' than others. It does not matter here whether this linear model is adequate, whether we have to supplement it by allowing for fluctuations in the threshold—cyclothymia—or replace it by some account that allows the same nature, in some cases, to be the most easily depressed and the most easily elated. James's point is that these men feel more acutely something all men are aware of: 'Let us then,' he says, at one stage in his exposition, 'turn our backs on the healthy-minded':

> Let us rather see whether pity, pain, and fear, and the sentiment of human helplessness may not open a profounder view and put into our hands a more complicated key to the meaning of the situation.[36]

To Tolstoy it seemed for a while that manly suicide was the only answer: Wittgenstein, not in a mood of special depression, told Pinsent that in all his life there had hardly been a day when he had not at some time or another thought of this. Yet, to his problems, especially, suicide could not be the answer. If his trouble was his failure to reconcile himself to the world, he would above all be failing by committing suicide. Thus, some time later, he said:

> If suicide is allowed, then everything is allowed. If anything is not allowed, then suicide is not allowed.
>
> This throws a light on the nature of ethics, for suicide is, so to speak, the elementary sin.
>
> And when one investigates it, it is like investigating mercury vapour in order to comprehend the nature of vapours. (*Notebooks* 10.1.17)[37]

The argument is similar to Schopenhauer's: suicide is the supreme assertion of the will and at the opposite pole from the renunciation that could alone give release. For some reason like this, Wittgenstein, in these Cambridge years, would occasionally talk to Russell and Pinsent not directly of suicide but of his conviction that he had not long to live. Such premonitions are not uncommon and little attention is paid to them unless subsequently fulfilled. They usually express—in Wittgenstein's case they surely did—the strong conviction that life as it is *cannot* go on, a conviction which, like many of the results of reflection on life, is literally meaningless.

36. *The Varieties of Religious Experience*, p. 136. (The quotation in the body of the text is slightly rephrased.)

37. Wittgenstein there adds: 'Or isn't suicide too, in itself, neither good nor evil?' ('Oder ist nicht auch der Selbstmord an sich weder gut noch böse!'), but what we here want to bring out is the argument *against* suicide as he saw it. For another argument, see the letter to Engelmann of 20.6.20.

Not to be sorry for death—*eine Bejahung des Todes*—was one of Wittgenstein's most fundamental attitudes. All his Cambridge friends heard of it: it was, for example, one of the Wittgenstein enigmas that Moore and Hardy tried to puzzle out. One thing worked in the contrary direction; his need to have achieved something.

> He is morbidly afraid he may die before he has put the Theory of Types to rights, and before he has written out all his other work in such a way as shall be intelligible to the world and of some use to the science of Logic. He has written a lot already—and Russell has promised to publish his work if he were to die—but he is sure that what he has already written is not sufficiently well put, so as absolutely to make plain his real methods of thought etc:- which of course are of more value than his definite results. He is always saying that he is certain he will die within four years—but today it was two months. (Pinsent's Diary 17.9.13)

> He talked again tonight about his death—that he was not really afraid to die—but yet frightfully worried not to let the few remaining moments of his life be wasted. It all hangs on his absolutely morbid conviction that he is going to die soon—there is no obvious reason that I can see why he should not live yet for a long time. But it is no use trying to dispel that conviction, or his worries about it, by reason: the conviction and the worry he can't help—for he is mad. It is a hopelessly pathetic business—he is clearly having a miserable time of it. This evening too he was worried horribly that perhaps after all his work on Logic was no real use: and then his nervous temperament had caused him a life of misery and others considerable inconvenience—all for nothing. (Pinsent's Diary 20.9.13)

He expected death because he had no right to live: he feared it only because he needed to produce some great work to give some meaning to the life he had already led—to make up for or to justify the irritation he had caused others and the contempt he had felt for them.

These thoughts and this motivation remained with him up to the time of the composition and publication of the *Tractatus*. Not only his attitude towards that work but his remarks in it bear witness to these preoccupations. But we shall see that there is an advance in his intellectual attitude towards them, evident in his remarks there about the sense of the world, about ethics and the mystical. Some way out was at least visible. Only glimmerings of such a prospect appeared before the war in his remarks on conversion and his conversation with Moore (of which we have only the barest report) on saintliness.[38] Thus Russell thought it a considerable change (for the worse) that religious and mystical themes played so large a part in Wittgenstein's thinking after the war.

38. On 'conversion' see above p. 114. 'Conversion' and 'Saintliness' are the titles of two main sections of *The Varieties of Religious Experience* after the account of the sick soul.

The discussions of Wittgenstein's spiritual and moral state throughout this Michaelmas Term 1912 continued alongside, indeed they partly arose from, discussions of philosophy. Russell read to the Aristotelian Society in London his paper 'On the notion of cause'[39] and to the Moral Sciences Club in Cambridge his revised paper 'On matter'. Wittgenstein did not attend the former, but at the latter he was, according to Russell, the only one who understood it. The members of the Club were on the whole interested in the validity of the instinctive belief in the existence of unperceived perceptible qualities which Russell eventually had recourse to. Wittgenstein, we saw when discussing the April version of the paper,[40] was more interested in Russell's attempt to show from how little the whole of physics might validly be inferred. Russell was not yet bold enough to assert that only my own sense-data need be supposed actually to exist—this was the view he first published in 'The relation of sense-data to physics' written in January 1914,[41] and then only as a programme for the future, something he believed but could not fully establish. But he did provide, particularly in his revisions to the April paper, many ingenious suggestions of how principles of physics could be understood in terms of differences in our sense-data. This contained, if it did not fulfil, the promise of a 'construction' of the world of physics on a basis of sense-data. It is clear that Wittgenstein discussed these problems with Russell—his early reading of Boltzmann and perhaps Hertz must be remembered and his acquaintance with Mach's work. In January 1914 he was to send Russell the suggestion (followed by a suitable argument):

Isn't what the 'principle of sufficient reason' (law of causality) says simply that space and time are relative?

The suggestion echoes a revision inserted in the 1912 paper where Russell says (with a rather different argument):

The real purpose of such rather vague principles as 'same cause same effect' or the 'uniformity of nature' seems to be that absolute time must not appear in any scientific law.

Derivation or influence is not an important point here: we are drawing attention to the fact that the two philosophers were concerned with the same problems. Similarly there is a parallel between Russell's destructive criticism of the notion of causality in 'On the notion of cause' and Wittgenstein's dismissal of belief in causality as superstition in the

39. Printed in *PAS* 1912–13 and in *Mysticism and Logic*. The paper was delivered on 4 November.
40. p. 106 above.
41. But perhaps he announced it to Wittgenstein in a letter to Vienna at Christmas, for Wittgenstein replied (LW to BR January 1913), 'I cannot imagine your way of working from sense-data forward.'

Tractatus (5.1363). Certainly Wittgenstein was the fiercer proponent of the view that there was no necessity outside logic and certainly his account of the nature of logical truth (which left no room in the realm of the a priori for 'principles' like those of induction or causality) had great influence on Russell. But it was on a Russell who was already attempting on his own account to clarify and purify the rather too miscellaneous collection of a priori truths assumed by *The Problems of Philosophy*.

Discussion of the problem of matter and of the nature of logic proceeded *pari passu*. We even find a most interesting set of logical jottings by Wittgenstein (with one '$\sim p$' in Russell's hand) on the back of a paper of Russell's entitled 'Matter—the problem stated'. The paper appears to date from shortly after the paper read to the Moral Sciences Club. Not all the jottings are easily intelligible—there may be logical devices implicit which were not expoited later, there may also be mistakes or false starts, but the following four ideas which are important for the presentation of logic in the *Tractatus* can be traced. (1) The idea of representing the truth-possibilities of a pair of propositions in a tabular form, thus:

$$
\begin{array}{cc}
p & q \\
W & W \\
W & F \\
F & W \\
F & F \\
\end{array}
$$

(cf. *TLP* 4.31). (2) The idea of correlating with such a table of truth-possibilities a further column indicating which (if any) of the truth-possibilities are allowed and which (if any) excluded. This will yield what was later called a 'truth-table' giving the truth-conditions (*TLP* 4.431) of a proposition which is a truth-function (*TLP* 5) of the original pair of propositions. Assuming a conventional order of truth-possibilities, it is possible to write this column alone down as a row and still indicate a particular truth-function (*TLP* 4.442). Thus either

$$
\begin{array}{ccc}
p & q & \\
W & W & F \\
W & F & W \\
F & W & W \\
F & F & W \\
\end{array}
\qquad \text{or} \qquad \text{F W W W } (p,q)
$$

will express the proposition that Russell wrote as $p \supset \sim q$ (say 'p only if not q'). This step towards the third idea is clearly implicit in the jottings. (3) There are 16 different ways of filling in this third column, 16 different rows that can be written down representing all the possible truth-functions of a pair of propositions. Wittgenstein does this in full at *TLP* 5.101 and sketches a way or perhaps two ways of doing so in these jottings, thus:

$$
\begin{array}{cccc}
W & W & W & W \\
W & W & W & F \\
W & W & F & W \\
W & F & W & W \\
F & W & W & W \\
\\
F & F & F & F \\
F & . & . & .
\end{array}
$$

(4) Wittgenstein was particularly interested in the fifth of these truth-functions, which he writes as $p \text{ |} q$ and equates with $\sim p \text{ v} \sim q$ (it is also equivalent, as can be seen above, to $p \supset \sim q$). The natural explanation of this interest is as follows. Each of these truth-functions is equivalent to certain applications of the propositional connectives of *Principia* (v, $\sim$, etc.) to a pair of propositions; and each application of these connectives to a pair of propositions is equivalent to one of these truth-functions. But the various connectives are also definable in terms of one another. Thus Whitehead and Russell defined all the others in terms of $\sim$ and v (thus for example $p \supset q =_{Df} \sim p \text{ v} q$). Now, if we employ a single sign for the connective represented by the fifth row ($p \text{ |} q$ in Wittgenstein's new symbolism), we shall have a connective with the property that all the other connectives can be defined in terms of it alone (for example $\sim p =_{Df} p \text{ |} p$ and $p \text{ v} q =_{Df} p \text{ |} p . \text{ |} . q \text{ |} q$).[42]

The use of a striking and ingenious method of presentation to make a philosophical point is very characteristic of Wittgenstein, but it seems that he did not at first see his way to using these ideas to present or recommend his views on the nature of logic. They do not appear in the *Notes on Logic* of 1913 or the *Notes dictated to Moore* of 1914, where other devices are used. Yet the jottings are certainly earlier than both, since

---

42. Two changes introduced by the *Tractatus* should be noted. Wittgenstein there adopts a different, now slightly unusual, order for tables of truth-possibilities:

$$
\begin{array}{cc}
p & q \\
\\
W & W \\
F & W \\
W & F \\
F & F
\end{array}
$$

He wished to consider truth-functions of an arbitrary number of propositions and probably considered that this order made the construction of truth-tables easier and certain generalizations more intuitive. The other change is that the fundamental operation there (*TLP* 5.5, cf. 5.474, 5.1311) is joint negation, corresponding to the connective 'neither ... nor ...' or the truth-function WWWF(p,q) in the above account. This is the only other connective possessing the property described above.

Wittgenstein did not see Russell between the composition of *Notes on Logic* and the end of the war.

These jottings are a valuable reminder of how little we know about the genesis of the *Tractatus* and how misleading the fragmentary preliminary work we have can be. Without this accidental find it might easily have been supposed that the devices of truth-tables and the fundamental logical operation occurred to Wittgenstein after the reflections recorded in the wartime *Notebooks*, whereas it now seems as if he recurred, at the time of composing the *Tractatus*, to an old device (recorded perhaps in one of the lost or destroyed notebooks).[43] We have already stressed how early Wittgenstein's fundamental ideas came to him: another way of looking at the matter is that the *Tractatus* was an attempt to make use of everything of value that had occurred to him.

Wittgenstein himself laid no claim to novelty in detail: the idea of the tables was Frege's; Wittgenstein's innovation was to use this sort of schema as a symbol for the proposition not as an explanation of it.[44] The discovery of the two single connectives in terms of either of which all others could be defined was made by Sheffer. The idea of acknowledging this seems to have been discussed, but perhaps it was thought too obvious.

For his part Russell hoped to make significant advances in logic. We have a first sketch of a paper 'What is logic?' 'which I think may be really important with luck' (BR to OM, 13.10.12). There is little doubt that it represents fairly accurately the position that Russell and Wittgenstein had reached at this time, and it outlines 'the complex-problem' which was to exercise Wittgenstein during the Christmas vacation. Logic, on the view taken, was the study of the forms of complexes. It did not deal with judgements (which are a matter for psychology) nor with propositions (which can be false and hence cannot be anything objective but must be mere forms of words). Complexes will be recognized as identical with the true or asserted propositions of earlier discussions.[45] We might say (as before) that complexes were facts, except that there are complexes whose existence is logically necessary, and it is natural to be reluctant, as Russell was, to speak of necessary or logical facts.

> In a complex [Russell writes], there must be something which we may call the form, which is not a constituent, but the way the constituents are put together...

43. Similarly we know that Wittgenstein inserted in manuscript in the typescript of the *Tractatus* the method of representing truth-combinations by means of brackets used at 6.1203 to show that a certain expression was a tautology. Here too he was not recording a new idea but reviving an old one, already expounded in LW to BR November–December 1913 and implicit in *Notes on Logic*.

44. *Wittgenstein's Lectures on the Foundations of Mathematics* (ed. Diamond), p.177.

45. p. 90 above.

Logic deals with those forms which yield complexes however the variables are determined.

Russell finds it necessary to assume 'forms' as a primitive idea. A symbol composed entirely of variables symbolizes a form but is not itself a form. This leads, however, to a number of questions.

What is a part of a form? Are there simple and complex forms? ...
   In every proposition of logic, some expression containing only variables is said to be always true or sometimes true. The question 'what is logic?' is the question what is meant by such propositions.

The question is a most fundamental one—and typically philosophical. If an answer to it could be given, it would not carry us a step further *in* logic. For that reason many a 'bourgeois thinker' (Wittgenstein's term later for Ramsey) would hurry over this part of the inquiry, anxious to make advances in the subject. But Wittgenstein's aim—and Russell's here—was that of clarification and they delayed the man who would press on, with frustrating questions: What were complexes? How were they composed? What was their form? What were statements about forms of complexes, that is to say statements composed of apparent variables, really about? These were the questions Wittgenstein variously referred to in 1912 as 'the Complex problem' and 'the apparent variables business' and their profundity can be gauged by considering the difficulty of answering the question with which Russell's fragment ends:

Consider (x): hum.(x). ⊃ .mort(x). [in words: whatever x may be, if x is human x is mortal]. This seems to require that 'Soc is hum. ⊃ .Soc. is mortal' should have a *form* with respect to Socrates, and that this form should be *necessary*. Then we state that, if x is any other entity, there is a complex having [the] same relation to x as [the] above has to Socrates. But this is again a general statement, and can't be the *meaning* of the original statement, or else we get an endless regress.

There may be errors in this: it may involve a confusion of necessity with general validity, but it is much to Russell's credit that he acknowledged here his own failure to account for the necessity of logic.
   Russell's hopes fluctuated—'It is difficult but I feel I must have another go at it' on the 13th October and 'Can't get on with "What is logic"—I feel very much inclined to leave it to Wittgenstein' on the 14th.[46] Throughout the term Wittgenstein kept coming in with new ideas on logic, his health and spirits varying directly with his skill in

46. Both quotations are from letters to Lady Ottoline.

hitting on them. For the vacation Wittgenstein returned to Vienna by way of Jena, where

> I had a long discussion with Frege about our Theory of Symbolism of which, I think, he roughly understood the general outline. He said he would think the matter over.
> The complex problem is now clearer to me and I hope very much that I may solve it. (LW to BR 26.12.12)

It seems very probable that it was on this occasion that Frege put to Wittgenstein a general objection to Russell's talk about complexes, to which Wittgenstein reverted many times in conversation and alluded àlso in his notebooks. Frege asked him whether, if an object is part of a fact about it, the fact will be bigger than the object. At the time he thought the remark silly, but later he came to see the point of it. It was in fact an attack on the whole notion of explaining the meaning of propositions by saying that there were complexes corresponding to them—a way of speaking that Wittgenstein did in fact abandon in the course of 1913. Partly the difficulty lay in the confusion made by Russell and at this time Wittgenstein between a complex and a fact. As Wittgenstein said much later in 'Complex and Fact':

> ... a complex is a spatial object consisting of spatial objects. (The concept 'spatial' admitting of a certain extension.)...
> To say that a red circle consists *of* redness and circularity, or is a complex with these constituents, is a misuse of these words and is misleading. [Frege was aware of this and said it to me.]...
> The part smaller than whole—applied to fact and constituent, this would lead to an absurdity.[47]

Facts were, therefore, quite different from complexes and must be talked about in a quite different way. Russell had always betrayed an uneasy consciousness of this, but had failed to resolve the difficulty. It was to be a major difference between him and Wittgenstein, whose *Tractatus* begins with the notion of fact (*Am Anfang war die Tatsache*, so to speak). Even then many problems remained common to them: whether there were negative facts corresponding to true negative propositions; and how false propositions could have meaning, since it seems that there were by definition no facts or complexes corresponding to them and so on.

Conversations with Frege thus sowed the seed of one of Wittgenstein's most important ideas. Another, as he told Russell, came to him independently:

---

47. 'Complex and Fact' (June 1931), *Philosophical Remarks* p.302 and *Philosophical Grammar* p.20.

There cannot be different types of things! In other words whatever can be symbolized by a simple proper name must belong to one type. And further: every theory of types must be rendered superfluous by a proper theory of symbolism. (LW to BR January 1913)

If 'Socrates is mortal' is analysed into 'Socrates', 'mortality' (both proper names), and the copula, we need a theory of types to tell us that 'Mortality is Socrates' is nonsensical. But if instead we analyse it into 'Socrates' (a proper name) and '($\exists$ x).x is mortal' (a symbol for a quality which is at the same time a copula) we should find it impossible to produce the nonsensical pseudo-sentence referred to. The suggested analysis may not be the best possible: what is certain, Wittgenstein thought, is

the fact that all theory of types must be done away with by a theory of symbolism showing that what seem to be *different kinds of things* are symbolized by different kinds of symbols which *cannot* possibly be substituted in one another's places. (id. ibid.)

This was in many ways a puzzling idea: it seemed to deal in a very cavalier fashion with one of Russell's most laborious achievements, and it did so in a way that led to much misunderstanding—Was Wittgenstein recommending the construction of an ideal symbolism which would prevent the formulation of nonsensical or paradoxical statements 'a logically perfect language', as Russell put it in the introduction to the *Tractatus*? If so, must one not already have some theory of what the conditions to be fulfilled by a logically perfect language would be? Or did he mean that ordinary language, if the rules for its correct use were understood, already prevented such formulations? If so, what sort of study or inquiry would reveal the rules for the correct use of ordinary language, since our first inclinations are obviously an inadequate guide?

It would be interesting to know when his best *thoughts* came to Wittgenstein. Those reported in letters naturally tend to come from times at which he was away from his normal discussion-partners. But his later notebooks, and his habit of bursting in on Russell, say, with the new ideas of the vacation, suggest that a new way of looking at things usually occurred to him somewhere in comparative isolation, and that discussion was important for him first to provide the fodder for his reflections and later to enable him to find the exact expression for their results.

It is remarkable that Wittgenstein managed to strike a good vein of thought on the occasion of this particular Christmas visit to Vienna. He found his father *very* ill, there was no hope of recovery, he told Russell, his thoughts were lamed, he felt out of his mind, he needed[48] (what he did not get quickly enough for his comfort) a letter from Russell. (Two kind letters from Russell did soon arrive.)

We have essentially only Ludwig's own account of the last days of his father. His sister Hermine tells us in general terms of the trials of the long illness, of the self-sacrifice of the mother, of her total devotion to the father, of her long-pretended ignorance of the fatal nature of the disease, and of how, at the end, she simply let this mask fall. The illness grew rapidly: Ludwig was in doubt whether he ought to wait for the end or return for term.

> He has not yet any pains, but feels on the whole very bad having constant high fever. This makes him so apathetic that one cannot do him any good by sitting at his bed etc. And as this was the only thing that I could ever do for him, I am now perfectly useless here. So the time of my staying here depends entirely on whether the illness will take so rapid a course that I could not risk to leave Vienna; or not. (LW to BR January 1919)[49]

Then on the 21 January a letter to Russell that ought to be quoted in full:

> Dear Russell,
>   My dear father died yesterday in the afternoon. He had the most beautiful death that I can imagine; without the slightest pains and falling asleep like a child! I did not feel sad for a moment during all the last hours, but most joyful and I think that this death was worth a whole life.
>   I will leave Vienna on the 25th and will be in Cambridge either on Sunday night or Monday morning. I long very much to see you again.
>   Yours ever
>   Ludwig Wittgenstein

Pause and note the importance attached to the manner of death. Ludwig too was to die in his sixties, of cancer, after a period of illness, and a longer period of premature retirement. He was to die—this surprised some—content with his life as well as with his death: it seems to have been so with his father too. We have seen that Ludwig, in 1913, had thought often and was to think constantly of death—until perhaps some climacteric in his middle years. Some things he feared—death might come too soon, his life or his work might not be in order, he might be tempted to take his own life, he might (this was the war) not have

48. LW to BR 26.12.13, 6.1.13: 'von allen guten Geistern verlassen' in the latter means 'out of my mind'.

49. Probably about 11 or 12 January, because it mentions a letter already written to Wittgenstein's tutor, whose actual date is 10 January. The English is understandably shaky: perhaps 'not yet' means 'no longer'.

behaved decently. A good life should issue in a death one could welcome: perhaps, even, a good life *was* one that led to a good death. Such, so it seemed to Ludwig, was the death of Karl Wittgenstein, the energetic and tempestuous, in an atmosphere of calm and order. Respectful obituaries appeared in the *Neue Freie Presse* and even in *The Times*—'The Carnegie of Austria' he was called: Russell and the others had not known how important a man he had been in the world. He was buried in the Zentralfriedhof of Vienna in the grave destined for many of his family. The business of dividing up his large fortune into a widow's portion and equal shares for the five surviving children slowly began. Ludwig was to feel the effects of this later; also, perhaps, the loss of a central ordering force in his life, to whose wishes all his plans had to be referred; but for the moment the natural course of things seemed to be to return to his required residence at Cambridge, to his work, and to his friends— Russell, Pinsent, and perhaps Moore—his chief support at this time. The Wittgenstein family, that elaborate organism which owed so much to Hermann Christian and the *Geschwister* Wittgenstein, but was set up chiefly by his father would continue to function: it was a background for him but did not at the moment require anything of him.

Russell was impressed by the new ideas Wittgenstein brought back from Vienna. He played more and more with the idea of leaving work to him: once he had got Wittgenstein to the point at which he could teach mathematical logic (this would involve some degree or qualification, for form's sake) he himself would leave Cambridge. The letters from Vienna alone were enough to make him think that Wittgenstein would soon be ready to take his place. He talked less and less of finishing 'What is logic?'—instead, when Wittgenstein convinced him that the early proofs of *Principia* were very inexact, he consoled himself with the thought:

fortunately it is his business to put them right, not mine (BR to OM 23.2.13)

'Ten years ago', he said in the same letter, 'I could have written a book with the store of ideas I have already, but now I have a higher standard of exactness.' Thus, even though he returned in May to the project of an introduction to logic in order to make references in his general work on epistemology intelligible, he seems to have had little confidence in it. Moore's diary mentions a tea-time conversation with Wittgenstein on 19 May about 'whether R's textbook of logic would be good'. (Not until 1918—in prison and in a different frame of mind—did Russell actually write his *Introduction to Mathematical Philosophy*.) Pinsent records, for example, how Russell called on him one day when Wittgenstein was already there:

He and Wittgenstein got talking—the latter explaining one of his latest discoveries in the Fundamentals of Logic—a discovery which, I gather, only ocurred to him this morning, and which appears to be quite important and was very interesting. Russell acquiesced in what he said without a murmur. (Diary 4.2.13)

Wittgenstein was thus acknowledged as an equal. He was taken to see the Whiteheads and Jourdain, with differing success. The Whiteheads were in poor health and he in bad humour: they formed an unfavourable impression of him, which, despite Russell's attempts to show them sympathetic or touching letters from Wittgenstein, is still reflected in Whitehead's later anecdotes about Wittgenstein. The meeting with Jourdain (evidently the first meeting, despite the 1909 correspondence we have referred to above) was more successful. It led to further discussions and a measure of collaboration. Jourdain, in this a bit like Keynes, was a connoisseur of the rare and brilliant. He was a devoted admirer of Frege, whose work he had summarized in some articles which are still of interest, and indeed had persuaded Frege to provide some comments of his own.[50] Now he wrote to Frege as if reporting the opinion of a valued colleague:

> In your last letter to me you spoke about working at the theory of irrational numbers. Do you mean that you are writing a third volume of the *Grundgesetze der Arithmetik*? Wittgenstein and I were rather disturbed to think that you might be doing so, because the theory of irrational numbers—unless you have got a quite new theory of them—would seem to require that the contradiction has been previously avoided; and the part dealing with irrational numbers on the new basis has been splendidly worked out by Russell and Whitehead in their *Principia Mathematica*. I say that we were disturbed, because we felt that you could not possibly, at this time, now that the theories you were the first to develop have been worked out by others, write a third volume that would be anywhere near your first and second in originality and brilliance. You must forgive me for speaking like this; it is only because I feel that your work on the foundations of logic is so wonderfully fine that I should regret to see its continuation into a domain that has already been cultivated by others. (PEBJ to GF 29.3.13)

Some time later Wittgenstein undertook to revise Jourdain's translation of part of Frege's *Grundgesetze*, but owing to Wittgenstein's absence, prolonged by the war, this office was in fact performed by J. Stachelroth.[51]

---

50. *Quarterly Journal of Pure and Applied Mathematics* 43 (1912) 237–269 reprinted in *Frege: Philosophical and Mathematical Correspondence* (1980).

51. Jourdain's translation of most of the Preface, the Introduction, and seven sections of the text appeared in the *Monist* 25–27 (1915–17).

One sign of Wittgenstein's professional status is that he was able, and was asked, to write a review of a conventional textbook of traditional logic. Pinsent helped him to translate his review out of German:

> He has written the Review in German and gave me a rough translation. But it was very difficult—the construction of the sentences is so different, I suppose, in German to what it is in English. And he insisted on the translation being fairly literal. (Diary 11.2.13)

The review (which bears no traces of these difficulties) is perhaps worth printing here: Wittgenstein's first known publication, confident and trenchant in style, a proof of his competence at the sort of task he later shunned, an example also of his preference for the epigrammatic and dismissive:[52]

> In no branch of learning can an author disregard the results of honest research with so much impunity as he can in Philosophy and Logic. To this circumstance we owe the publication of such a book as Mr Coffey's 'Science of Logic': and only as a typical example of the work of many logicians of to-day does this book deserve consideration. The author's Logic is that of the scholastic philosophers, and he makes all their mistakes—of course with the usual references to Aristotle. (Aristotle, whose name is so much taken in vain by our logicians, would turn in his grave if he knew that so many Logicians know no more about Logic to-day than he did 2,000 years ago.) The author has not taken the slightest notice of the great work of the modern mathematical logicians—work which has brought about an advance in Logic comparable only to that which made Astronomy out of Astrology, and Chemistry out of Alchemy.
>
> Mr Coffey, like many logicians, draws a great advantage from an unclear way of expressing himself; for if you cannot tell whether he means to say 'Yes' or 'No,' it is difficult to argue against him. However, even through his foggy expression, many grave mistakes can be recognised clearly enough; and I propose to give a list of some of the most striking ones, and would advise the student of Logic to trace those mistakes and their consequences in other books on Logic also. (The numbers in brackets indicate the pages of Mr Coffey's book—volume 1—where a mistake occurs for the first time; the illustrative examples are my own).
>
> 1. [36] The author believes that all propositions are of the subject-predicate form.
> 2. [31] He believes that reality is changed by becoming an object of our thoughts.

52. The work reviewed was P. Coffey: *The Science of Logic* (London, 1912). Coffey, a professor at Maynooth, did indeed propound scholastic philosophy in the form then current in theological colleges. The review was printed in *The Cambridge Review* 34 (1912–13) 351, a periodical which printed serious book-reviews (notably some by Jourdain and Russell) alongside the news and controversies of the university. Professor Coffey is unlikely to have had sight of it. It has been reprinted in *The Cambridge Mind*.

3. [6] He confounds the copula 'is' with the word 'is' expressing identity. (The word 'is' has obviously different meanings in the propositions—

'Twice two is four'

and 'Socrates is mortal'.)

4. [44] He confounds things with the classes to which they belong. (A man is obviously something quite different from mankind).

5. [48] He confounds classes and complexes. (Mankind is a class whose elements are men; but a library is not a class whose elements are books, because books become parts of a library only by standing in certain spatial relations to one another— while classes are independent of the relations between their members).

6. [47] He confounds complexes and sums. (Two plus two is four, but four is not a complex of two and itself).

This list of mistakes could be extended a good deal. The worst of such books as this is that they prejudice sensible people against the study of Logic.

Note also the absolute confidence in the superiority of the new logic, together with the implication that logic was a subject in which advances ought to be made.

All the signs were that Wittgenstein would, as it were, put his shoulder to the wheel and pass through all the stages then normal in the career of a young philosopher. Just as Moore delivered a course of lectures at Morley College in 1910,[53] so Wittgenstein, it was planned, should lecture at the Working Men's College, also in London. There, in the birthplace of workers' education, where F.D. Maurice originally, and the author of *Tom Brown's Schooldays* more recently, had taught the manliness of Christianity and the christianity of socialism, Wittgenstein too was to perform his own part in that atonement by means of education that the rich then felt obliged to make. Ten years later he would have scoffed at the idea of assisting the working man by any kind of academic training, let alone by philosophy, but for the moment he evidently felt (in the words of his advice to F.—p. 111 above) that an introduction to philosophy would help them to see what honest thought was. When October 1913 came he was out of England for a number of reasons and the lectures were not given.

Meanwhile, throughout the Lent and Easter terms of 1913 Wittgenstein continued to come to Russell with fresh and good ideas on the foundations of logic. To Moore too, on his good days, he would explain probability, or Russell's theory of classes, or the analysis of a proposition.

53. Now published as *Some Main Problems of Philosophy*.

As in Michaelmas Term, there were periods of depression, though shorter ones. He came to Russell in May to say that logic was driving him into insanity:

> I think there is a danger of it, so I urged him to let it alone for a bit and do other work—I think he will. He is in a shocking state—always gloomy, pacing up and down, waking out of a dream when one speaks to him. (BR to OM 2.5.13)

And from Vienna he wrote to Russell:

> I am as perfectly sterile as I never was, and I doubt whether I shall ever again get ideas. Whenever I try to think about Logic, my thoughts are so vague that nothing ever can crystallize out. What I feel is the curse of all those who have only half a talent; it is like a man who leads you along a dark corridor with a light and just when you are in the middle of it the light goes out and you are left alone. (LW to BR 25.3.13)[54]

> It is an awful curse [Russell commented on this letter] to have the creative impulse, unless you have a talent that can always be relied on, like Shakespeare's or Mozart's. (BR to OM 29.3.13)

Wittgenstein's difficulty seems to have been especially acute: it is as if he wanted to grasp or comprehend the whole of a difficult subject in a single act of insight—to find, as he puts it in his *Notebooks* (20.1.15), the word that will break the spell. It happened there was at that time a wave of interest in hypnotism in Cambridge. A number of dons were submitting themselves to it. Pinsent tells us:

> Wittgenstein has been having himself mesmerized—by Dr Rogers here. The idea is this. It is, I believe, true that people are capable of special muscular effort while under hypnotic trance: then why not also special mental effort? So when he (Wittgenstein) is under trance, Rogers is to ask him certain questions about points of Logic, about which Wittgenstein is not yet clear, (—certain uncertainties which no one has yet succeeded in clearing up): and Witt: hopes he will then be able to see clearly. It sounds a wild scheme! Witt: has been twice to be hypnotized—but not until the end of the second interview did Rogers succeed in sending him to sleep: when he did, however, he did it so thoroughly that it took $\frac{1}{2}$ hour to wake him up again completely. Witt: says he was conscious all the time—could hear Rogers talk—but absolutely without will or strength: could not comprehend what was said to him—could exert no muscular effort—felt exactly as if he were under anaesthetic. He felt very drowsy for an hour after he left Rogers. It is altogether a wonderful business. There can be no

---

54. This was the letter that Russell showed to the Whiteheads to make them think better of Wittgenstein.

'Auto-suggestion' about it—as Wittgenstein once found himself getting drowsy etc:, when he didn't think Rogers was trying to mesmerize him at all:—just after an attempt had failed, and when he (Witt:) thought the séance was over and was preparing to go away—just talking about other things for a moment before leaving. (Diary 15.5.13)

His sister Gretl told Ludwig a similar story about her own experiments with a hypnotist. It is tempting to think that both brother and sister were exceptionally strong personalities—that they lived, as it were, at a degree of tension not easily relaxed but once relaxed not easily restored. The dilettante's interest in the powers of one's own mind is also characteristic of both brother and sister: at one time they used to exchange dream-reports. Characteristic too is the perversity, the resistance to the hypnotism when it was officially being applied, though it was their own idea to undergo it. In so far as Wittgenstein's experiment was serious it throws some light on his conception of the nature of his task: it was something to be discharged not by patient and cumulative removal of partial problems but by some great insight achieved as a result of effort.

One feature of Wittgenstein's method of work was his need to involve another person—Pinsent and Jourdain are examples, but Russell was of course the chief sufferer or beneficiary. It was to affect Russell's work severely for another ten years—indeed the association with Wittgenstein may be put alongside that with Lady Ottoline and the new pre-occupations of the First World War as one of the chief influences on Russell's career.

It was an influence that he almost sought to avoid. He began to feel that Wittgenstein was narrow and uncivilized,

rather too much the champion of a party—that is when judged by the highest standards (BR to OM 6.3.12)[55]

He found himself no longer talking about his own work but only about Wittgenstein's:

When there are no clear arguments but only inconclusive considerations to be balanced, or unsatisfactory points of view to be set against each other, he is no good; and he treats infant theories with a ferocity which they can only endure when they are grown up. (BR to OM 23.4.13)

For this reason apparently he did not at first tell Wittgenstein of the direction of his own researches. He began to think, in May 1913, both that the subject of theory of knowledge would be the best for some lectures he was to give next year in America and that he ought in any

---

55. The background for this criticism is explained on p. 115 above.

case to write a work on that subject—to solve the problem, in particular, of dreams (i.e. of how we are to know that all our experience is not mere dreaming) before he could hope to tackle the subject of matter. It is not clear whether the lectures he had in mind were the Lowell Lectures he was due to give at Boston in 1914 or the lectures he would concurrently be giving at Harvard. In the event he gave as Lowell Lectures material written from September 1913 on, subsequently published as *Our Knowledge of the External World*, while he used his theory of knowledge material in Harvard. After only a few days of sketching his plan (no writer can read Russell's letters without envy!) he began to write on 7 May and saw no reason why he should not go straight to the end.

> It all flows out [he wrote next day]. There will be an introductory chapter, which I shall probably leave to the last—the first substantial chapter, which I have nearly finished, is called 'Preliminary description of experience'... If I go on the scale on which I have begun it will be quite a big book—500 pages of print I should think. It is all in my head, ready to be written as fast as my pen will go. I feel as happy as a king. (BR to OM 8.5.13)

He did indeed go ahead at the pace he had set himself—ten pages a day—or even faster. By 21 May he had already written six chapters.[56] Wittgenstein was told of the project of a book on the theory of knowledge a week after the actual writing had begun. It shocked him, Russell says,

> he thinks it will be like the shilling shocker, which he hates. *He* is a tyrant, if you like. (BR to OM 13.5.13)

Now, on the 20th, he had come to Russell with an objection to Russell's former theory of judgement

> He was right, but I think the correction required is not very serious. I shall have to make up my mind within a week, as I shall soon reach judgement. (BR to OM 21.5.13)

He reached 'the Day of Judgement' by the 24th and was full of confidence:

> I got a new way of dividing the subject—quite new and much more searching than the traditional divisions. ... any number of really important new ideas came to me. (BR to OM 23.5.13)

---

56. The six in fact that appeared as articles in *The Monist* January 1914–April 1915. The work as a whole (or all that was written) has now been published under the title *Theory of Knowledge* as volume 7 of the Collected Papers of Bertrand Russell.

By the 26th he had finished the crucial chapter—'On the understanding of propositions'—and was some way into the next when Wittgenstein came to see him.

> We were both cross from the heat—I showed him a crucial part of what I have been writing. He said it was all wrong, not realizing the difficulties —that he had tried my view and knew it wouldn't work. I couldn't understand his objection—in fact he was very inarticulate—but I feel in my bones that he must be right, and that he has seen something I have missed. If I could see it too I shouldn't mind, but as it is, it is worrying, and has rather destroyed the pleasure in my writing—I can only go on with what I see, and yet I feel it is probably all wrong, and that Wittgenstein will think me a dishonest scoundrel for going on with it. Well, well—it is the younger generation knocking at the door—I must make room for him when I can, or I shall become an incubus. But at the moment I was rather cross. (BR to OM 27.5.13)

All the indications are that this was an objection raised by Wittgenstein to Russell's theory of judgement even in its new form, but it was connected with just those problems—the nature of propositions, their forms, what their truth consisted in—that Russell wanted to leave to Wittgenstein.

When Wittgenstein wrote saying he could express his objection exactly, he put it as follows:

> I believe it is obvious that, from the proposition 'A judges that (say) a is the Relation R to b', if correctly analysed, the proposition '$aRb.\text{v} \sim aRb$' must follow directly *without the use of any other premiss*. This condition is not fulfilled by your theory. (LW to BR June 1913)

Sometime that same summer he wrote down:

> Every right theory of judgement must make it impossible for me to judge that this table penholders the book. Russell's theory does not satisfy this requirement.

or, as he said, more briefly in September

> The proper theory of judgement must make it impossible to judge nonsense.[57]

In the relevant chapter Russell explains that understanding is a relation which holds between a subject, the various constituents of a proposition,

---

57. Both remarks now occur in *Notes on Logic*, for the composition of which see below and my article in *Revue internationale de Philosophie* 26 (1972) 444.

and the logical form of the proposition. It might be represented therefore by $U(S,A,B$, similarity, $R(x,y))$—a relation holding between a subject S, the object A, the object B, the relation *similarity*, and the logical form $R(x,y)$. Believing or judging is another such relation. There are various specifications of what sort of relation understanding is: these would generally apply to believing also; their chief function is to show that the relation proceeds from the subject to each of the other terms and then arranges them in a certain way. The difficulty Wittgenstein alludes to arises because there is nothing in the specification of the relation U to show that the objects must be objects, the relation a relation, or the logical form one which it would be possible for the objects and relations (supposing them to be such) to figure in. Why is it—what is there in the specification given of the relation U (understanding) or B (believing) to make it the case—that the subject cannot take any arbitrary and ill-assorted set of objects of acquaintance and 'understand' or 'believe' them to be combined in any logical form that he chooses? What is it, in other words, about understanding or believing that makes only a proposition a possible object for them?

It seems indeed easy to say that a relation is not *called* understanding or believing unless it is the relation of a subject *to* a proposition. But anyone who says this must already know what a proposition is. Russell's position in *Theory of Knowledge* was that the world contained complexes (corresponding to true beliefs) and true and false beliefs: it did not contain propositions, true and false: these had to be constructed out of, abstracted from, the complexes and states of mind already mentioned. If, however, as is surely the case, the notion of proposition is prior to that of the state of mind consisting in belief, this part of Russell's programme collapses.

This is the only objection of Wittgenstein's to which we have an explicit contemporary allusion, but in Wittgenstein's own writings over the next years many of the themes discussed—many of the positions contested—were taken from the *Theory of Knowledge* manuscript.[58] We must suppose that there were a number of discussions of its contents and that it provided a good part of the matter for Wittgenstein's reflections during the productive year to be described in our next chapter.

After Wittgenstein's 'attack' of 27 May Russell continued to write, no more slowly but with less heart. He felt that he had overcome Wittgenstein's difficulty, but only superficially. Besides he did not want to steal Wittgenstein's ideas—and even a difficulty was an important idea. If the difficulty were not solved, it made a large part of the book he meant to write impossible, perhaps for years to come. The result was something it was very difficult to be honest about: 'the first time in my

---

58. Some instances are indicated in my 'The *Grundgedanke* of the *Tractatus*' in G. Vesey (ed.): *Understanding Wittgenstein* (1974).

life that I have failed in honesty over work. Yesterday I felt ready for suicide,' he wrote to Lady Ottoline on 20 June 1913. By this time he had paused in his writing, after 350 pages, meaning to leave Part III, on inference, until the autumn, but in fact he was to write no more of this book. He had already stopped indeed when he received Wittgenstein's 'exact expression' of his objection—in an invitation to lunch received on 11 June. The objection, he told Wittgenstein, 'paralysed' him.[59] He spent, in all, an anxious summer—until he returned to England from holiday and began (on 1 September) writing his Lowell Lectures—his 'popular lectures' as he called them in a letter to Lady Ottoline.

Looking back on these events, in 1916, Russell told Lady Ottoline:

> Do you remember that at the time you were seeing Vittoz I wrote a lot of stuff about the Theory of Knowledge, which Wittgenstein criticized with the greatest severity? His criticism, though I don't think you realized it at the time, was an event of first-rate importance in my life and affected everything I have done since. I saw he was right and I saw that I could not hope ever again to do fundamental work in philosophy. My impulse was shattered like a wave dashed to pieces against a breakwater. I became filled with utter despair...

'I soon got over this mood,' Russell said, much later, in a footnote about the letter,[60] but the date of the letter itself proves that his despondent conviction that all fundamental work in philosophy was logical and he himself no longer fit to do it lasted from the summer of 1913 until at least 1916.

These differences over the manuscript only accentuated the difficulties that Russell and Wittgenstein found in their friendship. Despite the criticisms Russell was convinced that his book was good 'because it gives an example of scientific method where previous writing has been unscientific'. In the same letter he reflects ruefully on Wittgenstein's effect on him:

> He affects me just as I affect you—I get to know every turn and twist of the ways in which I irritate and depress you from watching how he irritates and depresses me; and at the same time I love and admire him. Also I affect him just as you affect me when you are cold. The parallelism is curiously close altogether. He differs from me just as I differ from you. He is clearer, more creative, more passionate; I am broader, more sympathetic, more sane. I have overstated the parallel for the sake of symmetry, but there is something in it. (BR to OM 1.6.13)

And a few days later:

59. Wittgenstein answers some such remark in his letter LW to BR 22.7.13.
60. The letter is reprinted in Russell's *Autobiography*, vol. 2, p. 57.

I had an awful time with Wittgenstein yesterday between tea and dinner. He came analysing all that goes wrong between him and me and I told him I thought it was only nerves on both sides and everything was all right at bottom. Then he said he never knew whether I was speaking the truth or being polite, so I got vexed and refused to say another word. He went on and on and on. I sat down at my table and took up my pen and began to look through a book, but still he went on. At last I said sharply 'All you want is a little self-control'. Then at last he went away with an air of high tragedy. He had asked me to a concert in the evening, but he didn't come, so I began to fear suicide. However, I found him in his room late (I left the concert, but didn't find him at first), told him I was sorry I had been cross, and then talked quietly about how he could improve. His faults are exactly mine—always analysing, pulling feelings up by the roots, trying to get the exact truth of what one feels towards him. I see it is very tiring and very deadening to one's affections. I think it must be characteristic of logicians—he is the only other one I have known intimately. (BR to OM 5.6.13)

There may be logicians' faults; but more probably it was a question of which person kissed and which turned the cheek. A few days later again, on 10 June, they went together to the Choral Symphony. This was when Wittgenstein told Russell that hearing that symphony with him was one of the great moments of his life. It is possible to picture the enthusiasm he felt: the gramophone was young, stereophonic reproduction had not been thought of, a performance of the Choral Symphony was an event. All the same, Wittgenstein was in an exceptionally receptive and enthusiastic state of mind—it was only three months since he had told Pinsent of a performance of it:

It would seem almost as though the chorus of the 9th was symbolic of a real turning point in his life! That he had found consolation at last. (Diary 5.3.13)

There is, or was, a certain pattern to the ending of the Cambridge year—the concert and the heightened personal relationships are part of it. So in 1913, there was a demonstration at the Psychology Laboratory in which Wittgenstein took part; there were visits from relations—Pinsent's family came to Cambridge and Wittgenstein, a preoccupied host but otherwise in good form, gave them tea in chemical beakers; Wittgenstein's mother came to London and Russell and Moore went to lunch with her at the Savoy. We know nothing of what passed between them, but during the war Russell was able to write to her a letter of exactly the appropriate tone, inquiring about her son.

Wittgenstein's own calendar (he always developed one) required a visit to Manchester to see his friend Eccles (whether this was the year in which he went across the water to Eccles's home in Coleraine is not clear). It was from Manchester that he wrote to Keynes about the benefaction designed for Johnson and described above, showing that he had already begun to think about some of the consequences of the fortune he had inherited.

And so, in July, back to Austria and the Hochreith. After one of his most energetic years he was to start on one of his most retired; after one of his most eventful on one of his most productive.

1. Hermann Christian Wittgenstein –
   grandfather (Mrs Clara Sjögren)

2. Karl Wittgenstein – father
   (Mrs Clara Sjögren)

3. Family portrait for silver wedding of Karl and Leopoldine Wittgenstein – Ludwig in sailor
   suit (Dr Thomas Stonborough)

4. Karl and Leopoldine with Hermine Wittgenstein on the Hochreith (Mrs Clara Sjögren)

5. The infant Ludwig Wittgenstein
   (Mrs Clara Sjögren)

6. Paul and Ludwig Wittgenstein
   (Mrs Clara Sjögren)

7. Ludwig at his sewing machine (Mrs Clara Sjögren)

8. The family at table on the Hochreith – housekeeper, Mining, Grandmother Kalmus, Paul, Gretl, and Ludwig (Mrs Clara Sjögren)

9. Head of Ludwig Wittgenstein by Michael
   Drobil (Dr Franz Richard Reiter)

10. David Pinsent ca 1913
    (heirs of Ludwig Wittgenstein)

11. *Right:* Portrait of Margaret
    Stonborough by Gustav Klimt
    (Munich, Neue Pinakothek)

12. Alleegasse, the music room (Dr Thomas Stonborough)

13. The Hochreith in early days – the *Blockhaus* (Mrs Clara Sjögren)

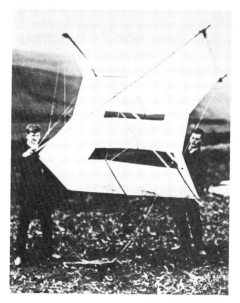

14. Wittgenstein and Eccles with a kite
(Dr Thomas Stonborough)

15. Wittgenstein's ship, *Goplana*, in Galicia
(Kriegsarchiv, Vienna)

16. Wittgenstein's military identity
card (heirs of Ludwig
Wittgenstein)

17. An artillery advance in the Bukowina (Kreigsarchiv, Vienna)

18. A family gathering during home leave – Kurt, Paul, Hermine, Max (Salzer), Leopoldine, Helene, and Ludwig (Mrs Clara Sjögren)

6 Norway 1913–14

LETTERS to Russell suggest that July and most of August were spent on the Hochreith—a usual pattern. The weather was 'constantly rotten' (LW to BR 22.7.13).

> The weather here is most abominable, it rains all day like mad. Just now a crash of thunder came down and I said 'Hell!', which shews that English swear-words are well in my bones. (LW to BR summer 1913)

The undergraduate slang and the mild swear-words are a characteristic sign of good spirits. His work was going exceptionally well. In the same letters he says that he felt nearer than he had ever felt before to the solution of all his problems.

Delayed by flu he arrived in England in late August for a holiday with Pinsent. Pinsent indeed, less favoured than Russell, had been waiting with some anxiety for a letter. A trip to Spain had been planned, but now Wittgenstein suggested other possibilities.

> He was very anxious to shew no preference for any particular scheme and that I should choose unbiased: but it was obvious that his choice was Norway, so I eventually settled on that. I am not sure I shouldn't have preferred the Azores—the voyage would have been very pleasant—but the voyage was precisely what Witt: disliked, as he was sure that we should meet crowds of American tourists, which he can't stand!... Why Wittgenstein should have suddenly changed his mind at the last moment I can't think! (Diary 25.8.13)

The plan was to go to Bergen and to make short walking tours etc. from there.

Before they left, Wittgenstein had business in England: a visit to Cambridge—we hear of tea with Moore and—much more important—a visit to the Whiteheads at Marlborough and a meeting with Russell in London. Pinsent was the first to hear of Wittgenstein's 'truly amazing' discoveries in logic.

> They have solved all the problems on which he has been working unsatisfactorily for the last year. He always has explained to me what he has been working at, and it is exceedingly interesting to see how he has gradually developed his work, each idea suggesting a new suggesion, and

finally leading to the system he has just discovered—which is wonderfully simple and ingenious and seems to clear up everything. (Diary 25.8.13)

Russell too was impressed—'extraordinarily good work' (BR to OM 29.8.13)—and (so Wittgenstein told Pinsent) Whitehead too:

It is probable that the first volume of *Principia* will have to be re-written, and Wittgenstein may write himself the first eleven chapters. That is a splendid triumph for him! (Diary, August 1913)

We shall make a guess how far he had got with his discoveries when we come to review his work during this year. Far enough at all events to make him feel that he could announce them to Russell and Whitehead. Probably it was chiefly Whitehead's blessing that he needed: Russell already recognized that the fundamentals of Logic were 'Wittgenstein's job' and was now enormously relieved at his progress:

You can hardly believe what a load this lifts off my spirits—it makes me feel almost young and gay. The oppression before was intolerable and affected my relation to you very much. (BR to OM 29.8.13)

On Wittgenstein's side it is probable that the preference for Norway which Pinsent detected was really for solitude and the opportunity to continue working. It turned out to be more like a reading-party than a holiday. They were well enough provided with money though not as lavishly as in the previous year: Wittgenstein brought £70 for the two of them and also carried a Letter of Credit. They travelled comfortably— single rooms at Grand Hotels, Second Class only when there was no First Class. As before, Wittgenstein tended to avoid fellow-passengers, while Pinsent was more solicitous about their feelings. It was on this trip that the incident of the intrusive smoker (see above pp. 121–2) occurred. Arrived in Bergen they looked for a small place on a fjord

where we can be quite alone from Tourists (upon this Ludwig is very firm). We want to settle down in such a place for say 3 weeks—and do some work (I at Law and Ludwig at Logic)—and get some walking and sailing on the Fjord also if possible. (Diary 3.9.13)[1]

---

1. Pinsent appears in the list of Wranglers for 1913. Two years earlier he had obtained a First Class in Part I of the Mathematical Tripos also. According to the first Lord Adrian (his future brother-in-law) he would have liked to put in for a Fellowship at Trinity, but was dissuaded by Barnes (the future heterodox Bishop of Birmingham). So after Part II he began to read for the Bar, as we here see. An uncle (later Lord Parker of Waddington) was already a chancery judge.

They found such a place at Östensö, as it was then usually called (Wittgenstein at first and Pinsent always referred to it as Öistensjö: today the spelling is Öystese).

A tiny village in a little bay of the Fjord (Hardangerfjord) with hills rising straight behind. It seems the ideal place we want.

They took two bedrooms and a sitting-room and spent three weeks there, almost exclusively in one another's company while the hotel gradually emptied. First there was their work: Pinsent would read Roman Law or whatever it happened to be: Wittgenstein would 'mutter to himself in a mixture of German and English and stride up and down the room all the while' (Diary 3.9.13). This *was* work for Wittgenstein—the effort of concentration on problems that he saw plastically before him. Books by others, or even his own notes, were not necessary for him. His notebooks were the distillate of long periods of concentration—and anything prepared for publication was yet further distilled. Thus he could work perfectly well while sailing with Pinsent—as, later, he speaks of working while peeling potatoes.

For recreation they sailed or went clambering on the rocks—Wittgenstein was rather clumsy at both. In the evening they would play dominoes:

We always begin by playing proper dominoes, and end up by building wonderful systems with the domino-pieces—with ingenious arrangements for knocking them down—also constructed out of domino-pieces! (Diary 7.9.13)

On one occasion Wittgenstein went to Bergen to make some necessary purchases and brought back also a couple of volumes of Schubert songs, which they performed in their usual way.

There were one or two scenes at first—we have mentioned the intrusive smoker; one in particular when they arrived at Östensö:

Later we went out for a stroll. I took my camera with me which was the cause of another scene with Ludwig. We were getting on perfectly amicably—when I left him for a moment to take a photo: And when I overtook him again he was silent and sulky. I walked on with him in silence for half an hour, and then asked him what was the matter. It seemed, my keenness to take that photo: had disgusted him—'like a man who can think of nothing—when walking—but how the country would do for a golf course'. (Diary 4.9.13)

A wounding remark—though not every non-photographer will think it as neurotic as Pinsent did. Actually the rift was quickly repaired: Wittgenstein was penitent and disgusted with himself, while Pinsent regarded such incidents as fits of madness that Wittgenstein was incapable of avoiding. But their relationship seemed now to be solidly based:

> He says that at times last year [on their Icelandic holiday] he was even uncertain whether to like or dislike me—but that since then we have got to know each other much better and he is never uncertain now. (Diary 2.9.13)

And in fact there was even less friction than Pinsent feared. The dominoes alone show that with Pinsent Wittgenstein could be in that vein of simple and childlike gaiety which we find him in with his sister Helene and with some later friends, but not (or not clearly) with Cambridge friends from this early period. This year, as opposed to the previous one, there was no planning to spend some of the time apart. It was a nuisance, Pinsent thought, when Wittgenstein had to make his separate journey to Bergen. It is significant too that about this time (as the diary entry for 4 September shows) they began to use each other's Christian names—we shall follow their practice when speaking just of the two of them.[2]

Ludwig managed for most of the time to be quite cheerful, David thought: and on his side 'Pinsent is an enormous comfort to me here,' Wittgenstein wrote to Russell. One thought haunted him, however, and comes in the same letter:

> I very often now have the indescribable feeling as though my work was all sure to be lost entirely in some way or other. But I still hope this won't come true. Whatever happens don't forget me! (LW to BR 5.9.13)

Curiously enough, he did nearly lose his portmanteau with all his notebooks on the voyage out, part of a general absent-mindedness—he misplaced a travelling rug on the way back and a letter to Russell on the next journey out. Anxiety about his work was a recurrent shadow on his talks with David: he would explain his progress with the theory of types ('the beastly theory of types' (letter of 5.9.13)) but could be gloomy and unapproachable when there were serious difficulties. It was in these days (17 and 19 September) that he told David of his fear that death would

---

2. For comparison: Russell and Moore and Wittgenstein remained such to one another all their lives. (Moore is perhaps a special case: no one called him George, his family called him Bill, his wife Moore.) After 1925 'My dear Keynes' was always addressed by and always replied to 'Ludwig'.

take him with his work unfinished or with no valuable work accomplished —we have quoted the passages above (p. 158).

David would try to convince him that his work could not be entirely useless and had some success in calming him. Ludwig was in a mixture of moods. On one expedition

> We had a long conversation about this holiday and holidays in general. Ludwig says he has never before enjoyed a holiday as much as this. He is almost certainly speaking the truth—but it is curious considering how depressed he has been at times lately: but I suppose these fits of depression are always with him and nothing exceptional. He has certainly been very cheerful indeed when he has not been depressed. (Diary 23.9.13)

Suspended between elation at his results and doubts about their completeness or presentiments about their future, Ludwig hit on two plans. The first he put to Russell:

> Types are not yet solved but I have had all sorts of ideas which seem to me very fundamental. Now the feeling that I shall have to die before being able to publish them is growing stronger in me every day and my greatest wish would therefore be to communicate *everything* that I have done so far to you *as soon as possible*. Don't think that I believe that my ideas are very important but I cannot help feeling that they might help people to avoid *some* errors. Or am I mistaken? If so don't take *any notice* of this letter. I have of course no judgement at all as to whether my ideas are worth preserving after my death or not. And perhaps it is ridiculous of me even to consider this question at all. But if this is ridiculous please try to excuse this foolishness of mine because it is not a superficial foolishness but the deepest of which I am capable. I see that the further I get on with this letter the less I dare come to my point. But my point is this: I want to ask you to let me meet you *as soon as possible* and give me time enough to give you a survey of the whole field of what I have done up to now and if possible to let me make notes for you *in your presence*. (LW to BR 20.9.13)

He goes on to make suggestions for a meeting in early October. As for the plan—to stimulate himself to write by the presence of a colleague— we shall come across something like it later in the dictation of the *Blue Book* and the *Brown Book*, the method of composition of the latter being strikingly similar to that planned in 1913. The idea that Russell should be given something for publication after Wittgenstein's death had already been canvassed (see our quotation from Pinsent on p. 158).

We shall see shortly how the meeting went. It was preceded by Wittgenstein's telling Russell and Moore of a plan first mentioned to Pinsent:

Ludwig was very cheerful this morning, but suddenly announced a scheme of the most alarming nature. To wit: that he should exile himself and live for some years right away from everybody he knows—say in Norway. That he should live entirely alone and by himself—a hermit's life—and do nothing but work in Logic. His reasons for this are very queer to me—but no doubt they are very real for him: firstly he thinks he will do infinitely more and better work in such circumstances, than at Cambridge, where, he says, his constant liability to interruption and distractions (such as concerts) is an awful hindrance. Secondly he feels that he has no right to live in an antipathetic world (and of course to him very few people are sympathetic)—a world where he perpetually finds himself feeling contempt for others, and irritating others by his nervous temperament—without some justification for that contempt etc: such as being a really great man and having done really great work... He has not definitely made up his mind—but there is great probability of his adopting the scheme eventually. (Diary 24.9.13)

Some sign of hesitation is to be seen in the fact that on the next day he worked with David on a paper which was to form the introductory lecture of the course to be given at the Working Men's College (see p. 170 above).

Perhaps the arrangements for, or as it turned out the cancellation of, this course was part of the business he had to deal with in London in early October. He arrived in Cambridge on 2 October and at once told both Moore and Russell of his firm intention to leave Cambridge and retire to Norway. In an anecdotal letter (not to Lady Ottoline) Russell described what followed:

Then my Austrian, Wittgenstein, burst in like a whirlwind, just back from Norway, and determined to return there at once to live in complete solitude until he has solved *all* the problems of logic. I said it would be dark, and he said he hated daylight. I said it would be lonely, and he said he prostituted his mind talking to intelligent people. I said he was mad, and he said God preserve him from sanity. (God certainly will.) Now Wittgenstein, during August and September, had done work on logic, still rather in the rough, but as good, in my opinion, as any work that ever had been done in logic by anyone. But his artistic conscience prevents him from writing anything until he has got it perfect, and I am persuaded he will commit suicide in February. What was I to do? He told me his ideas, but they were so subtle that I kept on forgetting them. I begged him to write them out, and he tried, but after much groaning said it was absolutely impossible. At last I made him talk in the presence of a short-hand writer, and so secured some record of his ideas. This business took up the whole of my time and thought for about a week. (BR to Lucy Mary Donnelly, 19.10.13)[3]

Russell liked nothing better than a good story—or, at any rate, than telling a good story. In his *Autobiography* he gives an even more syncopated version:

> At the beginning of 1914 he came to me in a state of great agitation and said: 'I am leaving Cambridge, I am leaving Cambridge at once.' 'Why?' I asked. 'Because my brother-in-law has come to live in London, and I can't bear to be so near him.' So he spent the rest of the winter in the far north of Norway.[4]

Moore's diary, Russell's letters to Lady Ottoline, and Wittgenstein's to Russell all are not only silent about, but seem to preclude, a visit to Cambridge at the turn of the year. So Russell, looking back over seventeen years, has probably misplaced the October conversation. The selection from it of a colourful detail not mentioned to Lucy Mary Donnelly is a trick of memory or of style. As a fact, Gretl and her husband Jerome Stonborough did move to Besselsleigh, a large country house near Oxford, about this time and Wittgenstein did deeply disapprove of his brother-in-law. The idealistic young beauty had married an American, rich (though not richer than she), cultivated, an amateur scientist (he provided his own laboratory); like her father in his preference for a grand style of life and his ability to impose himself on any gathering and to alter its tone by the force of his personality. Later, certainly, her family resented his dominance and she suffered from the moroseness of his temperament. Eventually they lived almost always apart. Fleeing all contacts, Wittgenstein may have mentioned this one in particular.

The need to work undistracted is a sufficiently rational motive and in the event Wittgenstein did achieve much during this stay in Norway, but the other arguments mentioned, even to Pinsent, seem more like pretexts covering a retreat from his friends. We are reminded of his father's running away from home; and we note a pattern in Wittgenstein's own life—away from home to Linz (as far west as possible); away from Berlin ('Enough!' *Nichts mehr davon!*) apparently when too great emotional demands were made; he was to quit his family later for reasons within

3. Mr Kenneth Blackwell kindly provided me with a copy of this letter: he comments on it in *Russell*, 197. The whole series of events is discussed, on the basis of somewhat inadequate information in my 'Bertrand Russell and Ludwig Wittgenstein's "Notes on Logic"' in *Revue Internationale de Philosophie* 102 (1972).

4. This section of the autobiography seems to have been written about 1931. There is some reference (see p.96) to revisions in 1949, but throughout the text of the autobiography there is no reference to any event involving Wittgenstein later than the publication of Julian Bell's skit, in 1930.

himself, going into lodgings, or into a gardening job, or an obscure village; there was to be another migration to Norway; he was to leave a wartime job in Newcastle not in order to return to Cambridge but to live in comparative isolation in Swansea; then towards the end of his life he resigned his chair and sought more and more remote parts of Ireland. Sometimes these retreats were productive—essentially we owe what is now called *Philosophical Investigations* to those of 1936 (to Norway) and 1944 (to Swansea)—but not always. No doubt many different factors influenced these distinct occasions, but it seems likely that on each of them the need to be relieved of the pressure of human relationships played an important part. Surely it was so in 1913–14. During that year in Norway he quarrelled with two of his best friends and it is probable that he deliberately made no provision for David to visit him in the course of the year. These retreats had the same complex motivation as the neat parcelling of his life between various friends and activities, the beginnings of which we have already observed. To be sure, too much intimacy was a hindrance to work; but perhaps it was also important that work could serve as a hindrance to too much intimacy.

Wittgenstein arrived in England on 1 and left on 11 October. Into this time he fitted five or six long conversations with Russell and two or three with Moore. Russell as usual was divided between exasperation and admiration:

> He is more intellectually intimate to me than anyone I have ever met, and yet I shall be thankful to see him go. (BR to OM 8.10.13)

Wittgenstein's plan of going to Norway did not on reflection seem too bad, Russell thought. He would come back when he had written something and finish his residence for his degree, and thus qualify to be Russell's successor. Meanwhile Russell attempted to secure a record of what Wittgenstein had already achieved. There were apparently at least two sessions with stenographers—one in Birmingham[5] with a German stenographer, another in Cambridge with a secretary of P.E.B. Jourdain's. Russell himself tried to write down some of Wittgenstein's remarks; and of the four manuscript translations in the Bertrand Russell Archive it is likely that some are translations of words dictated to Russell and some translations of manuscripts actually written by Wittgenstein, though it is impossible to tell which. At all events, we have from these eight days seven pages of typescript and 23 pages of manuscript (Russell's translation of Wittgenstein's German), constituting *Logic* or *Notes on Logic*, Wittgenstein's first philosophic work. As will appear

5. Russell's letter to Lady Ottoline of 9 October mentions that Wittgenstein was spending that day dictating in German in Birmingham. This confirms Russell's recollections of 1958, expressed in a letter to J.P. Griffin, see *RIP* 102 (1972).

shortly Russell's translation and ordering of the material into the form it has in the 1960 edition of *Notebooks 1914–16* was done only in February 1914, but essentially the work dates from the autumn of 1913. The content is a matter for later discussion, the method of composition should be remarked on immediately: Wittgenstein had notebooks in which he wrote down from day to day the end-result of his thoughts. From these notebooks he would select and dictate, or select and compose. The *Summary* (seven pages of typescript evidently based on the dictation in English of 9 October) contains rather syncopated versions of remarks that reappear in the *Tractatus*: Wittgentein must have been either translating freely from, or recollecting, his notebook formulations. The four manuscripts translated by Russell contain a number of propositions which in the German original must have taken almost exactly the form that we find again in the *Tractatus*.[6] It is natural to suppose that Wittgenstein kept the notebooks from which he read out or copied these remarks and that they were among the notebooks from which he eventually selected the remarks of the *Tractatus* itself.[7]

Wittgenstein's furniture, his books, and some of his papers were put in store; a casket with contents of real or sentimental value was entrusted to Russell; Moore made ready to move back into the abandoned set in Whewell's Court. Wittgenstein's Cambridge life was wound up, for longer even than he supposed, and on the 11th he left London for Norway.

He will have been in Bergen by Tuesday 14th. It seems he had thought of going to the Lofoten islands in the far north[8] (hence no doubt, Russell's remarks about how dark it would be). So hasty were his plans that the inn where he had meant to stay turned out to be closed for the winter. He contented himself with going as far north as Skjolden, deep inside Sognefjord, north of Bergen.

So far as we know, pure chance took him to that particular spot. Even if he had been in Norway before (as Engelmann believed),[9] this was the first stay in Skjolden that his friends there recall. Skjolden was to provide him with a hermitage throughout his life. It was a small commune in the

6. For an illustration of this see *RIP* 102 (1972) 451.

7. See G.H. von Wright's 'Origin of Wittgenstein's *Tractatus*' in *Prototractatus*. Von Wright quotes from a letter of Paul Engelmann's to F.A. von Hayek: 'His manuscript volumes were large office-books bound in black and green striped cloth, of the kind used in Austria as ledgers... The Tractatus is the final selection from seven books of this kind, which he destroyed after the appearance of the book.' My conjecture is that at least one of these notebooks contained *Notes on Logic* material, and it seems to be more probable that this material was copied out of a notebook than copied into one.

8. See LW to BR 17.10.13, with the notes in *Briefe* p.35.

9. Engelmann (in a letter to Hayek) argued that Wittgenstein had been in Norway in early 1911, because Wittgenstein told him he had read in Norway a poem in fact published in *Die Fackel* in February 1911. A visit in February is highly improbable: we have seen that Manchester University re-elected Wittgenstein to his Research Studentship in 1911, which is scarcely compatible with absence during the preceding academic year. Any stay must have been a short one (no Norwegian, or little, was learnt—see LW to BR 29.10.13).

furthest recess of the largest fjord in Norway. Beyond it were the mountains and the great glacier. All who have been there speak of the contrast between the black waters of the main fjord and the blues and greens of the various lakes and inlets. For long stretches trackless mountains come down to the water's edge. In level patches there would be stands of conifers, scattered houses, then mostly wooden, and pasture and fruit-trees both yielding richly in the startling summer of that latitude. Again and again in his letters from Norway Wittgenstein mentions the view. Engelmann singles out Norway before the war as an occasion when Wittgenstein's surroundings mattered a great deal to him,[10] and in 1936 Wittgenstein wrote to Moore,

> I can't imagine that I could have worked anywhere as I do here. It's the quiet and, perhaps, the wonderful scenery; I mean its quiet seriousness. (LW to GEM October 1936)

New roads have made it slightly more accessible, but when Moore came in March 1914 Wittgenstein and he took a train from Bergen to Myrdal, ski-ed[11] to 'Fua' (perhaps Flåm is meant, for they spent the night there in an hotel kept open specially for them!) then by steamer to Sogndal, then by skis to Solvron, thence by motor-boat to Skjolden.

The circumstances of Wittgenstein's life there are not altogether clear. Curiously enough he gave 'c/o Halvard [really Halvar] Draegni' as his address, but as he explains to Russell in the same letter he had got 'two nice rooms here in the Postmaster's house' and was being looked after very well indeed. Hans Klingenberg, the postmaster, was regarded as a man of some education. His son is now a schoolmaster in Skjolden and his daughter followed him in the local post office. The Draegni family had a factory where fruit-juice was bottled. When Moore was there (and presumably at other times of which we have no record), Wittgenstein would go to their house to make music. One of the Draegnis— Arne—was a particular friend. Friends too were Arne Bolstad, later a market-gardener, a mere boy in 1913, when, however, he saw a fair amount of Wittgenstein, and Anna Rebni, a schoolmistress who, later at any rate, put up summer visitors on her farm some way from the town. They seem to have played in Wittgenstein's life the role of quiet, simple people, with modest needs and education and means, honest and plain-dealing Tolstoyan figures. Only with Anna Rebni (whom he respected greatly) have we any trace—and that much later—of the

---

10. *Letters from Ludwig Wittgenstein with a Memoir*, p.60: Engelmann perhaps underestimates the importance of physical surroundings to Wittgenstein. His love of the Cambridge and Vienna water-meadows; his choosing to live in a tower; his journeys to remote parts of Ireland are all examples of a certain taste for quietness.

11. In his diary Moore appears to speak of 'skyds'. Perhaps some form of sledge is meant.

storms that usually punctuated his friendships. In the course of his life Wittgenstein learnt to speak Norwegian well, as well as being able to read the literary language of Ibsen and Bjoernson: it is natural to assume that he acquired most of this facility during that first year.

All the same, we have seen his own statement that he hardly met a soul, and his time in Skjolden must have been a great contrast to the years in Cambridge. After a fortnight's influenza, he found it an ideal place to work in:

> All sorts of new logical stuff seems to be growing in me, but I can't yet write about it. (LW to BR [November 1913])

New ideas were pressing in on him so fast that he had hardly the time or the patience to answer the questions Russell put to him about the result of his week's dictation and discussion in England. Russell sent Wittgenstein a typescript with some questions about it and also asked questions about a manuscript. Evidently the typescript was the result of the dictation to Jourdain's secretary and is still preserved as the nine-page 'Summary' in Russell's version of the *Notes on Logic* mentioned above, while the manuscript was the German original of some of the material now represented by the four manuscript translations in the Bertrand Russell Archives.[12] Russell was fascinated by the work: he made Whitehead read it—along with an exegesis by himself (now apparently lost)[13] and Whitehead thought just as well of it. But Wittgenstein was moving on to new problems: he struggled with identity; he discovered, as we shall see, his decision procedure for the propositional calculus—he thought that it would fairly easily apply to the whole of logical truth; quite incidentally he brushed aside the axioms of infinity and of reducibility. It was a time for talking about the fundamental question, the big problem:

> I wish to God that I were more intelligent and everything would finally become clear to me—or else that I needn't live much longer!... It's extraordinary, isn't it, what a huge and infinitely strange subject logic is? Neither you nor I knew that, I think, a year and a half ago. (LW to BR 15.12.13)

Wittgenstein was by now writing to Russell in German. No doubt the October conversations about his work had convinced him at last of Russell's mastery of that language. At first he hesitated, uncertain

---

12. The questions that Wittgenstein reminds Russell of in R.21 and answers in R.20, so numbered in *Letters to RKM*, both probably early November 1913, can easily be related to the Summary and to the 3rd and 4th Mss (so-called).

13. BR to OM 18.10.13.

whether to call Russell *Sie* or *Du* but Russell, as might be expected, quickly solved this problem for him. He depended enormously on Russell's letters—'Write *soon*!', he would say, 'Every letter of yours gives me infinite pleasure!', 'Your letters are a great boon to me. Do not feel sorry for writing to me so often.' 'Pray for me and God bless you! (If there is such a thing.)'[14] Russell was the recipient of his hopes and fears as well as of his thoughts. For his part Russell confided often in Lady Ottoline how relieved he was that Wittgenstein was away, yet he also sent her Wittgenstein's letters, to get her impression of Wittgenstein's state, or reported how Wittgenstein seemed. Wittgenstein was in his thoughts because he could not get over the criticism of *Theory of Knowledge* and because he was concerned about Wittgenstein's spiritual and mental health, but one has the impression once again that he was not involved with Wittgenstein in the way Wittgenstein was with him. Wittgenstein was conducting, in parallel, a correspondence with Frege.[15] It is another instance of his liking for keeping friends in separate compartments that he did not tell Russell of this correspondence nor of the visit he planned to Jena, though it was planned as early as 22 October. To Russell he only said that unfortunately he had to visit Vienna and his mother at Christmas. The fact that he also wanted to communicate his results to Frege en route, just as he had done earlier to Russell, was not mentioned. At least three letters preceded the visit: the first prompted the objection from Frege that Wittgenstein placed too much weight on *Bezeichnung* (perhaps *mode of* signification is meant): Wittgenstein replied with remarks on what was requisite for setting up a list of fundamental concepts for logic—no doubt he here brought in his objections to an interdefinable set of primitive signs, which appear in *Tractatus* 5.42 but can be traced back to 1913. A further letter (29 November 1913) brought what Scholz thought important objections against Frege's theory of truth particularly in connexion with the assignment of meaning to functions—read 'truth-functions' and we have here an anticipation of *Tractatus* 4.431. The visit followed ('before Christmas' according to Frege, hence presumably en route to Vienna): it was of great interest to Frege. He took down Wittgenstein's views in four pages of handwriting and wrote four sides of a letter continuing their discussion. We find him seeking Wittgenstein's address from Jourdain at the end of January—Wittgenstein must have been oddly silent about his intention to return to Norway. Jourdain seems not to have replied until

---

14. LW to BR October–December 1913, R.19–23.

15. What Frege retained was destroyed in the war and we only have Heinrich Scholz's notes on its general nature. Wittgenstein retained some of Frege's letters until at least 1936, when he declined to make them available to Scholz, saying that they had an *Erinnerungswert* for himself—a sentimental value—but were of no general interest. None have been found among his papers.

April, so that the correspondence, having faltered, was probably not renewed until after the war.[16]

Here we must revert to the account of his visits to Frege that Wittgenstein gave to R.L. Goodstein. After the visit from Manchester:

> Wittgenstein returned to England very disheartened, but a year later he sought another interview with Frege and this time he 'wiped the floor with Frege, and though they met for tea many times after they never discussed philosophy again'.[17]

Memory is impressionistic and an anecdote aspires to point, not perspective. We have seen that the first meeting did not result solely in discouragement. We must now observe that, though a certain reversal of roles may have taken place, it was, in the first place, over three visits, not two; since there was a visit in 1912 which Wittgenstein at the time described in terms that exclude a feeling of defeat on either side.[18] And even this third visit did not in fact give Frege a distaste for further discussion with Wittgenstein. We have seen that by his account given to Geach Wittgenstein was never allowed to discuss anything *except* philosophy with Frege;[19] and that the last conversational interchange between the two was about whether it was easy to think of numbers as objects. (It is quite possible, by the way, that this last interchange took place in 1913. No later visit is attested and the one planned for December 1919 did not in fact take place.)

It is idle to try to reconstruct the exact sequence of events in 1913. Probably Wittgenstein's account to Goodstein reflects his youthful certainty about his new solution set against Frege's habits of reserve and Frege's need to think over a new set of ideas. What it does not reflect—the perspective which only other anecdotes and remarks can give—is the enormous respect Wittgenstein retained for Frege, a respect which may have been partly owed to the fact that Frege did not belong to the Cambridge world of brisk and sometimes rather knockabout discussions.

From Frege Wittgenstein went to Vienna. The visit could not be avoided:

16. This reconstruction of the correspondence is based on Scholz's notes on items (a) to (f) in the Wittgenstein-Frege correspondence he had available to him; and also on the Jourdain-Frege correspondence where it is preserved or Scholz's notes on it where it is not. See Frege, *Briefwechsel* (1972), pp.264–8 and *Philosophical and Mathematical Correspondence* (1980), pp.109–33.

17. In *Ludwig Wittgenstein: Philosophy and Language* (1972), edd. Alice Ambrose and M. Lazerowitz, pp. 271ff. See also pp. 75 and 83 above.

18. See p. 74 above. 'I had a long discussion with Frege about our Theory of Symbolism of which, I think, he roughly understood the general outline. He said he would think the matter over.' LW to BR 26.11.12.

19. See p. 83 above.

The fact is, my mother very much wants me to, so much so that she would be grievously offended if I did not come; and she has such bad memories of just this time last year that I have not the heart to stay away. (LW to BR [November–December 1913])

Despite the anniversary of his father's death Wittgenstein had made some half-hearted attempts to stay away, telling his mother that he would have to use skis for a good part of the journey. To judge by his later life it was unusual for him even to think of being away from the family at Christmas: later memories are all of his last-minute irruption shedding presents. On this occasion, too, there is no doubt that he, the last-born, the gentlest of her surviving sons, will have sat with his mother, as was his custom, while she made music or while he read to her. But the cost was great. His mother, at best, was someone he had to support, not a source of strength to him. Last year his father's last illness had 'lamed his thoughts'; now, without that object of concentration, 'life among people' made work impossible for him. While still in Norway, he had thought he was going mad, the slow progress of his work had lowered his spirits, he had longed for everything to become clear to him or else for death to overtake him. There his whole life had seemed summed up in his work. Sometimes he thought he could do nothing, at other times that he would make a little progress and then be finished—then die, that is, and have his work published for him by Russell. Now back among his family he felt that his problems were not simply those of logic but ones rooted in himself. Back at home and quite unproductive, hoping only for a return to his solitude, he described his state to Russell:

Here I feel different every day. Sometimes things inside me are in such a ferment that I think I am going mad: then the next day I am totally apathetic again. But deep inside me there's a perpetual seething, like the bottom of a geyser, and I keep on hoping that things will come to an eruption once and for all, so that I can ... into a different person. I can't write you anything about logic today. Perhaps you regard this thinking about myself as a waste of time—but how can I be a logician before I'm a human being! *Far* the most important thing is to settle accounts with myself![20]

He gave a second account of the effect of the visit after his return:

20. LW to BR ?December 1913 (*Briefe*, 1980, pp.47–8); previously dated to June/July 1914 but it seems to suit his Christmas mood and to precede the January letter ('once again no logical news'). R. Rhees (ed.): *Recollections of Wittgenstein*[2] (1984), p.191n questions my translation of the last phrase—*mit mir selbst in's Reine kommen*. Perhaps it would be better to say 'to put my own house in order' (metaphorically understood, of course).

It is VERY sad, but I have once again no logical news for you. The reason
is that things have gone terribly badly for me in the last weeks. (A result of
my 'holidays' in Vienna.) Every day I was tormented by a frightful *Angst*
and by depression in turns and even in the intervals I was so exhausted
that I wasn't able to think of doing a bit of work. It's terrifying beyond all
description the kinds of mental torment that there can be! It wasn't until
two days ago that I could hear the voice of reason over the howls of the
damned and I began to work again. And *perhaps* I'll get better now and be
able to produce something decent. But I *never* knew what it meant to feel
only one step away from madness. —Let's hope for the best! (LW to BR
[January 1914])

Yet there is a striking parallel between his problems with his personality
and his problems with logic. The ferment in him is sometimes clearly
psychological, whereas at other times it slips over into 'the big question'.
The parallelism is a theme that runs through his notebooks and letters
'Logic *and* his sins', we have seen already, could preoccupy him at the
same time (p. 156 above). What he looked for in philosophy was *das
erlösende Wort*—the formulation that would solve a problem, but also the
word of redemption, the word that would deliver us from evil.[21]
Conversion in its various senses is what he wanted both in logic and in
life. *The* fundamental problem of logic had to be solved and he had to
become a new person. In quite what respects, we can only guess: his aim
was to be simple, direct, fundamental, understanding, strong; above all
to be himself, not to be pretending to be any of these things. Yet other
people, his family, precisely those for whom these qualities were needed,
induced feelings in conflict with all these ideals, feelings which could at
best be concealed. As to why these problems were felt particularly
acutely at this time, it is natural to suppose that his father while alive
had provided a framework of expectations within which Ludwig could
live: now he was forced to define his own personality in a largely female
family to whose standards he did not feel ready to submit. We shall
return more than once to the parallel between his emotional moral life
and his philosophical development.

   As usual in his case, the difficulty of making sense of the events of this
year in Wittgenstein's life is not so much the nature of the stimulus as the
intensity and violence of the response. Other men have reached maturity
just as their fathers died. Other men have felt compelled to remove from
their families and from environments which were their families writ
large. Other men even, though few, have suffered the throes of seeming
to see the answer to some great question and of struggling to formulate it.
These things are inseparable from life, work, and growth; and most men
are sustained by the positive elements in them. Not so Wittgenstein,

21. For *das erlösende Wort* see *Notebooks* 20.1.15.

whose thoughts turned to suicide more than ever during this year and who, in an unhappiness that was quite clearly more than theatrical, struck at the roots of friendships that supported him.

The first friendship to be assailed was that with Russell: a year after losing one father, he rejected another. It is impossible now to say which of the gods brought them into contention. Russell blamed himself: 'I have been too sharp with him,' he wrote to Lady Ottoline when he reported (obviously) the receipt of Wittgenstein's letter of January or February 1914 quoted at length below. Wittgenstein had written an earlier letter, now apparently lost, which tried at great length to resolve fundamental differences between the two men: and perhaps it was Russell's reply to this that was feared to be 'too sharp'. The best guess one can make is that the matter concerned in the first instance Russell's lectures in America (later published under the title *Our Knowledge of the External World*).

> Perhaps they will give you [Wittgenstein had written] at any rate a more favourable opportunity than usual to tell them your *thoughts* and not *just* cut and dried results. (LW to BR [January 1914])

Perhaps this remark drew from Russell some comments on the contrast between his own readiness to publish and the perfectionism that kept Wittgenstein from completing any piece of work. Or Russell may have touched on one of the points concerning which (as we have already seen) he was critical of Wittgenstein—narrowness, intolerance, excessive absorption in thinking about himself. At all events, in order to understand the significance of the episode it is important to remember that contemporary documents show Russell to have felt indeed some impatience and even some resentment towards Wittgenstein but to have thought of him with a constant anxious affection and with some perception. We ought not to be guided by Wittgenstein's letters alone; still less by the tone of Russell's much later comments.

Whatever the occasion of the quarrel—*der Streit* as Wittgenstein called it—Russell asked Wittgenstein to behave as if nothing had happened. Wittgenstein replied:

> But I can't possibly carry out your request...: that would go clean contrary to my nature. *So forgive me for this long letter* and remember that I *have to* follow my nature just as much as you. During the last week I have thought a lot about our relationship and I have come to the conclusion that we really don't suit one another. *This is not meant as a reproach!* either for you or for me. But it is a fact. We've often had uncomfortable conversations with one another when certain subjects came up. And the uncomfortableness was not a consequence of ill humour on one side or the

other but of enormous differences in our natures. I beg you most earnestly not to think I want to reproach you in any way or to preach you a sermon. I only want to put our relationship in clear terms *in order to draw a conclusion.* —Our latest quarrel, too, was certainly not simply a result of your sensitiveness or my inconsiderateness. It came from deeper—from the fact that my letter must have shown you how totally different our ideas are, E.G. of the value of a scientific work. It was, of course, stupid of me to have written to you at such length about this matter: I ought to have told myself that such fundamental differences cannot be resolved by a letter. And this is just *one* instance out of *many.* Now, as I'm writing this in complete calm, I can see perfectly well that your value-judgements are just as good and just as deep-seated in you as mine in me, and that I have no right to catechize you. But I see equally clearly, now, that for that very reason there cannot be any real relation of friendship between us. *I shall be grateful to you and devoted to you with all my heart for the whole of my life, but I shall not write to you again and you will not see me again either.* Now that I am once again reconciled with you I want to part from you *in peace* so that we shan't some time get annoyed with one another again and then perhaps part as enemies. I wish you everything of the best and I beg you not to forget me and to think of me often *with friendly feelings.* Goodbye!

> Yours *ever*
> Ludwig Wittgenstein[22]

I dare say his mood will change after a while [Russell commented]. I find I don't care on his account, but only for the sake of Logic. And yet I believe I do really care too much to look at it. (BR to OM 19.2.14)

And indeed Russell did write again, hoping Wittgenstein would relent: a letter that touched even that severe judge:

Dear Russell,

Your letter was *so* full of kindness and friendship that I don't think I have the *right* to leave it unanswered. So I have to break my resolution. Unfortunately, however, I can't put what I have to say to you in a few words and I have scarcely any hope that you'll really understand me. The chief thing, I must tell you again, is that our quarrels don't arise *just* from external reasons such as nervousness or over-tiredness but are—at any rate on *my* side—*very* deep-rooted. You may be right in saying that we ourselves are not so very different, but our ideals could not be more so. And that's why we haven't been able and we shan't *ever* be able to talk about anything involving our value-judgments without either becoming hypocritical or falling out. *I think this is incontestable*; I had noticed it a long time ago; and it was frightful for me, because it tainted our relations with one another: we seemed to be sitting side by side in a marsh. The fact is, we

---

22. LW to BR February 1914, *Briefe* (1980), p.50. The heavily emphasized 'E.G.' in the middle of the letter suggests that it was indeed some instance of diverging professional standards which occasioned the quarrel and was then taken by Wittgenstein as symptomatic of fundamental differences.

both of us have weaknesses, but especially *I* have, and my life is *FULL* of the ugliest and pettiest thoughts imaginable (this is *not* an exaggeration). But if a relationship is not to be degrading for both sides then it should not be a relationship between the weaknesses on either side. No: a relationship should be confined to areas where both people involved have clean hands, i.e. where each can be completely frank without hurting the other. And that's something *we* can do ONLY by restricting our relationship to the communication of facts capable of being established objectively, with perhaps also some mention of our friendly feelings for one another. But any other subject will lead, in our case, to hypocrisy or to falling out. Now perhaps, you'll say, 'Things have more or less worked, up to the present. Why not go on in the same way?' But I'm *too* tired of this constant sordid compromise. My life has been one nasty mess so far—but need that go on indefinitely? —Now, I'll make a proposal to you: let's write to each other about our work, our health, and the like, but let's avoid in our communications any kind of value-judgment, on any subject whatsoever, and let's recognize clearly that in such judgements neither of us could be *completely* honest without hurting the other (this is certainly true in my case, at any rate). I don't need to assure you of my deep affection for you, *but that affection would be in great danger if we were to continue with a relationship based on hypocrisy and for that reason a source of shame to us both.* No, I think the honourable thing for both of us would be if we continued it on a more genuine basis. —I beg you to think this over and to send me an answer only when you can do it without bitterness. Feel assured in any case of my love and loyalty. I only hope you may understand this letter as it is meant to be understood.

Yours ever
L.W.
(LW to BR 3.3.14)

The quarrel was made up but the friendship was ended: Wittgenstein would no longer lay bare his heart to Russell. Their correspondence would indeed contain some warm expressions of regard, but the content of it would be philosophical or factual rather than personal.[23] Relations between the two men did not become bad—there was still to be a good deal of collaboration. Perhaps later there were harsher judgements on both sides but the correspondence and some reported conversations show that, within human limits, Wittgenstein did maintain the promised attitude of gratitude and loyalty.[24]

23. I am assuming the dating of the the 'geyser' letter argued for in fn. 20 above. Russell's attitude can be gauged from his letter to Wittgenstein of 5 February 1915; from a wartime letter to Wittgenstein's mother; and from a number of references to Wittgenstein in his letters to Lady Ottoline.

24. This is perhaps the place to comment on Ronald Clarke's remark that Russell and Wittgenstein did not get on at least partly because Russell disapproved of Wittgenstein's homosexuality (*Life of Bertrand Russell* (1975), p.172). What Russell is said to have said, forty years later, is slender evidence; and every contemporary indication speaks against it. It was Wittgenstein who ended the friendship and at a time when he was alone and evidently not in a homosexual

The year in Norway was a crucial one also for Wittgenstein's relation with Moore. Moore, as so often in his life, was miserable about his work and told Wittgenstein so. He got a kind reply:

> I think the cause of it is that you don't regularly discuss your stuff with anybody who is not yet stale and is really interested in the subject. And I believe that at present there is no such person up at Cambridge. Even Russell—who is of course most extraordinarily fresh for his age—is no more pliable enough for *this* purpose. (LW to GEM 19.11.13)

They ought to have regular discussions when Moore made his planned Easter visit to Norway. (Moore had 'rashly'—to use his own word—promised such a visit when Wittgenstein left in October.) The prospect frightened Moore—as indeed did many aspects of his friendship with Wittgenstein. At first he neglected to send an account of Johnson's paper at the Moral Sciences Club. Then when he did respond (at great length) to Wittgenstein's reminder, he was 'afraid to open' Wittgenstein's reply, though 'very pleased' when he did so. This was the letter of 18 February again urging him to come. Moore set himself to find out from Russell what Wittgenstein's latest views on logic were. It was an opportune moment to do so, for Russell had just finished 'translating and copying and classifying the notes of Wittgenstein's work'—clearly those taken down or written in the autumn (see pp. 186f. above) in preparation for his lectures on logic at Harvard. Russell thought of Moore as going to visit Wittgenstein in the hope of understanding him.[25] G.H. Hardy was also drawn into the discussions. None the less Moore's nerve failed him again (it seems) and he offered the excuse of a paper he had to write.

> Wittgenstein's telegram asking me to do paper there makes me very uncomfortable ... write Wittgenstein. (Diary 10.3.14)

What Wittgenstein proposed and how he attempted to put Moore's mind at rest can be seen from his letter presumably sent off at the same time as the telegram:

> Why on earth won't you do your paper *here*? You shall have *a sitting-room* with a splendid view ALL BY YOURSELF and I shall leave you alone as much as you like (*in fact the whole day if necessary*). On the other hand we

relation with anyone. Russell spoke frankly to Lady Ottoline both of Wittgenstein's faults and of men's being in love with one another when for some reason he found it irksome (see e.g. p. 118 above): he never combines the two themes. His comment on Pinsent and Wittgenstein's 'talking to one another and ignoring the rest of the world' at one of his evenings (BR to OM 16.5.13) sounds amused rather than embittered. As for whether Wittgenstein was generally regarded as a homosexual, see p. 150 above, from which it is apparent that kind friends were quicker to suspect Russell of jealousy than Wittgenstein of intrigue.

25. BR to OM 28.2.14.

could see one another whenever both of us would like to. And we *could* even
talk over your business (which *might* be fun). Or do you want *so* many
books? You see—I've PLENTY to do myself, so I shan't disturb you a bit.
(LW to GEM March 1914)

Moore's apprehensions are easily enough explained: we have seen
how he was apt to find or to fancy Wittgenstein disgusted or
disapproving. He was in any case a shy and sensitive man, not easily able
to support weeks of constant contact with another single human
being—he had done it for years in Edinburgh with a great friend
(Ainsworth), but we know of no other example before his marriage.
Finally he had presumably already heard of the quarrel with Russell (he
told Curle—another great friend—about it 'perhaps indiscreetly' in
May, and Russell was in America from early March).

Whatever their cause, the apprehensions were overcome. Moore left,
by way of Newcastle, on 24 March. After much sea-sickness he arrived at
Bergen at 10 p.m. on 26 March and was met by Wittgenstein, who
talked, so Moore's diary puts it, till 1 a.m.[26] They stayed in Bergen
another day, shopping in the morning; then Wittgenstein talked till 6.30
p.m. More shopping and dinner till 8: 'he abuses me till 12.15.' A strange
reception, it may seem, for a guest: a stranger still reaction from an older
man to a younger. It is as if all Wittgenstein's moral force had been
banked up over the winter and was now loosed irresistibly on Moore. But
indeed at all times Wittgenstein had the power to make others suffer
under the awareness not of his superiority but of their own shortcomings.

They left the next day, a Saturday, by the route already described
(p. 188 above). Discussion was endless: physical things, Plato, suicide,
misfortune, the bad. And so to Skjolden, where Moore unpacked and
established himself in the hotel—with his sitting-room no doubt. At this
point his nature rebelled: they walked by the lake that evening and
quarrelled; and Moore (whom later only philosophy could anger) lost his
temper.

Moore was to stay in the little town for a fortnight. Generally he
would work in his hotel until 2, when he would go to Wittgenstein's
lodgings for dinner. Then there would be discussion ('*he* discusses,'
Moore says in his diary) until 5, when tea would be brought. Then they
would go for a walk or first play the piano. For the remainder of the
evening Wittgenstein would talk. Visits were exchanged with the
Draegnis (father and son), partly for the purpose of piano-playing; and
no doubt the four-handed arrangement of Brahms's *Schicksalslied* that
Moore had been asked to bring was then used. With Wittgenstein alone
Moore seems to have played Schubert, as usual. One boat-trip on the

26. These details are all taken from Moore's diary. Comparison with the letters shows that the
visit occurred a week later than Wittgenstein originally planned it.

fjord was made. The passive role accepted by Moore, or at any rate allotted to himself in his diary, will again be noted. In one respect it bore fruit: from 1 April on Moore began writing to dictation. 'Wittgenstein on Logic' fills two small exercise books full and a few pages of a third; it is now printed in the volume entitled *Notebooks 1914–16*. Its content falls to be discussed later along with that of *Notes on Logic*. For present purposes it is only necessary to say that it was an advance on those notes, both in being better organized or more fully organized by Wittgenstein himself; and in introducing new notions which carried forward and made it possible to clarify the account of logic implicit in those notes. The most important of those new notions were those of tautology itself and (a key notion, perhaps even throughout Wittgenstein's philosophical life) of what is shown rather than said by a proposition:

Logical so-called propositions *show the logical properties of language and therefore of the Universe, but say* nothing

is the opening of the first exercise book. The novelty of the notes dictated to Moore; and the circumstance that they seem to have arisen partly out of questions which worried Moore, Russell, and Hardy are important for understanding what followed.

At the end of the fortnight Wittgenstein, with his usual good manners, took Moore back the two-day journey to Bergen and saw him off on the boat, after champagne for their parting supper and endless talks. By the 17th Moore was again in Trinity:

Cambridge at 2½. Unpack; bath; shop etc. till Hall. Hall at end next Capstick, MacTaggart opposite. Read New Statesman. (Diary 17.4.14)

A don's life.

Ten days later Moore met W.M. Fletcher in Hall. We have mentioned Fletcher already as Wittgenstein's tutor. This time Moore congratulated him—either on his Sc.D. degree or on his appointment as secretary of the newly formed Medical Research Council (both occurred about this time). He also put to Fletcher a question about Wittgenstein which we can reconstruct as being the question whether Wittgenstein's treatise on logic would serve as the dissertation required of a Research Student if he was to obtain the B.A. degree. He wrote off the next day to Wittgenstein and on 11 May got the following reply:

Your letter annoyed me. When I wrote Logik I didn't consult the Regulations, and therefore I think it would only be fair if you gave me my degree without consulting them so much either! As to a Preface and Notes;

I think my examiners will easily see how much I have cribbed from Bosanquet. —If I'm not worth your making an exception for me *even in some* STUPID *details* then I may as well go to Hell directly; and if I *am* worth it and you don't do it then—by God—you might go there. (LW to GEM 7.5.14)

A breathing example of the directness and rudeness of which Wittgenstein's friends sometimes spoke: an example too, we are bound to think, of paranoia and lack of proportion. For the facts were these: the regulations required an applicant

to state, generally in a preface to his dissertation and specifically in notes, the sources from which his information is derived, the extent to which he has availed himself of the work of others and the portions of the dissertation which he claims as original.

Moore had not framed these regulations, nor was it his office to enforce them; he was merely reporting the view taken of them by an experienced university administrator. He may, of course, have seemed lukewarm or despondent or detached in his letter to Wittgenstein: it was often to be a cause of offence to Wittgenstein that his English friends seemed to put rules and procedures before the claims of friendship. Every Austrian is an exception and Wittgenstein was an exception even among Austrians.

Moore was shattered:

Wittgenstein's letter at lunch: makes me feel sick and can't get it out of my head. Very miserable first part of walk. . . . (Diary 11.5.14)

Walk Parallelogram [Moore's quaint name for one of his usual walks]: still can't help thinking of Wittgenstein's letter. (ibid. 12.5.14)

Concert $3\frac{1}{2}$–$4\frac{1}{2}$ then think of Wittgenstein's letter till Hall ... Go on thinking of Wittgenstein before and after Hardy's lecture. (ibid. 13.5.14)

Walk Madingley $2\frac{1}{4}$–$4\frac{1}{2}$, very pleasant but can't help thinking of Wittgenstein's letter first half. . . (ibid. 14.5.14)

Békássy comes to tea ... asks about Wittgenstein's logic. Hall between Fletcher and Hardy: ask Fletcher about Wittgenstein. (ibid. 15.5.14)

A fortnight later Moore had his great friend Curle to stay and the talk was chiefly about Wittgenstein (this was when he repeated the story of Russell's quarrel). Somewhat similarly we find him in October (though of course many things had changed by then) telling Desmond MacCarthy 'all about Wittgenstein'. The excerpts, like Russell's letters, show how far Wittgenstein was from being neglected or forgotten or held in low esteem by them all. They also show the inadequacy of Moore—the older man—to deal with so passionate a friend. Fifteen years later, when they met again, Moore, married and better established in his own life, was able to stand up to Wittgenstein and became a central and stabilizing figure in his life.

'Logik'—von Wright supposes that the Germanic spelling may indicate a work written in German: it is more likely to indicate a letter written in haste.[27] It seems to me, in fact, a probable conclusion that the dissertation shown to Fletcher was the actual set of dictated notes that we now refer to as 'Notes dictated to Moore'. It was these that Wittgenstein expected Moore to show and explain to Russell in order to acquaint Russell with his discoveries in Norway.[28] Had he had another manuscript, fit or thought to be fit for a dissertation, he would surely have shown that instead. The other possibility, of course, is that Moore simply described to Fletcher a manuscript shown to him by Wittgenstein.[29] It makes little difference—the content must have been roughly the same since the notes dictated to Moore were an attempt to sum up Wittgenstein's views on logic.

Evidently Moore returned no answer to Wittgenstein's letter and there was silence between the two men until a remarkable letter of 3 July 1914 from Vienna:

Dear Moore,
   Upon clearing up some papers before leaving Skjolden I popped upon your letter which had made me so wild. And upon reading it over again I found that I had probably no sufficient reason to write to you as I did. (Not that I like your letter a bit *now*.) But at any rate my wrath has cooled down and I'd rather be friends with you again than otherwise. I consider I have strained myself enough now for I would *not* have written this to many people and if you don't answer this I shan't write to you again.
                    Yours, etc. etc.
                    L.W.[30]

A lame apology, but an apology nonetheless—and it might have had its effect if the war had not intervened.

Wittgenstein's letter comes. Think I won't answer it because I really don't want to see him again. Doubt if I oughtn't to. (GEM Diary 13.7.14)

27. Note on M.4 in *Letters to RKM*, p. 150. Von Wright is correct, however, in pointing out that the work entitled Logic or Logik was still in progress in February and March 1914, and so cannot have been identical with *Notes on Logic*, as I at one time supposed.

28. Letters to Russell of summer 1914, winter 1914–15, and May 1915. Moore was disgusted when Russell told Wittgenstein of Moore's inability to explain the notes to him: 'he has no right to say this, because he has never tried to get me to explain them.' Moore's Diary for 20.1.15.

29. There is reference to this in the letter received by Russell in January 1915—*Mein Manuskript, welches ich damals Moore zeigte...* 'The manuscript of mine that I showed to Moore at the time').

30. Von Wright supposes (*Letters*, p. 151) that 3 July is the date of receipt—but Moore's diaries show that that was 13 July.

Hall next Russell who asks about Wittgenstein and talks about their quarrel. Makes me doubt again whether I oughtn't to write to Wittgenstein. (ibid. 23.7.14)

There was talk about Wittgenstein in the intervening years, but no contact until their accidental meeting in 1929, which falls to be described later.

After Moore's return to England in April, Wittgenstein stayed on in Skjolden until the tourist season, which he was anxious to avoid. He was certainly in Vienna at the beginning of July. Writing to Russell at some time in May or June he says that his work has made great progress in the last four or five months, but also that he is now exhausted; he implies that he has not made any progress beyond the position as he explained it to Moore. This agrees with the wartime letter to Russell (quoted above) which speaks of a manuscript shown to Moore and of one written during the war—with the implication that nothing much came in between.

Thus the late spring and early summer in Norway seem to have been a time of recuperation. Wittgenstein began to plan for a yet longer stay in Norway, perhaps an indefinite one. Some distance above the fjord there was a lake, skirted on one side by a road, on the other by a mountain. On that mountain—accessible only by boat across the lake—Wittgenstein built himself a house 'miles from anyone' (*in der Einsamkeit*) as he told Russell. My translation here is a bit free—the house was about a mile from the village, though the journey would be quite a long one. The plan Wittgenstein drew for Moore is reproduced in editions of his letters.[31] The house was of wood, 27 feet by 24 feet, a hundred yards from the lake. At some point (for he lived there later) Wittgenstein fixed up a rope-railway with pulleys to bring water and other supplies up to the house from the lake. The entrance was on the side away from the lake, under a gable, into the living-room; opening off this room on the right were a bedroom and a kitchen.[32] The litle house had a wonderful view across the lake and the fjord to the south-west and itself looked cheerful enough in the summer when overgrown with creepers and surrounded by greenery. But it would take the temperament of a hermit or even a stylite to live there through a winter: some courage too—Wittgenstein was of a nervous enough disposition to spit into the lake for luck when he took his little boat across on a stormy day. There is some conflict of testimony whether Wittgenstein stayed there at all in 1914 but he can hardly have stayed there long. It was only built after Moore's departure (Moore did not know its site when he wrote in

31. *Letters RKM* (1974), p.166, *Briefe* (1980), p.199.
32. The house was taken down in 1957 and re-erected in the village (where it may still be seen) in a slightly altered form.

1936) and the plan was to bring furniture up from Christiania (Oslo) after the summer.

Dis aliter visum, one is inclined to say about all plans of that summer; but Wittgenstein was the last person to view the future with confidence. Everything he did was somehow provisional: it is symptomatic of this that at various times he wanted to give away the house, make it over to someone else, notably to a comrade during the war which delayed his return to it. In that spring of proverbial false security, he had discussed with Moore what he would do in case of a great war. People used to be impressed, perhaps a little too readily, by Wittgenstein's prescience. He always expected the worst, so his correct forebodings were naturally remembered. He even preferred bad news, his sister Gretl used to say. One of his favourite quotations was from Gottfried Keller:

Always remember, when things are going well, that they don't have to.

7 The War 1914–18

AUSTRIA is now our theme, Austria and the last days of an empire and culture whose variety, whose failings, and whose charm mirrored human nature itself. Through those last days and through their sad aftermath, Wittgenstein was to live, largely by choice, among his countrymen, sharing at times (largely by choice) dangers, privation, and humiliation, at others the rarefied idealism and carefully unostentatious wealth of his family. Janik and Toulmin called their book *Wittgenstein's Vienna* and dealt with the city in the period before the First World War:[1] a more important concept from the biographical point of view is Wittgenstein's Austria—the history and life of the country that he lived in between the ages of 25 and 40. These are the really formative years of a man's life and in them his mood of prevailing pessimism became established but also his vision of what could or might be saved from the general decline. In these years the last traces of the little Wittgenstein that went to Berlin disappeared. Nieces and nephews saw him before the war as a sunny and charming uncle, afterwards as a figure of authority and too often of disapproval. After the collapse of 1918—the breakdown or *Zusammenbruch* —Wittgenstein too went through a period of despair and of comparative estrangement from his family. Throughout the 1920s, despite false starts and setbacks, there was development and germination. And the end-result was a kind of harmony of spirit which made it possible for him to take up his real work again. More fortunate than his country he was not limited by a geographical situation; but we shall see in a later volume how the events of the 1930s in Austria were also reflected in his personal life.

As so often with historical events, we seem to be seeing patterns rather than causes. The development that the war brought about in Wittgenstein seemed to be a necessary one for him. Years later he made a point of discussing his war-experiences at length with a nephew and when the nephew made some remark of pacifist tendency, he said of the war: 'It saved my life; I don't know what I'd have done without it.'[2] Russell was shocked by the mystical and religious tendencies that he found in Wittgenstein after the war. These can in part be explained, we shall see, by the pressures of the war itself and by accidents during it, yet they also contributed an essential element to the book on which he had been working since 1911. Even the philosophic silence that he observed in the

1. London and New York 1973.
2. Professor Felix Salzer (personal communication).

1920s, which can easily, and to some extent truly, be ascribed to despondency, had also its philosophic justification, both in the doctrines of his first book and in the deeper view of thought and language that his immersion in other activities gave him. 'For internal as well as external reasons...' (*Aus inneren and äusseren Gründen!*...), Wittgenstein was fond of saying to explain (or refuse to explain) one of his actions; and we too usually have to look at them in both lights.

Wittgenstein had returned to Austria; for the July and August, as it seems, for he meant to go on a holiday with Pinsent in September and to make a short visit to England before returning to Skjolden. At the end of July he came down from the Hochreith to Vienna for a meeting which, in the event, determined many of his friendships and interests over the succeeding years.

Admirer as he was of Karl Kraus, he had read Kraus's reference to *Der Brenner*, a literary and intellectual periodical published in Innsbruck. 'That the only honest periodical in Austria comes out in Innsbruck ought to be known, if not in Austria at least in Germany, whose only honest periodical also comes out in Innsbruck,' said Kraus. Its editor, a few years older than Wittgenstein, was Ludwig von Ficker, a writer himself, but chiefly one with a nose for what was good—with *Spürsinn*, as Wittgenstein himself called it. In *Der Brenner*, fortnightly since 1910, there had appeared poems, criticisms, stories, articles of philosophical or social interest, comments on events of the time. There was no one theme: Karl Kraus was an obvious influence and the name of the journal was meant to indicate an opening from German into Mediterranean culture. There was no political tendency in the magazine but a sustained attempt to achieve authenticity in art and life. Names now familiar to historians of literature occur in those early numbers—Theodor Däubler, Peter Altenburg, Albert Ehrenstein, Else Lasker-Schüler, above all, perhaps, Georg Trakl. Some but not all of these would have been to Wittgenstein's taste; but it is natural to suppose that he was affected by the frequent discussions of Dostoevsky and the translations into German (the earliest translations easily available) of Kierkegaard. Wittgenstein actually mentions that he himself was struck by what Ficker had written on Kraus.[3] The magazine seems to have been an attempt to do in a less personal and individualistic manner—in a less fastidious one too—what Kraus also was attempting: something very Austrian, and something, we can now see, very Wittgensteinian—to achieve a kind of moral reform of life and thought without attempting to alter the conditions of life. The unworldliness can be seen as a reflection of the actual political impotence of the intellectuals of the time, or as a reflection more generally of the

---

3. A small selection of *Brenner* articles about Kraus had been published in 1913, *Studien über Karl Kraus*, and was advertised in *Die Fackel*, which Wittgenstein surely saw.

rottenness of the Austro-Hungarian Empire;[4] but it can also be seen as an important discovery, the discovery that the revolution needed (however impossible it might be) was not one in institutions but one in the thinking and the sensibility—Kraus would say, in the language—of men.

It was not by accident, then, that Wittgenstein turned to Ficker for help in the following matter. He wanted to arrange for 100,000 crowns (over £4,000 in the sterling of those days) to be distributed among Austrian 'artists' (*Künstler* was the term used, and it gave rise to some misgivings—Were only graphic or plastic artists meant, like those Wittgenstein's father had aided?).[5] Ficker would know, he said, the best and the most needy. He had recently inherited a large fortune, he explained in a second letter, and it was the custom (perhaps he meant that of his family) to devote a sum to charitable purposes. Kraus (we have seen this for ourselves) was the connexion that had led him to Ficker. Could a meeting be arranged?

Ficker in fact arranged to go to Vienna when Wittgenstein would next be there. Meanwhile he inquired of his Viennese friends and heard (not always without irony) of the identity of Karl Wittgenstein and the patronage he had extended to the arts. No trace of this irony was felt by Ficker when the meeting actually took place:

> I had travelled through the heat of the day and darkness was falling when the taxi stopped at the the open garden gate of a mansion among the parks of Neuwaldegg. The building itself was some way back from the road and was only indistinctly visible, but the terrace in front was brightly lit and there, already awaiting me, stood the young benefactor, a modest figure, reminiscent perhaps of Alyosha or Prince Myshkin in Dostoevsky. No sooner had he noticed me than he came to meet me, down the few steps and along the wide gravel path. He greeted me warmly and led me into the house. He seemed in the best of spirits at supper too, which a servant brought us, and though there was something awkward in his manner of speech he seemed possessed by a deep need for communication. I soon saw that I had to do not only with a lover of the fine arts but with a thinker...[6]

Wittgenstein told Ficker how he mant to go back to his wood-cabin in Norway in order to sift and clarify his thoughts.

4. So, if I understand them, Janik and Toulmin in the book referred to above.

5. The correspondence is printed in L.W. *Briefe an Ludwig von Ficker* with many helpful notes by W. Methlagl and G.H. von Wright. It is also included in *Briefe* (1980) and is translated in *W. Sources and Perspectives*, ed. C.G. Luckhardt (1979).

6. L. Ficker in the last number of *Der Brenner* 18 (1954) 238, 'Rilke und der unbekannte Freund'—the article is a mixture of unique memories and simple confusions about dates and the order of events.

It was not until the next morning, as they walked in the park that reached right up into the hills—the private *Wienerwald* of the Wittgensteins—that Wittgenstein came round to the reason for Ficker's visit. It seems likely from the correspondence that he had the cheque ready and it was simply a question of its division among beneficiaries. Ficker at once proposed 20,000 crowns each for Rilke and Trakl. It seems that Wittgenstein already admired Rilke[7] and was prepared to accept the suggestion of Trakl, knowing perhaps little of him at that time. He only stipulated that an amount (10,000 crowns) should go to the *Brenner* itself. For the rest, Wittgenstein left the decision to Ficker and it seems that Ficker largely followed the following list (it still survives):

Georg Trakl	20 000 Kronen
Rainer Maria Rilke	20 000 Kronen
Carl Dallago	20 000 Kronen
Redaktion *Der Brenner*	10 000 Kronen
Oskar Kokoschka	5 000 Kronen
Else Lasker-Schüler	4 000 Kronen
Adolf Loos	2 000 Kronen
Karl Borromäus Heinrich	1 000 Kronen
Hermann Wagner	1 000 Kronen
Josef Georg Oberkofler	1 000 Kronen
Theodor Haecker	2 000 Kronen
Theodor Däubler	2 000 Kronen
Ludwig Erik Tesar	2 000 Kronen
Richard Weiss	2 000 Kronen
Karl Hauer	5 000 Kronen
Franz Kranewitter	2 000 Kronen
Hugo Neugebauer	1 000 Kronen

All the beneficiaries except Hauer, Kranewitter, Kokoschka, and Rilke were contributors to *Der Brenner*, and Rilke, perhaps in consequence, did contribute something to the single volume that appeared in 1915. There is no reason to attribute to Wittgenstein any particular attitude towards the individual beneficiaries unless we find one expressed by him: apart from Trakl, Rilke, and the *Brenner* itself, he left the whole matter to Ficker. He acknowledges a letter of thanks from Dallago (the philosopher) and when later he is sent a collection of thanks to the unknown benefactor, he tells Ficker:

I am sending back the acknowledgements, with the exception of the lines addressed to me by Hauer and the kind and noble letter from Rilke. I didn't need the other letters as acknowledgements; and as thanks I found

---

7. Friends say that he found Rilke's later work unsympathetic.

them—to be frank—extremely distasteful. A certain ignoble almost fraudulent tone, etc.

Rilke's letter to you touched me and gave me great pleasure. The affection of any noble-minded human being is a mainstay in the unstable equilibrium of my life. I am quite unworthy of his splendid gift, which I will wear next my heart as a sign and reminder of that affection. Could you convey to Rilke my most heartfelt thanks and my complete devotion? (LW to LvF 13.2.15)

This letter, of course, was written after several months of war, and some of the sourness may be attributed to that. But in general Wittgenstein, who saw things in black and white, was only too liable to regret some of the benefactions that he had authorized. In a letter to his friend Paul Engelmann in 1917:

I received today from Zurich two books by Albert Ehrenstein—the one who used to write in *Die Fackel* (once I helped him financially without really wanting to). Now he returns the favour by sending me his *Tubutsch* and *Man Screams*. Dog-dirt, if I'm not mistaken. And such stuff is sent to me out here! (LW to PE 31.3.17)

Since Ehrenstein was also a contributor to *Der Brenner*, it is tempting to suppose that Ficker's plans were changed and his name substituted for one of those on the list we have preserved—though then Wittgenstein would have had little justification in disavowing the benefaction. It is also possible that he made further benefactions—perhaps through Kraus. It is worth reflecting on the scale of his generosity: his yearly income (known from his military papers) was 300 000 crowns (say £7,500) and, from what we know alone, nearly a third of the first year's income was being given away. As for Wittgenstein's hostility to Ehrenstein, Engelmann himself explains it[8] by a dislike for expressionism and any reader of the books in question can see (to use Engelmann's quotation from Plato) that they are not 'conducted in the rhythms of a decorous and manly life'. Ehrenstein's pacifism (the reason why the books were sent from Zurich) may have been an additional reason for distaste in this case, but Wittgenstein tolerated it readily enough in Engelmann, to whom this very letter was addressed. As for Dallago and Haecker, we can gather from a later letter of Wittgenstein's only that he thought himself every bit as well worth publishing as they were.[9]

Walter Methlagl has described[10] how these wholly unforeseen gifts were received by the beneficiaries. Perhaps two should be picked out: Trakl had been in complete despair because of his inability to support his

8. P. Engelmann: *Letters from Ludwig Wittgenstein with a Memoir*, p. 85.
9. LW to LvF 4.12.19.
10. In *LW: Briefe an LvF* (Salzburg, 1969).

sick sister; from this trouble at least his mind will have been relieved in his own last days—for such they proved to be. Kokoschka's letter to Ficker will perhaps be of some interest to historians of art:

> Despite your declining all thanks, I must allow myself to send you mine from the bottom of my heart.
>
> You can scarcely imagine what this great help has done for me by way of freeing me from cares—something I have wanted and struggled to achieve for years but which never turned out to be possible has now occurred.
>
> I can work and my powers will not be squandered in the struggle for existence.
>
> If I am now called up, I shall have carried my plans a good distance forward.[11]

Kokoschka was to be supported again later by the Wittgenstein family—so far, that is, as purchasers may be termed supporters. Though he had little to do with the selection of beneficiaries, Wittgenstein's idea of distributing among *individuals*, who were worthy of support and in need of it, was in his father's tradition. Where he differed from his father was in not insisting on making the selection for himself.

The meeting with Ficker had two other important consequences for Wittgenstein. The first was friendship: Ficker, some nine years older than himself, was for a short time to take the place of the older friend, vacated by Russell, later filled by Moore in England (though with less intimacy) and by Hänsel in Austria. It was a figure he often seemed to be in search of. Indeed the other consequence of the meeting with Ficker was perhaps another example of it. Ficker took him down on that Sunday, after they had discussed their business, to the Café Imperial where they met the architect Adolf Loos. Loos was famous, indeed controversial, at the time as the architect of the building on the Michaelerplatz, directly opposite the magnificent baroque gateway of the imperial palace. It avoided all ornamentation—it was known as the house without eyebrows because it had not even dripstones above the windows. At once Wittgenstein engaged him in a lively discussion on the principles of modern architecture—lively, that is, as far as content went, since its actual conduct was slowed down by Loos's deafness. This is the first indication we have of Wittgenstein's interest in architecture though he had, of course, designed furniture in England and a simple traditional cabin in Norway. We remember only his advice to his sister on how to draw. He was not quite the universal man of the renaissance: it was rather that he would take up someone else's subject, someone else's ideas, and do it or make them better. We shall discuss later, and illustrate, his own house

11. ibid.. p. 54.

and his collaboration with Loos's pupil Engelmann; that house too lacks all ornament and employs the Loosian device of interlocking split-levels to prevent the division of the interior space into 'floors' though only in the lower storeys: but in other respects, notably the tall and narrow windows and doors, it is unlike Loos's work and reminiscent, though remotely, of Cambridge.

In some ways the contact with Loos was more important than that with Ficker—to Ficker Wittgenstein must write, but Loos was always in Vienna and the acquaintance could be kept alive and could introduce Wittgenstein into the periphery (on one occasion the centre) of the Kraus circle. As a small part of his life Wittgenstein was on the way to becoming a Viennese intellectual, with his favourite café—in his case the Café Museum near the art schools, its interior designed by Loos. Loos the individual, like many friends, seems to have incurred Wittgenstein's displeasure in the difficult years after the war; but the side of Wittgenstein's life he represented did not disappear for good.

Ficker went back to Innsbruck on 28 July—the day of the declaration of war on Serbia. Wittgenstein's family came to Vienna—no doubt he himself simply stayed there. All was confusion—his brothers Kurt and Paul had regiments to join. But what was Ludwig to do? David Pinsent mentions an attempt to obtain non-combatant work. If there is any basis for this, it will presumably be that Ludwig thought his double rupture (which had excused him military service) might disqualify him from a fighting arm. Several days passed before this was resolved. It was on 7 August (the day after the declaration of war on Russia) that he enlisted as a volunteer gunner for the duration—his double rupture is simply not mentioned on the documents under the heading for bodily defects. Wittgenstein commented on how incredibly friendly the authorities were: people who were asked for advice daily by thousands, none the less gave friendly and detailed answers. How cheering this was—it reminded him of English conditions![12]

It was a time of confusion as well as of enthusiasm: the Austro-Hungarian mobilization had begun late—on 31 July. They were involved in a race with the Russians, who, fortunately for them, were almost equally slow. One of the main aims of the High Command was to strengthen the forces in Galicia and to make such advances as they could into Russian territory in order to forestall the Russian cavalry who were thought to be ready to sweep through Galicia.[13] A small advance into

12. The diary from which these reactions of Wittgenstein's are quoted is described shortly below in the text. Dates are often confirmed and other details given by the relatively very full documentation available in the *Kriegsarchiv* and the *Innenministerium* in Vienna.

13. Wittgenstein's campaigning on the Eastern Front took place in the Austrian provinces of Galicia and Bukovina and to a small extent in the then neighbouring provinces or governments of Russia. The places mentioned are now largely in the Soviet Union, partly in Poland. Between the two wars they were largely in Poland, partly in Rumania. In my text, except where there is an English

Russian territory did in fact begin on 6 August itself and the use of troops from the Cracow garrison for this purpose was authorized. From this larger view it is not surprising that Wittgenstein's medical examination was a formality, that his education and his knowledge of mathematics were completely overlooked, and that within two days he found himself attached to a Garrison Artillery Regiment in Cracow and instructed first and briefly in the working of an antiquated mortar and then in that of a searchlight (for his regiment had a searchlight detachment) on a small river gunboat captured from the Russians (the *Goplana*, as it continued to be called). This travelled down the Vistula into Russian territory. He was on active service within ten days and by 1 a.m. on 18 August we find him called up to the bridge in his nightclothes to man the searchlight—a post of obvious danger, though on this occasion it turned out to be a false alarm.

With what spirit he went into the army, we can collect from various witnesses. David Pinsent thought of him as patriotic. His sister Mining speaks of his wish to defend his country but also—she is very emphatic on this point—'he had the intense wish to assume some heavy burden and to perform some task other than purely intellectual work'.[14] Arvid Sjögren who came to know him during the war and was perhaps his greatest friend immediately after it gives a similar explanation: he wanted to share the burden that fell on others.[15] Similarly Paul Engelmann (who as a friend came second to Arvid Sjögren about this time) speaks of Wittgenstein's repeated refusal to accept privileges—though we shall see that this could not be followed out in practice.

As for patriotism, it is clear that Wittgenstein accepted military service as a civic duty and that he felt identified with his country. But this by no means connoted confidence in victory. On 25 October, commenting on a senseless rumour that Paris had fallen, he wrote:

> It makes me feel today more than ever the terribly sad position of our race—the German race. Because it seems to me as good as certain that we cannot get the upper hand against England. The English—the best race in the world—*cannot* lose. We, however, can lose and shall lose, if not this year, then next year. The thought that our race is going to be beaten depresses me terribly, because I am completely German.[16]

name place-names follow the form given in Austro-Hungarian war-maps and documents (usually a slightly Germanized Polish). I have allowed myself to regard 'Lwow' as the English for 'Lemberg'.

14. In her *Familienerinnerungen*, p. 108.

15. Personal communication.

16. See below for the notebook from which this remark is taken. It will be evident enough from previous chapters how far Wittgenstein was 'German'. With Wittgenstein's attitude here towards national character contrast his excoriation of Malcolm in 1939 (M. Malcolm, *Memoir*, p. 32). Perhaps both the times and Wittgenstein had changed.

In conversation with Groag and the others later in the war, he said that he was sure the Allies would defeat the Central Powers. They would just laugh, he said, at Kaiser Karl's proposals (these must have been those of the letter of March 1917). He also said that he thought the German generals had a good grasp of their job, but the Austrian generals knew nothing.

Some of these remarks we have already quoted are taken from a remarkable document consisting of a diary, in clear for a few pages and then in code, contained in the three notebooks whose philosophic content is reprinted in *Notebooks 1914–17*. The diary, though not a very full one, runs from 9 August 1914 to 22 June 1915 and then from 29 March to 19 August 1916. It seems highly likely that there were three further notebooks from the time of the First War, no doubt similar in content to those we have.[17] We have seen (p. 56 above) that the practice of writing down thoughts about himself on bits of paper began in his Berlin days and also that in 1929–30 he could speak of not having made notebook entries 'for so many years'. It is possible that there were personal notes among the manuscripts left in England in 1913, manuscripts which he was insistent should be burnt. It is also possible that there were such in 'the large book' in which—pupils and neighbours noticed—he would write at night in the 1920s. But all these are lost. What we can infer from the corpus of notebooks preserved is that he felt the need to make personal notes most strongly when he was not among friends—as in the First War, so in Norway in 1936–7. Thus of the motives mentioned in 1929–30, that of creating a substitute for a person in whom he could confide was perhaps the strongest. It would be inappropriate to transcribe the whole diary here even if space permitted it, so a remark based on a reading of the whole may be in place: the wartime entries have great immediacy and openness. It is impossible to believe that any important elements of Wittgenstein's moral, emotional, or even sensual life (above the level of consciousness) have been concealed. At some points reading it is like hearing a death-bed confession.

Code-entries begin on 15 August, perhaps because Wittgenstein was about to go towards enemy territory. The code is a simple one (a = z, b = y, etc.): all the same he shows a comparative facility in using it from the first, so that he had perhaps practised it earlier. The aim was of course not concealment for ever but concealment from anyone who casually picked up the book.[18]

17. See von Wright's account of the origin of the *TLP* in *Prototractatus*. He calculates that there may have been three or four more wartime notebooks. See below p. 264, where I explain why I think there were three.

18. One of the 1930s notebooks has instructions *written in code* about how it is to be disposed of in case of Wittgenstein's death. There are also other subtler indications that the remarks written down in the 1930s and 1940s were thought of as a kind of testament or autobiography meant to be read by others.

So much for our chief source. The light it throws on his attitude when entering the army supports what his sister says. The prospect excited him: it would be a crucial test for his character—an ordeal by fire—a test whether he had the necessary strength not to lose his energy and good spirits. Other and severer tests were to come in battle. There is every sign that as tests he welcomed them. At the same time, he meant to work, that is, to continue with his philosophical thinking during the war. The first philosophical entry in his notebook occurs on 22 August, but there are several references to work's being done before that date. Clearly 'work' meant reflection and perhaps writing down something on a slip of paper—entry into the notebook was the second or third stage. The results of his work from before the war were evidently contained in one large notebook, which he had left with his father's secretary in Vienna for safe-keeping. His wartime notebooks, in like manner, carry instructions suggesting that they too, when completed, were left in Vienna and were intended to be sent to Russell after the war, if Wittgenstein himself did not survive it.

The first days in the army—who that has experienced them can forget the confusion and the novelty, the mass of events that press in on one, the sense of complete isolation from one's earlier life? Each day seemed like a week. Wittgenstein would wake up and fancy himself still in some dream that he was back at school. The humble duties of a recruit he could perform with an ironic smile to himself, but some of the physical hardships suited him particularly badly—to avoid bed-bugs he planned to sleep out of the barracks; but the food in the canteen, which he found uneatable, soon upset his stomach, which was never strong. As so often, he was his own enemy: a lieutenant who came across him in the canteen (and recognized him no doubt as an educated man) was surprised: why was he not in the mess? Having graduated from a *Realschule* Wittgenstein was entitled to the distinctive stripe and the privileges of an *Einjährigfrei- williger*, perhaps we should say a cadet though there was another rank with that title in the Austro-Hungarian army. During the war the commission might be expected within months and in the meantime there was a life shared to some extent with the officers. Pride seems to have kept him from claiming these privileges though he sorely needed them. He was merely amused when the other *Einjährigfreiwilligen*, learning of his background, addressed him as *Herr Kollege* and urged him to make himself one of them.

With the captain, Wittgenstein, perhaps because of his unmilitary bearing, had less success than with the lieutenant in the canteen. He was sent to the comparatively humble task already described on the *Goplana*. No question of privileges here—though he probably none the less incurred the suspicions of his uneducated comrades. For his part he found them impossible to get on with. Stupid, coarse, and above all men of ill-will, he thought. It was not true that men were necessarily made nobler by some great common aim. On the contrary; although external circumstances, the voyage down the Vistula and the shipboard tasks could have made this the happiest of times the men themselves made their work into drudgery.

It was not easy for Wittgenstein to see that the others were only too accustomed to physical labour and that the thought of doing it for no adequate pay and with the prospect even of danger, to be incurred by them—Poles and Czechs for the most part—in a German war, will have soured them even beyond the ordinary harsh conditions of their peacetime life. Then, especially on the ship, there was the problem of constant proximity. The smell, the continual noise was too much for him. He tried sleeping on deck, but it was too cold. Later he seems to have had a cabin to himself—or perhaps *the* cabin to himself, since, being the searchlight orderly, he had to be on watch all night and to sleep during the day, which kept him to a certain extent away from the others. When winter-quarters impended, he, who normally avoided all privileges, sought leave not to sleep in the barrack-room. (In the event a new posting in December made that easily possible.)

The picture was not wholly black—a change of crew brought improvement, and he allowed some exceptions to his sweeping condemnations of meanness. But, as a rule, he despised his shipmates: in a crisis they would get drunk and, as for himself, they plagued him. No doubt his status was unclear to them: it was a great surprise when he returned (after six weeks on the ship) with the stripe of an *Einjährigfreiwilliger*, which the captain had eventually instructed him to assume. They made it impossible for him to get work done properly: when the searchlight would not function and he wanted to approach it slowly and in a considered manner, as was his wont, they pushed him aside. What was he to do? He felt betrayed and completely dependent on others as he had not felt since his schooldays in Linz. The important thing, in his own words, was not to lose hold of oneself (*sich selbst nicht verlieren*), not to give in to others. Perhaps this could be done by enduring everything, trying to view everything as an observer, doing one's work humbly and not involving oneself in what went on. If he tried to defend himself he was bound to fly out at them. But withdrawal was hardly possible in practice: he could not work with people and have *nothing* to do with them—something must be said, questions must be asked, rude and inadequate answers must be endured. Besides 'unaccountably', *unbegreiflicher-weise*, (surely only Wittgenstein would have viewed the matter in this way) it was no easy matter to cut oneself off from others. Not that he felt drawn to any of them in the least, but the habit of being friendly with people was so strong.

Sometimes he ascribed his inability to be on good terms with them to the lack of the necessary vulgarity; but on another occasion he contrasted himself with the lieutenant:

A very nice man. He can have to do with the biggest scoundrels and be friendly without losing any of his dignity. When we hear a Chinaman talk, we are inclined to think his speech nothing but inarticulate gurgling. Someone who understands Chinese will recognize it as *language*. Similarly I often cannot recognize the *human being* in a man. (Diary 21.8.14)

With the non-commissioned officers immediately in charge of him he was not on good terms either—perhaps because of too haughty a demeanour. He resented it bitterly (and naturally) when one of them tried to suggest to an officer that he had behaved in a cowardly fashion, though he had actually performed his task faithfully. A later talk with the non-commissioned officer cleared the air a bit. But, as with the drunkenness of the soldiers, so Wittgenstein's fastidiousness noted and felt all the customary faults of petty authority. A siege was expected in Cracow:

The worse the situation becomes, the cruder are the NCOs. Because they feel that they can give free rein to their meanness unchecked by the officers, who are now losing their heads and no longer exercise any control to keep things on the right path. Every word you hear now is a piece of abuse. Because there is not the slightest reward for decency any more, so that people abandon even the small amount of it that may still be left to them. It is all extremely sad. (Diary 11.11.14)

There was the occasional officer with whom he got on well. The first commandant of his ship was one such and would talk to him about all sorts of subjects. There was the lieutenant in the canteen whom we have mentioned. Another lieutenant came on board at Tarnobrzeg and seemed not to be stupid. Wittgenstein was delighted to be called *Du* by him—the form of address used by one officer to another. One of these officers must have been the Lieutenant Molé who wrote to Ficker and described a fine summer's night on deck, when Wittgenstein peeled potatoes and discussed philosophy with animation.[19] But among the officers too there was much to depress him: overhearing a conversation between a later commandant and another officer, he wrote:

What mean voices! You can hear all the viciousness of the world croaking and snarling in them. Meanness wherever I look. Not a *single* heart with feeling in it in sight! (Diary 9.11.14)

19. L. Ficker in *Der Brenner* (1954) 237; cf. *LW: Briefe an LvF*, p. 19.

He longed for a friend to whom he could say everything and pined for David Pinsent in particular. But even within his own country the letters were uncertain and slow: he quoted Karl Kraus's joke—'we are cut off from the outside world by the Military Post.'[20] It was 10 November before he even learnt that he could write to England via Switzerland and 21 December before he had a letter from David: in his excitement he kissed it and in the following month the receipt or failure of a letter from David was the most important matter for a diary entry.

It is sad to have to begin the account of a new phase in Wittgenstein's life with another recital of difficulties with his fellow-men. It is important to see that the feelings recorded are those neither of a saint nor of a curmudgeon. They are confessions written down by one who in this area as in others was trying to embody a moral ideal. It is almost as if the war came to him as an especially good occasion for this, as if that were why he was so excited on enlisting at the prospect of his future life. Much of the accounts of Wittgenstein's life in these years must be an attempt to trace the lineaments of that ideal. One feature of that ideal explains why he mentions so often the extent to which the behaviour of those around him grated upon him. He wanted to make himself independent not only of material circumstances but also (what was even more difficult) of other human beings. On the same day that he heard the mean voices of the officers, he had a postcard from his uncle Paul, of the sort that ought to have refreshed and heartened him:

> But in the last few days I have been *a subject for depression*! I have no real pleasure in anything and my life is full of anxiety about the future! Because I am no longer at peace within myself. Every failure in decency in my environment—and there's always something of that kind—inflicts a wound deep inside me, and there is always a new wound opened before an old one has healed. Even at times—like the evenings nowadays—when I am not depressed, I still don't feel properly free. Only occasionally, and then very fleetingly, have I the taste for work. Because I can't bring myself to feel at ease. I feel myself as dependent on the world and so I have to be afraid of it even when for the present nothing bad is going to happen to me. I see myself—that self in which I was once able to rest secure—as a distant country, now vanished, that I long for. —The Russians are advancing fast on Cracow. The entire civilian population is having to leave the city. Things look very bad for us. *God help me*!!! (Diary 9.11.14)[21]

---

20. *Von der Mitwelt durch die Feldpost abgeschnitten, Briefe an LvF*, p. 25.

21. 'A distant country': the German text is indecipherable though the general sense is clear. 'that self in which I was once able to rest secure': it is difficult to think what period Wittgenstein might be referring to. Perhaps 'in which I might be able to etc.' (*könnte* rather than *konnte*) is what is meant. But 'vanished' (*von mir gewichen*) speaks against that.

This passage will serve us as a key and as a reminder that Wittgenstein's inner life was determined simultaneously by a number of moments that we are bound to separate in our exposition. We have dwelt on his relations with his comrades, but we can note also the implicit references here to the dangers of the war (the approach of the Russians), to its privations (Wittgenstein was less depressed in the evenings, he thought, because, though tired still, he had then at least the prospect of sleep), to the importance for him of his philosophic work, and to the strength that he found through prayer.

The operations in which Wittgenstein was involved during the first four months of the war were of the following nature. It was thought (as said above) that the Russian armies would sweep through Galicia in the direction of the Silesian industrial districts and, behind Cracow, the Moravian gap, which was the road to Vienna. A false appreciation led to the view that their attack would come from the direction of Lublin. Conrad, the Austro-Hungarian Chief of Staff, accordingly ordered an advance into Russia in the direction of Lublin on the left and Chelm on the right. Dankl's I Army to which Wittgenstein's regiment was attached formed the left wing of this advance, and on its left was the Vistula, along which Wittgenstein's vessel sailed. There was as yet no Eastern Front: scattered bodies of skirmishers created intermittent alarm but the main bodies of troops met only occasionally and by accident. Ignorant armies clashed by night.

I Army, therefore, moved into Russia, and we find an entry to this effect in Wittgenstein's diary for 17 August, presumably meaning that his vessel had gone down the Vistula beyond Sandomierz, where the Austro-Hungarian frontier took a turn to the south-east, following roughly the line of the San. The Russian cavalry—the Cossacks, as the Imperial and Royal troops called them—were very skilful at harassment, at creating the impression of being a much larger force than was the fact. Hence, no doubt, the alarms to which Wittgenstein was subject. The function of his vessel, to judge by his occasional references and by the obvious probabilities of the case, was to provide mobile fire-power to assist river-crossings or troops involved in engagements in the vicinity of the Vistula or its tributaries, and also on occasion to transport troops and matériel. The searchlight would be needed, sometimes to assist in the directing of fire, sometimes for navigation, and sometimes to enable works on another vessel to be continued at night. In the first case particularly, and in the second to some degree, the searchlight and hence its orderly would be an obvious target for enemy fire. Wittgenstein was very conscious of the danger but, as is often the case in combat, he was much more disturbed by the possibility that the searchlight might be extinguished, for whatever reason, in which case the whole responsibility would have fallen on him.

To return to the general picture: Dankl's army had some success against the Russians at the battle of Krasnik (23–25 August) and on 2 September Wittgenstein heard of a big five-day battle—presumably the battle of Komarow, in which the Austrian IV Army defeated the Russian V. But meanwhile, on another front the results of Conrad's false appreciation of Russian intention and of his tardy decision to devote his troops to Galicia rather than to Serbia were becoming apparent: in battles on the Gnila Lipa and the Zlota Lipa (tributaries of the Dniester that Wittgenstein was to know well later) the Austro-Hungarian III Army and elements of II Army, arriving from the Serbian front, were driven back by much stronger Russian forces. It was in the east, not in the north, of Galicia, that the Russians had planned to advance. Thus Lwow fell and Przemysl held out only for a while as a surrounded fortress. This news disheartened the otherwise successful I Army, which in any case began to feel increased Russian pressure (as the slow mobilization in that country began to take effect). This pressure was particularly strong along the Russian right, which was formed by the Vistula, with Wittgenstein's vessel on it. Conrad had various plans—it might have been an excellent idea to press on in the north (in the sector of I and IV Army) and to turn the Russian flank, but Hindenburg, for the Germans, was not at that point prepared to commit further German forces to support adventures in the East: the general plan (in so far as there was a unified general plan) of the Central Powers was still to achieve decisive victory on the Western Front first. Conrad in fact did allow I Army to continue to advance for a while, but switched IV Army in the direction of Lwow, thus opening a potentially dangerous gap between the two Armies. This, and other, events forced a general retreat. I Army moved back between 11 and 15 September to the lower San, but found this position untenable. On 12 September Wittgenstein speaks of bad news and a state of instant readiness. On 13 September they abandon the ship to the Russians. On 15 September they re-occupy it and sail upstream as far as the Dunajec (the tributary on which Tarnow stands) with the Russians on their heels. On 16 September they hear heavy gun and rifle fire. It was then planned to sail further, to Cracow itself, but for a day or so they feared that the frontier (here the Vistula itself up which they must sail) was occupied by 'Cossacks'. In the event they reached Cracow safely enough by 19 September—the Russians had been beaten back from the river sufficiently far not to harass them.

By 28 September the Austro-Hungarian forces as a whole had fallen back to the line of Gorlice and Tarnow. Wittgenstein—whose notes give a picture of the morale of the forces that corresponds very well with events—reports that in Cracow a siege was now expected and that there were many cases of dysentery.

This was the first advance and retreat in which Wittgenstein was concerned. Another was shortly to follow, because the Central Powers saw that some steps must be taken to restore the Imperial and Royal Army as a fighting force after the heavy casualties and loss of matériel involved in this retreat. By a remarkable feat of logistics a new German army—IX, under Hindenburg—was assembled on Dankl's left, and an advance on Warsaw in conjunction with the Austro-Hungarian I Army was planned. Wittgenstein heard about it on 4 October and set off for Russia on 6 October. At Szczuczin on 7 October the Russians were still 80 km away but as Wittgenstein and his comrades moved towards Sandomierz and halted at Tarnobrzeg they heard artillery in the distance. At Sandomierz itself they could see and hear the shells. Still under barrage they were meant to advance to Sawichost on 10 October and protect the German crossing of the river. Various such plans—which Wittgenstein would hardly have survived had they been carried out—were formed and cancelled in the next few days. But, while the Central Powers advanced, the Russians had been gathering their 'steam-roller' and on 13 October Wittgenstein's vessel—as part of a general retreat—got the order to make its way back, by night, to Sandomierz, which it did, with grenades flying over it. For the rest of October their vessel plied between Tarnobrzeg and Sandomierz on various errands, until on 28 October it broke a wheel and had to be towed back to Cracow. They reached Cracow on 5 November. This was in fact about the date that saw the completion of the retreat of the Central Powers forces in this theatre: the planned drive towards Warsaw had been completely frustrated by the advance of the steam-roller from Warsaw. Here, in front of Cracow, the Imperial and Royal I Army was to stay for the winter. The Russians were advancing fast, the civilians were evacuated, firing could soon be heard at the fortifications. The best that could be expected was a long siege. Battles long ago, soon forgotten except by the most specialized military historians, fought over remote territory by the forces of two vanishing empires: these were to divide Wittgenstein from his later pupils in Cambridge more completely even than the experience of the trenches marked off his English contemporaries from their juniors.

It was a more open war than that on the Western Front: in Galicia there was no tight network of communications. Hence the surges to and fro (much greater ones were to come in the following years) as one side or the other gained local superiority. Hence too some of the discomfort: Wittgenstein's ship in particular could not easily be provisioned, and they had to rely often enough on local purchase in a region impoverished even when no army was feeding off it.

Wittgenstein was sick sometimes, tired often; on one occasion he mentions not changing his boots or clothes for four days: on another he had to man the light in his night clothes, in that inhospitable climate a chill task even in autumn. Later, but particularly in the siege, he mentions the ice and the walk sometimes to the sanitary facilities. But for the most part he was cooped up on board the small vessel. He observes very acutely and frankly how the sensuality that hard work might repress would return when there was inadequate opportunity for physical movement.

Like the barely tolerable companions, the physical hardships were felt by Wittgenstein chiefly as a hindrance to attaining the right state of mind. The war seems to have provided him paradoxically with the possibility of a new life by focussing his expectations and his attention on danger and death. Remembering his remarks about his father's death being worth a whole life, we may say that the war 'saved his life', as he put it, by confronting him with the simple task of preparing himself for a good death. Describing his first experience of action he says:

> Suddenly woke about 1 a.m. Called for by the Lieutenant who says I must go to the searchlight straightaway: 'no getting dressed'. I ran to the bridge almost naked. Icy wind, rain. I was certain I was going to die on the spot. Turned on the searchlight. Went back to get dressed. It was a false alarm. I was *frightfully* agitated and groaned audibly. I felt the terrors of war. Now (in the evening) I have got over the terror. Unless I change my present bent of mind I'll strive with all my might to stay alive. (Diary 18.8.14)

More than once later he complains about the difficulty of finding the courage to accept life as it is, to 'live for the spirit', when he was exhausted by cold and lack of sleep and an empty stomach.

One help that he found is indicated in the words just quoted. On 1 September he began reading Tolstoy's *The Gospel in Brief* and within a couple of days felt that he was drawing great profit from it. As so often with an influential book it fell into his hands by accident. He went into a small bookshop in Tarnow,

> which, however, seemed to contain nothing but picture postcards. However, he went inside and found that it contained just one book: Tolstoy on the Gospels. He bought it merely because there was no other. He read it and re-read it, and thenceforth had it always with him, under fire and at all times. (BR to OM 20.12.19)[22]

At one time he was a byword among the soldiers for carrying it—'the one with the Gospels' he would be called. The Christianity that he found in Tolstoy seemed to him the only sure way to happiness, but it was not

---

22. This is from Russell's account of his first meeting with Wittgenstein after the war.

an easy way. Man must renounce the flesh, the gratification of his own will, must make himself independent of outward circumstances, in order to serve the spirit which is in himself and in all men. This spirit makes all men the sons of God and the only true life for a man is communion with that spirit, without any concern for his own wishes or for the past or future: the only true life is life in the present. For a man living not the personal but the common life of the spirit, there is no death.

These themes occur in Wittgenstein's notebooks throughout the war, and of course later in his *Tractatus*: Tolstoy's Christianity with a particular stamp given to it by Wittgenstein.

> The news gets worse and worse. Tonight there will be instant readiness. I work every day, more or less, and with fair confidence. I say Tolstoy's words over and over again in my head: 'Man is powerless in the flesh but free because of the spirit.' May the spirit be in me! In the afternoon the lieutenant heard shots in the vicinity. I became very agitated. Probably there will be an alarm. How will I behave when it comes to shooting? I am not afraid of being shot but of not doing my duty properly. God give me strength! Amen. Amen. Amen. (Diary 13.9.14)

What he added to Tolstoy—the particular way in which he saw Tolstoy's teaching—was his intense awareness of his identity with the spirit in him: this was that self that he was always anxious not to lose, not to make a present of to the mean natures that surrounded him. Thus on the day after the last entry he wrote:

> Today, very early, we abandoned the ship with everything on it... The Russians are on our heels. Have lived through frightful scenes. No sleep for 30 hours, am feeling very weak and can see no external hope. If it is all over with me now, may I die a good death mindful of my self. May I never lose myself. (Diary 13.9.14)

And two days later:

> Now I might have an opportunity to be a decent human being, because I am face to face with death. May the spirit enlighten me. (Diary 15.9.14)

Generally before action he prays like this: God be with me! The spirit be with me! Sometimes he fears that the spirit has forsaken him or speaks of an icy cold within him. If only he could for once sleep properly before things came to a head! He has to struggle to attain the right state of mind:

> I still do not understand how to do my duty just because it is my duty and to reserve all of the human being in me for the life of the spirit. I may die

in an hour, I may die in two hours, I may die in a month, or not for a few years. I cannot know about it and I cannot do anything for or against it: *such is this life*. How then ought I to live in order to hold my own at that moment, to live amid the good and the beautiful until life stops of itself. (Diary 7.10.14)[23]

It is difficult to estimate how far he was successful in attaining his aim. Of his intellectual work, whose progress may give some clue, we shall speak shortly. Generally his spirits were good in the immediate prospect of action: he would only pray in the way described. But there were times of depression:

> Periods of indifference towards my external fate alternate with ones in which I long again for external freedom and peace, in which I am tired of carrying out any and every command, willy nilly and in complete uncertainty about the immediate future. In short, there are times when I cannot simply live in the present and for the spirit. One ought to enjoy the good hours of life thankfully, as a boon, and otherwise face life with indifference. (Diary 12.10.14)

It will be seen that it was not danger that depressed him. On the same day, after writing the above, he heard that they were that night to sail under the Russian positions to Sawichost in order to land troops and matériel:

> Tonight then. —We are supposed to fire with Quick Firing guns and machine-guns, more to make noise, I am told, than to hit anything. I gather too that it is going to be a dangerous affair. If I am supposed to guide the searchlight, then I shall *certainly* be lost. But that does not matter, because only one thing is necessary! We sail in an hour. *God is with me*! (Diary 12.10.14)

In fact they sailed upstream to Nadbrzesze and then, by a reversal of orders, back to their original position. It was a dangerous enough day of heavy gunfire from both sides. Wittgenstein was elated, in the best of humour the whole time and intoxicated by the thunder of the guns. 'I am spirit and that is why I am free,' he wrote.[24] In danger and in depression his spirit, his share of the spirit, supported him, if it did not quite conquer. Depression, the harder of the two to combat, came from

---

23. *Das geistige Leben*: I have translated this as 'the life of the spirit'. It could *include* intellectual life—and in some authors (but not in Wittgenstein) this would be its meaning. *In jenem Augenblick zu bestehen*: if *jedem* were the reading the meaning would be 'to exist at every moment'.

24. *Ich bin Geist und darum bin ich frei* (Diary 13.10.14). It might be translated 'I am *a* spirit' but other passages make clear that the meaning is that *the* Tolstoyan spirit is in him, God is with him.

such sources as we have already seen—the hard conditions of his life, bad news about the war, a reverse for the Central Powers, the news (in fact some false rumour) that his second adoptive country, Norway, had now allied itself with the enemy, anxiety about his family—was his mother still alive?—or bad news concerning it. In particular he heard that his brother Paul the pianist was a prisoner of the Russians and had lost his right arm (we have already mentioned how he overcame this (p. 30 above) but Ludwig could not at the time foresee the event):

> I cannot help thinking of poor Paul the whole time—so suddenly *deprived of his occupation*! How terrible! What philosophy it would take to get over that! If only there is some solution other than suicide!! (Diary 28.10.14)

(Philosophy and *his* occupation, as we shall shortly see, were essential to keeping Ludwig somehow in equilibrium.) Depression is the element in his inner life that yet remains to be described. Sometimes the depressions seemed to Wittgenstein without cause (*grundlos*), most frequently they were occasioned by the bad terms he was on with his fellow soldiers and his own failure to achieve impassivity in this particular. He longed all the more—though it ought not to be necessary—for someone with whom he could speak openly. Ficker told him that the poet Trakl was in Cracow and as they fell back on that city his hopes rose. He wanted to call on him immediately they arrived there, but had to wait until the next day and then he was shattered to learn that Trakl had died three days before of a heart-attack. It came to be thought that Trakl had taken poison which was available to him as a hospital orderly, and the exact circumstances of Trakl's death have been much discussed.[25] Ficker wrote to ask what had happened—somehow a human reaction—but Wittgenstein replied that when the one important thing had been told him he felt a reluctance to inquire further into the circumstances. (LW to LvF 16.11.14)

Ludwig longed all the more for David—'I wonder whether he thinks of me half as much as I think of him?' (Diary 11.11.14). Trakl had perhaps presented the idea of a spiritualized friendship, of the warmth and sensitivity that was missing from his military life. When such opportunities came, in 1915 and 1916, he accepted them eagerly, but for the moment, in Cracow, he had to endure the friction with his comrades without such support. The situation was a little easier for him in that carrying out his garrison duties left him the opportunity, evidently not his while the *Goplana* was under way, to sit alone in his quarters and collect his thoughts ('collect myself', *mich sammeln*, is what he said). He had the opportunity to get himself into a better state of mind, to lay

25. For one account see Stupp: *Südostdeutsche Semesterblätte* 19 Sommersemester (1966), pp. 32–9.

firmer hold upon that spirit which was in him, which was him, if he but so lived as to be it. We have already seen many instances of his speaking so: another indication that he so thought is that he turned now for help to Emerson's *Essays* (it seems that books were available in Cracow, for he bought a volume of Nietzsche there, and Emerson too was read in Central Europe at the time).

The *Essays* are still sometimes recommended for style: Wittgenstein surely read them primarily for content—they even open with a favourite thought of his in these years:

> There is one mind common to all individual men. Every man is an inlet to the same and to all of the same. ('History', in Emerson's *Works*, 1888, p.1)

The mystical and moral implications of this are worked out in 'Self-Reliance' and 'The Over-Soul':

> A political victory, a rise of rents, the recovery of your sick, or the return of your absent friend, or some other favourable event, raises your spirit, and you think good days are preparing for you. Do not believe it. Nothing can bring you peace but yourself. Nothing can bring you peace but the triumph of principles. ('On Self-Reliance', ibid. p.21)

> Let man, then, learn the revelation of all nature and all thought to his heart; this, namely, that the Highest dwells with him; that the sources of nature are in his own mind, if the sentiment of duty is there. But if he would know what the great God speaketh, he must 'go into his closet and shut the door', as Jesus said. God will not make himself manifest to cowards... The soul gives itself, alone, original, and pure, to the Lonely, Original, and Pure, who, on that condition, gladly inhabits, leads, and speaks through it. ('The Over-Soul', ibid. p.66)

A taste for Emerson was an indirect sign of fidelity to his own traditions—Emerson shared with Carlyle a deep respect for the German genius: he detected in Goethe what was lacking in French, English, and American writers—'an habitual reference to moral truth.' Like Goethe he looked for a lofty conception of the world without the trappings of religion. The actual result, called Transcendentalism by its more sectarian adherents, was derived ultimately from Kant: transcendental knowledge, originally, was the understanding's awareness of the conditions of its own knowledge; for these thinkers it was the moral and mystical guidance that the soul could obtain by the consideration of its own nature. As for Emerson's style, the constant near epigrams, the elevation of the language, the poetical and rhetorical treatment of philosophical themes, all have parallels in Wittgenstein's preferred reading—in Lichtenberg, St. Augustine, Schopenhauer and others. His own style is more pared down—he was chaster in what he wrote than in what he read—but one cannot read Emerson without being reminded from page to page of the *Tractatus* and the wartime *Notebooks*.

Poetical and epigrammatic also was Nietzsche. Within a month of reading Emerson Wittgenstein bought volume 8 of Nietzsche's works in Cracow—presumably from Naumann's Leipzig edition, where volume 8 contains *inter alia* 'Der Antichrist' the first book of the intended *Der Wille zur Macht*.[26] The volume also contains 'Der Fall Wagner', 'Götzen-Dämmerung', 'Nietzsche contra Wagner', and Nietzsche's poems. Parallels and faint echoes are worth looking for in all, but it seems to be 'The Antichrist' that Wittgenstein refers to when he says:

> I am strongly affected by his hostility against Christianity. Because his writings too have some truth in them. To be sure, Christianity is the only *sure* way to happiness; but what if someone spurned this happiness? Might it not be better to perish unhappily in the hopeless struggle against the external world? But such a life is senseless. But why not lead a senseless life? It is ignoble?—How can it be reconciled with the strict solipsistic position? But what must I do in order that my life shall not be lost to me? I must be conscious of it always. (Diary 8.12.14)

Just as Nietzsche took the Schopenhauerian analysis of the will seriously, but instead of renouncing the will affirmed it, so also he took seriously the Schopenhauerian version of Christianity espoused by Tolstoy—'only one thing is necessary, resist not evil'—and branded it as the enemy of humanity and of reality itself. Nietzsche seemed important for Wittgenstein because Nietzsche's starting-point was the same as his own. Just as we have seen that he said of Weininger that you could take every sentence in his works and negate it, so Nietzsche was a possible attitude towards a set of questions. These questions arose—for Nietzsche and Tolstoy and Emerson and Wittgenstein—from taking as a starting-point the rejection of the miraculous and the mysterious in Christianity. It was all part of the legacy of David Friedrich Strauss. What Nietzsche attacked in Strauss was the particular set of values that he relied on in

---

26. The preface to *Der Wille zur Macht* begins with the words:'This book is the property of the very few. Perhaps indeed not one of them is yet on earth.' (*Dies Buch gehört den Wenigsten. Vielleicht lebt selbst noch keiner von ihnen.*) Surely this is echoed in the preface to the *Tractatus*, and even more strikingly in Wittgenstein's later remark that he thought he was writing for a race of men who would think in a quite different way from us. A later judgement of Wittgenstein's on Nietzsche—that he alone among philosophers touched the problems of our culture that Goethe and Beethoven knew: but then he was more of a poet than a philosopher—is quoted above, p. 33. *Der Antichrist* itself begins with the impressive evocation of the strangeness and novelty of Nietzsche's doctrines. 'Let us look one another full in the face. We are Hyperboreans—we know well enough how aloof our life is. "Neither by land nor by sea shalt thou find the road to the Hyperboreans", so much about us Pindar already knew. *Our* life, *our* happiness is beyond the north, beyond ice, beyond death... We have discovered happiness, we know the road, we have found after thousands of years the way out of the labyrinth.' Similarly, Professor von Wright points out to me, *Zarathustra* is subtitled *Ein Buch für alle und niemanden.*

order to determine what remained of Christianity when these elements had been removed. All of Wittgenstein's mentors believed, like himself, that they could isolate what was true in Christianity by asking what *said* something to them, that the spiritual measure of inspiration is the depth of thought, and that every peasant knows in his heart how to live according to God's word. Nietzsche was alone in envisaging the opposite, as it were the Titanic, answer to the problem.

Problem and answer: these were Wittgenstein's concerns in his work also, if we use the word, as he did, for the philosophical activity that accompanied—it might be said supported—his military duties, the danger, the depression, the loneliness, the physical privations, and the spiritual struggle for a stable equilibrium. When he joined the army Wittgenstein wrote almost as if philosophy was one of the purposes of his doing so: 'I am very excited about my future life. Shall I be able to work now?' (*Notebook* 9.8.14). The thought is: Will this change restore my ability to work? It will be remembered that his house-building in Norway during the summer of 1914 was the result of a lull in his philosophic powers. His work went together with his spiritual progress. He works with confidence (*Zuversicht*) and constantly repeats Tolstoy's words about freedom through the spirit. Work was a boon—*Die Gnade der Arbeit!*—he exclaimed more than once. In the middle of hardship one could reteat into oneself and work, but the work must not be simply a way of getting through the time but must be undertaken in a devout spirit in order to make life possible.[27] It followed that he felt better when he worked—his depression left him. But conversely if he was not at peace with himself, he could not work:

> All morning I did my best to work but in vain. Clarity of vision refuses to come. I think a lot about my life. And that is an additional reason why I cannot work. [He goes on to reflect that he has not yet cut himself off sufficiently from the other members of the crew.] (*Notebooks* 13.11.14)

The ability to work goes in cycles and the determination of them is generally an inner one. Headaches, tiredness, shells overhead, and danger often occur on days when he also worked better than usual. We have already noted that he could work, presumably in the sense of thinking out the solutions to his problems, while peeling potatoes: it led him, in fact, to volunteer for that fatigue.

By a trick of the mind which was very characteristic of him, he assimilated his philosophical tasks to military situations:

27. I interpret here the notebook entry for 12.11.14, which brings several themes together. 'The important thing is not to lose hold of oneself!!! Pull yourself together! And do your work not as a pastime but devoutly, in order to live! Do no one an injury!' The idea of work as a retreat is implied in the entry for 2.11.14: 'It is bitter cold: it is a real piece of good fortune that one has oneself and can always take refuge in oneself. Much work done. What a boon work is!'

A great deal of work done: no success as yet but great confidence. I am laying siege to my problem. (*Notebooks* 24.10.14)

Worked the whole day. Stormed the problem in desperation. But I will leave my blood in front of this fortress rather than withdraw with nothing accomplished. The greatest difficulty is to retain captured forts long enough to sit quietly in them. And until the city has fallen, it is *impossible* to go on sitting quietly in one of the forts. (*Notebooks* 31.10.14)

As he wrote this he was on his way to Cracow where he would be himself besieged while, in Eastern Galicia, Przemysl, the model of a stonghold protected by a ring of detached forts, was long to hold out against the Russians. It is as if he did not distinguish clearly between his various problems or tasks; to acquit himself with dignity in battle and in military life; to produce the philosophical solution that he was searching for, and to put his life finally right, by making himself independent of fate and of other people. He seems to have regarded each of them as an opportunity to justify his life. It is perhaps typical, therefore, that he thought of each as something to be done once and for all: he adhered, as it were, to the theory of the 'knock-out blow' that was popular in military thinking just before the first war. It was as if he thought there was just one task to be performed—to meet death without disgracing himself, to break through to the solution of all his philosophical problems by a *coup de main*. This was not just a trick of style or fancy but a deep-seated habit of thought, which Russell detected. We have already seen how Wittgenstein used to think of logic *and* his sins; now, as Russell remarked after the war, his attitude to philosophy was affected by the fact that he had to compete with the dogmatism of shells and bullets. At heart he did not distinguish between *der erlösende Gedanke* in different spheres—the word or thought that would deliver him from fear or anxiety, from fastidious irritation with his comrades, and from the frustrating struggle with continually elusive problems of logic. It was for this reason that one problem might interfere with another—as he said shortly afterwards to Engelmann:

How can I be a good philosopher when I can't manage to be a good man?

Tractatus and *Notebooks* show how the problems interacted: the philosophical solution *was* the solution to the problem of life; in both areas it was a matter not simply of not asking for the wrong thing but of not asking for anything. What we notice in the early days of his journal is a similarity of structure in his approach to the problems. He treats philosophy as if it were a war: only victory will do—only a definitive solution which will enable us to set the problems aside. This is said in the preface to the *Tractatus*, of course, but the same idea is present in the analogy of the siege. As long as the defenders were in their main fortress, the detached forts alone were of no use to an attacker, but if he abandoned them and they were re-captured by a sally, they could again be used to keep him out of range of the fortress. What the fortress stood for was the general view (*der Überblick*), the solution, the great discovery, that Wittgenstein at this time constantly felt he was on the point of making. It was on the tip of his tongue, but he was always somehow frustrated.

> Winter is setting in... Once again no clarity of vision. Yet I am obviously on the point of solving the most profound problems, so much so that the solution is practically under my nose!!! The thing is, my mind is simply blind to it just at this moment. I feel that I am at the very gate but cannot see it clearly enough to be able to open it. This is an extremely remarkable state which I have never experienced so clearly as at present. (Diary 16.11.14)

The lack of a general view meant that he saw only details without realizing how they fitted into the whole: what he ought to see, he felt, was that each problem was the main problem.

'Only one thing is necessary'—as Tolstoy put it, following a traditional text now once again favoured by critics[28]—the maxim served for life, for philosophy, and for war. Wittgenstein's later philosophy too is characterized, no doubt, by a unity of method, but the thought then is that philosophy constantly returns to bewitch us, it cannot be laid once and for all. Now however in the First War he thought of a breakthrough, a definitive solution. In the war—even perhaps because of the war: it is as if the war and its way of thinking came at the right time and put him into the right circumstances, as if he went along with the war, anxious, as we have seen, to see what would become of his life. He let it affect, if not dictate, his thought. By a similar habit of thinking he often wonders whether he will get as far as the discovery that he feels to be impending: impossible to say that he meant distinctly either 'Shall I be killed first?' or 'Will my intellectual powers desert me?' Just as he often did not indicate whether he was suffering from a physical or a spiritual ailment, and spoke of being lost or going under without indication whether physical or moral death was meant. He hurt his leg, and felt that it lamed his thoughts. This attitude was part of his solipsism, which in his case was not an intellectual exercise but a moral and mystical attitude. Everything that he was involved in was seen as part of what passed before, what constituted the world for, a mind or soul, and the task of that mind or soul was to accept and thereby harmonize that multiplicity. For that reason, he felt the power of Nietzsche, because Nietzsche also was able to grasp life and experience as a whole towards which some

28. From the reply to Martha at Luke 10.42.

definite attitude must be taken; but on the other hand, Wittgenstein could not accept Nietzsche's attitude of defiance of putting oneself at odds with the world. 'How can it be reconciled with the strict solipsistic position?', we have seen him asking (p. 225) and can now see why. One thing only was necessary, to live for the moment and for the spirit in himself. This theme will recur, and—what is bound to matter most in a philosopher's biography—we shall see it decisively affecting the form and content of his first work.

Wittgenstein was apt to set dates for himself—or to assume that dates had been set—by which a specific task must be achieved. Even in peacetime he expected death to put an end to his activity. The year before, in Norway, he had led Russell to suppose that he would commit suicide in February. Now he thought, as November came to a close, that his fertility too was at an end. *Meine 3/4 Monate*—the three or four months of productivity that he had promised himself at the beginning of autumn and the war—*sind um*—were over. It is with premonitions as with suspicions—if enough are voiced or felt, some will be strikingly confirmed. In four months he had written 32 printed pages worth of philosophy; in the next five he was to write 9. It is possible that he was conscious of a longer-term cycle in his inspiration than the day-to-day fluctuations we have noted. It is interesting that—in a way he could not have foreseen—these four lean months coincided with the opening of a new phase in his army life in which both his duties and his relations with his fellows were to engage much more of his attention.

He was indeed in some despair in this latter respect at the end of November: how could he support such comrades and such superiors in the close quarters of a siege? A kindly commandant promised him at least a room to himself. There was talk of his joining the balloon section. When this came to nothing Wittgenstein went to the garrison head-quarters and by good fortune an Oberleutnant Gürth who was there overheard a reference to his knowledge of mathematics and had him assigned to his section, housed in a factory. Within a few days, actually on 9 December, he had become a member of the 'Auto.-Artillerie' detachment of the Garrison Workshop (dealing, evidently, both with vehicles and with ordnance), and on the next day enjoyed for the first time in four and a half months the luxury of being alone, in a proper room, and with a bed to sleep in.

As happens from time to time in army life he had found a home, almost a family, such as he was to come to rest in from time to time throughout his life. His work was at first tedious enough—to make a list of all the vehicles in a certain barracks and the like—and he would usually have to spend the whole day in the office—*G.T.K.* (*Ganzen Tag Kanzlei*—'Office all day') became a typical entry in his Diary. Better things awaited him; but the most significant of them was that he was at once invited to meet and put on equal terms with some of the officers, men of background and tastes to some degree comparable with his own. That first evening he had supper in Gürth's lodgings to meet a captain (no doubt Captain Scholz) whom Gürth had told about him. He had supper with five officers: Gürth had originally seemed 'very nice', now the captain seemed 'infinitely likeable' (*unendlich sympathisch*) and the others 'extremely friendly' (*riesig liebenswürdig*). They talked until half past ten and parted very cordially. A small enough event but a boon to one brought up amid every refinement of correctness and considerateness and now for some time forced to have to do with the uneducated and crude. Before meeting Gürth Wittgenstein himself had noticed the pleasure he took, once back in Cracow, in drinking two cups of coffee every evening in a cafe: 'The respectability of the atmosphere does me good' (*die wohlanständige Atmosphäre tut mir gut*). Now he found himself constantly invited to officers' messes and evidently treated as a person of interest and distinction. Not that the officers all came up to his requirements. On one day he comments:

> Spent the evening with many officers in the café. Most of them behaved like pigs. Even I drank a tiny bit more than was necessary. (Diary 27.1.15)

And when Gürth on a journey stopped for supper with a captain who was 'infinitely unlikeable', Wittgenstein made his excuses the moment they got up from table. Even when he was in good spirits he would from time to time feel his loneliness like a cold shiver running down his back. But he had now some support in the men that surrounded him. Gürth was obviously a friend and Captain Scholz was a particularly agreeable host: on one occasion Wittgenstein mentions music-making until midnight —exactly his idea of an evening. Anything of this sort was a great boon in surroundings where it was a noteworthy event to meet and sit in a cafe with a young man who had been in the University or Polytechnic in Lwow.

At the New Year Gürth went on an official journey to Vienna and took Wittgenstein, whose chief comment is that they spent many very agreeable hours together and that he was now very curious about his future life. It is significant of his attitude towards his family that meeting them again after so long and so anxious an absence elicits no further comment than that his mother was understandably extremely surprised and pleased and that he wanted to record that his own moral standing was now considerably lower than, say, at Eastertime. He gives the impression of being uneasy with his family but made at least two visits in this short time to the old composer Labor.

Gürth soon realized that he had found a remarkable new assistant and brought him forward as best he could. Wittgenstein was surprised to

find himself almost immediately promoted *Militärbeamter* (really desig-
nated a clerk not actually given a rank) and then shortly afterwards
Adjutant (again not a rank but an assignment to the Oberleutnant as
assistant). More important and more interesting was his appointment on
3 February 1915 to have oversight of the forge. He saw that this would
lead to difficulties—his exceptional status, enjoying the support of the
Oberleutnant but no official rank had already led to some heated
moments and he had thought that it was up to him to take some decisive
step. But now he said simply

> May the Spirit help me! It will be very difficult. But don't give up! (Diary
> 3.2.15)

Nevertheless within a few days he found himself in very strained relations
with one of the officers, Cadet by rank and thus presumably rather
young. There is a reminiscence of the young man who was so dangerous
for Wittgenstein in the laboratory at Manchester.

> It is possible that it might come to a duel between us. All the more then
> live a good life and follow your conscience. The spirit be with me. Now
> and in whatever the future may bring! (Diary 11.2.15)

It is curious that Wittgenstein felt powerless to avoid such an outcome:
perhaps both the intensity of his anger and disapproval and the respect
he felt for the established procedure were in play. All the same, from
what he later said about single combat,[29] it is hard to believe that he
ever meant to draw aim himself. But even to let the other man do so...
Perhaps either the institution is too remote from us, or we are simply
betraying an inability to see Wittgenstein as not in charge of a situation,
as twenty-five years old.

He reports unpleasantness—obviously not always on this level—again
and again. He worked long hours in the forge and his position there was
quite unsatisfactory. No doubt he had the responsibility for what
happened but the men (he mentions *die Mannschaft*) were ill-disposed
to take instructions from one equal or inferior to them in rank. It is likely
also that he was sufficiently sure of his technical judgement to seem
overbearing. There was much to anger and offend him and he felt that
he was wasting his inner powers. It got in the way of his thinking. He
had long talks with Gürth about it but (as he thought) these came to
nothing.

---

29. One of the pieces of advice he gave Drury when he went into the Second War was that if it
ever came to hand-to-hand fighting Drury must just let himself be killed.

The consequences were as always—his spirits were troubled, he felt isolated, not in his right mind. He would quote Goethe to himself:

> Feiger Gedanken,
> Bängliches Schwanken,
> Ängstliches Zagen,
> Weibliches Klagen,
> Wendet kein Elend,
> Macht dich nicht frei.

which (correcting a slight misquotation) may be translated:

> Cowardly thinking
> Means hesitant shrinking
> And womanish quailing
> And timorous wailing:
> These cure no troubles,
> These won't make you free.[30]

but it helped little, he was near to weeping, he thought of suicide, he felt that the externals of his life, the meanness of those around him, had invaded his inner self and filled it with hate so that there was no possibility to make room for the spirit. Various plans occurred to him—to go to the Front as an infantryman, or to join the Light Infantry (the *Kaiserjäger*) where Ficker was. Russell sent him the address of Dziewicki, a philosophical correspondent of his in Cracow, and Wittgenstein called on him within days ('a nice old man', 'a most genial young man' (i.e. a young man of genius) were their mutual impressions), but when he did so he expressed gloomy forebodings. It is clear that his mind ran on leaving the workshop and almost equally on entering some combatant arm and being killed.

Wittgenstein must clearly have been the best-qualified person in the workshop. On 22 April he mentions having complete oversight of it and even if this was during a temporary absence of Gürth's it argues a high degree of responsibility. Gürth tried to alleviate the awkward situation in various ways. He applied for a promotion of some kind for Wittgenstein, and in the meanwhile gave him provisionally the title and allowed him to wear the uniform of a *Landsturmingenieur* a reservist's post and presumably intended for maturer men. This application (which we shall describe) finally came up for a decision at the beginning of 1916, but in the meantime Wittgenstein's activity as 'the engineer' continued, successfully enough, but with a considerable sense on his side that he was

---

30. *Feiger Gedanken* etc. from Goethe's *Lila*. *Von allen guten Geistern verlassen*, literally 'abandoned by all good spirits': a phrase Wittgenstein used also at the time of his father's death, LW to BR 6.1.13.

being exploited—that is, presumably, that his abilities were being made use of without his receiving the necessary protection, in rank or standing, against inconveniences.

One consolation was that his ability to work returned, though slowly. He had felt exhausted and dead in this respect. It would need a miracle to make him produce anything: some outside force must lift the veil from his eyes. But by the middle of February he noticed that there was no day in which he failed to think (even if only fleetingly) about logic. Despair and gleams of hope alternate, until on 17 April he briefly notes: '*Arbeite*' ('Am working'). Such notes recur, and it is indeed notable that from this time on the philosophical entries in his notebooks become longer and more continuous, until in June, when the current notebook ends and we are temporarily deprived of evidence about his day-to-day activities, he was working almost as productively as in the first months of the war.

The inconclusive winter fighting in the Carpathians and the fall of Przemysl in the middle of March affected the morale of the Cracow garrison. The lull from then until the end of April, on the other hand, was a time of intense activity in the workshop. An offensive was preparing, part of whose aim was to restore the confidence of the Austro-Hungarian forces. When it came—in Wittgenstein's sector it was known as the breakthrough at Gorlice-Tarnow—it was preceded by an artillery barrage on a scale hitherto known only on the Western Front, for which every piece of ordnance available must have been required. It throws light on Wittgenstein's comments on German and Austrian commanders that the offensive in this sector was in fact led by the German General Mackensen and that the artillery tactics were devised by the German Colonel Bruchmüller ('Durchbruchmüller' as he was inevitably nicknamed). The pressure on the workshop did not cease with the offensive, because it was determined to push forward as far as possible in order to weaken decisively the Russian position in the Carpathians—and indeed with some hope of crushing them in the East altogether, though the German High Command were divided on this point. For these purposes and indeed in general it was necessary for the outnumbered Central Powers to maintain and exploit their superiority in matériel. It was in this haste and under this pressure that Wittgenstein suffered his first injury of the war: as he told it later to Arvid Sjögren he had to intervene when a colleague (one cannot exactly say a subordinate) had carried out some foolish operation. In the resulting explosion of the barrel under treatment, he suffered shock and a number of injuries—the scar of one was observable on his forehead for the rest of his life. He had to spend some time (it was now July) in hospital.

Fortune had favoured Mackensen's offensive, it had proved possible to release further troops from the Western Front; Przemysl and Lwow were recovered and by September the Central Powers had established a line running almost due north from Czernowitz to Riga. A huge salient consisting of most of Poland and Lithuania had been captured and in prisoners alone the Russians had lost 750,000. At this point it became necessary to withdraw troops to the west, where French attacks were expected; thus the front in the East was stabilized. Wittgenstein in the meantime had moved forward probably in August to a workshop train at Sokal north of Lwow, a railhead of the Austro-Hungarian system. Here he was to spend the winter.

We lack at least one notebook here but we have an independent account of Wittgenstein's life there in a letter from Dr Max Bieler,[31] which gives a convincing picture not only of Wittgenstein but of the sort of friend he attracted.

In 1915 I was employed as a doctor in a military hospital on the Russian front. Then I was ordered to take over a Red Cross Hospital Train whose commandant was sick. The train stood behind the front in a forlorn railway station at a place called Sokal, north of Lwow. Since things were at a comparative standstill on the front, the train was empty and I was able to recover from my intensive work in the hospital. Opposite my hospital train a military workshop train was standing, where vehicles, guns, etc. were repaired. I introduced myself to my neighbour, the commandant of the workshop train, and he kindly proposed that I should eat not in the mess of the local headquarters but in that of his train. I accepted gladly.

Among those present at the first meal—who were all officers—a slender man about 25 years old and without military rank. He ate and drank little and did not smoke, whereas the others stuffed themselves with food and drink and made a great deal of noise. When I asked my neighbour about him, he told me that the man was called Wittgenstein and was attached to the train as an engineer. I was glad to find a university man among the empty-headed young professional officers, especially one whom I found immediately likeable (I too eat and drink little and do not smoke). He gave the impression of not belonging to his surroundings—he was simply present there because he had to be. I think he found me likeable too, because after the first supper he invited me to see his compartment in the train.

This is how our friendship began, which lasted several months and led to daily conversations of hours at a time (without alcohol or cigarettes).

After some days he proposed that we used the familiar *Du*.

We talked about philosophical and metaphysical themes and these sometimes absorbed us so completely that we lost sight of place and time. I remember one comical incident. It was New Year's Eve 1915. The local Commandant had invited us all to the Officers' Mess for the New Year's

---

31. The letter, dated 30 September 1961, was addressed to Dr George Pitcher, who was at that time contemplating a book like the present one. With extreme kindness he made me aware of it and placed it at my disposal.

celebrations. When supper was over, getting on for 10 o'clock, the two of us retired to Wittgenstein's room in order to resume yesterday's theme. At about 11 o'clock the officers from the train let us know that it was time to set off in order to arrive at the party in good time. Wittgenstein conveyed to them that they should simply go and we would follow immediately. We quickly forgot about the invitation and the time and continued our discussion until loud voices became audible outside. It was our comrades, returning merrily at 4 a.m.—and we thought it was not yet midnight. The next day we had to make our excuses to the local commandant and pay him our New Year's compliments belatedly.

I once told Wittgenstein that when I reflect on the fundamental principle it seems to me that I am dealing with a kind of kaleidoscope in which, every time a wheel is turned, a new board comes into view with the answer to my question written on it. Only the mechanism of the wheel is defective. Just when the last board with the solution of the cardinal question is due to appear in my field of vision, it falls irretrievably into the depths as a result of the faulty mechanism. Our concern was: how could one repair the mechanism? Would one ever be in a position to do it?

The winter of 1916 was very severe. The hardships on the front were very great and the dearest wish of the soldiers was that the war might soon come to an end. Once when we were talking about this, Wittgenstein told me that he had just had a letter from Russell in London in which Russell had told him that the war would last a long time yet. . .

In April (?)[32] 1916 Wittgenstein suddenly received orders to leave for the front. It was a heavy blow for us both. He took with him only what was absolutely necessary, leaving everything else behind and asking me to divide it among the troops. On this occasion he told me that he had had a house built beside a Norwegian fjord where he would sometimes take refuge in order to have peace for his work (I think also that Russell had visited him there). He now wanted to make me a present of this house. I refused it and took in its place a Waterman's Fountain Pen. Among a few other books he took with him *The Brothers Karamazov*. He liked this book very much. We often spoke about the figure of the *starets*.

. . .

In one of our animated conversations Wittgenstein said to me 'You will become a great disciple but not a prophet.' I could say of him that he had many of the traits of a prophet but absolutely not the traits of a disciple. He was sometimes snappish but never overbearing.

. . .

Bieler is speaking of Wittgenstein in a most favourable constellation of circumstances. Perhaps, indeed, one of the most important features was precisely that he had (in Bieler himself) a disciple. It is interesting to contrast the content of the immediately preceding notebook with the

32. It was in fact in late March: the hesitation does Dr Bieler's memory credit. Similarly he is uncertain below about a visit by Russell to Norway: in fact Moore was the visitor and the house referred to was not yet built.

subjects that he and Bieler discussed. In June 1915 Wittgenstein wrote perhaps the most arid and strictly logical of the remarks from which his book was drawn. We cannot doubt that at the same time his mind was full of reflections about life and its meaning of the kind to which Tolstoy and Dostoevsky gave rise. These perhaps *could* only be discussed with another. To go over them, to develop metaphors, to extract lessons was essentially work for two together. It was like making music together rather than recording something for an impersonal posterity.

As well as a disciple he had a protégé. Not being an officer he had no claim to an orderly, Bieler told Pitcher in another letter. But the commandant of a local camp for prisoners of war assigned a young Russian to act as his servant.

> Constantin was a good boy and took care of Wittgenstein with great zeal. Wittgenstein treated him very well and in a short time the lean, frail, and dirty prisoner of war was transformed into the most fleshy and cleanest soldier of the whole garrison.

This was the Constantin of whom Wittgenstein would occasionally tell anecdotes when he was a schoolmaster—how completely he had preferred Wittgenstein's comfort to his own, how he had been a prodigious drinker, and so on—simple Russian characteristics of the kind to appeal to Wittgenstein (the farmers who overheard were principally surprised by the presumption of a schoolmaster in having had a servant).

From Bieler's account one would guess that the personal difficulties Wittgenstein had felt in the workshop in Cracow no longer bulked large in his life.

His work had entered on a new phase. Previously it had been embodied in a large pre-war notebook (presumably identical with the manuscript shown to Moore at Easter 1914) and a manuscript consisting of two notebook volumes written during the war. There were also of course the notes he had dictated to Moore in Norway. The notes were fundamentally right, but were hard to understand; and Moore (so he was led to believe) had been unable to explain his ideas to Russell.[33] His notebook entries of May (he felt) were yet harder to understand than the Moore notes. 'The problems are becoming more and more lapidary and general and the method has changed drastically.' The plan was to explain these to Russell after the war or to have them sent to him should he not survive. On one occasion he vowed that his manuscript must be printed whether anyone understood it or not.

By October he was not only pleased with the success of his recent work but was engaged in summarizing his results and writing them down

---

33. Moore was indignant when he heard of this (from reading LW to BR (received Jan. 1915)). Russell, he said in his diary, had not asked him to explain Wittgenstein's ideas to him.

in the form of a treatise (the German word is *Abhandlung*, which was indeed used in the German title of the *Tractatus*). In his letter to Russell of 22 October 1915 he refers to 'the final summary written in pencil on loose sheets of paper' which Russell must not be put off by, though it would be hard to understand. This was probably the first of about three preliminary versions of the *Tractatus*.

As far as we can judge in default of diary entries the period in the workshop train was one of relative calm and progress. The sudden departure for the front did indeed signify being pushed out from a sort of haven into open and stormy waters where he would again have to find himself and where he would for the first time experience the full horrors of the war. The departure came about in the following way. With Gürth's support—no doubt at his prompting—Wittgenstein made application in the autumn to have his status as engineer somehow legitimized. His civil studies—two years at Berlin, three at Manchester and two at Cambridge—entitled him to the *venia legendi* in England: further he had a year's work experience now in an artillery workshop. Gürth, in the report that accompanied this application, emphasized that Wittgenstein, despite his double rupture, had hastened to enlist at the beginning of the war, that he had made no use of his volunteer status, that he had undertaken humble tasks—those of a sanitary orderly and the like, until he had quite accidentally come to Gürth's notice in the artillery workshop. He had been allowed to wear an officer's uniform to overcome disciplinary difficulties. For months he had done good work there and on the train. In July (an appeal to sympathy) he had been badly hurt when a gun-barrel exploded. He wished indeed to go to the Front as a gunner, but clearly he was of great use in the workshop unit. In a further document attention is drawn to his total unfitness at three medical inspections (presumably those before the war): his recurrent hernia and his astigmatic short-sightedness (it was implied) made him quite unsuitable for front-line service.[34]

It is possible to sympathize with the authorities in their dilemma. No blame attached to Wittgenstein they emphasized (clearly Gürth's actions on the other hand were regarded as questionable). Wittgenstein was extremely employable (*äusserst verwendbar*—a masterpiece of military vocabulary since it suggests no suitable employment for him) but promotion to Landsturmingenieur was impossible—for one thing he was in the army proper or Landwehr, not in the Territorial Army or Landsturm. Another possibility that had been floated—Artillerie Zeugs-Akzessist in der Reserve—was intended for soldiers with 12 or 13 years' service. Wittgenstein could clearly not retain the title and uniform of an Ingenieur, nor otherwise stay with the train. So he packed what was

34. The file on this application is among the documents collected under Wittgenstein's name in the Kriegsarchiv in Vienna.

absolutely necessary, gave away everything else, and left like one who did not expect to return to normal life. (It is striking that correspondence with Russell and Ficker stops with the year 1915 and is not resumed until after the war. A letter written to Russell on 28 April 1915 seems not to have arrived.)

He went to the 4th battery of the 5th Field Howitzer Regiment on about 21 March. (When howitzers and field-guns were no longer grouped separately, this regiment was renamed Field Artillery Regiment 105.) The regiment's headquarters were at Olmütz in Moravia. The battery at the time he joined it was evidently on its way to the front, being attached to the 24th Infantry Division which had recently been transferred to VII Army under Pflanzer-Baltin, one of the best Austrian generals. The general situation on the Eastern Front at this time was that the Central Powers had little hope of knocking out the Russians by a large-scale encirclement. A further advance into Russia (given the almost unlimited possibilities of Russian withdrawal) would only extend their line without bringing any compensating advantage. For this reason the Western and the newly opened Italian Fronts were preferred and the forces on the Eastern Front correspondingly weakened. In the Austro-Hungarian sectors of the front this took the form of a reduction in the number of pieces of artillery available and a lowering in the quality of the troops engaged. To some extent German-Austrians and Magyars were replaced by troops from the minor nationalities whose loyalty could not be relied on. Conscious political sentiment was rare at this time but it was most common among troops from the Czech lands when mustering, so that traces of it may have been felt by Wittgenstein. On the front morale was low because of the positional warfare that had gone on since the line had been established in September, with no prospect of change for the better.

Wittgenstein's notebook for this period has survived and gives a picture of one of the hardest times of his life. The physical conditions alone were too much for him and he was forced into all sorts of exertions that he was unaccustomed to and ill-fitted for. He seems to have contracted food-poisoning and to have suffered from other illnesses. His commandant spoke of sending him back to the rear. In his sufferings after the food-poisoning life had seemed attractive; but he felt that if he were to be sent away from the front he would commit suicide. He used later to say that the war alone saved his life: its dangers (it seems) forced him to want life in the ordinary way and its duties removed from him the choice whether to go on living and the responsibility for doing so. Long marches, nights of coughing, heavy physical work left him unable to work and completely a-sexual, and gave him the sunken face that was to mark him for the rest of his life no longer as a serious young man but as one who had suffered deeply.

As before, the troops were his greatest difficulty. Fortunately the officers liked him well enough and protected him to some degree, but the other ranks (he thought) almost all hated him, just because he was a One-year Volunteer with the status we have described. He found them drunken and stupid and mean; evil and heartless; it was almost impossible to find a trace of human nature in them; he does not hate them but they nauseate him; they are caricatures of humanity, a mean riff-raff; indeed he seems to say that human beings in general are miserable scoundrels. A moving letter from David Pinsent makes him aware that he is living in exile among monsters. Thus he flies out against them in his notebook: partly of course in order not to fly out at them in reality. He knew that it was useless to be angry with them and, as on the *Goplana*, he struggled to remain impassive. He blamed himself for his failures: he was a weak man, he was not a saint, his discontent with his surroundings was the sign of a bad life. He ought to try to understand his fellow men rather than hate them. Those among whom he found himself were not mean or stupid but enormously limited: they were intelligent enough in their own circle but they lacked character and hence amplitude: 'A true believer's heart understands everything,' he said, with allusion, perhaps, both to himself and to them.

His notebook has as much self-exhortation and prayer as that written at the beginning of the war.

> Now comes inspection. My soul shrivels up. God give me light! God give me light! God give light to my soul! (Diary 29.3.16)

> Do your best. You cannot do more. And be cheerful. Be content with yourself. Because others will not prop you up or at most only for a short time (then you will become burdensome to them). Help yourself and help others with all your strength. And at the same time be cheerful. But how much strength ought one to use for oneself and how much for others? It is difficult to live a good life. But the good life is something fine. Yet not my will but thine be done. (Diary 30.3.16)

As before the prayers to God for help and the resignation into the hands of God redouble when he finds himself in battle. This happened on about 21 April—a month after he joined the battery. He was at first employed on the gun position, where there would be heavy physical work and (at his rank) nothing that required his particular abilities. It is worthy of remark how little training was thought necessary. Twice he was sent up to the observation-post, once during a surprise bombardment, both times he came under fire.

> Thought of God. Thy will be done! God be with me.

> God is all that man needs. (Diary 29 and 30.4.16)

He had in fact asked to be sent permanently to that position and (very sensibly) his application was granted. It is clear that he was an excellent aide in the observation post and the loneliness suited him temperamentally:

> I am like the prince in the enchanted castle in the observation post. (Diary 5.5.16)

There was another and more questionable attraction:

> Tomorrow perhaps I shall be sent out, at my own request, to the observation post. Then and only then will the war begin for me. And—possibly—life too! Perhaps nearness to death will bring light into my life. (Diary 4.5.16)

Here he had defined and accurate tasks of spotting and plotting on the map enemy positions, of observing and directing the fire of his own guns; all leading up to the sound of the barrage, which, later, he always remembered with excitement. Enemy fire and that of his own side did not distract him, but (by one of the illogicalities that he permitted himself) he complained bitterly in retrospect about the constant shouting into the field-telephone—though of course the passing of messages back is the raison d'être of an observation post.

The constant danger of death meant that he prayed constantly—when he had danger to face and when he had survived it. If he lost heart (*verzagt würde*), if his soul flinched when he heard a shot (note the implication that his body did not), it was a sign of a false conception of life. It was a sin and a weakness, just as his irritation with his fellow-men was a sin. He was deep in sin, but God would forgive him. If his spirit were stronger he would be happier. He must think of the goal of life. 'Only death gave life its meaning' he said during his first days in the observation post (his remarks at the time of his father's death will be recalled p. 166). This has at least two senses—only the prospect of death makes life desirable; only facing death is worthwhile in life. Wittgenstein had acted on the latter in making his way to the position of greatest danger: he was bound to experience the former too. It was as if he was determined to put himself in the most difficult situation. It would somehow overrule or cancel out his failures to master his weakness of getting angry with his comrades if he could overcome this apparently much greater and much more immediate temptation. Or, on another plane, he needed to become master of himself: he could do so in a way satisfying to himself only if he succeeded in some considerable task. He was putting himself into danger in order to force himself to be a decent human being as he conceived it.

This is perhaps the place to comment on the question whether Wittgenstein was in fact a saint, as his sister Mining sometimes believed. The answer seems to be, as he himself thought, that he was not: but he had the concept of being a saint and was aware how far he fell short. This made him (saint-like in this) anything but a comfortable companion; also he was sometimes an inspiration to others and sometimes a hero. The diary entries were not written for self-justification (certainly Wittgenstein would have looked askance at such a motive) nor is it our business to judge his life in this respect. As far as they were written for us they were meant to show the sense of his life—not its success but its point. What we must try to see from them is the nature of his ideal: what it meant for him to lead a good life and to purify himself ('ein gutes Leben führen und mich läutern', Diary 26.7.14).

Positional warfare continued throughout May, but toward the end of the month it became clear that a Russian offensive was imminent. Ammunition and troops were being brought up in large quantities and numbers to practically every sector of the Russian south-west army group. On 27 May Wittgenstein expected an attack 'today or tomorrow': the circumstances made him nervous—as is commonly reported of the Austro-Hungarian troops at the time:

Very disturbed sleep in the last weeks. Constantly dreaming of my duties. Dreams that bring me to the brink of waking. (Diary 28.5.16)

In fact the offensive came on 4 June and though it extended over the whole Russian south-west front the main areas in which it developed were at Luck to the north and at Okna immediately north of the Dniester, where Wittgenstein was stationed. The Tsar had agreed on a summer offensive to relieve his Western allies of some pressure. That however had been planned for July. Now there came a call for an earlier move in order to save the Italians. Of the Russian army group commanders only Brusilov was prepared to undertake this. The nature of the offensive (known as the Brusilov offensive and one of the most considerable Russian victories of the war) was as follows. The troops of the Central Powers (for there were a certain number of Germans in these sectors) were in strongly prepared positions. It was proposed to bombard these with mortars and artillery and to advance wherever a breakthrough of the front line seemed to have been achieved. Naturally this was expected and the defence plan was to keep the infantry in foxholes protected from the drumfire barrage until the breakthrough actually took place, when they would emerge quite fresh to engage their exhausted assailants. Meanwhile the defence's artillery engaging in counterbattery fire would reduce the effectiveness of the drumfire barrage. What Brusilov correctly anticipated was that the drumfire of

the attackers would prevent the observation and disrupt the communications on which the defence plan depended; and the confusion—
literally the smoke of battle—would make it very difficult for the
defending infantry to emerge from their foxholes at precisely the right
time. Moreover, because of the defence uncertainty about where the
main thrust would develop, there would be no substantial reserves
available behind the line to counter and contain it. This is connected
with a feature affecting morale: it was common to speak then of
Durchbruchsfieber, the panic that overtook troops on either flank of a
breakthrough: they had, after all the immense rounding-up of Russians
in 1915 as an example. It was not so much the quality of the
Austro-Hungarian troops as the fact that they were committed to a plan
which depended too much on the front line's holding that led to
Brusilov's success. He was aided, of course, by the multi-lingual
character of the army he was attacking and perhaps by some failures in
generalship.[35]

Wittgenstein had just been promoted *Vormeister* (something like
Lance-Bombardier). His division was on the left flank of XI Corps and
therefore just south of the Benigni Group (soon after renamed VII Corps
and given Wittgenstein's division), a collection of troops of very mixed
origin, who however held out very well against some of the best Russian
troops in the battle of Okna. We have two reports recommending
Wittgenstein for a decoration which give a picture of his duties and
conduct in this battle: the longer runs:

> Volunteer Wittgenstein was attached to the Observer officer during
> the engagements in front of Casemate JR77 (Cardinal Point
> Saro(?Sanvo?)krynicznyi) and the Cavalry Strongpoint Hill 458 from 4–6
> vi 16.
>   Ignoring the heavy artillery fire on the casemate and the exploding
> mortar bombs he observed the discharge of the mortars and located them.
> The Battery in fact succeeded in destroying two of the heavy-calibre
> mortars by direct hits, as was confirmed by prisoners taken. On the
> Battery Observation Post, Hill 417, he observed without intermission in
> the drumfire, although I several times shouted to him to take cover. By
> this distinctive behaviour he exercised a very calming effect on his
> comrades.[36]

The decoration recommended was the Silver Medal for Valour 2nd
Class, a considerable distinction for one of such humble rank. That

35. For a recent account, written very much from the Russian point of view and emphasizing
'Habsburg-Bourbon incompetence' in the Austro-Hungarian command see Norman Stone: *The
Eastern Front 1914–17*, 1975.

36. The other recommendation merely adds the detail of infantry fire and varies the spelling of
the 'Cardinal Point'.

decoration was in fact conferred on him in October, but evidently for a previous engagement of which we have no details. The present recommendation seems to have resulted in the Bronze Medal for Valour, also conferred in October.[37]

The Cavalry Strongpoint referred to did in fact hold out for some time and delay the Russians, but on 10 June a breakthrough took place to the north west of Wittgenstein's position and Pflanzer-Baltin was forced to withdraw, the Benigni group moving west and XI Corps moving south-west (across the Dniester where necessary) to the line of the Pruth and later to that of the Sereth. Wittgenstein presumably went with his division in the latter direction.

Here now, as at Luck to the north, the Austro-Hungarian army was in full and chaotic retreat. Many were lost: by 12 June it has been calculated Pflanzer-Baltin had only 3500 men at his disposal of the 16,000 that there should have been in Wittgenstein's formation. Wittgenstein himself later told a nephew of his long retreat from this offensive, in which he sat utterly exhausted on a horse in an endless column, with the one thought of keeping his seat, since if he fell off he would be trampled to death.

'Colossal exertions in the last month' Wittgenstein wrote on 7 July. There are, naturally enough, no diary entries to give us any hint exactly which operations he was engaged in. The south-western retreat of much of VII Army allowed the Russians to advance into Bukovina in mid-June. Wittgenstein's division took part in this fighting and then in the battle of Kolomea from 24 June to 6 July. In the event the Austrians were forced back into the Carpathians, where they spent the rest of the campaigning season. In one of his rare notebook entries Wittgenstein mentions being in the mountains:

> Terrible weather. In the mountains, bad, quite inadequate shelter, icy cold, rain, and mist. An excruciating life. Terribly difficult not to lose oneself. Because I am indeed a weak human being. But the spirit helps me. The best thing would be if I *did* fall sick; then at least I should have a little peace. (*Notebooks* 15.7.16)

Hardship and danger made him fear that he would lose himself, his portion of the spirit. His comrades too often added another difficulty to be overcome.

Throughout July and August Pflanzer-Baltin made a number of counter-offensives in the region south of the Dniester. These were in so far effective that they confined Letchitski, his Russian opponent, more or

---

37. Documents in the Kriegsarchiv in Vienna under Wittgenstein's name. His *Hauptgrundbuchblatt* signalizes the award of the Silver Medal as being 'for the second time' but it does not in fact list an earlier time and Wittgenstein himself in an official report mentions only one.

less to the area originally won. The Russians were held off from the passes into Hungary (which were more important for public opinion than for any military purpose). Finally this army at least demonstrated that the Imperial and Royal forces could not be written off. True, they had suffered a severe reverse; in many sectors they had to be stiffened by the infusion of German formations. Many Austro-Hungarian troops now came under Hindenburg's command and even Pflanzer-Baltin in the south had to accept von Seeckt (the archetype of a Prussian officer) as his chief of staff, as later did the Archduke Carl, the Austrian commander-in-chief in the south. Still, the Russians were held and their failure in the war was precisely that the Brusilov offensive was their greatest victory. Their last throw had achieved only partial success.

Wittgenstein evidently played a normal part in these operations. We hear of his being under fire, of messing with the infantry (he castigates himself for minding being sent to mess with the men rather than with the officers as promised and for trying to obtain his rights), of a three-day journey to a new position. Towards the middle of August he heard that he would shortly be sent back to the rear for training and he welcomed this, to all appearances because at present he was surrounded by meanness. Normal training must continue even in war—or even more in war; and Wittgenstein with his skill and his courage was an obvious candidate for a commission. It may also have played a part that the severe fighting in his sector now seemed to be coming to an end, so that he could be released.

Wittgenstein had been continuously in the field for five months. The notes he made, both philosophical and personal, are few, but they testify to a change in his thinking as great as that which he himself saw in his countenance. In April he made a handful of notes (barely a page and a half of print) on propositions, functions, and objects—the topics of his previous wartime notes. In May there are a few scribbles that do little more than raise questions, except for one extremely interesting remark about the modern illusion that the laws of nature explain natural phenomena. The ancients (for whom God and Fate played the part now reserved for the laws of nature) were to this extent clearer, that they recognized a clear terminus—they did not think that *everything* could have grounds given for it. (These remarks are used in *Tractatus* 6.371–2.) Wittgenstein is beginning to make general remarks about the *Welt-anschauung* of his time. It was the beginning of July[38] before he could write anything again—the reason for his silence we have seen in his campaigns. But during that May of mounting tension and that June of

38. 1 or 4 July (though 11 seems to be written) appears to be the real date of the remarks ascribed to 11.6.16 by the editors of *Notebooks 1914–17* even in their second edition. There are also a couple of scribbled formulae, apparently from late May. The code diary also is silent between 29 May and 6 July.

rout he had reflected (he tells us on 6 July) a great deal on every possible subject. 'Oddly enough I cannot establish the connexion with my mathematical modes of thought.'[39] The difficulty can be seen from the remarks with which he reopens his philosophical notes:

> What do I know about God and the purpose of life?
> I know that this world exists.
> That I have a place in it like that of my eye in its visual field.
> That there is something problematic about it, which we call its sense.
> That this sense is not situated in the world but outside it.
> . . .
> The sense of life, i.e. the sense of the world, can be called God.
> And connected with the image of God as a father. (*Notebooks* 1(4?).7.16)

Throughout the rest of the notebook—some twenty printed pages—reflections on life, on religion, on ethics, on the will, on solipsism are interspersed among (and indeed outweigh) his more customary discussions of the general form of a proposition and the nature of an operation. It is significant moreover that these reflections are no longer of such a personal character as the prayers and self-analysis of his earlier notebooks—and that they are not written in cypher. It is as if he had bridged—or was about to bridge—some gap between his philosophy and his inner life. Indeed he seems to say this on 2 August:

> Yes, my work has broadened out from the foundations of logic to the essence of the world.[40]

We have mentioned above (p. 77) that the implications for *Weltweisheit*—for the philosophy of life—of his technical philosophy were not always apparent to him, though no doubt they were unconsciously part of his motivation. But now, in this the worst summer of danger and defeat, somewhere between the shells and the bullets, he began to feel that the two were connected; that grasping the essence of propositions or of an operation had something to do with adopting the right attitude towards life. No longer does his attitude towards his philosophy merely exhibit the same structure as his attitude towards life: the two are now identified. The critic of Russell is fused in the reader of Dostoevsky.

Wittgenstein's first philosophy (and much of his later personality) is the fruit of that campaigning season, but for fruition was also required the succeeding autumn, comparatively free of military exertions and annoyances, but full of intellectual and personal factors which combined

39. This occurs in a code pasage.
40. 'Ja meine Arbeit hat sich ausgedehnt von den Grundlagen der Logik zum Wesen der Welt.' *Notebooks* 2.8.16 (Miss Anscombe's translation seems to me to miss the point here.)

and intensified the amalgamation of religion and logic that was to surprise Russell so much after the war. These factors also evoked contradictory elements in his attitude towards others—the affectionate and dependent alongside the authoritarian. The roulette-wheel of military life now released him from banishment and allowed him to fall for a while into another of the 'families' we have mentioned. It was, perhaps for the first time, a family in which he was at least the elder brother, if not the uncle or the father.

The circumstances can be reconstructed as follows. Wittgenstein was posted from his regiment to a Reserve Officers' School in the town of Olmütz in Moravia but first went on leave to Vienna. There he met Loos[41] who gave him the name of a young pupil just then convalescing in that very town. This was Paul Engelmann.

Engelmann has given his account of the meeting that resulted and begins by describing the physical setting—the town itself.

> It was in my time still an entrancing ruin of bygone days arising out of the spiritual ruin of the twentieth century. A childhood spent between the flaking town houses grouped round two vast market-places, or in one of the crooked little lanes tightly crammed into the inadequate space of a former fortress, in houses with dark vaulted stairways, in flats consisting of a few huge and gloomy rooms with badly dilapidated floors of varnished boards, inhabited by the last off-shoots of old and slowly dying burgher families—such a childhood will endow a man with a musical ear, as it were, for things past which must elude those brought up in more ordinary surroundings.[42]

Engelmann does not say, perhaps he did not feel, that to the Viennese Olmütz was a byword for provincialism, a remote German outpost in the Czech lands. This was part of the reason for the intensity of its cultural life. It is striking how many of the thinkers of the last half-century of the Dual Empire came from such small towns—Freud, Mach, Husserl, Gomperz, Loos from Moravia, Kraus from Bohemia (even the German writers of Prague, Rilke and Kafka, are a related phenomemon). Theirs was a German culture, its last efflorescence matching the Czech national revival, which eventually overtook it. It was a Catholic culture—the churches and pillars and statues of the Counter-reformation were in every square, the saints' days were observed, every Olmützer knew of the

41. An undated notebook entry (in cypher) of about this time probably refers to this meeting: 'Am depressed. Alone, alone! Thank God. Loos is alive.' Whether Wittgenstein is glad to be alone after the campaigning or depressed to find himself isolated even at home is not clear; but perhaps the second is the more probable interpretation and the thought is that Loos had been a refuge from his family, as Labor may have been when Gürth took him to Vienna at the beginning of 1915.

42. P. Engelmann: *Letters fom Ludwig Wittgenstein with a Memoir* (Oxford, 1967). I was also in correspondence with P. Engelmann and have further been able to consult Dr Heinrich Groag and Dr Max Zweig, survivors of this period.

unique rank and privileges of the archbishop. And it was a culture to a large extent transmitted by Jews, some few being converts like Archbishop Kohen of Olmütz or for a while Kraus himself, most of them still Jews as far as registration went but willing to embrace the essence, or what they took to be the essence, of Christianity. So it was, at all events, in the small group of young people to whom Wittgenstein was now brought.

Engelmann, who introduced him to them, had many of the qualities Wittgenstein looked for in a disciple. He was gentle, not self-seeking, even ineffectual, but above all painfully critical of his own failings. By profession he was, or was training himself as, an architect, more particularly an *Innenarchitekt* or interior designer. He was small, was generally considered likeably ugly, and his health was not good.[43] In 1915 he was invalided out of the army after only a few days. In one respect he thought himself very different from Wittgenstein. At the outbreak of war he had shared in the general upsurge of patriotic feeling, which we have traced in Wittgenstein's notes; but with time he became convinced of the justice of Karl Kraus's opposition to the conduct of the war by the Central Powers. He helped Kraus to collect the newspaper cuttings that made up so much of the wartime *Fackel* and were then, in many cases, used in the phantasmagoric and unperformable drama *The Last Days of Mankind*. These were, typically, official reports, which by their very wording, without commentary, revealed the barbarity of the authorities and the corruption of the press. One often-cited example is the following report from 1916:

Berlin, 22 September.
The Wolff bureau reports: One of our U-boats hit in the Mediterranean on 17 September a packed enemy troopship. The ship sank within 43 seconds.[44]

To which Kraus merely added the title 'With watch in hand'. There is something Austrian about the fact that this bitter satire on the official propaganda was commonly carried by officers at the front, while British officers were satisfied with broadsheets reprinting pieces by Dickens, Macaulay, Shakespeare, and Scott. The Austrians were called upon to show courage without confidence in the value, let alone the success, of their cause. It was natural for them to emerge with a sourer and more realistic view of the nature of human societies and, on the internal side, with a sense of duty not supported by a general confidence in the group

43. On the whole Wittgenstein naturally preferred good looks but he also liked to 'take up' someone, to see something where others did not: 'All Luki's swans are geese,' his sister Gretl used to say.
44. *Die Fackel* 437–42, October 1916, p. 121.

they belonged to, with a conscience focused on motive and manner
rather than effect—the precursor of what was later called inner
emigration. We have seen signs of this attitude in Wittgenstein: it
reflected a more hopeless moral situation than that facing his English
contemporaries and many of his differences from them in the 30s and 40s
can be traced back to it. But Engelmann's reaction was not that of
Wittgenstein; he went further even than Kraus. Kraus is said to have
admitted later that he had from the first hoped for the defeat of the
Central Powers. Engelmann was not against one side in the war: he was
a pacifist completely. In his memoir he refuses to describe his activities,
and only claims that their effects were not quite as fanciful and
imaginary as Wittgenstein, like many others, assumed at the time.[45] He
is not here speaking of the effect of Kraus's *Fackel* but perhaps of
incidents like the following. Once when he was sick in bed a new
transport for the front was at Mass (as the custom was) in the church of
St. Maurice outside his house. He rose from his bed and went into the
church and exhorted the men in the name of the Holy Spirit to lay down
their arms. This, naturally, he did in German and it is unlikely that the
Czech troops understood it. In a kindly way the officer in charge simply
told Englmann to be off and took no further action. Engelmann, back in
bed, was greatly relieved, and, as soon as he could be moved, his friend
Groag took him to Vienna and then to Zell-am-See, returning only when
all might be supposed forgotten.

Engelmann's whole circle was an unworldly one—children of
commercial or professional families, all aspiring to devote themselves to
the arts or to things of the mind. Engelmann's own father was not a
success in business and made a living but not on the level that the family
had achieved in the past. His brother was a gifted and satirical cartoonist
under the name Peter Eng and a sister was a painter also and deeply
depressive. Engelmann was to spend his life on small but choice
commissions, on private publications and on composing, in exquisite
hand-writing, his own collection of the best German poems, which he
feared might otherwise perish. All were at odds with the world, rather as
Engelmann's mother, the warm centre of intellectual evenings in their
slightly shabby flat, resented the richer but more recently arrived
burghers of the town.

Of the circle too were the cousins Zweig—Fritz the musician and
Max the writer; Max studied the law but devoted his life to writing
dramas written according to the strictest rules of unity. He did not take
over his father's practice in Prossnitz but spent the greater part of his life,
with Engelmann, in a sort of exile in Israel, where German culture must
indeed have seemed precarious. Lastly there was Heini Groag, already

45. P. Engelmann: *Letters*, p. 73.

mentioned, the most practical perhaps and the most amusing. He wished for a stage career but eventually became a successful lawyer: traces of the idealism of his youth remained in his devotion to pacifism, until survival in Moravia, first as a Jew, then as a bourgeois, necessarily preoccupied him.

These now became Wittgenstein's circle too, and by degrees were associated with his family—in the twenties Engelmann would be called on for architecture and design, Groag for a legal task, Groag's cousin when an engineer was required, and so on. They were, we have said already, a family to him. Like them he was inclined not to practise the skills that had made his family rich; and his own family, like their small group, spent its time making music, performing plays, discussing books and poems. It was like being back with Gretl and her friends. Except that here he could set the tone: where she had taught him not to believe, he could lead them to the passages of Tolstoy and Dostoevsky that came closest to his ideal of religion. And here was the benign motherly figure of Mrs Engelmann to approve of everything. And Engelmann himself, earnest and self-accusing was just such a disciple as he needed. Wittgenstein still stammered but Engelmann's companionship enabled him—served, he used to say, as a forceps—to bring the words out. Indeed Engelmann was so familiar with his thinking that he would come out first with the correct formulation. Or Wittgenstein would use the sharp mind and phenomenal memory of Groag to develop his ideas. With one or the other (Groag or Engelmann) he would leave the evening's gathering and each would accompany the other home in turn, prolonging the conversation well into the night. Here surely there was respite from battle, here surely the hearts with feeling that he had cried out for on the Vistula.

For them, certainly, these were unforgettable days. Here came a man from Vienna only a little older than themselves but already knowing so much, bringing the answers to their questings from remote realms of logic and mathematics where lucidity and certainty seemed to be possible. They were in awe of him of course: he had seen and suffered more, he bought his uniform from the best tailor in Olmütz, he came from one of the first families of Vienna—it never occurred to them that he was nearly as Jewish as themselves, he had talked on equal terms with the great. He came to them with a mixture of attitudes very characteristic of him—on the one hand an engaging modesty and the politeness—more than the politeness, the *Liebenswürdigkeit*, the engaging charm—of his family, on the other hand a severity of moral judgement and a brutality or directness in its utterance which alarmed them. One respect in which he stood apart from them was that he took no part whatever in the amorous intrigues to which a circle devoted to the life of the mind lends itself. They thought he had no relation to women, while for his part he told one of them—not a close friend—'You are like pigs rolling in filth.' They knew him well enough—at least Groag did—to ask him about his evident need to keep others at a distance: it was then that he recited Schopenhauer's parable of the porcupines and their conflicting demands, for warmth and to avoid one another's prickles (above, p. 44). And so it was with himself—he had need of their comfortable and contentious evenings, but in the middle of it all he would cast imploring looks, perhaps to Groag, wanting the other to take him away. (Here, to be sure, the severe stomach troubles from which he suffered at this time provide an alternative explanation; but an unconvincing one since he could talk happily with a single friend.) Perhaps indeed Wittgenstein's difficulty was that of finding the correct distance—either he was shunning all contact, as when he wanted to live in the high tower of the *Rathaus*, or he was so involved in his friends' lives that their failings rankled.

To these young people Wittgenstein was chiefly a guide: they played and read and talked all their lives—but the time with him remained in their memories. He set the tone. He was not the performer but the critic whose judgement mattered. Fritz Zweig would play to them, Fritz who was later to be conductor of the Berlin opera: Wittgenstein's role was to be leader of the audience. When the neighbours above stamped on the floor (it was 9.30 when the concert began) Mrs. Engelmann began to demur but Wittgenstein insisted that the neighbours ought to be happy to hear such music. He led the audience at their plays—no one thought he might act but his presence and participation made their performance of the *Malade imaginaire* into a memorable occasion.

As often with Wittgenstein what was enjoyed and explored was a limited repertoire of the great creative artists of the past: Molière was performed, Shakespeare too we hear.[46] Fritz Zweig would play them Bach on the organ of the synagogue: humming and playing the piano at the same time he would render vocal and orchestral pieces by Mozart, Schumann, Schubert, and Brahms. (We are reminded of Wittgenstein's whistling with Moore and Pinsent—and he did indeed whistle for Engelmann too.) The younger men execrated Wagner and this was tolerated by Wittgenstein. So too with poetry: the most severely classical poems of Goethe and Mörike, Engelmann points out, were what Wittgenstein required as an antidote to the poems of Albert Ehrenstein, when these were sent to him at the front (p. 260 below). It was to Groag that Wittgenstein praised Schiller's passion for freedom (p. 34 above) and to him also that he said of Grillparzer, 'We do not know how beautiful he is' (p. 35 above); and every day in their time together he talked to Groag of Goethe. Engelmann tells (like other witnesses) of

46. 'I often think of you, of the *Midsummer Night's Dream* and the second ballet in the *Malade imaginaire* etc.' LW to PE 31.3.17.

Wittgenstein's admiration for Gottfried Keller with his exact fit of expression and feeling. The same quality seemed to Engelmann to be present in a poem of Uhland's which in Karl Kraus's phrase was 'so clear that no one understands it'. *Graf Eberhards Weissdorn*, romantic in theme, classical in the precision and reticence of its presentation: Engelmann rightly attached great significance to Wittgenstein's few lines of comment on this poem:

> The poem by Uhland is really magnificent. And this is how it is: if only you do not try to utter what is unutterable then *nothing* gets lost. But the unutterable will be—unutterably—*contained* in what has been uttered. (LW to Engelmann 9.4.17)

Two things are noteworthy here: that Wittgenstein's feeling for literature is wedded to one of the central ideas of his philosophical work—what is shown by a proposition cannot also be stated explicitly in it; and that the idea seems to have been suggested by Engelmann—Wittgenstein in the letter is agreeing with him. In their conversation Engelmann had not aspired to do more than follow at a distance the logical conceptions that Wittgenstein was developing but he felt he was able, because of his own spiritual crisis at the time, to grasp the motives that led Wittgenstein to write the book he was engaged on. That book was to be a reaction against sensationalism and psychologism in philosophy: it was of a piece with Wittgenstein's rejection of most of contemporary literature. It was the reactionaries that he turned to—Kraus first, and through him Weininger and the critic Kürnberger, from whom Wittgenstein used to quote the phrase later used as the motto of the *Tractatus* (curiously enough he would not say where the quotation came from: it was in fact quoted also by Kraus).[47] That motto is typical of the circle he found himself in or perhaps created. They too thought for a while that everything worth saying could be said in a few words. 'One thing is necessary'—the keynote of the Tolstoyan Christianity that Wittgenstein had discovered at the front—was now applied to the intellectual life generally. It seems probable that the approach was in the broadest sense linguistic: Engelmann seeks to draw a parallel between Kraus's taking his opponent at his word, convicting him out of his own mouth by what is made manifest in what he says, and Wittgenstein's critique of philosophical language;[48] it seems likely also that it was during this time that Wittgenstein read or reflected on the *Nachwort* to the Grimms' fairy tales by Paul Ernst, which influenced him so powerfully with its account of how language misleads us—graphic modes of expression and

47. Wittgenstein often discussed Kürnberger with Heinrich Groag, to whom I owe this point.
48. Paul Engelmann: *Letters from Ludwig Wittgenstein*, pp. 124–7.

metaphors being taken literally.[49] Wittgenstein in both cases goes beyond his sources: he detects and dissects nonsense, not mere deception or deceptiveness. There is some speculation in these suggestions, however: what Wittgenstein certainly dwelt on in this Olmütz period was a theme common to Weininger and Kraus, the idea that logic, ethics, and aesthetics were one. Wittgenstein often discussed Weininger's chapters on these themes at Olmütz, and he echoes them in the *Tractatus* when he says that ethics and aesthetics are one. Engelmann points out two aspects of Kraus's work that are relevant here: Kraus insisted that works must not be judged by one-sided aesthetic canons and that a moral defect will generally be manifest in an aesthetic fault in an artist's work: but clearly more than this was meant by Wittgenstein and his friends. The general lines of their thought can be recovered from his 1916 notebooks:

> The work of art is the object seen *sub specie aeternitatis* and the good life is the world seen *sub specie aeternitatis*. This is the connexion between art and ethics. (*Notebooks* 7.10.16)
>
> Is it the essence of the artistic way of looking at things that it looks at the world with a happy eye?
>
> Life is serious, art is gay. [Schiller]
>
> For there is certainly something in the idea that the end of art is the beautiful. And the beautiful *is* what makes happy. (*Notebooks* 20–21.10.16)

A way of looking at things: we shall see later that this is connected with the notion of something that can only be communicated in a special way, shown or manifested but not said. What is shown in art is perhaps what Engelmann describes as a solution.[50] This accords with Wittgenstein's liking (manifested admittedly at a later date) for a 'happy ending' in films and also for his *penchant* for the edifying in poetry—a slight limitation in taste not indeed required by but consentaneous with his views. As for ethics, the point is that there too—i.e. in the world as a whole—there is a solution to be seen, by eyes that are prepared for it.

We shall shortly describe what that solution seemed to the Olmütz circle to be. It is less clear (from Engelmann's memoir and from the reports of survivors) how they understood the identity of logic with ethics and aesthetics. Wittgenstein made some of them read Frege and he talked to them about Kant and Schopenhauer, with whom they had, like

49. Max Zweig was a great admirer and follower of Paul Ernst, a neo-classic writer and critic. Groag recalled his being much talked about at Olmütz. Wittgenstein later told Rhees that he would have liked to include Ernst's name in the preface of the work in later editions, for the reason given in our text. Wittgenstein may, however, have known Ernst's *Nachwort* earlier: Russell's library has a copy of the relevant edition of the tales, probably one of Wittgenstein's pre-First War books, which Russell bought.

50. P. Engelmann: *Letters*, p. 93.

himself, the normal educated man's acquaintance. 'In the words of the great Kant' he would quote from time to time: Engelmann gathered that Wittgenstein did not believe in the existence of synthetic propositions a priori.[51] Now there was indeed a parallel between Wittgenstein's aim and Kant's: the one wanted to abolish reason to make way for faith, the other to remove the whole of ethics and religion from the area of speculation into that of the inexpressible; but the concentration on logic important for Wittgenstein is lacking in Kant. The point was to show that logical statements too (the best that philosophy could aspire to) said nothing. Logic therefore did not present us with a set of truths independent of experience: it was in this like ethics, so that he could say, in July of that year,

> Ethics does not treat of the world. Ethics must be a condition of the world, like logic. (*Notebooks* 24.7.16)

Logic is thus the paradigm of the inexpressible: there is something to be seen but nothing to be said. At the time of his Olmütz discussions he was experimenting in his notebooks with the notion of an operation (later discussed in propositions 5.21–5.254 of the *Tractatus*) and this emphasis is naturally and correctly reflected in Engelmann's account of Wittgenstein's thought (*Letters etc.* p.104). The knowledge of forms of propositions and their relations, which is what logic gives us, is really the recognition that one proposition can be produced out of others by certain operations. That it can be is not a logical *fact* and seeing that it can be is not a logical *experience*.

There it was a matter of how one looked at things, just as in ethics it was a matter of how one willed (*Notebooks* 29.7.16: 'Here everything seems to turn, so to speak, on *how* one wants.') This variant on Schopenhauer's views appears in Wittgenstein's notebooks at this time and in his conversations with his friends. It is as if behind the ordinary life of wanting and willing there was a deeper life and a truer will for which success and failure in the ordinary life ought to be indifferent. Thus he said to Groag, in a conversation later repeated in a letter to Engelmann:

> We are asleep. Our life is like a dream. But in our better hours we wake up just enough to realize that we are dreaming. Most of the time, though, we are fast asleep. I cannot awaken myself! I am trying hard, my dream body moves, but my real one *does not stir*. This, alas, is how it is! (LW to PE 9.4.17)

---

51. P. Engelmann: *Letters*, p. 125.

How quite to accommodate such thoughts within a Schopenhauerian framework is uncertain; Wittgenstein himself said at this time 'I am conscious of the complete unclarity of all these sentences' (*Notebooks* 2.8.16) but the general outlines of his thought at the time and of its reflection in his conversations with his Olmütz friends are not in doubt. Ethics, the good, the happy, the harmonious life were not marked by any objective feature, by anything within the sphere of the will conceived as an agent altering the facts of the world. The good life is marked on the contrary by a metaphysical or transcendental feature—by an attitude of the willing subject in the deeper sense, an attitude which can surmount and accept the misery of the world and can regard its amenities as boons granted by fortune which can always be renounced. As with Schopenhauer the impression remains that misery predominates in the world and that death is not simply to be faced but even welcomed. 'Nothing better could have happened to him' (*Es könnte ihm nichts besseres passieren*) was Wittgenstein's comment when they spoke of the death in battle of an Olmütz friend. But he seems to have rejected suicide rather for Schopenhauer's reason (that it was the supreme act of self-assertion of the will—here the ordinary will). Thus he says that if suicide is allowed, everything is allowed. But he hesitates and asks, 'Or perhaps even suicide is in itself neither good nor evil?' (*Notebooks* 10.1.17—the last entry preserved in his wartime notebooks). He was disturbed, he told his Olmütz friends, by the suicide of Weininger. (His later letters to Engelmann indicate that for a period suicide was never far from his thoughts and also that he thought suicide involves a *misuse* of the will.)

A whole spiritual attitude is not easily described: it is probable that Wittgenstein and his friends also felt that they were exploring and creating it and had never quite fully grasped it. Acceptance and resignation before the facts of the world were only a part of what they aspired to: indeed it was much more the heights and depths within one's own soul that they sought to be reconciled with. Every reader of Wittgenstein's letters—particularly those to Engelmann—will recognize the theme: 'the state of not being able to get over a particular act' (*wenn man über eine bestimmte Tatsache nicht hinweg kommt*) is mentioned in the very letter in which Wittgenstein analyses the sordidness of suicide and we have seen the same sort of preoccupation in the earlier wartime diary. Of the same kind is the admiration that Engelmann reports (*Memoir*, p.80) for the self-knowledge of the pilgrim in Tolstoy's story who admits that 'Sin got the better of me' and does not try to excuse his action. In the other scale is the enthusiasm Wittgenstein felt for the exclamation that Dmitri Karamazov—even and precisely he, the libertine—makes when he says: 'Hail to the Highest—also within me!' Dostoevsky was preferred as a teacher even to Tolstoy, probably because the sense of something good in human nature even in its depths, of happiness to be found even in a life that it would be a blessing to be rid of, is stronger in him. In July of 1916 Wittgenstein uses Dostoevsky to illustrate and explain the attitude towards the will and the world that we have mentioned. Right willing gives a meaning to the world without altering anything in it.

> And to this extent [he says] Dostoevsky too is right when he says that the man who is happy is fulfilling the purpose of existence.[52]

The essential feature of this attitude in Wittgenstein's view is the renunciation of an influence upon what happens, so he goes on to refine on Dostoevsky:

> Or one could also say that the one who fulfils the purpose of existence is he who needs no further purpose other than life. That is to say, who is satisfied. (*Notebooks* 6.7.16)

The elder in Dostoevsky tells the woman of little faith that this happiness will be achieved, and that the answer to all her questions and doubts will be found, only by active love of our neighbours. It is clear that for him, as for Wittgenstein, results do not matter, but he is more specific about the aim with which one should live, whereas Wittgenstein, at a higher level of abstraction, as it were, simply says that we must be in agreement with the world. Life itself, his thought seems to be, will from moment to moment provide us with something we clearly ought to aim at. If we depart from this we shall have a bad conscience.[53]

As in his notebook reflections, so in his conversation with his Olmütz friends, the ethical went over into the religious. They would read the Bible—chiefly the New Testament—together: 'It must be more than human inspiration,' said Engelmann as he read passages to Groag. Wittgenstein thought it best read in Latin. The great building blocks of that language always appealed to him, but there was also the remoteness, the hieratic quality that Latin lent to the text, quite the opposite of that familiarity with the sacred which he so much disliked. Thus the New Testament was not a set of precepts for life, but its tone or approach, properly dwelt on, were those appropriate for life. 'I know nothing of religion', he told Groag, 'but there is surely something right in the concept of a God and of an after-life—only something quite different

---

52. *Notebooks* 6.7.16: the reference is presumably to *The Brothers Karamazov*, pt. 1, bk. 2, ch. 4, where the elder Zossima says, 'Men are made for happiness and he who is completely happy has a right to say to himself: I've carried out God's sacred will on earth.'

53. Concretely conscience speaks like Dostoevsky's elder: 'When my conscience upsets my equilibrium, there is *something* with which I am not in agreement. But what is that? Is it *the world?* ... For example: it makes me unhappy to think that I have offended so and so. Is that my conscience?' *Notebooks* 8.7.16

from what we are capable of imagining.' Engelmann's poem,[54] in which the soul after death realizes that flames that surround it *are* the love of God, represents the same attitude. In seeing this, the soul wakes from a dream—our life *is* a dream as Wittgenstein said to Groag. Religion would give one a right view, a waking view, of the world, and, with it, an acceptance of fate—if his manuscripts went astray, it was God's will[55] (there was also modesty here about the value of his work, Groag thought); while the war was welcome because it forced one to realize one was in God's hands. There remained the problem of behaving decently (the word *anständig* again) in the field, as in ordinary life. On this point Wittgenstein shared his scruples chiefly with Engelmann. Both were given to self-castigation, as can be seen from the correspondence between them (though this was even more a theme for talk).

Wittgenstein's military training proceeded smoothly enough, with minor interruptions. He was not studying hard enough (*Ich bin ein Schweinehund.*) He suffered from gastric flu. Engelmann carried gruel from his mother to Wittgenstein's lodgings on the outskirts of the small town: 'You overwhelm me!'—'No, I overwhelm myself!' (Engelmann had spilt some of the gruel on his own topcoat.) The humour and the care for the sick friend were very much to Wittgenstein's taste. The flu was evidently a recurring affliction, because Wittgenstein described Dr. Hahn's medicine as 'the only one that has ever helped me'. In later life he ate bland foods—what a child would like, he said—and sometimes explained that his simple diet was in no way penitential but was what he preferred. It was rather that of an ulcer patient and it seems likely that the hardships of the war had accentuated a pre-existing diathesis.

On 1 December 1916 Wittgenstein was given the rank of Fähnrich in der Reserve for the duration of the war (later back-dated to 1 October 1916): he had previously been a Kriegsfreiwilliger Kanonier with the title of Vormeister (from 1 June 1916) and Korporal (from 1 September 1916). In his new rank as officer he remained attached to the 4th battery of the 5th Field Howitzer Regiment (later 105 Field Artillery Regiment), which he had joined from the workshop in March 1916. The course at the Reserve Officers' School seems to have been over before Christmas and Wittgenstein left for leave in Vienna, first wrapping up carefully his Christmas presents for Engelmann's mother and delivering them in a laundry-basket.

His stay in Olmütz was at an end, but he was to return there occasionally, since it was the depot of his regiment; and in any case he kept in touch with his Olmütz friends. Even in Vienna one of his first acts was to call on Loos, with a commission from Engelmann. Fritz Zweig

54. Printed in P. Engelmann: *Letters* and in L. Wittgenstein: *Briefe*, p. 79. Wittgenstein liked it well enough to want to read it to his sister Mining.
55. Undated letter to Engelmann: *Letters*, p. 7; *Briefe*, p. 79.

was also there and called on Wittgenstein. Engelmann arrived just after Wittgenstein himself left but his friendship with the Wittgenstein family—into which he was soon completely adopted—probably began about this time.

About this time, too, according to Hermine Wittgenstein, Ludwig made a gift of 1,000,000 crowns to the state for the purchase of a 30 cm calibre mortar.[56] The dating seems correct: Ludwig's income is put at 300,000 crowns per year in one of the forms that Gürth made out when urging his promotion and three or four years of modest living might have left him with a surplus of this order. Hermine makes gentle fun of her brother for the unpractical manner of this donation. The state had no way, she says, of using this money for the purpose intended, so it was put into the Emperor's (by now Kaiser Karl) Charitable Fund and vanished in the later inflation, wasted, just as the K.600,000 given for cancer research after her father's death had been wasted through lack of proper supervision. No more wasted, one would have thought, than any money taken by the state in taxes, and thus as much a contribution as the million given by Paul, who (like his father for once) actually saw to the manufacture of military greatcoats. Still it is true that we have here another example of how Wittgenstein distanced himself from his money and left the management of it to others. The other aspect to note is the simple patriotism of the gesture, which completely ignored the pessimism about the outcome of the war that Wittgenstein did not conceal from his Olmütz friends.

Wittgenstein was on active service again from 19 January. His battery was now attached to a Croatian division, 42 HID, of the Honved or Hungarian Territorial Army (successsively commanded by Lieutenant-Field-Marshals Šnjarić, Lipošćak (March–June 1917), and Mihaljević) in the XIII Corps (FML von Csicserics) and III Army (Colonel-General von Tersztyánszky)—the names, and those of the towns and rivers involved give some idea of what it was like to belong to the Dual Monarchy. In general the Austro-Hungarian troops in this sector were in the same positions in which they had halted the flagging Russian advance when Wittgenstein left for his training course. The early part of 1917 was a period of comparative silence between the Carpathians and the Dniester, with occasional minor attacks by 42 HID (and 5 ID with other batteries of Wittgenstein's regiment) across the Bystrzyca Solotwinska towards Bohorszcsany. In March there was a flurry of patrolling activity. It was much hoped that the February Revolution would affect the supplies, the state of preparedness, and the morale of the opposing troops. At the very least information was required. Wittgenstein, in fact, volunteered to lead a patrol against Drwiniacz on 15

---

56. *Familienerinnerungen*, pp. 109 and 112ff. Probably the Austrian 12-inch howitzer, which even the Germans used for its mobility, is meant.

March, the day of the Tsar's abdication. We hear this from a citation, which says that the patrol was undertaken in very difficult weather conditions and that valuable information was brought back.[57]

In fact the troops opposite 42 HID and III Army generally were not at this point greatly affected by Red or other propaganda. There were even some slight Russian advances, and war-maps show Wittgenstein's division still opposite Lachowce at the end of June. At this point it was clear that a Russian attack was imminent (the last major one of the war, as it turned out) and III Army's reserves, Wittgenstein among them, were grouped at Rosulna awaiting it. They were thus involved on the flank of the battle of Stanislau-Kalusz in which the Russian 8 Army under Kornilov drove the Austro-Hungarian forces back from the line of the Bystrzyca Solotwinska as far as that of the Lomnica, where (in Wittgenstein's sector) a stand was made at Ldziany. This Russian advance enjoyed some success. An entire Czech regiment defected. Above all, there was a threat to the East Galician petroleum fields. German troops reinforced III Army and General Kritek was given command. The stand was successful. At Ldziany itself the part played by defensive fire in beating off an attack on 42 HID is particularly commented on in the official history.[58] A further citation for Wittgenstein is preserved covering these days (10–20 July 1917). He was awarded the Silver Medal for Valour first class 'for carrying out admirably the duties of an Observer Officer ... under heavy fire. Heavy losses were caused to the enemy in decisive moments. Fire was directed onto threatened positions which were otherwise invisible to the Battery Commander.'[59] This was not, of course, a context for understatement, but the confidence felt in Wittgenstein by his immediate superiors is very evident. We find it again in an account drawn up, partly by him, partly by them, of his activities from 30 September 1916 to 30 September 1917. Under the heading 'Suitability for next level of command' Lt.i.d.R. Scholz writes:

> Suitable to be a troop-commander. In view of his special qualities of character and his misgivings (no doubt unfounded) regarding other forms of service, his employment in a framework other than that of an observer would not be of much use. Conduct outstanding, especially in the engagements round Ldziany.

Scholz also mentions, under another heading, Wittgenstein's good influence on subordinates, especially effective in battle.[60]

57. *Verzeichnis über ... Tapferkeitsmedaillen* of FHR5 in 3 Army Kriegsarchiv, Vienna.
58. *Oesterreich-Ungarns letzter Krieg* VI.278
59. *Verzeichnis über beauftragte Auszeichnungen* FHR 5, 3 Army, Kriegsarchiv, Vienna.
60. *Vormerkblatt für die Qualifikationsbeschreibung*, Kriegsarchiv, Vienna.

This offensive was the Russians' last. It had been ordered by Kerensky in the hope of a success that would recommend his war policy. It was conducted by Brusilov, then, after his defeat at Zborów, by Kornilov who was shortly to attempt a military coup d'état. It failed because of the chaotic state of the Russian forces. The infantry morale was low. Officers had lost their authority and 'delegates' had little effect. As General Fox reported to Lloyd-George,[61] co-ordination and the organization of artillery support and of supplies was inadequate. The Austro-Hungarian III Army crossed the Lomnica and began to advance on 23 July. Wittgenstein's own official record of his employment shows him following the movements of 42 HID, crossing the two branches of the Bystrzyca, assisting 36 ID at the capture of Starumia (24 July), advancing to Kolomea, Kniaze, and finally at the rate of 10 or 20 kilometres a day along the course (roughly) of the Pruth towards Czernowitz. Here, 20 km WNW of the city, they were held up for a day or two—the Russians wanted to save their supplies and the Imperial and Royal forces were hampered by their lack of fodder (the fuel of those days) and of rail connexions. But not for long. On 3 August Wittgenstein took part along with his own division and 5 ID in the capture of the city.

Though small, a city, indeed, with three cathedrals, a synagogue, a university, a medley of races, religions and languages, but a centre of culture. It changed hands more than a dozen times in the First World War, after which it became a small town in Rumania. It is now a small town in the Ukraine. Not glory, perhaps, but something passed away, and Wittgenstein saw it do so. His English friends, in their 'unbesieged cities' (Rilke's phrase) had no such experience.

Here and round here Wittgenstein spent the rest of the autumn, in positional warfare and in one limited advance (to capture a height called Dolzok on 27 August), which seems to have put an end to the artillery duel in that sector. There were no particular strategic goals to be pursued locally and the bulk of 42 HID was moved north but Wittgenstein remained, by his own account, until the armistice signed by the Bolsheviks took effect on 29 November.

He had been in the field continuously since January and we have little record of his intellectual and spiritual life—a postcard and two letters to Engelmann before the main engagements of the year, two postcards and two brief notes after them.[62] Back in the field, he is able to work again (after the depression of his Christmas leave). Disgusted by books of

---

61. D. Lloyd-George: *War Diaries*, vol. 2, p. 1527.

62. 78–81 and 82 and 84–86 in the Suhrkamp volume of Wittgenstein letters. 83, the letter that mentions the manuscript lent to Groag and the poem written by Engelmann, I am inclined to date to early 1918. When it was written Wittgenstein had recently seen Engelmann and was shortly going to see his own sister Hermine. Neither condition held in early 1917. Also Groag's recollection was that the manuscripts were lent him at the end of 1917. This is of some importance for the pre-history of the *Tractatus*.

Ehrenstein's sent to him, as we have seen,[63] he asks for an antidote in the form of Mörike's poems and some of those of Goethe. 'Drawing on the purest well of classical German poetry,' says Engelmann,[64] and it is true that many of the Goethe poems by which the desired volume is identified (the *Venetian Epigrams*, the *Elegies*, and the *Epistles*) are written in classical metres, but note that the volume also includes (in those *Roman Elegies*) Goethe's declaration of independence from the morality, the pre-occupations, the responsibilities, even the taste of his time and of his own past, in favour of a simpler life strongly marked by eroticism. Perhaps Wittgenstein could identify in some ways not only with the sage of Weimar but with the idyllist of the room off the Corso. Certainly there are parallels between the unconventionality of Goethe when he returned from his Italian Journey, and that of Wittgenstein after the war—the deliberate informality of dress of both is only the indicator of a more radical break with the past. Engelmann himself stresses the value placed on Mörike, which we have already touched on—the perfect fit of style and content p. 34 above) and so on, but the poems of Goethe mentioned here show that Wittgenstein's taste was regulated by something more complex than the 'rhythms of a decorous and manly life', of Engelmann's Platonic phrase. Mörike did seem to Wittgenstein to be closely related to Goethe, but more perhaps to the Goethe of *Iphigenie*.[65] The Uhland letter already quoted (p. 251) should teach us caution, however, in all such interpretations.

Apart from these poems Wittgenstein asks for a portable but legible Bible. He reports on two further occasions that he is able to work—or that his brain is working (April and August—the latter occasion being that of the Austrian advance we have just described) but we have no notebook covering the period. He wishes he were better and cleverer (*gescheiter*), which two are the same thing, and he repeated to Engelmann his remarks about living in a dream that we have already touched on but in general he indicates that it is impossible for him to set down the personal things that he has to say.

We know, or can infer, that his work had advanced so far that he could leave with Groag a manuscript of numbered remarks like those later used in the *Tractatus*: perhaps this happened at Olmütz on Wittgenstein's way back to Vienna.[66] Likewise we know, or can infer, some of the effects of his thinking about his own nature.

---

63. pp. 208 and 250 above. Engelmann himself had scruples about Ehrenstein, too much of a poseur, perhaps:

> Man ehrte gern den Ehrenstein
> Nur seine Werke stören ein',

he used to say (a *Schüttelreim* with the Viennese 'ein'' for 'einen').

64. P. Engelmann: *Letters*, p. 85.

65. A letter to Russell of January 1914 (no. 35 in *Briefe*) makes this connexion.

66. Groag's recollection supports this date and also the description of the manuscript just given.

There's a difference (he writes at the time to Engelmann) between how I am now and how I was when we saw one another. in Olmütz; and the difference is that I am a little more decent now. By that I only mean that I am a little clearer about my lack of decency than then. (LW to PE 16.1.18)

One solution that he tried over this winter was that of having himself transferred to the infantry. Perhaps he also tried to revert to the ranks, but nothing seems to have come of that. The attempt to change his arm was more serious. There was some occasion for it in that the Austro-Hungarian army was re-grouping as the war in the East had come to an end. Also in that winter there was a reorganization of infantry divisions and a renumbering of artillery regiments. Still Wittgenstein's request was a very odd one: the staff officers could hardly adjust to an officer's wanting to move to employment which was not less but more dangerous. Wittgenstein went as far as General Löbl, with whom his sister Gretl had connexions, and a conversion-course for him was evidently approved.[67] Comments on his success in it and on the pleasure of having him near home were exchanged between his sisters, Gretl in Switzerland (she was an American national and had gone into exile) and Mining at home. But to the sisters' relief it was eventually decided that he should remain in the artillery. The grounds for this sensible decision are not known, but his own motives for seeking the change were obvious to his friends: he wanted to be in the position of greatest danger. *Eine Bejahung des Todes*—an acceptance of death, certainly, but also a way of putting himself in a position where he would be forced to live up to his own standards. The letter just quoted continues, perhaps with a reference to plans such as this:

If you reply that I have no faith, you are *quite right*, only I had none earlier either. It's obvious that a man who tries to invent a machine for becoming decent has no faith. But what am I to do? (LW to PE 16.1.18)

Wittgenstein, now promoted Leutnant i.d.R., duly left for the Italian front and seems to have arrived on 10 March. He was detached from his own Czech regiment and posted to a Mountain Artillery Regiment (GAR 11), Galician troops, part of 11 Army (General von Scheuchen-stühl). He was stationed at the north east of the plain of the Veneto and thus on the right flank of the Austro-Hungarian position in the Trentino, where the general strategy was to descend and, in concert with another similar attack across the Piave, to capture as much of the plain, with its

---

67. The incident is known from the recollection of the late Dr Groag, communicated orally, and from the letters of Margaret Stonborough to Hermine Wittgenstein (seen when in the possession of Dr T. Stonborough).

wealth of supplies, as might be possible. Save that for the present there was no offensive. The defeat at Caporetto the previous October had by no means been decisive. The Italians had rallied even on the Piave, and in January they took two Austro-Hungarian positions in the Asiago area, from which repeated counterattacks could not drive them. Both Austro-Hungarians and Italians were under pressure from their allies to launch an offensive. That of the Austro-Hungarians was planned for April but occurred in June; that of the Italians, pre-empted by the Austrians in June, actually occurred in October. Until June the Austro-Hungarians were reorganizing and marshalling the troops arrived from Russia (Wittgenstein himself was on a training course in May) and in the meantime engaged in positional warfare, rendered particularly uncomfortable in the mountains by the rigour of living conditions and communications. Wittgenstein used to recall that on arrival he found that the troops had to reach their posts by a funicular meant for goods. As he nerved himself to the ascent he was much helped by a quiet figure sitting in the corner of the shed who simply said 'Don't be afraid' (*Fürchte dich nicht!*).[68]

His health seems to have suffered. We find him asking Engelmann for a prescription to deal with his gastric flu and at some point in the year his mother in Vienna received a letter from a brother officer, stiff but well-meaning, to tell her that Wittgenstein was in hospital at Bolzano. Perhaps there were health grounds for the long leave that he was given in the summer.

But first he had to take part in the Austrian offensive. Conrad, now a Field Marshal but no longer Chief of Staff, was to attack from Asiago and Monte Grappa with 55 divisions, while at the same time Boroevich attacked with 51 across the Piave. A third, preliminary and diversionary attack from the Stelvio region into North East Lombardy came to nothing. Italian sources and the German observer with the Austrian forces (General von Cramon) agree that the Austrian spirit and technical preparation were excellent. Discipline was good, racial harmony prevailed. There was probably an underestimate of Italian powers of resistance and it was a mistake, at the highest level, not to concentrate on a single offensive, in the plain.[69] On Conrad's front, the Asiago plateau, the brave title Radetzky Offensive was chosen.

Wittgenstein went forward with the first wave on 15 June, as observer for an advancing battery. A recommendation for a decoration describes him reporting on the tactical situation in the middle of fierce machine-gun and artillery fire. Two of his patrol were wounded and he saw to their evacuation despite the drum-fire. He then made his way back to

68. Recollection of the late Arvid Sjögren, communicated orally.

69. See P. Broucek (ed.): *Ein General im Zwielicht* (the memoirs of E. Glaise von Horstenau), vol. 1 (1980).

the new gun-position, which was itself under heavy fire. One shell buried the Gun Position Officer and three of the gun-crew. Wittgenstein took over and directed the rescue-work at the risk of his own life. When orders came to withdraw the gun to the start-line, he did so in good time despite the intensity of the drum-fire.

> His exceptionally courageous behaviour, calmness, sang-froid, and hero-ism won the total admiration of the troops. By his conduct he gave a splendid example of loyal and soldierly fulfilment of duty.

The Gold Medal for Valour (Officers) was recommended, the highest award possible, but one of the independent witnesses, an Oberst Denzer, objected that the effect of the action (that on the enemy was meant) was very slight. The guns were often silent for hours. A Gold Medal would be too much. In the event Wittgenstein was awarded the Band of the Military Service Medal with Swords, itself a high distinction, and this method of measuring valour by success afforded him at any rate some later amusement. Ironically enough, his opponents here were British troops.

His heroism cannot have been common, but his experiences were a microcosm of the offensive. The attack had been known to be imminent and the enemy were well-prepared. Everywhere they brought down devastating counter-battery fire: guns were silenced, concentration points heavily shelled, communications and the moving up of reserves made difficult if not impossible. The Austrians were attempting to advance into wooded hills honeycombed with machine-gun nests. Observation of enemy positions and of the effect of their own fire was almost impossible. On 16 June Conrad was forced to withdraw to his original position: there was not a single division, he said, which could for the time being be regarded as capable of fighting.

The offensive on the Piave was forced back also and by some estimates the Austrians lost some 100,000 men in all. The wider repercussions of this on morale in the army, on the Hungarian parliament, on the war as a whole do not fall to be considered here. What affected Wittgenstein is that the Italians too had suffered and were in no position to counter-attack. The Austrians managed to put up a discouragingly stout resistance to one or two local attacks in the Asiago sector, but the Italian supply services were in any case heavily strained. On the Piave front their losses had been heavy. Both armies fell back, therefore, on their original positions, the Austrians to recover, General Diaz on the Italian side to amass reserves and to mature a more ambitious plan, whose execution in October we shall have to describe later.[70]

---

70. For accounts of this offensive see L. Villari: *The War on the Italian Front* and the article 'Italian Campaigns' in the 12th edition of the *Encyclopaedia Britannica*, vol. 31.

Soon after the Asiago offensive Wittgenstein went on leave. The indications are that this lasted from 5 July (when he made out his section of a Vormerkblatt für die Qualifikationsbeschreibung) to the end of September. It is not clear whether so long a period had its rationale in ill-health, exhaustion, or accumulated entitlement. Wittgenstein's development seems more than once to have undergone a sharp acceleration during the war and this leave was certainly an eventful one, marking in some ways a break with his old life and the beginnings of a new role.

One shadowily attested but very important event almost certainly belongs to it,[71] and perhaps to its beginning: Wittgenstein's uncle Paul came across him unexpectedly at a railway station (Salzburg is the obvious possibility) in a state of great mental anguish. In fact Ludwig was on his way to commit suicide somewhere in the mountains (of the Salzkammergut, one supposes). Paul, the man of the world, frowned on by severer aunts, had a genial liking for his nephew and even his nephew's philosophy, which is perhaps what made it possible for him to persuade Ludwig to come instead to Hallein, where Paul had a house. Useless to ask for the reasons of the suicide plan. Wittgenstein felt alone in the world now: news had come of the accidental death as a military test-pilot of David Pinsent, his friend in England. The saving environment of active service was being left behind. Now he was going back to his family, to an atmosphere and a set of pressures that, objectively, he had avoided for many years.

At Hallein, and in August on the Hochreith, he brought to completion the work of the last six years, preparing and sending for publication (unsuccessfully on this first attempt) more or less the final version of his *Logisch-philosophische Abhandlung*, later christened by Moore *Tractatus Logico-philosophicus* and often known simply as the *Tractatus*.

Something, but inevitably not enough, is known about the physical origins of this work. It was extracted, Engelmann said, from seven large notebooks and this is testimony of one who was with Wittgenstein on the Hochreith that summer. Three notebooks certainly survive and have been published: we have quoted from them freely above.[72] Von Wright calculates that the gaps in the dating allow for four more lost notebooks, but such calculation is dangerous both a priori and since we know that Wittgenstein's rate of entry in his notebooks (though perhaps not his rate of 'work' by which he meant the mental solution of problems) fell during periods of active service. Engelmann may have been mistaken in his recollection, or, more probably, he may have included the notebook now called the *Prototractatus* in his reckoning. This contains an early version of

71. The event was during the war and near Salzburg. He was there in July 1918 and there is hardly another time free in the war years.

72. *Notebooks 1914–16* (actually 1914–1917). The second edition is a slight improvement on the first as far as the German text is concerned.

the *Abhandlung* arranged in an interesting manner. The work was to consist (as the *Tractatus* finally does) of propositions, aphorisms or remarks of at most paragraph length, numbered so as to show their logical relations. n.1 was to be a comment on n, n.11 on n.1, and so on. The most obvious exemplar of this system of numbering is *Principia Mathematica*. It will be remembered that Russell wanted Wittgenstein to rewrite the first chapters of that work. The implication that these philosophical propositions have the lack of ambiguity and the quite definite logical relations of the lemmata, definitions, axioms, and theorems of a logical system is, though paradoxical, quite certainly intended. For composition this method of numbering (like the Dewey classification) has the merit that a number, an afterthought, can always be inserted between any two existing numbers—thus between n.11 and n.12 we can insert first n.111 then n.112 (or n.1101), then n.1121 (or n.1111 or n.1102 or n.11001), and so on (other series are obviously possible). The *Prototractatus* notebook *indicates* such numbers for the propositions composing it (which seem to have been copied directly or indirectly out of the dated notebooks that have been preserved and others like them) but does not itself put the propositions in the desired order.[73] Rather it writes out first the pivotal propositions 1, 2, 3, 4, and 5 (6 and 7 as it happens come later) on an early page and follows them by propositions intended as comments on them—following sometimes the order in which they occur in the original notebooks, sometimes simply the order in which they occurred to Wittgenstein's mind or else some other principle of order not now divinable. It is, in short, an early version in which Wittgenstein worked out the desired order of his remarks. Since it is written in large part in field-pencil, I am inclined to suppose that it was composed actually at the front. One possibility is that it was done at Asiago. Perhaps Wittgenstein used also a yet earlier numbered treatise lent to Groag (as we have mentioned on p. 260 above) and requested back earlier that year. The other possibility is that the *Prototractatus* was the manuscript lent, or was among the manuscripts lent, to Groag, and this is indeed supported by the principle of economy. In that case it will date in essence from his time at the front in 1917.

At all events I suppose Wittgenstein on his way back from Italy to Vienna to have arrived at Salzburg with our manuscript. Its arrangement was not ideal, some renumbering was necessary, a preface needed to be written, and the like. But essentially his views had reached a maturity and a completeness that demanded publication. Now at Hallein he sat down with the volume and revised the numbers and the text. He added a preface—much what we see in the *Tractatus* today, but with a tribute also to his Uncle Paul. A dedication to the memory of

---

73. The original and the intended order can both be seen in facsimile and in print respectively in the published *Prototractatus*, ed. myself and others (London, 1971).

David Pinsent was added on an early page, next to a quotation from the feuilletonist Kürnberger, possibly borrowed, as we have seen, from Karl Kraus. The dedication is our first record of Wittgenstein's great loss. There is a moving letter to Dame Ellen in the possession of her family.

The content and the significance of the work we shall review in another chapter. Here we are concerned with its effect on Wittgenstein's summer and his spirits. The stages we can be sure of are these: an intermediary version must have been prepared, on the basis of the now revised manuscript and then altered, by renumbering and a certain amount of addition or subtraction of material, into a form from which a typist (presumably in Vienna and probably in the family office in the Alleegasse) could make the two very slightly different typescripts that survive of the *Abhandlung* together with a third one.[74] Two typings may have been needed to allow for the production of carbon copies, giving Wittgenstein perhaps four (or at most six) copies in all. Between Hallein, Vienna, and the Hochreith, the work was finished in August. 'My life's work' he was to call it when he could again write to Russell: 'containing all my work of the last six years. I believe I've solved our problems finally. This may sound arrogant but I can't help believing it.'[75] He sent off a copy immediately to the Viennese publisher, Jahoda.

Jahoda because Karl Kraus's publisher. Wittgenstein saw his work as a contribution to the aims of *Die Fackel* (we shall see later how he put this sort of point to Ficker) and hoped or suggested that Kraus would or should be consulted about publication. He was in touch with the Kraus circle: Loos was a friend and Engelmann, the former adjutant of Kraus, was in Vienna and visited Wittgenstein on the Hochreith at this very time.

74. There must have been a third typescript and von Wright recollects seeing it, accompanied by a copy of Russell's introduction, in Gmunden in 1952. This was probably an earlier translation of the introduction since the copy of Russell's introduction used by Ostwald is known to have been lost. In any case it or its translation into German would naturally have been attached to the Engelmann typescript, which is demonstrably that from which the Ostwald printing was done.

75. LW to BR (13.3.19), see also letter of 12.6.19.

8   Captivity and Return 1918–20

It was to the end of empire that Wittgenstein went back—*finis Austriae*, and nowhere seen more dramatically than in the field. September, to be sure, was a lull or stay of execution. Victualling was a little improved after the harvest. A British and French attack in the Asiago sector was beaten off. Probably Wittgenstein was still in Vienna:[1] on the 22 September, in a last formal act, the Military Medal won in June was conferred on him. But the end of the month, when he was back in Italy, brought with it the armistice in Bulgaria, the sudden defencelessness of Hungary, the demand of the Magyar troops to return home, the declaration that Austria-Hungary would become a federation of free states, and finally the request for a general armistice.

This last the troops heard of on 5 October, and from that date on the Archduke Joseph and the other commanders had the hopeless task of persuading troops of various nationalities to stand firm for the sake of reasonable peace terms. And these were troops with torn uniforms and one set of linen, constantly informed by enemy propaganda of the national difficulties at home. In Wittgenstein's sector what was feared as much as a worsening of the peace terms was the unforeseeable effect of allowing hungry and leaderless troops to make a hasty retreat along the one line back home—as many did, Croats, Bosnians, Czechs, Hungarians, perhaps above all, but many Austrians too.

These difficulties became particularly acute after the Allied attack of 24 October in the Sette Comuni (the district round Asiago). This was actually a feint, because the real breakthrough was intended to be on the Piave. At first 38 Honved ID (to which Wittgenstein's battery was attached) managed to hold the British and Italians and even to win back Mount Sisemol. Wittgenstein's correspondence with Engelmann and with a prospective publisher continued until this date. Perhaps (one shudders at the risk) the only corrected copy of his *Abhandlung* was sent him, rejected, at this time.[2] It is always amazing how the small change of life—letters, minutes, promotions, decorations—continues to circulate amid the gravest crises. But soon Wittgenstein's division, and all Hungarian troops in XI Army had to be promised their return home. There were refusals to reinforce and resistance by regiments to the very approach of officers from higher formations: only the artillery kept up

---

1. His sister Gretl supposed him to be there on 16 September, GS to HW 16.9.18. His first field postcard to Engelmann is dated 9.10.18.
2. LW to PE 22 and 25.10.18

the idea of a continuous line. And this was more or less held in the Asiago sector until 30 October. On the Piave, however, the great crossing took place on 24 October and by about 29 October the victory of Vittorio Veneto was secure. The Austrians sued for peace and a general retreat from occupied territory was ordered.

Peace did not come immediately, but the mass return home had already begun. Troops tended to break up into national groups, to wear national colours, sometimes to set up soldiers' councils and to depose officers of the wrong nationality. It was in circumstances of this kind that Wittgenstein's brother Konrad (or Kurt) took his own life. Family stories vary: it may have been because his troops would not serve, or because he refused to commit them to a hopeless action, or simply to avoid the shame of surrender and captivity. All were clear that a highly developed sense of honour was his motive.

Meanwhile many, even high-ranking officers, got on the next train to leave. Heinrich Groag had the presence of mind to tell a witless engine-driver to put a plate saying 'Olmütz' on the front of his train. In this way one detachment at least got home. Not so Wittgenstein: it is hard to think that his sense of obedience would have allowed it. He duly fell back on Trent and was overtaken by the British and French advance, really a walk-over, which began on 1 November. Trent was occupied, by the Italians, on 3 November and all Austro-Hungarian troops there were declared prisoners of war. On the Austrian side the belief was that the armistice had begun 36 hours previously, when indeed the announce-ment was made that terms had been agreed.[3] In those 36 hours 300,000 troops were made prisoner, of whom 30,000 died in captivity. On 3 November also, back at home, the Emperor Charles handed over command of his armies; and, not exactly abdicating his powers and prerogatives, he placed them at the disposal of his peoples.

Thus it was rather to their surprise that the captured Austrians found themselves sent, officers and men separately, not back home but into prison camps. Franz Parak went by slow stages to Cassino, under the monastery.[4] Wittgenstein went first perhaps to Verona,[5] then at some point to Como, and came on to Cassino only in January 1919.[6]

Parak has described the cheerless scene: two rows of huts, a camp road, a parade ground, high walls around, the bitter cold in winter,[7] the

3. This was the Austrian view, which accounts for Hermine Wittgenstein's phrase 'he was taken prisoner in that strange armistice'. No doubt the Allies were strictly justified.

4. F.Parak,'Als ich mit Wittgenstein in der Gefangenschaft war', *morgen* Kulturzeitschrift aus Niederösterreich 33 (1984)

5. Here Wittgenstein borrowed 100 *lire* from an Oberleutnant Sturm: he was to remember and repay it, with much incidental punctiliousness, in 1925: see LW to LH 23.9.25.

6. So Hayek in his unpublished sketch, relying on Hänsel, whose movements were the same as Wittgenstein's.

7. They slept under their kitbags, Ludwig told Arvid Sjögren, and he had never been so hungry in his life.

sun that drove them into their narrow rooms and onto their iron bedsteads in summer, the constant hunger. One day Parak noticed a new arrival:

> He had a thin face and a noble profile, was of middle height, and, to judge by his figure and general appearance, was not yet thirty years old. His tunic was green and open at the neck, with his shirt collar turned over it. He wore breeches, tucked into puttees. He was bare-headed and his hair seemed slightly curly. But the really striking thing about him was his manner of speaking: it conveyed an extraordinary definiteness. There was a characteristic movement of his head too: usually it was bowed, but from time to time he would throw it back and direct his gaze into the distance. This was Ludwig Wittgenstein.

Parak notes that with the end of the war military standards of judgement were dropped and the prisoners valued each other much more for what they had been in civilian life or could contribute in lectures, readings, or conversation to the relief of the enforced idleness. Not all elements of Wittgenstein's background were immediately apparent. If anything he seems to have been more informal and shabby in appearance than the others. When the conversation turned to Klimt and in particular his portrait of Margaret Stonborough, Wittgenstein's reference to her as 'my sister' amazed Drobil—'Are *you* a Wittgenstein?'

The subject of this conversation was typical enough and is perhaps of a piece with the change noticed by Parak. In many cases captivity—to some extent the mere fact of defeat—engenders, by a natural displacement, a spiritualization. In numerous prisoner-of-war camps in and after both world wars (when conditions at all allowed it) lectures and performances would be organized, books would be eagerly sought after, and the intellectual discussion of personal and religious problems would deepen friendships in a way not so easily attainable in normal or family life.

So, at least, it was at Cassino: not always, of course, at the highest level. We hear of a former, or perhaps would-be, actor who read poems with exaggerated expression: 'One can't listen,' said Wittgenstein; 'it's like having an electric shock.' There was also an exhibition of pictures painted in the camp: all but one were dismissed by Wittgenstein: a good picture, he said, should have the effect of a box on the ear. Parak also tells of some journalistic philosophy lectures that Wittgenstein avoided: but he did attend (for reasons which will appear) some pedagogical lectures on logic and educational theory, apparently a co-operative venture based on the textbook with that title by Anton Hergeth. He told Parak, forgetting Dr Coffey or perhaps indulging in harmless affectation,[8] that, though he had written his own logico-philosophical treatise, he had no idea what a textbook of logic contained. In the event he found much to criticize in the lectures; naturally enough, since the Herbartian tradition, to which this textbook belonged, was familiar only with so-called Aristotelian logic: it had a limited insight into the variety of logical forms and, partly in consequence, regarded logic as a mere preliminary to philosophy, whereas the very title of Wittgenstein's work implies that he found the whole of philosophy contained in logic.

But to all these public functions Wittgenstein characteristically preferred personal contacts with a small group or with an individual. We remember his asking, 'Shall I find a friend?', when he arrived in England, and the importance to him of the Olmütz group. He sought out suitable companions, Parak, for example, whose short story written in the prison camp, full of lyricism and home-sickness, Wittgenstein asked to see. Others he had found already in regimental life or earlier captivity. Of these the most important to him throughout his life was Ludwig Hänsel, a profoundly Catholic figure, who was to have an influential career in Austrian education. After release, Wittgenstein sometimes stayed with the Hänsels, used their house for his books and correspondence, and interested himself deeply in the well-being and moral education of the Hänsel children. For the present, Hänsel's seriousness and his philosophical education and aspirations made him an ideal companion.[9] The two would take chairs out on to the barrack square or under the holm oaks and read Kant together in the mornings. Books they seem to have got from a library that 'a Swiss society' (the Red Cross?) had presented to the camp. It was difficult for individual prisoners to have books sent them. Later, as we shall see, Wittgenstein was lucky enough to obtain special permission for just this. Previously not even his beloved *Grundgesetze* was in his possession and he had to recite from memory to convince Hänsel of the glories of its preface.[10] It was a comradely relation: 'Du, Hänsel' was the form of address for the rest of their lives. Such too was the relation with another friend who long remained such, the sculptor Drobil (we still have some of his later drawings of Wittgenstein and a head in relief; also the bust that Wittgenstein modelled in his workshop). The few notes and letters of Drobil that remain are terser than Hänsel's—it is the contrast of the maker with the thinker—but both men belonged to the small class of

8. Wittgenstein frequently took himself to task for having misrepresented himself, and perhaps there was some justice in this.

9. Hayek reports that Wittgenstein first knew Hänsel (at Como presumably) as a lecturer on logic, where he heard him in silence, but afterwards expounded symbolic logic to him.

10. He asks Engelmann to send a copy in May (LW to PE 24.5.19) but there is no reference to its arrival and LW to PE 31.10.20 may imply that there were difficulties about bookpost from the new Czechoslovak Republic.

those who spoke with Wittgenstein as equals rather than disciples, and the officers' style of greeting rather typifies this.

Parak's was a different case, as he himself engagingly makes clear. He was, one might say, 'taken up' by Wittgenstein, who was interested in Parak's writing and in his being a schoolmaster. He allows us to see that he was overwhelmed by Wittgenstein. Parak, in return, read the typescript that Wittgenstein had with him: they walked round and round the barrack square after a day of rain and, as Parak expressed his enthusiasm, Wittgenstein took his arm. Thereafter they would meet in the afternoons: Parak would join the group—Hänsel, Drobil, Jungwirth —to which Wittgenstein read *Crime and Punishment*; or else he and Wittgenstein would separately have a discussion of that book or of other literary matters; or they would whistle together, two voices, taking a theme from a Bach fugue chosen by Wittgenstein, Bach being his favourite composer at that time. The literary conversations (convincingly sketched by Parak) belong to the history of Wittgenstein's development and will be touched on shortly, but to grasp the nature of Parak's relationship with Wittgenstein (the forerunner of many similar ones) we must show how it too developed.

In the heat of the summer Wittgenstein (like many of the others) lay on his bed and brooded, meditating, Parak thought, revisions of propositions in his book. Actually we can see from the typescript that hardly any were made: he may, rather, have been preoccupied by internal problems, 'mein Inneres' as he put it.[11] At all events Parak felt that his own visits were now unwelcome and that in general Wittgenstein was avoiding him to a greater extent than moodiness would account for. He managed to broach the matter, with an interesting result. He acknowledged that he himself (like Wieland when Goethe arrived in Weimar) was as full of Wittgenstein as a dewdrop of the sun. Though only seven years older, Wittgenstein, he felt, was enormously his superior in talents and culture: impossible not to open up every pore to drink in as much of this knowledge as possible. Easily irritated and fastidious, Wittgenstein in time withdrew like a sensitive plant from this degree of attachment. The metaphor seems to have been Wittgenstein's, who went on to say that he had known only one other person of Parak's kind—his own mother. Wittgenstein's family noticed his attitude of holding her at arm's length and we can read it in his letters to the family: *Viele Grüße an die Mama*, as if 'Regards to Mama' were enough! We are bound to remember the *Nichts mehr davon!*, 'Enough of that!', of Berlin days. There were to be other examples of women approaching too close, and of men being taken up (rather as Goethe, with the same *arrière pensée*, speaks of a flower's being taken up)[12] and planted in Wittgenstein's garden, not always to flourish.

11. LW to PE 25.4.19.
12. *Gefunden*, '*Ich ging im Walde…*', of his wife.

Perhaps it can be said, echoing but not quite agreeing with Malcolm,[13] that it was Wittgenstein's tragedy that he intensely craved for affection but could rarely tolerate the way it was expressed. Our concern in these pages is to see the development of such features and the factors that affected them. One change effected, or rather one development promoted in Wittgenstein, by the war and the prison camp was the maturity, the command, the power over others that led to cases like Parak's—a happy case, be it said, on Parak's side at least: circumstances soon parted the two, but Parak's memories remained warm and positive. The clarification of their relationship was evidently a well-judged one, well effected.

There are other developments in Wittgenstein about this time that Parak's account enables us to identify. Their conversations ranged from criticism of Parak's own work, through comparisons of Dostoevsky with other authors to the discussion of Wittgenstein's religion and his projects in life. As so often in his case, it is easiest to start with the aesthetic aspect. Not all his judgements of value have equal importance. If at that time he thought Haydn the equal of Beethoven and anyway preferred Bach to both, there were soon to be times when Beethoven, or Schubert, was everything. To some extent composers must be explored one at a time. Perhaps we can read something more into his critical remark about Wagner's music—that one cannot translate word for word from one language into another. This I take to mean that the literary goals, the message desired, are too mechanically rendered in music by Wagner: a move away, this, from Wittgenstein's youthful identification with the *Mastersingers* and a move towards an inexpressive art, where what matters is not what is said but how it is said. This was indeed the burden of his criticisms of Parak's writing. This or that adjective (Wittgenstein could trace its true place and its origin to a story of Keller's) did not fit what Parak meant. Parak had not imagined things clearly. When Parak protested that the whole *content* of his story (it was his second and, he thought, better one) was being lost, Wittgenstein replied, *Die Sprache ist alles*, 'The language is everything', or, to paraphrase Hofmannsthal,[14] the whole difference lies in *how* a thing is said.

In practice what said most to Wittgenstein, perhaps especially at this time, were works in which there was a strong sense of a moral lesson, but chastely presented. The Uhland poem praised to Engelmann, the Keller stories in general, are examples. To Parak he would rather read out a

---

13. *Memoir* (1984 ed.), p.81. Malcolm speaks of 'his need for love together with the harshness that repelled love'. I speak rather of something in him that did not want love.

14. 'Aber in dem Wie, da liegt der ganze Unterschied,' says the *Marschallin* towards the end of Act I of *Der Rosenkavalier*: what matters is how one accepts the inevitable.

parable by Mörike than dwell on a passage where, Parak felt, Goethe managed to give literary expression to sexuality.[15]

This issue arose from their reading of *Crime and Punishment*, the question being why Dostoevsky shows only the saintly side of Sonia, while the sinful side is barely touched on, though of course it forms the essential background to scenes such as that where the prostitute reads to the murderer from the Gospels. The friends, and Wittgenstein especially, dwelt on this book for the sake of their own lives. Parak thought Wittgenstein had found Tolstoy's religion not satisfying. Too much should not be made of these changes of emphasis: Wittgenstein was to come back to Tolstoy.[16] Still Dostoevsky is certainly the one cited in his later war-time diaries, and indeed just *The Brothers Karamazov*, which, he told Parak, was yet greater than *Crime and Punishment*. It was Dostoevky's 'deeply religious attitude' that recommended him to Wittgenstein. Parak, with a true writer's eye, connects another of their conversations with the latter book. Wittgenstein had described himself as reborn, and Parak dismissed the hypothesis of reincarnation (because Wittgenstein had already said that it was pointless to think about, or to seek to atone for, a former life that we could not remember), but he recalled the remark when reading the last paragraph of *Crime and Punishment*:

> But now a new history commences: a story of the gradual renewing of a man, of his slow progressive regeneration, and change from one world to another—an introduction to the hitherto unknown realities of life.

This then was the change in Wittgenstein that Parak believes took place. A religious conversion: a felt rebirth, which led Wittgenstein to give up all his possessions and to lead a quite different life, a life devoted to these other, inner, religious goals. Parak points to the contrast between Wittgenstein's life before and after the war in point of luxury, comfort, and the opposite. Parak attributes much to the collapse of the empire that had formed the background and base for the rise of the Wittgenstein family. Some weight must be given to this, even if Wittgenstein had known from the beginning of the war that defeat would be the outcome. The reality, no doubt, had a more powerful effect than the expectation. Another factor was that Wittgenstein needed to recover from the war: to master all those experiences a retreat inwards was required. Leavis recalled that in 1930 he had recognized Wittgenstein as a kindred spirit, tense and electric with the experience of the war,

15. *Das Märchen vom sicheren Mann* as opposed to Gretchen's monologue, *Wie könnt' ich sonst* etc.'

16. For example, to use the *Simple Tales* in his teaching, itself a Tolstoyan (as well as a Dostoevskian) project. Also Wittgenstein's relation to his family and his wealth was to be more like Tolstoy's than Parak (p.14) allows. Neither were free.

like Leavis himself.[17] But perhaps most significant is what we have already observed. The war was a release to Wittgenstein. Hardship and danger concentrated his mind on the only essential thing and the demanding tasks of every day—*Schwerer Dienste tägliche Bewahrung*, as it were—made life with his fellow men possible. He was no longer seeking what to become; he knew now what he had to be.

Such, at this time, seems to have been his state of mind. Outwardly, of course, he had to become something, and the choice seemed to lie, Parak tells us, between the priesthood and the life of a schoolmaster. But four years study of theology would have been too much, and Wittgenstein planned to apply for entrance to the last year of a teachers' training college. 'I'd most like to be a priest,' he told Parak, 'but when I'm a teacher I can read the gospel with the children.'

All this is to sum up in a few words (as that final paragraph from Dostoevsky does) a hard-won state of mind, inseparable from a deep and painful self-reproach and a sense of the sinfulness of past attitudes and actions. We have noted the passage in Kügelgen where the respectable man becomes a miserable sinner. Wittgenstein understood this from his own experience. In prison camp and around that time we find him dwelling on the importance of acknowledging one's sin—Sonia urges this on Raskolnikov, and the saintly pilgrim in Tolstoy is the one prepared to admit that sin got the better of him.[18] The brooding in the prison camp and the allusions to his inner state in his letters to Engelmann all fit into this pattern. A year or so later his sister expressed to Hänsel her sorrow that she had as brother an unhappy saint rather than a normal human being who was happy,[19] recognizing that this sort of unhappiness is one of the marks of a saint and has little to do with the gravity of any sins actually committed. It does not make sense to ascribe the title of saint in virtue of one phase in a life, but that this was a deeply religious phase in Wittgenstein's life is unmistakeable.

He had always been, of course, a man of high principle; and such he remained. Examples are his request to be transferred to the Other Ranks camp at Cassino when typhoid broke out there; also a continued refusal to accept privilege, the description of which will bring us to the contacts that existed between the prison camp and the outside world.

His family had, of course, been searching for him. Gretl was in Switzerland and had powerful friends among those exiled there by the war: soon too she was to be involved in the work of Mr Hoover's US Food Administration. With whatever recommendation, she wrote immediately in November seeking an 'exchange' for Ludwig (a straightforward release must have been meant). She had no success, but hoped

17. Personal communication.
18. Parak (p.15) speaks of the first example, Engelmann (ch. 3 of his *Memoir*) of the second.
19. HW to LH 13.12.20.

he would be the better treated for her intervention.[20] It seems that his exact whereabouts were not known (or became unknown again) for in a later letter she reports that her researches concerning Lukerl have come to nothing.[21] By January, at any rate, contact with him seems to have been established and a little money and some cigarettes[22] could be sent to him. The prisoners depended on their officers' pay, duly given them by the Italians, which was barely enough to cover messing. (For this reason Wittgenstein's promotion to Oberleutnant, gazetted for 1 November, was of importance.)

But more than this was sought. In March a distant relation in Zurich (the same Elisabeth Gräzer who had forwarded letters between the Wittgensteins and Russell) wrote on the prisoner's behalf to the Secretary of State at the Vatican, requesting a release on compassionate grounds—Wittgenstein's mother having lost all other sons but one (and that one maimed in the war) and being in the poorest of health. No one in the family, said Frau Gräzer, knew of this application.[23] Would the cardinal use his great influence? The cardinal was all politeness and attention. Signora Gräzer's was a noble and charitable act on behalf of an afflicted mother and the Holy See would do whatever was in its power to help: and, in fact, he did have letters sent to the Archabbot of Cassino (in case anything could be done locally) and, more effectively, to Baron Monti, the head of the *Fondo per il culto* (the usual channel for communications between the Holy See and the royal government, not yet officially recognized). He in turn invoked the Prime Minister's office, and though family reasons (being universally applicable) could not be recognized as grounds for release, Wittgenstein, along with two (only two) other Austrians, was to be given a special medical examination to determine whether release was indicated, with an assurance that generous criteria would be applied. Profound expressions of thanks and paternal benediction were exchanged. Wittgenstein's mother, finally hearing of it, was overjoyed.

They had reckoned without the prisoner himself. He refused any exceptional treatment and would return only when his comrades could.[24] He attributed the intervention to his family and was later[25] to reproach his mother, though she was probably in this case innocent.

Wittgenstein was dogged by privilege and by his friends: from England too efforts were made to obtain favours for him. Russell applied

20. GS to HW 30.11.18.

21. GS to HW 25.12.18 (unless this is actually a 1917 letter).

22. By now, it seems, Wittgenstein did smoke. Testimony of Arvid Sjögren.

23. The correspondence is contained in two files of the Secretariat of State, 1914 GUERRA, 244–2a, 89174 and 91234, copies of which were, with great kindness, made available to me by Dottoressa Liliana Albertazzi of Trent, their discoverer.

24. Parak, p.12

25. T.Stonborough, personal communication.

to Keynes who was in Paris at the Peace Conference and to Trevelyan, who had served in the Red Cross in Italy; Keynes applied to the Italian authorities in Paris (writing to Wittgenstein through them), Trevelyan to the scientist and explorer Filippo de Filippi.[26] There was little hope, though some, of obtaining Wittgenstein's release, much of securing permission for him to exchange learned correspondence and not merely short postcards. In the event, it was also made possible for him to obtain books, even bound books; hence the request to Engelmann for Frege's *Grundgesetze*:[27] Russell's *Introduction to Mathematical Philosophy* was sent in gatherings to speed it through the post.[28] Russell's book was actually sent in Keynes's name: Wittgenstein's English friends thought it prudent not to stress that Russell, the conscientious objector, was his sponsor.

And so contacts with his real friends, and in some measure his real life, began again for Wittgenstein. If only Russell would come and visit him! 'If you were on the other end of the world and I *could* come to you I would do it,' he said in a letter,[29] which Russell had copied for circulation to all who might help. Of course (and characteristically) Wittgenstein was being unrealistic: of all visitors to be allowed (and there were none) Russell would have been the last.

As always work and life went hand in hand: it was to explain his work that Wittgenstein burned to talk to Russell. His life's work, and he longed to see it published. It was galling to lug the completed work round in captivity and to see nonsense left a clear field outside and equally galling to think that no one would understand his work even if it did get printed! So he exclaimed in a letter to Russell.[30] Russell had already been sent the typescript, but the slender hope that he would understand it had now vanished: so at least the content of Russell's book (newly arrived, as we have just seen) suggested to Wittgenstein. Not a trace of understanding of the ideas on logic dictated to Moore in April 1914![31]

But for all this pessimism, the contact with friends and with philosophy was reviving. In May and June he speaks of inner suffering, of not working, of constant thought about what chance there was that he might become a decent human being:[32] by August he could even support Frege's letter, revealing that he too 'had not understood a word' of the typescript sent him.[33] Wittgenstein tells his sister Mining that he

26. Letters between the persons named, in the Bertrand Russell Archive, McMaster University.
27. LW to PE 24.5.19.
28. LW to BR 12 6 19, with note in *Briefe*, p.87.
29. LW to BR 13.3.19.
30. LW to BR 12.6.19.
31. See note 33 p. 236 above (and Moore's diary (20.1.15)) for Russell's failure to obtain an explanation of Wittgenstein's views from Moore.
32. LW to PE 24.5.19 and to HW 25.6.19.
33. LW to BR 18.8.19.

can now work and we see some results in his explanations sent to Russell.[34] The content of the book we shall consider elsewhere, but it is striking that Wittgenstein is intent on reducing the message he has to a single formula:

> The main point is the theory of what can be expressed (*gesagt*) by propositions—i.e. by language—(and, which comes to the same, what can be *thought*) and what cannot be expressed by propositions, but only shown (*gezeigt*); which I believe is the cardinal problem of philosophy.

It is relevant too that this insistence on the limits to the expression of thought come at a time when more than at any other life decisions were called for.

Rumour and news now indicated an early return to Austria, which Wittgenstein had feared would not be before Christmas.[35] They had come down to Cassino in cattle-trucks, Parak relates, now they were to return in second-class carriages. The Italian guards left at Villach. Parak changed on to a train for Lower Austria; Wittgenstein went with the other Viennese. The two were never to meet again. Wittgenstein's official date of release was 26 August 1919, but his first letter from Vienna is dated 25 August: he tells Engelmann that he is not very well—*es geht mir nicht gut*—as far as his state of mind is concerned.[36]

That this return was a crisis in his life will hardly be doubted. One of the great *Wandlungen* or transformations that marked his career, like that of his father, was preparing. So his sister Hermine felt (*Familien-erinnerungen*, p.111). It was only natural. The war, which had saved his life, which had served him as a machine for living decently was over. He had to find his feet somehow,[37] to find a place for himself in the world, not simply one prescribed by war or captivity.

It seems in the logic of things that he had to leave the ambience of his family, and at this time he could not do it by going abroad. They were poorer for the war, no doubt, but incomparably better off than the poor of Vienna in that harsh post-war winter of inflation and starvation. He had gone into the army to suffer with the people: he could not now return to privilege. Previously he had had various valid excuses: that the money was not his own but his father's, that he was doing logic, the thing that he was good at: now logic had been brought to completion. He must now manifest in his life what he had tried to convey, so indirectly, in his writing.

34. ibid. and LW to HW 1.8.19.
35. LW to HW 19.7.19.
36. LW to PE 25.8.19.
37. *Mich wieder zu finden*, 'to find something of myself again', in LW to PE 2.9.19.

So much to provide an outline of the motivation for the two first steps we know of after his return. He gave away his money to his brother and sisters; and he began to live in lodgings found for him in various houses. His address was no longer to be the address of 'the rich Wittgensteins': he dissociated himself from them, without losing touch, like some latter day Alexis, living below stairs in his father's house, *intactam sponsam relinquens.* The parallel that his sister Hermine draws[38] is with another Alexis, Alyosha in *The Brothers Karamazov.* Alyosha has no money, but unlike the careful Ivan, will never lack what is necessary, since others will gladly give to him, and he, just as naturally, will accept. We shall see that this last point is true and important, but true with qualifications.

The facts then were that he insisted on a division of his possessions. At first he simply came to the bank and announced, to general consternation, that he did not want his money.[39] Long discussions with the family lawyers were necessary before they could be brought to realize, as one put it, that he wanted to commit financial suicide.[40] In the course of these he insisted over and over again that in no way was the money to be kept aside, covertly reserved for him, as Onkel Paul explosively recommended.[41] All must go ahead as if Ludwig had not survived his father. (It seems there was an exception made in that Gretl, who had not suffered so much financially in the war, was not to be included in the new division.)[42] We find the same arrangements repeated in 1926 when the widow's portion of his mother fell to be divided:[43] once again Ludwig was insistent that nothing should slip through to him, and his insistence when something was important to him was really formidable.

There were those who smiled—'Ah sooy!' said Adolf Loos—when they heard that the gift was in favour of Wittgenstein's own family, but from several points of view it was the only possible solution. The money was not a heap of gold but a share in a set of interlocking properties and portfolios. A stranger or a charitable institution could not easily be a shareholder. Besides Wittgenstein's aim was to free himself of his inheritance, not to use it, however indirectly, for his own purposes. Finally, as he told Engelmann,[44] he did not think any good would come of devoting his wealth to humanitarian purposes.

---

38. *Familienerinnerungen*, p.110. The habit of seeing themselves as akin to characters in their favourite books went on in the family for several generations. Some were so named or nicknamed—Mining herself, for example, and among nephews we find a Pierre and a thinly disguised André, also referred to as der Sohn Bernhard, the 'son who can do no wrong' in *Soll und Haben.*

39. PE to F.von Hayek 8.3.53.

40. A phrase reported by Mr R.Rhees.

41. It was long before he could be reconciled with his nieces over this failure, as he saw it.

42. The family account, but confirmed by Wittgenstein in an undated letter to his sister Hermine (apparently after the crash of 1929).

43. Papers previously in the possession of Mrs Clara Sjögren.

44. Letter to Hayek already cited.

There was no criticism of his sisters in all this. They were sharply aware of the responsibilities of privilege. Gretl was probably at the time touring America campaigning for aid to starving Austria. She had sent in a trainload of condensed milk at her own expense from Switzerland. More benefactions were to follow. Hermine, in hospitals during the war, was now training herself to provide a day home for poor boys. Indeed later Wittgenstein was often to avail himself of the help of his sisters, freely given, for some charitable project of his own, always a personal project, be it noted, something undertaken for and by an individual, not a subvention to a charitable organization. Later still, similarly, Wittgenstein would apply to Keynes for assistance in some plan: Keynes took it good-humouredly,[45] which shows that friends could accept in Wittgenstein's case the proposition that it was right for him to use their money but wrong for him to keep his own.

Was there more behind this personal imperative than the need to share hardship? In this context a later notebook entry of his has been quoted: he would not like to see his family poor, because in their case they would be losing such *power* as they had.[46] It is implausible though that Wittgenstein meant to renounce power for himself: rather he wanted only what power he could produce for himself from his own personality. (We shall also later see him usually aware of what was his due in the way of earnings, frugal in spending them, generous in disbursing them as anonymously as possible.)

This matter of his money settled, he had to adopt a way of life. A religious life was not yet finally excluded. Hänsel used to tell of a visit to a friary (Brothers of Charity or Franciscans, both were envisaged) where Wittgenstein was put off by a surly porter; and there seem to have been a number of tentative inquiries, such as are no rarity for religious houses. In December when Russell met Wittgenstein (the meeting will be described later in the chapter), he found him incredibly changed.

> I had felt in his book a flavour of mysticism, but was astonished when I found that he has become a complete mystic. He reads people like Kierkegaard and Angelus Silesius and he seriously contemplates becoming a monk. (BR to OM 20.12.19)

Still, Russell judged that this was 'an idea not an intention'; Wittgenstein's intention was to be a teacher.

---

45. More good-humouredly than Wittgenstein could easily believe, as LW to JMK (May 1929) shows.
46. From a 1931 notebook: quoted in *LW, sein Leben in Bildern und Texten* (Nedo and Ranchetti), p.148.

If not religion, then teaching: so he had said in the prison camp.[47] In some ways it fitted his temperament very well: the Wittgensteins had, we have noted, a gift or a need to instruct, and a tendency to see all education as moral education. The two sisters, Mining with her day-home, and Gretl with her studies of psychology, exemplify it. Moreover we have already seen that Ludwig may have thought of himself as a sort of Alyosha, reading from the Gospel and inspiring his group of boys for all their lives.

And yet, was it not a misuse of his talents, the use, Mining said, of a precision tool to open a packing case? 'You remind me,' he said in a characteristic simile, 'of someone looking through a window who can't make sense of the strange movements of a passer-by outside. He has no idea of the violence of the storm outside nor of the difficulty the other has simply in staying on his feet.'

So he did see this choice of profession as demanded by his inner problems, not those (as has gratuitously been suggested)[48] of life amid the moral temptations of Vienna, for they were problems he had felt (and a decision he had come to) in the prison camp. They were his perpetual problems, exacerbated by the depressions of a defeated country. Was he honest enough with himself and with others? Could he endure others and their meanness (that also more evident in times of demoralization) without undue impatience? How could he react to the affection of his family felt to be stifling yet not brusquely to be rejected? These, and every scruple of a conscience that both aspired too high and criticized too minutely, we have been able to observe repeatedly. Why should they now not lead him into a sort of renunciation of the world, into the choice of a straightforward occupation, where there was no need to be only half-convinced of its value, no ambiguity about one's relation with one's fellow-men, and, as in the religious life, a certain freedom from distraction which was at the same time a freedom to devote oneself to an inner life of meditation and spiritual development?

And what other such occupation was open to him? There is every sign that he took seriously the lesson of his own as yet unpublished book—namely that he had now thought his way through to the end of philosophy and had nothing to add: he said as much to Keynes and Ramsey a year or two later. 'I have no longer any strong inner drive towards that sort of activity. Everything that I really *had* to say, I have said, and so the spring has run dry.'[49] In practice there was in any case no way of doing philosophy without returning to England, which could not be envisaged in 1919. Not only had he no standing in Austrian

47. This shows incidentally that it was not socialism and the Austrian *Schulreform* that inspired his choice of profession.
48. This hypothesis appears in W.W.Bartley III, *Wittgenstein*.
49. LW to JMK 4.7.24.

academic life, but he despised it: showing his, or any, philosophical work to a philosophy professor would be casting pearls..., he said.[50] Altogether he had little taste now for Austrian intellectual life. His letters to Ficker are irritable and a meeting with Loos, to whom he must have hurried just after his return, was a severe disappointment:

> I was horrified and nauseated. He has become infected with the most virulent bogus intellectualism! He gave me a pamphlet about a proposed 'Fine Arts Office', in which he speaks about a sin against the Holy Ghost.[51] This surely is the limit! I was already a bit depressed when I went to Loos, but that was the last straw![52]

Friends told also of a meeting with Kraus (surely not before the war) where Wittgenstein could not, or did not, restrain himself from saying, 'Of course, with your repulsive vanity, you wouldn't understand something like that.'[53]

Teaching may have been an honest choice, but was it itself a poor substitute for the religious life? It is possible to read such a view into Wittgenstein's remarks when he finds himself in the same state of mind as Engelmann:

> What happens, I believe, is this: we do not advance towards our goal by the direct road—for this we (or at any rate I) have not got the strength. Instead we walk up all sorts of tracks and byways, and so long as we are making some headway we are in reasonably good shape. But whenever such a track comes to an end we are up against it; only then do we realize that we are not at all where we ought to be.[54]

If so, this would be an instance of Wittgenstein's failing because of lack of faith. It would explain his later feeling that he had been called but had failed to respond. Still, some of the time it looks as if he thought he could become 'a monk in the world' as the *starets* desired for Alyosha.

For the immediate decision, a short stay at Neuwaldegg and a longer period on the Hochreith were enough (he left Engelmann guessing); then by 25 September he was already enrolled in the *Lehrerbildungsanstalt* (the

50. LW to LvF 22.1.20.

51. Failure by the state to recognize a true artist: so Loos in his preface to *richtlinien für ein kunstamt*, 1919.

52. LW to PE 2.9.19. *Verschmockt*, 'bogus beyond words', sums up pungently Wittgenstein's reaction to what he saw as profanation and hypocrisy. A dedication by Loos in 1924 shows that the two did not quite lose contact: he thanks Wittgenstein for the ideas he has had from him (*Anregungen*) and hopes that his friendly feelings are returned. (*Ins Leere gesprochen*, copy in the possession of the late Arvid Sjögren.)

53. Heinrich Groag, personal communication. Engelmann also speaks of a meeting, and says that Kraus took Wittgenstein for a madman, so violent was he towards Kraus's acolytes.

54. LW to PE 16.11.19: the interpretation is that of K.Wünsche: *Der Volksschullehrer Ludwig Wittgenstein*, pp. 44f.

Teachers' Training College—'so-called', as Wittgenstein ironically adds)
in the third district, just across the street from where he and Engelmann
would one day build a house for Mrs Stonborough. He was also lodged
nearby. 'My circumstances have changed quite generally, except that I
am no wiser,' he darkly says. The new address was to be changed twice
within a month.

The same letter ruefully records the difficulty of the regression
involved in attending such a college:

> So here I am sitting in a schoolroom again, which sounds funnier than it
> is. In fact I find it terribly hard; I can no longer behave like a grammar
> school boy, and, funny as it sounds, the humiliation is so great for me that
> I often think I can hardly bear it. (LW to PE 25.9.19)

In fact the normal student at such an establishment would be a young
pupil-teacher, with not even a *Matura* like Wittgenstein's, let alone a
trace of his high culture or of the wide frame of reference that his studies
and the war had given him. One is reminded of Ignatius of Loyola
learning Latin in Barcelona at the same age: 'Great captain turned
schoolboy' as the hymn has it. But, for Wittgenstein, it was not in fact to
be Linz all over again. The director recognized the distinction of this
strange ex-serviceman (not a quite unexpected figure in the aftermath of
war) and would gladly draw him into his office for conversation. His
intelligence and the power of his personality always won him a general
respect in educational circles. His background too was guessed at: it was
here that he dissociated himself from the rich Wittgensteins, claiming to
be only distantly related to them.[55] But this seemed to him a difficulty,
and of course his dissimulation made it worse.

The work at the college was simple enough. Wittgenstein was excused
all academic subjects on the evidence of his *Matura*, leaving him only
with specifically pedagogic subjects to cover, including singing, organ,
violin,[56] rural economy, and calligraphy. A letter written in rather stiff
Kurrentschrift, Gothic script, is preserved in Hänsel's family: Wittgenstein
all his life wrote a fair round Roman. The certificate from the college
characterizes his performance in this field as *befriedigend*, the third mark
of five: in all the other subjects named, *lobenswert*, the second. *Lobenswert*
too were his practice lessons—in some of them we hear of his reading
fairy-tales to the children: 'It pleases them and relieves the strain on
me.'[57]

---

55. LW to LH (September 1919).
56. Actually we later find him playing by preference the clarinet, learnt for this purpose.
57. LW to PE 19.2.20.

The textbooks used in the college are well described by Wünsche[58] as containing generalities designed to make the new teacher think through his aims in each lesson, prepare his material, look round for associations and devices to impress it upon the memory of his pupils. All of this Wittgenstein in his later practice conscientiously did. Less clear, and perhaps not relevant at this point, is whether his aim like that of traditional pedagogy was the assimilation of rehearsed material, or rather the winning of new skills through activity. It will be seen that this question, essentially the question whether he subscribed to the ideas of the new *Schulreform*, must be answered with a yes and a no. In practice he thought out his own methods of teaching, certainly departing from tradition in this, but there was also much in the *Schulreform* that he rejected, notably its attitude towards discipline and the voice to be given to children in the running of a school.[59] But that is for discussion in the context of his work when trained: for the present no more than lip-service, and little enough of that, will have been paid to its ideas in his college. And the practice of the college was one of training in the strict sense (*Abrichtung* rather than *Bildung*, hence perhaps Wittgenstein's irony noted above). Certainly in his later philosophy and in his attitude towards children, we can see him attaching importance to this as an element in human thought as well as in social life.

His own life in this period oscillated between involvement with his family and holding them at arm's length. His lodgings near the college were soon exchanged for the house of a family friend in Hietzing. Mima Sjögren, born Hermine Bacher, was the widow of a Swedish engineer, director of one of Karl Wittgenstein's steel mills: her father had been director of another. She had been a close friend of Ludwig's sisters since his early childhood. Now her sons too became part of the extended family, partly because it was felt she needed help and guidance in bringing up the boys alone. The Sjögrens shared, therefore, in the carefully planned festivities and they visited the Hochreith in the summer or the various large Vienna houses at the weekend. Mima would make small artistic contributions on these occasions, but more than that she was among them, the amateurs, much nearer to a serious artist, and was appreciated as such. Her gifts are still evident in a series of portraits. In photographs Mima stands out as an attractive and striking woman even alongside Margaret Stonborough. Two of the sons, Arvid and Talla, impinged in different ways on Ludwig.[60] Talla, tall, handsome and amiable, visibly a Swede, was typecast, in the way families have, or

58. op.cit., pp. 49ff.

59. See E.C.Hargrove: 'Wittgenstein, Bartley, and the Glöckel School Reform', *JHistPhil* 18 (1980) 453ff.

60. These impressions are largely based on the recollections of contemporaries, including the late Arvid Sjögren himself.

the Wittgenstein family at all events, as the less serious character: everyone would like him, but there would always be the problem what he would do He was an obvious victim for Mrs Stonborough's benevolent management of the lives of others. So he was seen at all events. (His part in Ludwig's life was to come much later.) Arvid, tall also but heavier, was quiet and offered more resistance. He had a candour of soul and self-sufficiency that promised to take him through life. Something in his seriousness, the literalness and directness of his vision, attracted Ludwig—they had met before only in wartime leaves, when Arvid was noisier, a schoolboy. Now he became the frequent companion—we shall see that in due course he accompanied Ludwig on his trips abroad. It was the beginning of a lifelong friendship, which continued even after Arvid was obliged to wean himself away: Ludwig demanded too much, he came to think. His friends had to be too attached to him, too absorbed in the friendship. Ludwig talked a great deal, certainly, about one's life, but needed a lot himself. He was put out if he arrived for a visit and the lamp outside was not lighted or when he found Arvid preoccupied by some carpentry he was doing for one of Ludwig's sisters. You needed calm to be Ludwig's friend. But Arvid had this and, just for the present, as we have seen, it suited him to be a disciple of Ludwig's, perhaps the first friend that can be so categorized, Pinsent and Engelmann being on a more equal footing than this almost nephew. A disciple, but a thinker too: Ludwig always saw this side of Arvid. In every book, every incident of life, that they discussed, Arvid would have his own perception. The influence then was a subtle one, not the imprinting of one personality on another. One practical decision that Ludwig contributed to was regretted later by some family members: he advised Arvid not to study, with the result that the boy became a mechanic rather than an engineer. It was to happen again and again that younger members of their circle were advised to take up simple practical occupations by Ludwig and his sister Gretl, and it obviously jumped with Ludwig's own inclinations at this period: the idea of an academic study of anything important is explicitly rejected in his book. Remarkable, though, is the willingness to intervene in another's life. 'The older generation,' Thomas Stonborough, a nephew, used to say, 'didn't stop short at the other person's rights.'[61] Later we find (by inference from a letter of Arvid's)[62] Ludwig chiding Arvid for not being concerned for ('not giving a shit for') the salvation or spiritual welfare of his friends. Arvid answers that he has to let others, even his fiancée, go

61. Personal communication.

62. AS to LW n.d. (perhaps 1931): *Daß ich ein bißchen auf das Seelenheil meiner Freunde scheiße, mag stimmen.* (This sort of vigour of language was characteristic of Wittgenstein's spoken expressions of opinion, as many friends relate.) The *first* half of Wittgenstein's letter had been concerned with Arvid's virtues.

their own way: in his best moments he can serve as a signpost (which just stands there). If Ludwig was more than a signpost in this matter of higher education, Arvid at the end of his life himself talked as if it was somehow meant to be so. Others regretted it more than he.

To this house, then, and these preoccupations, Ludwig came as a lodger in or towards November. His help with the education of the boys may have fallen in with the plans of others, his distancing himself from the Alleegasse with his own. Fruit of the stay was the lifelong friendship we have touched on—it gave him first of all company on a journey to Holland to meet Russell. But fruit also was a lifelong rift and awkwardness in his relations with Mima. Arvid himself thought she had fallen in love with Ludwig. Surely there must have been some difficulty for her in negotiating his need for warmth and his aversion to contact, the attraction and repulsion of Schopenhauer's porcupines, which Wittgenstein seems to have felt especially with women. And he was now at his most sensitive—we shall see it in the difficulties his sister Hermine has in dealing with him: easier for her to write to Dr Hänsel. At all events, Ludwig left Hietzing and returned to the third district, a change of home 'accompanied by operations which I can never remember without a sinking feeling'.[63] Thereafter relations were difficult: to be sure, a visit from her to him a year or so later was rather carefully planned, but in general his family were careful not to invite Mima when he was likely to be there; and we find her son Arvid doing the converse in an undated letter more than a decade later.[64]

The episode is characteristic in its mixture of what Wittgenstein, nearly always lamenting them, called inner and outer aspects. In this case someone else's behaviour or expectations impinged on him, and he had to carry out operations on the environment and on himself to become master of the situation, operations which gravely affected the inner life that he was striving to put in order.

It is in such a light that we must survey the main areas of preoccupation for him in this year of transition, a year in which it was only natural that he should have the greatest difficulty in finding his feet, as his family indeed saw. The first area, already partly covered, was that of family and friends. Detached from his family, he had yet to spend Saturday afternoon regularly with his mother,[65] and this presented a difficulty for reasons he had described to Parak in the prison camp. Hänsel and his wife provided a refuge, when measles or other family preoccupations would allow:[66] for this Hermine Wittgenstein thanked

63. LW to PE 24.4.20.
64. AS to LW n.d.: 'If Mama should be away just at the time when you're here,... I'd ask you to come to us.' At this point, mid-1930s?, Mima shared the Perrongasse house with her son and daughter-in-law.
65. LW to LH 24.9.19.
66. For the measles see LW to LH (March 1920).

them most touchingly, and also made presents of a kind most useful in days of hardship, with the most tactful explanation that these latter could of course not be regarded as in any way fulfilling her duty of thanks.[67] Hänsel, then, though not too often; and occasional visits to the sculptor Drobil; and a very occasional visit from Paul Engelmann,[68] with whom Wittgenstein felt he could really talk. This was hardly enough: in March, after a visit to Russell which falls into another context, Wittgenstein wrote:

> How much I'd like to see you again! I'm no longer in any condition to acquire new friends and I'm losing my old ones. It's terribly sad. Nearly every day I remember poor David Pinsent. Because, however odd it sounds, I'm too stupid for nearly everybody. (LW to BR 19.3.20)

His way of thinking, perhaps, made no sense for most people. (Arvid, the new friend, was an exception.) And yet his aim must be to accept others. Perhaps this helps us to understand his cry, to Engelmann this time, 'Normal human beings are a balm to me, and a torment at the same time.'[69]

The second area of preoccupation was the college and his training. We have seen the humiliations involved here were not easy for him and we find him in January 1920 both writing to Engelmann that he was in a state that was terrifying for him[70] and appealing to Hänsel for advice and even help:

> Things are not going particularly well for me, internally, because relations with my fellow-men constantly preoccupy me in an unpleasant manner. And so I toss around in my head the question whether I should stay here or go away, but still have come to no end-result. (LW to LH 16.1.20)

It looks as if this led to one of the attempts to enter a religious house, and thus that the attempt had at least some of its origin in a dissatisfaction with how he was treated in the college (perhaps this is what he meant by *das Meritorische meiner Angelegenheit*, the merits or details of his case, where he could not be helped)[71]—but the attempt will have had some of its origin also (which is most important) in his own inability to accept or deal with this circumstance. Inner or outer? It is impossible to say, and when Wittgenstein speaks of having contemplated taking his own life 'not from my despair about my own badness, but for purely external

67. HW to LH, a number of letters from 1919–20, printed in Wünsche: op.cit, pp. 327–9.
68. In the other scale we have sixteen letters LW to PE in the year in question.
69. LW to PE 16.11.19.
70. LW to PE 26.1.20.
71. LW to PE 21.6.20.

reasons',[72] it may have been circumstances like those at the college, which have a strong inner element, that he meant. It is perhaps significant that this letter to Engelmann is the very one already quoted which speaks of advancing, directly or indirectly, towards a goal. For a period in January Wittgenstein felt that rather than advancing, he was vegetating.[73]

A third area of preoccupation was the closing, so to speak, of the former phase in his life, the attempt to publish his work.[74] Here too some feeling that he was not getting his due was inevitable, for he was exposed to nearly every ill that authors are born to. Immediately on his return from captivity, he took what was probably the third typescript[75] of his work to Braumüller, who had been the publisher of Otto Weininger. Some recommendation from a philosopher was requested, which he easily persuaded Russell to provide. This received, Braumüller was prepared to take the book, but only if Wittgenstein would pay for the paper and the printing. Wittgenstein, however, had not got the money: he could indeed obtain it, but, as he told Ficker,

> I don't want to, because I think it's not decent behaviour, from a social point of view, to force a book on to the world (of which the publisher is a part) in this way. *My* job was to write the book: its acceptance by the world must proceed in the normal fashion.[76]

A fair enough reaction. But (as related in the letter just quoted though with a slight ambiguity as to the timing) Wittgenstein had also turned to 'a professor in Germany' (Frege, obviously) in hope to have his work published in a periodical there.[77] Frege's failure to understand a word of the work seems to have been overlooked, but not for long, since there ensued an exchange of correspondence which left Wittgenstein 'thoroughly exhausted from giving what are purely and simply explanations'.[78] In the end (we have only Wittgenstein's own account of the matter) Frege

72. LW to PE 16.11.19.

73. LW to BR 19.1.20.

74. Most of the information that now follows, and much more, is contained in G.H. von Wright: 'The origin of Wittgenstein's *Tractatus*', an introduction to *Prototractatus*, reprinted in his *Wittgenstein* (1982).

75. One was certainly with Russell, another probably with Frege.

76. LW to LvF (mid-October 1919). For this section the references can generally best be found in von Wright's essay just cited.

77. *Beiträge zur Philosophie des deutschen Idealismus*, where Frege's 'Der Gedanke' (sent to Wittgenstein in the prison camp) had been published. Wittgenstein's letters to Frege were lost in the Second War. We have only Heinrich Scholz's notes on their number and general content. These record about ten items of correspondence from the prison camp (among them this request), and four in the autumn following. (Frege's letters to Wittgenstein are also a sad loss, and a strange one. In the 1930s Wittgenstein told Scholz that he had only letters of a personal nature from Frege and was anxious to keep them. But nothing of this nature was found among his papers, though many personal letters from others were.)

78. LW to BR 6.10.19.

wanted him to 'mangle the work from beginning to end, and in short make it a different work altogether',[79] another impossible condition.

Now it was Ficker's turn. Was there any chance of publication in *Der Brenner*? If so, the manuscript would be sent.

> For the present I will only say this much: the work is strictly philosophical and at the same time literary: but there's no gassing in it.

Gassing, *das Schwefeln*, was the great danger both in literature and in philosophy and the only way to get a true view of just the questions that Ficker and Kraus were concerned about was to banish it. Wittgenstein's next letter to Ficker has often been quoted:

> My work consists of two parts: the one presented here plus all that I have *not* written. And it is precisely this second part that is the important one. My book draws limits to the sphere of the ethical from the inside as it were, and I am convinced that this is the ONLY *rigorous* way of drawing those limits. In short, I believe that where *many* others today are just *gassing*, I have managed in my book to put everything firmly into place by being silent about it.

'To put everything firmly into place'—a bold claim. No wonder that Ficker was not expected to see this at once. No wonder, perhaps, if he failed to see it. At any rate he excused himself to Wittgenstein, at first (evidently) expressing some doubt whether *Der Brenner* was the right place for the work, but offering to show it to a professor of philosophy (perhaps a teacher in a Gymnasium). A fierce letter—a *Brandbrief*,[80] Wittgenstein later called it—was the answer.

> I agree with you: I myself don't know where a home can be found for my work. If only I myself could find a home somewhere else and not in this lousy world. As far as I'm concerned you can show the manuscript to your philosophy professor (even though showing a philosophical work to a philosophy professor is the same as casting pearls...). However he won't understand a word. And now just one more request: make it quick and painless for me. Tell me no immediately rather than ever so slowly: that's Austrian delicacy and my nerves are at the moment not quite strong enough to endure it. (LW to LvF 22.11.19)

Ficker (as can be seen from Wittgenstein's later letters) immediately offered to be the publisher of last resort, despite the unusual character of the work and the consequent risk to his small publishing house. Again an offer that Wittgenstein could not accept: he would not risk 'the existence

---

79. LW to LvF in the letter just cited.
80. This usually means a peremptory letter, e.g. a dun's.

of any human being whatsoever' for the publication of his book. It would be different if Ficker himself thought the book worth it.

> Any book, even if it's written with absolute honesty, is from *one* point of view worthless: because really nobody need write a book, given that there are quite other things to do in the world. On the other hand I think I can say that if you're going to print Dallago, Haecker, etc. *then* you can print *my* book too. (LW to LvF 4.12.19)

Here Wittgenstein's preoccupation with *das Meritorische seiner Angelegenheit*, with the merits of his case, is very intelligible. To be noted rather is the kindness with which he overcomes his resentment:

> And now: all best wishes and don't fret yourself on my account. Everything is going to turn out all right.[81]

Similarly in January we find him telling Engelmann that Ficker will lose all he has if he does not stop publication of *Der Brenner*: *Kann man ihm helfen?*, Can anything be done for him?, is Wittgenstein's immediate reaction.[82] It was always his gift, or his curse, to respond at full strength in whichever direction: incapable of half-tones himself, he was impatient of them in others.

His despondency is intelligible too:[83] now he had been rejected, as it were, by Kraus (through Jahoda), by Weininger (through Braumüller), by Frege, and by Ficker. There was some possibility of Insel Verlag, since Rilke was ready to intervene on his behalf, but (perhaps correctly, since nothing came of it) Wittgenstein seems not to have put much faith in it. There remained whatever hope he might derive from prospective visits to Russell and Frege (for both were planned, and the former at least was eagerly anticipated).

The visit to Russell is a high point in this year. Perhaps because we see Wittgenstein intensely engaged in the 'active use of his reason', which only certain persons made possible for him,[84] and because on this occasion we can see him through other eyes, less jaundiced than his own. Russell had discussed the book sent him with Nicod, a brilliant young French philosopher of mathematics, and with Dorothy Wrinch, a pupil and protégée, later an eminent crystallographer.[85] Now he needed a

81. LW to LvF 5.12.19, though with the sardonic postscript, aptly dated 6.12.19, 'By the way is there a *Krampus* (St.Nicholas's shadow figure) to haul off naughty publishers?'

82. LW to PE 26.1.20.

83. Whether this was factor that led to thoughts of suicide is discussed below: the dates do not quite fit, since on 16 November when he wrote to Engelmann about such thoughts, he had not yet had Ficker's first negative letter.

84. He himself attributes this power also to Engelmann, LW to PE 29.12.19.

85. LW to PE 26.1.20. Most of these details, confirmed as here by letters, are most easily found in Russell's *Autobiography*, vol. 2, pp. 95ff.

discussion with Wittgenstein himself, and they decided on Holland for the meeting as being a neutral country . It may also have played a role that a cousin of Wittgenstein's was Austrian ambassador there. The decision, in any case, was made in October, and the procuring of a passport and an entry visa was not altogether straightforward. There was also, as can be imagined, some difficulty for Wittgenstein in financing the trip: both his renunciation of his own wealth and the general currency difficulties of those days will have contributed. Wittgenstein therefore asked Russell to sell for him all the books and furniture that he had left stored in Cambridge since before the war. In fact Russell bought it all (at a valuation). Some of the furniture was described above in connexion with Wittgenstein's rooms in 1912, and the books (now the property of the Bertrand Russell Archive) have in this way fortunately been preserved to give us an idea of Wittgenstein's exacting pre-war taste, as I have tried to show above. 'The best bargain I ever made', said Russell, for they were worth more than the Cambridge dealer supposed, who disliked the design of the furniture.[86]

Russell arrived in The Hague early in December. Wittgenstein turned up, the first opportunity, it seems, on 12 December. He brought Arvid Sjögren with him for company. Russell meanwhile had been joined by Dora Black, who came from Paris to discuss their future together. But the meeting of the two we are chiefly concerned with was exactly like pre-war Cambridge:

> Wittgenstein has arrived—just the same as ever—it is a great joy to see him—he is so full of logic that I can hardly get him to talk about anything personal. He is very affectionate and if anything a little more sane than before the war. He came before I was up and hammered at my door till I woke. Since then he has talked logic without ceasing for 4 hours...[87]

And so it continued for a week. They went through the book point by point and Russell found Wittgenstein 'glorious and wonderful, with a pasionate purity I have never seen equalled.'[88] Wittgenstein too was delighted, the more so because Russell promised to get his work published in England, in German and English, doing the translation and writing an introduction himself.

Meanwhile Dora Black worked on free thought in Dutch libraries and Arvid filled the time as best he could. All four would meet for meals, where the conversation (in Dora Russell's recollection) was superficial: Russell says Wittgenstein was quite witty, which perhaps comes to the

---

86. We know this fact, and the price paid (£80) from correspondence with Jolley (the dealer) in the Russell Archives (File W 51).

87. BR to Colette (Lady Constance Malleson) Friday (12.12.19).

88. BR to the same (16.12.19).

same thing. As regards the war Wittgenstein gave the impression of being both a patriot and a pacifist. He spoke of having fraternized with Russians on the Eastern Front and of his admiration for them. Wittgenstein was very proud, Russell said, and would not mention the privations of life in Vienna, or would laugh at them. He had no greatcoat but only a little mackintosh cape with no warmth in it.

We have already mentioned how astonished Russell was by the depth of Wittgenstein's mysticism. He suggested that what Wittgenstein liked best in mysticism was its power to make him stop thinking: but Wittgenstein would not agree. Still it was a happy meeting, as both men show in their letters at the time. (Russell's memoir[89] written later when differences had sharpened gives a more satirical view.)

Wittgenstein was at his best practically too, as he soon had to show, for Arvid contracted a severe influenza. The visit to Frege was cancelled and the two had to make their way back to Vienna by the uncertain trains of postwar Germany. At Passau it turned out that there were no passenger trains to Austria before the Christmas holiday, but Wittgenstein, with the force he was capable of, saw to it that room was found for them on a goods train, and on it he looked after his friend and brought him safely home.

For the publication of his book there now seemed to be no difficulty (though we have already seen that he had other preoccupations in January that weighed heavily upon him). With an introduction by Russell, any publisher would accept it, so, for example, Reclam, whom some friend of Engelmann's had recommended. And it seems they indeed would have done so, and when Russell's promised introduction arrived (none too promptly for Wittgenstein's taste) at the beginning of April, Wittgenstein set about having it translated for Reclam, though he saw at once that there was much to disagree with in it

> both where you are critical of me and also where you are simply trying to elucidate my views. But that doesn't matter. The future will pass judgement upon us. (LW to BR 9.4.20)

In the event when he saw the translation, all the refinement of Russell's style lost, he thought that nothing remained except 'superficiality and misunderstanding', and so he refused to have it printed, saying to Reclam that it might serve solely for their own orientation in regard to the work. Russell was not to be angry with him...[90] If Reclam should consequently refuse the work Wittgenstein would comfort himself with the following argument:

89. *Autobiography*, vol.2, pp.100-1.
90. There are many affectionate phrases in this very direct letter.

that that discrepancy is not the fault of life as it is, but of myself as I am. (*Letters &c*, pp.76–7)

If we take seriously Engelmann's account of what brought him and Wittgenstein together, and seriously also Wittgenstein's avowals of inner failure (taking this to be above all an awareness that he was not by nature suited to be perfect), we are as near as outsiders can be to understanding both the temptation to suicide (three brothers and his admired Weininger succumbed to it) and the fundamental betrayal of his faith that it would have represented. The multiple occasions for such a temptation that we have seen are all variant forms which this lack of self-mastery assumed.[93] It was a kind of despair at the human condition: at that time and place the climate of history favoured it, but we have also been observing how its roots were set in the whole process of Wittgenstein's formation.

'*Well, we shall see!*—', underlined as usual, was Wittgenstein's conclusion to the saddening letter last quoted, apart that is from his customary respectful greetings to Engelmann's mother. Something would happen. In fact, it came from himself: for the summer, instead of visiting Engelmann at Olmütz and then going on the Hochreith, he got himself taken on as assistant gardener at Klosterneuburg:

> I was longing for some kind of regular work, which, of all things I can do in my present condition, is the most bearable, if I am not mistaken. (LW to PE 19.7.20)

And there, indeed, he did in a quiet way flourish in the benign atmosphere of that wealthy foundation, like some great Cambridge college but with too few fellows, which dominates its little town and its wide vineyards, just far enough north of Vienna not to be easily visitable. There, even more of an Alexis now, he lived in a gardener's hut, near the canons' graveyard ('The dead don't talk,' he told Arvid), tired enough each evening not to feel unhappy, well enough fed by the head cook, who had taken him to her heart and gave him pastries, even meat sometimes, from the canons' table.[94] Meanwhile his applications for a teacher's post in Lower Austria were being considered.

---

93. W.W.Bartley's *Wittgenstein* ascribes much influence to guilt over homosexual episodes in the Prater (reached nightly from distant Hietzing?). I have not paid much attention to this hypothesis (such it must be, though with what foundation is not clear). It is above all an unnecessary one, as I hope to have shown, and it is in fact totally incompatible with the frank discussion of Wittgenstein's difficulties which I for one have had with close friends of his from that time. For that matter, would Engelmann's memoirs or Wittgenstein's own later confessions be conceivable on the Bartley view? For the best refutation, however, see Rush Rhees and J.J.Stonborough (a nephew) in *The Human World*, 1972.

94. LW to PE 20.8.20, to LH 10.8.20.

There we leave him for the moment and turn to his book. For himself it had been a time of crisis and his future state of mind was still dubious; but perhaps (as had been before his mind in the prison camp) a new history was commencing, a story of the gradual renewing of a man, of his gradual regeneration.

intellectually before the war and an enormous success during and after it. Wittgenstein was known to Ogden from the Russell circle and the Moral Science Club of pre-war years. Recently Ogden had put the results of his studies of language teaching to use in *The Meaning of Meaning*, written together with I.A. Richards, for its time an unusually concrete psychological and sociological account of language. At this point he was launched on a new publishing career: as editor both of *Psyche*, an international journal with a central interest in language, and of The International Library of Psychology, Philosophy, and Scientific Method published by Kegan Paul, whose very title conveys its manifesto. Jung, Vaihinger, Russell, Moore, and Hardy's *Mathematics for Philosophers* figured among the authors and books projected. The new sciences were to be brought to the aid of British culture, Cambridge voices were to be heard alongside the last word from Vienna or Trieste. The aftermath of the war seemed to promise a new science, a science of man. The interest above all in language was its hallmark. These ambitions of Ogden and his friends may fairly be said to have been realized.

This was the man to whom Dorothy Wrinch showed Wittgenstein's treatise shortly after the rejection from the Cambridge Press arrived.[7] He took no immediate action, so she went the rounds of Germany, with what result we have seen. Still, Ogden was more perceptive, showed more *Spürsinn*, than Ficker and in due course he put to Russell the idea of publishing the work. Russell scrupulously sought a second authority to publish from Wittgenstein. This was of course forthcoming and Wittgenstein in fact collaborated, marking up corrections in a copy of the *Annalen* publication, reading the proofs supplied by Ogden and also commenting on the translation as it was sent him. The translation seems principally to have been the work of Frank Ramsey, who in a short life was to make considerable contributions both to economics and the philosophy of mathematics. Not yet twenty years of age, but already recognized as a genius, son of an academic family, an Apostle, of course, and a protégé of Keynes's, he was on the point of leaving mathematics for the moral sciences, to give them their Cambridge name, and Trinity for King's. It was perhaps known that he had won at Winchester a German prize intended for non-specialists. Braithwaite describes him as sailing into Miss Pate's typing office in Cambridge and dictating the translation with Ogden at his side.[8] Russell's own version was used for those passages originally cited at length by him: Wittgenstein insisted that these translations had equal authority with the German text. There was also much consultation with Wittgenstein himself, conducted by Ogden. The idea of publishing the original with the translation *en face* was Russell's

7. So she told me, and it explains how Ogden was able to approach Russell about the book in the autumn following.
8. Personal communication.

but Ogden readily embraced it as an intelligible solution to a difficult problem. It was almost impossible, he said in his editor's note, to convey the literary and epigrammatic flavour of the original in any other way.

It is a nice question whether in their attempt to convey this flavour he and Ramsey overdid it or not. A whole generation of English-speaking philosophers came to know the work through a translation which seems to have been not so much liberated as shackled by the presence of the German on the opposite page. It reads as if made from a dead language, though that may be thought to assist the stylistic effect of a revelation which is certainly one of the aims of the original. A smoother, and perhaps more philosophical version has been attempted by the present writer with a colleague.[9]

Almost as influential as the translation was the title chosen, which even in German sometimes supplants *Logisch-philosophische Abhandlung*. That, the original title, seems to me deliberately chaste: 'a treatise—as it might be one of many—that goes about philosophy in a logical way'. It is understated in a way that the book itself is not. The first suggestion for a translation was *Philosophical Logic*, which indeed appeared in Kegan Paul's advertisements. This, of course, gets things just the wrong way round, and Wittgenstein poured scorn on it:

> I don't know what it means! There is no such thing as philosophic logic. (Unless one says that as the whole book is nonsense the title might as well be nonsense too.) (LW to CKO 23.4.22.)

So instead Moore's suggestion of *Tractatus Logico-Philosophicus* was accepted: 'not ideal,' Wittgenstein said, 'still it has something like the right meaning'. The allusion to *Tractatus Theologico-Politicus*, a work of Spinoza's more familiar for its title than for its content, was perhaps not altogether a happy idea: it is a work censured by Schopenhauer for its optimism and Wittgenstein will hardly have known it. He does indeed echo a phrase of Spinoza's (not from this work) when he equates the mystical view of the world as a limited whole with the view of the world '*sub specie aeterni*',[10] but the context in his *Notebooks* suggest that, as with many of his allusions, it is Schopenhauer's quotation of Spinoza that he is echoing here rather than the original.[11]

The new title reinforced the tendency of the translation to underline the dogmatic and quasi-biblical tone of Wittgenstein's work. There is, as has been suggested above, some justification for that: the work begins with a sort of creation-myth:

9. With D.F.Pears, 1961. In 1971 a second edition was published taking account of Wittgenstein's own wishes as expressed in the correspondence with Ogden (also published 1971).

10. *TLP* 6.45.

11. Cf. *Notebooks* 7.10.16 with *Die Welt als Wille und Vorstellung* vol.II (Frauenstädt) p.211.

come cosa salda.[12] The status of his own propositions is always in his mind. He was right to say to Ficker in a letter we have quoted that the work was strictly philosophical and at the same time literary. One aspect of its literary character is that, like a poem, it is not an indifferent vehicle for something expressible in other ways but shows or conveys something unique by its own form of expression. In Wittgenstein's own terms, it shows or manifests something—*sie zeigt etwas*, as we find him saying in the last sentence of the preface. The interesting thing, and the real riddle of the *Tractatus*, is that at the same time it does give expression to thoughts, claimed to be incontestably true. So the work is philosophical as well as literary, but it is in the nature of philosophy (according to the *Tractatus*) that its thoughts are ones whose point is to turn us away from philosophy. Thus, while Wittgenstein is convinced that his work contains, in all essentials, the final solution of the problems treated[13] and that its value in the first place consists in how well this is expressed, the very fact that he has the final solution enables him to say in the last sentence of his preface:

> And if I am not mistaken in this belief, then the second thing in which the value of this work consists is that it shows how little is achieved when these problems are solved.

A strange book, half of whose value consists in showing its own unimportance!

The reader will, I believe, find it invaluable to keep these literary characteristics of the work in mind as he reads it. The aphoristic style and the sometimes puzzling transitions of thought are part of its commentary on itself. They show something about the nature of philosophy—and that after all is the subject of the work. There are plenty of internal indications that its propositions are not to be taken quite *au pied de la lettre*. It is, of course, not the only philosophical work with such an aim. The self-doubt of the philosopher is to be found in many sceptical writings. Sextus Empiricus is echoed here, who tells us that, according to the Pyrrhonian, scepticism is not a set of dogmas but a way of life, and Plato devotes the last part of the *Phaedrus* to a demonstration that written works (and hence the very dialogue which teaches this) are not the way to convey the lessons of true philosophy, which is found only in the living speech and written in the soul of the participant. It is in the same spirit that Wittgenstein says:

---

12. 'Treating these shadows as material things', as Statius did Virgil's shade in Dante (*Purg.* 21.136).

13. Wittgenstein here echoes Frege's preface to *The Foundations of Arithmetic* p. v: 'I hope to settle the question finally, at least in essentials'.

Philosophy is not a body of doctrine but an activity.

Philosophy does not result in philosophical propositions but rather in the clarification of propositions.

It will signify what cannot be said by presenting clearly what can be said. (4.112, in part, and 4.115)

The idea of 'signifying' is important here. To be sure it is only one possible translation of *bedeuten*—Ogden and Ramsey had 'mean'—but at all events the idea is that nothing can be said. Philosophy is a sort of knowledge which can be presented only obliquely, as Heraclitus says:

The Lord whose oracle is in Delphi neither speaks out nor conceals, but gives a sign. (DK 22 B 93)

And to make the parallel with Plato even more striking, Wittgenstein seems to condemn the method of his own book:

The correct method in philosophy would really be the following: to say nothing except what can be said, i.e. propositions of natural science—i.e. something that has nothing to do with philosophy—and then, whenever someone else wanted to say something metaphysical, to demonstrate to him that he has failed to give a meaning to certain signs in his propositions. Although it would not be satisfying to the other person—he would not have the feeling that we were teaching him philosophy—*this* method would be the only strictly correct one. (6.53)

It is not unfair to see his whole philosophy as a kind of mystic revelation, remembering that mystic *means* what cannot or should not be spoken. He himself says so just before this last proposition:

There are indeed things that cannot be put into words. They *make themselves manifest.* They are what is mystical. (6.53)

The reading of the book, then, has a purpose: it is like an initiation into the mysteries, and when they are reached it can be forgotten.

These are, of course, only prolegomena; and while the reader of the present volume will not expect a substitute for reading the *Tractatus*, he may be surprised at an introduction that lays so much emphasis on its hidden content. The fact is, however, that a direct description of its doctrines (which many of my predecessors have attempted—*vestigia terrent*)[14] often leads to surprise at the sudden turn in the argument by which those doctrines are themselves invalidated. The edifice erected in

14. Norman Malcolm in *Nothing is Hidden*, 1986, (especially chapter 2) at least discusses views like mine, though he reaches an opposite conclusion. Earlier commentators often end up trying desperately to put the bathwater back with the baby.

combination, the other being that which is so combined—function and argument these are called in Wittgenstein's semi-technical vocabulary.[17] With them, equally present in every judgement, is the key to all that can be done with language. We are here speaking, it must be understood, of the theoretical limit of analysis. It is not pretended, it need not be pretended, that we can reach that limit. What is being said, through the remainder of the 3's, which we shall not rehearse in detail, is that the notions of representation, of sense, of possibility, of necessary consequence can only be anchored in our grasp of what is implicit in a proposition (we remember how central the problem of the proposition was in Wittgenstein's wartime notebooks). Thus when he says as the culmination of this section:

A thought is a proposition with a sense. (4)

he is drawing the conclusion that the laws of the sense of propositions are the laws of thought generally. No wonder the comment immediately follows that philosophy is nothing but critique of language.[18] We are here at the heart of the *Tractatus*. The essence of its account of propositions is contained in the propositions number 4.01–4.0641, which lead off with the picture theory:

A proposition is a picture of reality.
A proposition is a model of reality as we imagine it. (4.01)

It is an interesting circumstance that nearly all the arguments in this section were developed before the idea came to Wittgenstein that propositions might be seen as pictures. One might say that nothing hinges on this way of seeing them. The picture paradigm is a convenient way of summing up what must logically be true of a proposition. As so often, what looks like a premiss is a conclusion.

The real premisses are, for example, that we can understand the sense of a propositional sign without its having been explained to us (4.02). The proposition can do this only by having the correct multiplicity, only by representing, implicitly or explicitly, all the elements of reality that are relevant. It must, as it were, (this is an extension of one of Wittgenstein's own metaphors) build a model with bricks in the certainty that sufficiently similar bricks are available in reality. If it does this, the proposition will itself be enough to guarantee the possibility of

17. See 5.47, later in the book, for a very clear statement of this.
18. 4.0031. 'Not in Mauthner's sense,' says Wittgenstein, because Mauthner, in his large work with the title *Critique of Language*, set out to show various ways in which language misrepresented thought and reality, whereas, according to Wittgenstein, their general nature is identical with the possibilities afforded by language.

what it says, because (i.e. this is equivalent to the fact that) it has sense. And this means that there is a further stage, after the understanding of the proposition, which is the comparison of that proposition with reality (4.5). All this talk about sense and possibility, where we might wonder how Wittgenstein knew with such certainty what were the correct relations between these concepts, turns out to be a way of saying (or exploring the meaning of the fact that) a proposition is essentially something capable of being true or false. This is precisely what Wittgenstein told Whitehead in 1913:

A proposition has two poles, 'a' and 'b'

and when asked, mildly—for Whitehead was not without his satirical side—what 'a' and 'b' might be, replied 'in a voice of thunder':

'a' and 'b' are indefinable.[19]

In the *Tractatus* all this is put by saying:

A proposition can be true or false only in virtue of being a picture of reality. (4.06)

where Wittgenstein is telling us that this minimum condition for being a proposition, this bipolarity, entails the view of possibilities and logical space that is set out in the sections we have been summarizing.

It could be argued that the 4.06's, which give an account of what is required for truth (i.e. for truth-or-falsity) are the pivot of the *Tractatus*, the logical centre of the work. Wittgenstein himself picks out a slightly earlier proposition in our present context:

My fundamental idea is that the 'logical constants' are not representative; that there can be no representation of the *logic* of facts. (4.0312 in part)[20]

We remember that this echoes an early problem of Russell's and Wittgenstein's, and, perhaps for that reason it here serves as a turning-point, leading us into the negative side, the downward slope, as it were (though also much the longer part) of the book. We have seen that the principle of the representation of objects by signs makes possible the true-or-false proposition: in other words, our magazine of signs that can be combined without first inquiring as to the facts assures us of sense

---

19. This is the only anecdote about Wittgenstein in V.Lowe's life of Whitehead. It is taken from Russell's *Autobiography* vol. 2, p. 101.

20. Translation slightly modified. I have discussed this passage at, at any rate, greater length in 'The *Grundgedanke* of the *Tractatus*' in G. Vesey (ed.): *Understanding Wittgenstein* (1974).

but of those we apply none are really more complex than others.[22] We can certainly display the available truth-tables in a systematic way, and in other ways show how an expression for one possible assertion about our subject matter can be constructed out of that for another; but in doing so we shall be merely exhibiting features of our chosen system of signs, features which will vary in interest according as we ourselves, or those to whom they are exhibited, have failed to notice them. Not many will have had difficulty seeing, 'It is not not raining,' as another way of saying 'It is raining', but some more complicated correspondences or inclusions will at first escape all of us.

The notion of an operation thus introduced is characteristic of Wittgenstein. It has been comparatively little studied and, leading as it does to the apparent trivialization of logic and mathematics, it seems almost too ambitious. The difficulty is that it asks us to depart from a favourite model—that of the formal sciences as a set of truths. Wittgenstein is not so much contributing to the solution of a set of well-recognized problems as demanding a change in our whole approach. It may be put to the debit side that he does not then develop a whole system of logic and mathematics on a new basis. He is content with the insight itself—and this is in some ways intelligible, for it is a difficult insight. The idea that there are at least two quite different uses of language, one to put forward truths, another to exhibit features of language itself, is on the one hand attractive, but also something that we have to be forced to accept. Just as Wittgenstein says that everyday language has features that are designed to do anything rather than reveal its true logical form, so a great deal of our activity as regards the formal sciences—the writing of logic books, the examination of children in arithmetic—seems to presuppose that here too we can conjecture and get things wrong, while other parts of our activity—our reliance on self-evidence, the extraordinary freedom we have in our starting-points—seem to place us in a different world. The difference from factual enquiries is one that we sometimes seem to see clearly and then suddenly lose again.

An operation powerful enough to generate all truth-functions is defined at 5.5, and in the course of the the 5.5's it is shown that it will indeed permit the expression not only of any degree of complexity in the selection of truth-possibilities, but also, and by the same token, of general propositions. Given that propositions consist in the application of a truth-schema to a suitable material, or as Wittgenstein says in function and argument (which two cannot come together save by the application

---

22. This might be put by saying that in Wittgenstein's table of possible truth-functions of two propositions (if we ignore tautology and contradiction, which are not really truth-functions *of* the two propositions in question) all lines serve to define a proposition in exactly the same way: none is the *preferred* possibility.

of the logical constants expressed by truth-schemata), we do not need a further logical constant of generalization, as Frege and Whitehead and Russell supposed. By a suitable use of Wittgenstein's one logical operation we can apply truth-schemata to a propositional variable (to the sort of function that is implicit in every proposition) and obtain a generalized proposition of any desired degree of complexity. Thus, in a simple example, if we simultaneously negate the range of propositions indicated by, '*x* is both human and immortal' we obtain the proposition that all men are mortal. The essential move is made by supposing that a range of propositions can be specified by a function, i.e. by the use of a logical prototype (*Urbild*) such as '*x* has *F*': there is no need for the fictitious enumeration of all possible objects, $a, b, c, ...,$ in order to construct the equally fictitious proposition, $Fa \text{ v } Fb \text{ v } Fc ...$ (where F stands for 'is both human and immortal'), whose negation might be used to define the generalization in question.

In succeeding brief sections Wittgenstein attempts to show (and his attempt is at least interesting) that identity is not an extra logical constant requiring separate treatment, and that propositions of the form, '*A* judges that *p*' (which, as we have seen, caused so much trouble to Russell) can also be dealt with. This is not a relation of some independent subject A to a proposition, which would leave it open that A might inadvertently have the same relation to, might entertain, say, something not a proposition at all. Rather, A is nothing but a succession of thoughts, and when we specify one of them, there is no further question how it manages to be the thought of just the state of affairs it envisages: 'p', as Wittgenstein puts it, says—i.e. it cannot but say—that p. The occurrence of a thought is not established by taking the mental temperature, but by observing or understanding a proposition. It follows easily that a nonsense cannot be thought (technically that 'p or not-p' follows from p's being thought).[23]

If the subject of judgement is, in this way, a complex (and hence not really a soul at all—5.5421), it is perhaps natural that Wittgenstein should turn next to the topic of solipsism:[24]

The limits of my language mean the limits of my world.
　I am my world. (The microcosm.) (5.6 and 5.63)

At some point certainly Wittgenstein needed to make clear that there was not a metaphysical subject, outside both world and language and set over against them, an idea to be found in some form in Schopenhauer,

---

23. This interpretation is given at slightly greater length in my 'Language and Reality in the *Tractatus*', *Teoria* 5 (1985) pp. 140ff. It derives some plausibility from Russell's adopting it in the second edition of *Principia Mathematica*.

24. In *Prototractatus*, however, the topic is treated earlier, and that of judgement later.

apparently more technical problem how much of set theory is needed for how much of mathematics is still a central one and its investigation leads ever and again to surprising simplifications. And the basic issue between intuitionism and Platonism is still alive in a form which might lead philosophers to seek a fresh vantage point such as the *Tractatus*, in the infant days of art, aspired to give.

The answer to Russell's 'Problem of Matter' is as decisive in intention as that to the problems of the foundations of logic and mathematics. The *Tractatus* renders meaningless any attempt to describe the elements of reality. They are bound to be logical elements, incapable of any description. At a higher level, indeed, it is possible to paraphrase any statement of fact in physical terms, or equally to paraphrase it in terms of the sense data of an individual. These are merely arbitrary choices of a framework within which description can take place: neither is the correct one, though either may be illuminating for a particular purpose.[29] The claim that either represented the real furniture of the world would be metaphysical.[30]

On the question of the status of science, of that cognitive or intellectual value that had led Russell to aspire to a scientific method in philosophy, the *Tractatus* position is twofold. On the one hand, science (in the sense of natural science) alone has cognitive value, since it is the totality of true propositions. On the other hand, it provides us with the explanation of nothing. Darwinism gives the essence of the world as little as phenomenalism. Like Newtonian physics, or Hertz's, it is simply a choice, which might be made a priori, of the form in which we are going to express our general descriptions of the world. Various considerations, of convenience, of convention, and of tolerance of error or of complication in description, may decide us for one such possibility in preference to others, but the possibilities themselves are all clearly constructions implicit in language. Here, perhaps, Wittgenstein fails to do justice to the fertility of the scientist in the formation of new concepts and to the essential role in such formation of a corpus of experience and of interrogation of nature, concerted or consilient, by generations of scientists without which the conditions for the formation of such concepts would not exist.[31] Such misgivings do not affect the main point: the

29. Thus at 6.3751 a physicalist translation in terms of movements of particles is used to show why (i.e.how) it is contradictory to ascribe, say, redness and greenness to a single place in the visual field. When Carnap and Neurath made great play with the notion, Wittgenstein told Schlick that the *Tractatus* had already dealt with physicalism though not under that rebarbative (*scheusslichen*) name and with its usual brevity (LW to MS 8.8.32).

30. Thus, as Wittgenstein reminded Schlick in the letter just quoted, the *Tractatus* is directed as much against the metaphysics of the physicists (physicalism) as against that of the philosophers (of which phenomenalism would be one form).

31. Mach's *Theory of Heat* describes this well for one domain, but it is also evident, I think, in the work of Boltzmann and Hertz, so much admired by Wittgenstein. I have developed this theme in an address given at Kirchberg in 1986.

rejection of any claim by science to *explain* phenomena, if (that is) explanation is taken to be anything other than presenting the phenomena in some clear and easily grasped form. Of course, Mach had already effected this rejection: but Wittgenstein's position is of special interest in that it proceeds from purely logical considerations not from an empiricist prejudice.[32] This conclusion is besides important for the fundamental lesson of Wittgenstein's book. It is no accident that the account of science in the 6.3's culminates in 6.4:

All propositions are of equal value.

Just as factual propositions cannot explain in an intellectual context, so also they cannot give sense to the world. All the value of the world lies in the inexpressible, as we have already seen.

For the third range of questions that Russell and Wittgenstein had to deal with, those concerning the self, we have given the essence of the answer, or rather the new question, in the course of our exposition. It seemed that the self was bound either to be dissolved by phenomenalism into a series of conscious states or, if an idealist starting-point was taken, to absorb everything into itself, and result in solipsism. Wittgenstein adopts both positions, but draws the sting from both. The self of acquaintance is not an object known to me alone—rather as Russell thought that the real reference of the phrase 'The Iron Chancellor' was an object—call it O—known only to Bismarck, but is instead a series of thoughts which I of course can describe.[33]

Yet there is another attitude to the world, which is that of identifying with the metaphysical subject, of seeing the world, one might say, with the objectivity and neutrality of language itself. This, the refusal to identify with the interests of the individual human being, or to be exercised by hope and fear, is no doubt what, quite early in the War, he described in his diary as the strict solipsistic position,[34] and in his notebooks in the latter part of 1916 he returns again and again to this theme. It is less prominent in the *Tractatus* itself, yet there too he sketches an attitude to the world which renounces any special position for the empirical self and attributes no value to the holding, or the bringing about, of any particular states of affairs. The lesson is not itself so strange as the way it is taught. He has indeed found his way through the technical problems of logic in which he did not want Russell to find value: yet precisely in them he has also found his answer to the problems

32. This is why Schlick and some others regarded Wittgenstein as one of the founders of *logical* positivism (though the latter of the two words does not fit him very well).

33. In a book *The World as I Found it* there would be no mention of the subject, according to Wittgenstein (5.631).

34. In his code diary for 8.12.14 Wittgenstein asks whether the idea of leading a life without sense is reconcilable with the strict solipsistic position, clearly thought of as being the one he aspires to.